THE ENCYCLOPEDIA OF
WORLD WAR II
SPIES

PETER KROSS

BARRICADE
BOOKS

Fort Lee, New Jersey

Published by Barricade Books Inc.
185 Bridge Plaza North
Suite 308-A
Fort Lee, NJ 07024

ISBN: 1-56980-171-1

Printed in the United States of America.

First Printing

CONTENTS

INTRODUCTION

World War II was *the* defining event of the 20th century. From 1939 to 1945, the Western democracies, plus the Soviet Union, waged a global war against Germany, Italy and Japan. Students of the war know the great battles of the conflict: Stalingrad, Iwo Jima, the Battle of the Bulge, the North African campaign.

But while this combat between soldiers was waging, another covert war was being fought by spies on all sides. The names of these men and women were not known to the public at the time, their very nature making them anonymous. As the war progressed, these spies would turn the tide of battle, ensuring victory for the allies, and creating a legend that would live far beyond the conflict.

The purpose of this book is to tell the stories of these unsung heroes and villains, and how their exploits changed the course of the war. Spying is called the "Second Oldest Profession," and the men and women who took part in that ages-old endeavor could not have written a better script.

In these pages you will read about the men and women, their missions, and their impact on how the war was fought and won. You will learn about Moe Berg, a brilliant baseball player turned spy, who worked for the OSS, and almost killed a German scientist working on the atomic bomb. Commander Ian Fleming of the British navy had his own band of raiders who carried out espionage missions behind the lines. After the war, Fleming would introduce to the world his most famous agent, James Bond, 007. Dusan Popov, a fashionable playboy, learned of the plot to bomb Pearl Harbor but was turned away by J. Edgar Hoover because the FBI chief did not like Popov's womanizing. In these pages come the stories of ordinary women who worked for the OSS at home and abroad, bringing out downed flyers from occupied territory—of lawyers, writers, cooks, the cream of the crop of America's elite, all working for the OSS, America's first modern intelligence service. You will learn of the actions of traitors on all sides who decid-

7

INTRODUCTION

ed to sell out their country, for their own selfish reasons, and of men and women who just wanted to make a difference.

For the researcher interested in doing further study on this topic, let it be known that over the past decade, the CIA has declassified hundreds of thousands of pages of once secret OSS records and have turned them over to the National Archives. (This is called Record Group 226.) It would take several life times to go over all this material, but it is the best starting point in doing research of this type.

Due to time and length constraints, the author has had to limit the amount of material in this book. I have listed what I think are the most important spies and missions of the war and realize that a subject such as this can go on forever. If I have left out something important, apologies are due.

The subject of World War II is only studied peripherally in grade school, and only a little more in the higher grades. The story of espionage in the war is not studied at all. Here then is the hidden history of the conflict that is not taught in schools, yet is a powerful story in itself. History, though hidden, shouldn't be lost forever.

—Peter Kross
July 2001

A

Abwehr

The Abwehr, a word translated "to ward off," was an organization that conducted German military intelligence operations during World War II. It lasted from 1921 until 1944 but had its origins in the 1860s. After the German defeat in World War I, the Abwehr was set up as a defense organization, not the spy apparatus it later became. The Abwehr's first director was Major Frederick Gempp, a World War I deputy to the head of German intelligence, Walter Nicolai.

The Abwehr's first military success came in 1866 when Prussia, then a German kingdom, defeated Austria. During the Franco-Prussian War of 1870, the organization thwarted French military operations, and captured many prisoners. Its brilliant work led to a Prussian victory.

During World War I, the Abwehr was run by Walter Nicolai. He developed the group, instituting a school for spies that ran a vast network of covert agents inside allied countries. After the defeat of Germany, the spy network was disbanded. In the 1920s, Colonel Erich Fritz took command of the Abwehr and concentrated on airplanes as a means of warfare, rather than espionage. The Germany navy's intelligence section was being merged into the Abwehr in an attempt to consolidate its power. In June 1932, Captain Conrad Patzig was named the new boss but to his horror he later found himself at odds with Heinrich Himmler, an unforgiving Nazi military leader. He was replaced by Vice Admiral Wilhelm Canaris, one of Hitler's most controversial leaders. During the war, Canaris had attempted to make a separate peace with the West.

Canaris was able to run the Abwehr his own way, out of the reach of Hitler's minions. Unfortunately, he ran afoul of two of Hitler's most trusted aides: Reinhard Heydrich and Walter Schellenberg. With two Nazi leaders breathing down his neck, Canaris lived on borrowed time.

When a group of German military officers tried unsuccessfully to assassinate Hitler in 1944, Canaris was identified as one of those responsible. He was removed from office, and ultimately hanged.

(*See Also*: Canaris, Heydrich, Dulles, Schellenberg)

Allied Intelligence Bureau (AIB)

The Allied Intelligence Bureau was the forerunner of the Australian Secret Intelligence Service (ASIO). During World War II, the AIB was jointly operated by the United States and Australian military intelligence agencies, whose combined operations were focused on Japanese forces in the Southwest Pacific. Its commander was General Douglas MacArthur. MacArthur, in turn, gave orders to his Chief Intelligence Officer, Colonel Charles Willoboughy. Another officer in control of the unit was Colonel C.G. Roberts of the Australian Military Intelligence mission.

A vital aspect of the AIB's mission was the organization of Coast Watchers, whose job it was to battle Japanese units in New Guinea, the Solomon Islands and the Philippines. Additionally, the Coast Watchers were expected to infiltrate Japanese lines and collect intelligence on Japanese operations.

One of their most memorable operations was the destruction of a Japanese destroyer that obliterated the "PT 109," the PT boat captained by Lieutenant John F. Kennedy. An alert Australian Coast Watcher was instrumental in saving young Lieutenant Kennedy and his crew from Japanese capture.

The headquarters of the AIB was in Melbourne, Australia. It was made up of five departments, including those run by British and Dutch intelligence, sabotage operations, and a propaganda division.

When the Japanese captured the Philippines in the spring of 1942, General MacArthur fled to the safety of Australia, leaving the Coast Watchers quite literally on their own. Communication was established through powerful short-wave radios. Some of their most successful jobs were the hit-and-run raids against Japanese emplacements before General MacArthur's return to the Philippines.

In one notable failure, a 34-man team of Australian/Portugese agents was captured by Japanese forces on the island of Timor, in the Java Sea in September of 1943. The enemy used the captured AIB's radios to transmit false information to allied headquarters.

The AIB went out of business when the Philippines were retaken by MacArthur.

(*See Also*: Kennedy, John F.)

Astor, Vincent

Franklin D. Roosevelt had an interest in spying long before he became president of the United States in 1932. His first official espionage post was assigned in 1913 when the newly elected Woodrow Wilson appointed him Assistant Secretary of the Navy. As commander-in-chief, FDR was free to make use of his passion for espionage.

When the United States entered World War II, FDR used as many people as possible, in official and unofficial capacities, to conduct clandestine operations for the United States. One of the men whom the president sent out on intelligence missions was his old friend, Vincent Astor.

Astor was a New York neighbor of Franklin and Eleanor Roosevelt, and had their complete trust. At that time, he was the managing director of the Western Union Telegraph Company and was used by Roosevelt in that capacity for intelligence purposes. FDR appointed him liaison to William Stephenson, the head of the secret British Security Coordination service (BSC).

One of the first things Astor did was kill a proposed Vichy French wireless station intended for the Caribbean island of St. Pierre. The station would have enough power to communicate with other countries without being censored by the British wireless station on Bermuda.

Astor also worked closely with the Office of Naval Intelligence (ONI), relating information to the president. Astor's travels took him to the Marshall Islands, where he spied on the Japanese, and to the sunny islands of the Caribbean. But his most important contribution was as managing director of the Western Union Telegraph Company. Astor used his influence to monitor all cable traffic sent by German spies in New York to Latin America. Astor's agents also monitored the frequencies coming from the Swiss, Cuban and Mexican radio stations.

This amateur spy organization, consisting mostly of personal friends of the president, went by the code name *Room*. It was a tight group, unknown even to FBI Director, J. Edgar Hoover. Once the United States came into the war, *Room* was quietly disbanded and replaced by the Office of Strategic Services (OSS), headed by William Donovan.

(*See Also*: BSC; Hoover, J. Edgar; Donovan, William)

B

Bazna, Elyeza aka "Cicero"

The story of Elyeza Bazna, more commonly known as code name *Cicero*, is one of the compelling tales in the history of World War II espionage.

Bazna was a spy for the Germans. He provided some of the most important information gathered by a German agent. He was born in Albania and moved with his family at a young age to Turkey. As a young man, he secured a job as a valet to its British Ambassador, Sir Hugh Knatchbull-Hugessen.

Bazna took on certain sensitive jobs inside the embassy. He was able to read much of the confidential material that crossed the ambassador's desk and make a duplicate key to the dispatch box that contained the embassy's top-secret files.

On October 23, 1943, Bazna met with a German intelligence officer stationed in Ankara, Turkey. The officer, L.C. Moyzisch, received a phone call from the wife of First Secretary Jenke of the German Embassy, offering him an opportunity to obtain classified information. Moyzisch was interested and met his visitor, Bazna, who told him of his position as the valet to the British ambassador and offered to spy for the Germans on the spot, demanding £20,000.

Moyzisch went to the German Ambassador to Turkey, Franz von Papen about his midnight caller. Von Papen radioed Berlin for instructions and was surprised by the German government's quick concession to Bazna's demands. Bazna was given the code name Cicero, and his career as a double agent began.

Cicero was able to provide the German high command with the most explosive classified information, including the minutes of the Casablanca meetings between FDR and Winston Churchill as well as plans for the June 1944 D-Day invasion of France (Operation Overlord).

Unfortunately for Cicero, his career never really took off. His German masters did not believe much of what he had to report and declined to act on his information, then a secretary at the German Embassy who fled to the West betrayed him. Bazna denied any wrongdoing when confronted by the British Ambassador but was fired immediately.

He fled to South America with what he believed was his fortune. However, the British pounds paid him by the Germans were counterfeit, and he was arrested. After jail, he returned to Europe to live out his life. His case was named "Operation Cicero."

A book on Cicero's exploits, *Operation Cicero,* was published in 1950, as well as a movie called *Five Fingers* (1952). Bazna himself wrote his autobiography in 1962, entitled *I Was Cicero.*
(*See Also*: Operation Bernhard)

Bentley, Elizabeth

Prior to and during World War II, the United States was riddled with hundreds, possibly thousands of spies working for the Soviet Union. The Soviets were our allies against Germany, but Stalin saw the United States as one ally worth cultivating. Under the direction of the American Communist Party (ACP) headed by Earl Browder, communist agents burrowed into every facet of the American nation, including various departments of the U.S. government. One of these spies was a rather plain woman named Elizabeth Bentley.

Elizabeth Bentley (1906-1963), a graduate of Vassar College with an M.A. from Columbia University, joined the Communist Party USA (CPUSA) in 1930. After a trip to Italy where she witnessed Benito Mussolini in action she vowed to fight against fascism. Her lover recruited her into spying, a man named Jacob Golos, who headed one of the most important Soviet spy rings in Washington during the war years. Following Golos's sudden death, Bentley assumed leadership of the Golos network

It was assumed Bentley was merely a courier for Golos, but that was not the case. She was privy to all vital information and knew every employee's name. One of Bentley's primary jobs was as liaison between Golos and another Soviet spy group in D.C. headed by Gregory Silvermaster. Itzhak Akhmerov, the head of Soviet espionage in Washington, called Bentley an "intelligent, sober-minded, a quiet woman."

Bentley did all she could to separate her American communist cell from that controlled by the NKVD. This organization, literally *Naradnii Komissariat Vnutrennikh Del*, was the secret police of the Soviet Union from 1935 to 1943, and a forerunner to the KGB. Bentley withheld vital information from her Soviet bosses and kept much of the material gleaned from American sources for her own use.

Despite the fact that Akhmerov referred to Bentley as "one hundred percent our woman," she was undergoing a dramatic change of heart about Russia. When its government discovered her affairs with both a man and a woman in her organization any confidence they might have had in her soured.

According to the Venona tapes, an American espionage project, Soviet bosses said of Bentley, "Taking into account that Bentley won't go anywhere voluntarily and…may damage us here very seriously, only one remedy is left…get rid of her."

Bentley went to the FBI in November 1945 and told them her story. She exposed all of the agents she worked with in Washington: men in top posts of the Roosevelt administration—Lauchlin Currie, one of FDR's closest advisors; Harry Dexter White, Assistant Director of the Treasury; and dozens of Washington officials.

The defection of Elizabeth Bentley was a devastating blow to the Soviet spy operation in the United States. Many spies named by Bentley fled to Russia, breaking down a widespread espionage network in the country. After the war, Bentley would testify before the House Un-American Activities Committee (HUAC), which was investigating communist penetration of the American government by the Soviet Union. That investigation led to the 1950s McCarthy witch hunts that would dominate the American political scene for years.

(*See Also*: Browder, Earl; Golos, Jacob; Venona)

Berg, Morris, "Moe"

Of all the World War II spies, among the least understood to this day is professional baseball player and scholar, Morris "Moe" Berg.

Moe Berg was born in Newark, New Jersey, into a strict Orthodox family. As a youngster, he loved to play baseball and read books. He attended Princeton University, where he was proficient in German, Latin, and Greek. He was also a star athlete on the Princeton baseball team. On campus he was a loner, but organized religious services for its few Jewish students. He graduated magna cum laude in 1923 and, against his father's wishes, pursued a career in professional baseball. He was signed by the Brooklyn Dodgers for $5,000. While the rest of the team read the sports pages, Moe read the classics, played a mean shortstop, and at season's end made his way to Paris to attend the Sorbonne.

In 1924, he returned home and resumed a baseball career. He was sent to the minor leagues and the now defunct Reading Keys of the International League, after which he was picked up for $50,000 for the Chicago White Sox's 1926 season. Berg attended Columbia Law School, and during the next few years, he both played ball and got his law degree. New York Yankee manager Casey Stengel called him, "the strangest fellah who ever put on a uniform." Stengel was right on the money.

In October 1934, Berg played in Japan on an all-star American baseball team whose members included Babe Ruth, Lou Gehrig and Jimmy Foxx. Berg made the trip to Japan holding a letter addressed to the American consulate in Tokyo that instructed them to "provide Mr. Berg such courtesies and assistance as you may be able to render consistent with your official duties." The letter was signed by Secretary of State Cordell Hull. Moe Berg was an American spy.

When not playing exhibition games against the Japanese, Berg made clandestine trips all over Tokyo, photographing strategic sites in commercial and industrial areas, as well as sites near the naval base. During the war, Berg's photographs were used in General Jimmy Doolittle's raid against the Japanese mainland.

On January 7, 1942, Moe Berg hung up his spikes and catcher's mitt. His first foray into government work was his participation in Nelson Rockefeller's Office of Coordinator of Inter-American Affairs (OCI), where he was sent on a "goodwill mission" to political leaders in Brazil and Panama.

By April 1944, William Donovan had assigned Berg to the fledgling Office of Strategic Studies (OSS). He was in the Special Operations Branch of the OSS where his "travel was secret" and his expenses paid out of Special Funds, having presented a letter from Rockefeller verifying that he was on a confidential mission for the White House. He was authorized to carry a .45 caliber pistol and other OSS spy equipment.

Berg's next mission was one of the most important of the war. He was sent to Italy by submarine to monitor atomic research by high-level Italian scientists. Berg was part of the American government's secret plans to build an atomic bomb code-named "The Manhattan Project."

In June 1944, just as the allies invaded France at Normandy, Berg entered Switzerland on orders from General Leslie Groves. His job was to track down German scientists working on their own atomic bomb. Berg found that two of the top German scientists, Otto Hahn and Werner Heisenberg, survived an allied bombing attack on their headquarters at Dahlem, Germany.

The OSS had developed a plan to kidnap Heisenberg and kill him if necessary. Berg was sent into Switzerland as a "technical expert," to take in Heisenberg's lectures. In the end, Berg did not carry out his assignment, believing that Heisenberg was not involved in the development of a German bomb.

After the war, Berg continued secret work for the CIA and worked for NATO.

The events surrounding Berg's death are as mysterious as his life. He died on May 30, 1972 after a fall at his New Jersey home and was buried in an unknown location in Israel.

(*See Also*: Manhattan Project; Heisenberg, Werner)

Black Orchestra (Schwarze Kapelle)

The Black Orchestra was an organization of German military and civilian leaders whose goal was to rid Germany of Hitler and end the war.

When Hitler took over Germany, he promised to return the country to the world power it had been at the beginning of World War I. Despite harsh military and political conditions imposed upon Germany after the Treaty of Versailles, Hitler disregarded all international sanctions. The Western countries ignored Hitler's rearmament until German troops invaded Poland in September 1939, starting World War II.

Hitler's "Final Solution" led to the deaths of six million European Jews, as well as millions of others the German leader thought inferior. As these events unfolded, some members of the German military decided Hitler's policies would eventually mean defeat and decided to oust him.

A number of officers conspired with the Americans in anti-Hitler plots. The most notable was Abwehr Chief, Admiral Wilhelm Canaris. Canaris appointed a number of men to his staff and ordered them to make contact with the West. Among them was Fabian von Schlabrendorff, who, posing as a writer, made his way to London and contacted members of the British Secret Service.

Others who made overtures to the allies were Hans Bernd Gisevius, a Gestapo lawyer who met with U.S. spies in Switzerland; Dr. Joseph Muller; and an anonymous lawyer who went to the Vatican office of the Department of Extraordinary Affairs to enlist members of the pope's entourage. The major military presence working against Hitler was Colonel General Ludwig Beck, former chief of the German General Staff, now the unofficial leader of the Black Orchestra conspiracy.

When Hitler first resolved to take over Austria and attack Czechoslovakia, the Black Orchestra informed then British Prime Minister Neville Chamberlain. Chamberlain, however, sought a separate peace deal with Hitler, and was betrayed.

When it became obvious that Germany could not win, Beck, Canaris, and the others decided to assassinate Hitler. A number of German generals agreed to go along. They planned to do it at Hitler's military headquarters in Rastenburg, East Prussia on July 20, 1944. A prominent participant was the "Desert Fox" himself, Erwin Rommel, whose victories over the British in North Africa had made him a national hero.

The man who placed the bomb under Hitler's desk was Count Claus von Stauffenberg. After planting it, Stauffenberg made his way back to Berlin according to plan and awaited the news of Hitler's death. Unfortunately for Stauffenberg, Hitler escaped injury.

Immediately thereafter, the conspirators were arrested, shot, hanged or given the opportunity to commit suicide. Rommel took a poison pill, and Canaris was arrested and executed. The short-lived coup by the Black Orchestra ended in disaster.

Bletchley Park

Bletchley Park was the site of a confidential British code-breaking operation during World War II, from which British scientists, mathematicians, linguists, and musicians, broke German military codes and, most significant to the result of the war, cracked the Enigma codes of the German intelligence service.

The original site of Bletchley Park was established in 1860 by Herbert Leon, a wealthy Victorian businessman. It was located about 50 miles from London in a low-activity area. One of the advantages to Bletchley's location was the nearby highway that linked two British universities: Cambridge and Oxford.

Bletchley Park was nicknamed "Station X," and served as the evacuation area for members of the Secret Intelligence Service (SIS) in case London was overrun by the enemy. Its employees were dubbed "Little Kings," a reference to the many graduates of Cambridge that wound up working there.

It became fully operational in 1941, employing about 1,800 people. It was organized into a collection of huts, with one SIS officer per area, each chosen for their expertise. Much of the staff lived in private homes nearby, hiding what they did from their wives and friends.

The chief of station was A.G. Denniston, who ran the Government Code and Cipher School (GC&CS). However, Denniston gave overall command of the daily routine to Cmdr. Edward Travis, personal representative of Stewart Menzies, or "C," head of the British Secret Service. Travis was an ex-naval officer who brought the best and brightest of British minds to Station X. It evolved into the main resource for cracking worldwide German military codes and ciphers intercepted by British listening stations around the globe. By the end of 1943, the working population of Bletchley was 3,200. They operated around the clock in shifts, eating meager food and working in cold, dimly lit conditions, sacrificing to the cause of defeating Nazi Germany.

As the British began to decipher the German Enigma code, military specialists from the United States arrived at Bletchley to aid in the work. A delegation of U.S. code breakers arrived in 1941 under the direction of William

Friedman, a legend in the United States for his ability to break codes. The American delegation volunteered a copy of the *Purple* machine used by American cryptoanalysts to decipher Japanese codes.

A number of men who would later play an important role in postwar America came to Bletchley as part of the American delegation. Among them were William Bundy, future assistant secretary of state, and Lewis Powell, Jr., future Supreme Court Justice. The British "stars" at Bletchley Park were Alan Turing, inventor of the modern day computer, Gordon Welchman, and Hugh O'Dowd Alexander.

Every snippet of intelligence from every German source was catalogued, broken down and passed on to its relevant unit. If not for the scientists operating out of the GC&CS at Bletchley Park who cracked the *Ultra* code, the war's outcome might have been vastly different.

(*See Also*: Ultra; Enigma)

British Security Coordination (BSC)

Two years into the war, with Britain reeling from the Nazi blitzkrieg, Prime Minister Winston Churchill's government sought any means available to combat the German takeover of Europe. One of their most important strategies was the gathering of intelligence to keep one step ahead of Hitler's soldiers. In May 1940, the United States still had not entered the war, but President Roosevelt had meetings with his British counterpart. FDR gave Churchill 50 overage destroyers for British use, receiving in exchange 99-year leases on eight military bases in New Foundland and the West Indies. By 1941, he provided surplus guns and ammunition for their war effort and planned strategy in case the United States became a participant in the conflict.

One of the most secret plans between Winston Churchill and Roosevelt was the establishment of a secret British spy agency in the United States. The name of this operation was British Security Coordination (BSC). Writers have chronicled the wartime exploits of a Canadian named William Stephenson, aka "Intrepid," who ran the BSC.

Only a handful of American officials knew of the BSC, among them were President Roosevelt, FBI Director J. Edgar Hoover and William "Wild Bill" Donovan, who would shortly be appointed the country's first espionage chief, operating the Office of Strategic Services (OSS). FDR was kept abreast of Stephenson's BSC operation in New York and provided aid to the Canadian effort. The other person who mentored Stephenson was Donovan, in organizing a secret intelligence unit.

Although Roosevelt and Donovan were enamored of the BSC and its work, J. Edgar Hoover was not. Hoover told FDR he opposed the BSC, that their operation on American soil was an infringement on his own intelligence turf. FDR instructed Hoover to cooperate with Stephenson; he reluctantly agreed.

Stephenson established his BSC headquarters right on Fifth Ave., across the street from St. Patrick's Cathedral in New York. The BSC headquarters was just another obscure office in Rockefeller Center. The name on the door read "British Passport Control" and was in fact the office where British citizens came to get or renew passports. Its real purpose was as headquarters for a vast British espionage network that blanketed the Americas. It kept track of German agents in the United States, Canada, Central and South America, and foiled numerous German attempts to initiate terrorism on American soil.

The parent body of the BSC was the Security Executive set up by Winston Churchill. The Security Executive's job was to keep track of "Fifth Columnists," those who might be a security threat on British shores at the outbreak of the war. The man in charge was Lord Swinton, aka, Philip Cunliffe-Lister, minister for air from 1935 to 1938.

Another organization represented by the BSC in New York was the internal security service, MI-5, the British equivalent of the OSS. In time, though, a Canadian and Caribbean MI-5 pulled out of its cooperation with BSC.

The four main areas of interest to BSC were 1) Intelligence, 2) Security, 3) Special Operations, and 4) Passport Control. Later, Communication became number five, as BSC's agents used listening posts throughout the Americas and had to maintain communication with their agents. One of BSCs political functions was to influence American public opinion in Britain's favor. This was accomplished by courting prominent American journalists such as Walter Winchell and Drew Pearson, whose popular columns put Britain's struggle for survival in the best light possible.

When not working at his Rockefeller Center headquarters, Bill Stephenson lived at the exclusive St. Regis Hotel in Manhattan. He held private discussions there with members of the British military and political establishment who made their way to New York. On September 6, 1941, a group of men arrived at Stephenson's hotel to talk strategy. The group was composed of Tommy Davis, a top member of the British Special Operations Executive (SOE), whose job was to wreak havoc behind German lines; Noel Hall, director of London's National Institute for Economic and Social Research; an American doctor named Blake Donaldson; arctic explorer Vilhjalmur Stefansson; and A.J. Taylor. These men planned a training facility for agents to be schooled in the arts of combat and espionage techniques, and sent into enemy territory.

Once Bill Stephenson got his BSC under way, their mandate expanded. In time, BSC's agents investigated Americans who were allied with the

Germans, guarding American ports of entry and collecting information from the longshoremen who offloaded ships for anti-German splinter groups in European countries. This was followed by the establishment of a censorship station in Bermuda where British censors read American mail.

One of BSCs top priorities was to gain naval protection from the United States for British convoys sailing from the United States to England. That was one area where FDR was glad to cooperate. At the beginning of the war, American-led escorts braved the German U-boat threat by accompanying hundreds of British ships carrying war materials.

A sterling BSC contribution was the wireless war being undertaken by the British at Bletchley Park. BSC agents used new radio direction equipment to keep track of German messages to and from their military and diplomatic outposts around the world.

Stephenson's deputy at BSC was Colonel Charles Ellis, a former MI-6 officer whose history in intelligence preceded him. It was alleged by some in the secret services that Ellis had worked for the Germans before the war and should not be given the sensitive responsibilities he now had. But Stephenson trusted him.

Although FBI Director Hoover felt Stephenson's BSC was trespassing in America, he had a useful contact in the Canadian's BSC. FDR had given Hoover the responsibility to conduct counterespionage activities on behalf of the U.S. in South and Central America, coming directly in contact with BSC. Hoover's Special Intelligence Service agents were able to liaison with a number of BSC's agents and share information.

The FBI was not the only American intelligence service to work with BSC. Representatives from the navy and army aided Stephenson's agents in a wide range of activities. The BSC remained in New York until the war ended, serving as an extension of the British Secret Service, far away from the British Isles.

In speaking about his role as head of BSC, Bill Stephenson said this, "BSC became the only all-encompassing integrated secret security organization that had ever existed…anywhere, and myself the repository of secret information…beyond that of any other…involved."

(*See Also*: Donovan, William; Stephenson, William; Hoover, J. Edgar)

Earl Browder

From the 1930s well into the war years, the Soviet Union maintained a large cadre of spies and undercover agents inside the United States government. Many members of the Communist Party United States of America (CPUSA) held high positions in government departments, from aides to cabinet members, and secretaries in positions of influence. Others served as couriers in the nation's capital, going between party members and their underlings. The man in charge of the CPUSA was Earl Browder.

Browder's code name from Moscow was "Helmsman." He served the Soviets from 1930 to 1945. Browder's sister, Marguerite, also served in the foreign department of the NKVD in various European cities. Earl asked his bosses in the Soviet Union to release his sister from active duty because of "…my increasing involvement in national political affairs and growing connections in Washington political circles…." He received a reply from the head of the NKVD ordering Marguerite's release for political reasons.

Browder, born in 1891 in Wichita, Kansas, joined the Socialist Party, and was convicted of anti-war demonstrations in World War I. He served his first prison term in 1920. In 1921, he became a member of the CPUSA's Central Committee, and rose to the top in 1930. His second wife, Raissa Berkman, was also a CPUSA member.

In 1939, with communist infiltration of Washington getting the attention of Congress, Earl Browder and his brother William were called to testify before the House Un-American Activities Committee. They were asked whether their sister has been a member of the Third International, an organization uniting communist groups of various countries. They replied, "to the best of my knowledge, she is not now and has not in the past been officially connected with any government institution." The Congress investigated Marguerite Browder and found a false passport in the name of "Jean Montgomery." Her signature on her passport application was written in William Browder's hand.

The recently decoded Venona materials shed historical light on the extensive role Earl Browder played as head of the CPUSA and its relations with the Russian NKVD. The releases contain Earl Browder's name 26 times.

The tapes document Browder's involvement in espionage against the United States. For example, Browder used information from one of his inside sources in the Roosevelt administration, an employee of Undersecretary of State Sumner Wells. In May 1941, Browder passed a report written by Wells to Moscow concerning the U.S. reaction to political turmoil inside the Italian government. The NKVD also shared information with Browder, which he used to gain further intelligence from his huge covet network inside Washington.

The CPUSA was the vital link between the Soviet Union's spies in the government and the NKVD in Moscow. One of Browder's most influential agents was Jacob Golos who ran one of the most secretive Washington espionage rings. Another person who met frequently with Browder was Golos's lover and courier, Elizabeth Bentley.

According to newly released files, Browder also recruited foreigners to work with the CPUSA-KGB. One of these was Pierre Cot, a member of the radical party in France. Cot was a Soviet source dating back to his work as a Soviet agent in the Spanish Civil War. Cot came to work for Browder in Washington in September 1940.

Unknown to Browder, the FBI was keeping a very close watch on his activities. In 1940, he had been sent to prison for using a false passport on a trip to Spain at the time of the Spanish Civil war. He spent only 14 months of a four-year prison term before being given amnesty by FDR

In May 1944, at a Congress of the CPUSA, Browder got the delegates to disband the organization in favor of a Communist Political Association. This news did not go over well in Moscow and Browder was driven from his job. Following his firing, Browder tried unsuccessfully to communicate with Joseph Stalin through the KGB representatives in Washington but was rebuffed. However, after the war, Browder served as the Soviet Union's mouthpiece for a publishing venture in this country.

Earl Browder went from head of the most productive Russian-supported spy ring in the United States to pariah at Joseph Stalin's whim.

(*See Also:* Bentley, Elizabeth; Venona)

Guy Burgess

In the history of 20th-century spying, the most notorious group of Russian spies came to be known as the "Cambridge Five," a collection of highly educated British agents and members of the privileged class that spied for the Soviet Union. One of the members of this group was Guy Burgess. Over a period of 20 years, Burgess and the rest of the members of the Cambridge Five supplied the Soviets with troves of vital information spanning the pre-World War II years and beginning of the Cold War.

Guy Burgess was born in Devonport, England, to a Royal Navy family. His father had been an officer, and Guy tried to follow in his footsteps. At a young age, Guy went to Eton, then to the naval college at Dartmouth. He did not last long there and had to drop out (so the story goes) because of an eye disorder that prohibited him from entering the navy. The real reason for his dismissal, one that would haunt him the rest of his life, was his homosexuality. An affair had been discovered by school authorities.

He graduated Eton in 1930 and went to Cambridge University, where he was to meet the other members of the ring that would prove so disastrous to England. He studied history and fell in love with communist ideology. At Cambridge, Burgess joined a group called the Apostles, a secret group of anti-establishment youths. It was there that Burgess was first recruited by Russian agents, and found soul mates in Donald MacLean and Kim Philby, who were gay as well.

The man who actually recruited Burgess was Anthony Blunt, a young communist. In 1934, Burgess, Philby and MacLean took a trip to Moscow, where Burgess spent most of the time drunk. He was even arrested by local police. After his return, he joined an Anglo-German Fellowship Society and tried to get a job with the Conservative Party.

After graduation, Burgess went to work as a broadcaster with the BBC. During that time, Burgess was approached by British Intelligence. One of his tasks was to find information about the inner workings of the French cabinet. Burgess also worked for the Russians and hid the fact from the British.

In 1939, the year England entered the war, Burgess worked for MI-6 in an office that handled propaganda and subversion. Part of his assignment was to keep watch on the White Russian community in England. He also smuggled the private correspondence of Prime Minister Chamberlain to his Soviet bosses. He began to work for the British spy agency, Special Operation Executive (SOE). He scored his most successful coup (as far as the Soviets were concerned) when he recruited Kim Philby, his pal from Cambridge days, into British intelligence.

Living in London, Burgess held court with many local men and met often with Blunt and Philby, passing along information as he received it. In 1944, he joined the Foreign Office handling news broadcasts. For six years he sent information to Moscow, while deciding what news to pass along to the British people.

In time, Kim Philby was transferred to a top security job at the British Embassy in Washington. Burgess managed to get a similar assignment and joined Philby in giving Washington's most important secrets to Moscow. He lived with the Philbys and regularly drank to excess, once going so far as to insult the wife of William Harvey, an operator in U.S. intelligence.

In June 1951, Burgess learned that the British had discovered Donald MacLean's espionage. MacLean was living in London, but Burgess managed to return home and warn him. Burgess knew that once MacLean was exposed, he was next. Both men packed their bags and fled to Moscow. Burgess died there in 1963, suffering from arteriosclerosis.

(*See Also*: Philby, Kim; MacLean, Donald; Cairncross, John; Cambridge Spies)

C

COI (Coordinator of Information)

Among the warring nations in World War II, the only one that did not have an organized intelligence service was the United States. Most nations had a long history of operating a national security service. Prior to Pearl Harbor, the United States had nothing. Armed services, like the army and navy, used a limited number of people to collect and analyze such information for the government. But in Washington, as the war developed, in the fall of 1941, President Roosevelt decided the United States should keep track of Germany and Japan with a unified intelligence service under the president's jurisdiction. To that end, FDR appointed a friend, World War I hero William Donovan, as head of a new organization directly responsible to him. The name of the agency was Coordinator of Information (COI). COI directly preceded the wartime Office of Strategic Services, also headed by Donovan.

Part of Donovan's duty was to "collect and analyze all information and data which may bear upon national security; correlate such information and data; and make the same available to the President or to such departments...as the President may determine, and carry out when requested by the President, such supplementary activities as may facilitate the securing of information important for national security not now available to the Government."

Donovan set up COI's new headquarters in two small rooms across the street from the White House and Lafayette Park. They soon moved to larger quarters at the Apex Building. In its first year, the COI's budget was a measly $1,454,000. Most of it came from a secret fund operated by President Roosevelt, referred to as the Emergency Fund.

Many of COI's initial recruits were personal friends of Donovan, men from the upper echelon of society. Among them were playwright Robert Sherwood, whose play *There Shall Be No Night* would win the Pulitzer Prize;

Archibald MacLeish, the Librarian of Congress; authors Edmond Taylor and Douglas Miller; journalists James Warburg and Wallace Deuel; James Roosevelt, one of FDR's sons; John Ford, Hollywood director; and many more.

Of the many to inhabit the secret world of COI, only three would be the brains behind the organization: James Murphy, Colonel Edward Buxton and Otto Doering, Jr. Murphy had previously worked for Donovan at the Justice Department and would later be in charge of one of COI's most sensitive operations, *X-2*, a counterespionage service. Murphy would be part of some of the most crucial spy missions of the war. Ed Buxton was a World War I veteran, having served with the famous Alvin York, as his commander. He headed his Oral Intelligence Unit, which interviewed travelers from Europe. Otto Deoring had previously worked in Donovan's law office and acted as de facto chief of staff at COI. "It was Doering who supplied the organizational talent that enabled Donovan to construct his service in thirty months— against the thirty years it had taken the European powers."

As COI grew in importance, Donovan received a $10-million budget, no questions asked. It moved to larger quarters at the National Institute of Health, not far from the Lincoln Memorial. One visitor remarked that it "closely resembled a cat house in Laredo on a Saturday night, with rivalries, jealousies, mad schemes, and everyone trying to get the ear of the director...." Nonetheless it was an organization in the making.

Other visitors to COI came from England, where British spymasters popped in to see how their apprentices fared. Among those who lent their expertise was Commander Ian Fleming, James Bond author, and Colonel Charles Ellis, a top man in the British Secret Intelligence Service (SIS) who was sent personally by William Stephenson. The British helped COI trainees learn the fundamentals of organizing a spy network. They taught Donovan's men the techniques of secret warfare, radio-finding operations, the use of codes and ciphers, how to establish a hidden bank account, the use of explosives, how to conceal a murder weapon, in short, a how-to of secret operations.

In August 1941, COI would take on another, more dangerous role. Donovan was visited by a man named Wallace Banta Phillips. Phillips claimed he worked for the Office of Naval Intelligence (ONI), heading a secret compartment called the "K Organization," responsible for controlling secret agents in the field. COI was offered the operation.

Donovan, who had never met the hunchbacked Wallace Banta Phillips, was just a touch leery, but when he learned Phillips had been appointed special assistant to the director of Naval Intelligence when Germany attacked America's European allies, Donovan named him Director of Special Information Service. The SIS was the cover for a network of agents in Europe. Thus, the COI became engaged for the first time in espionage operations. What Donovan didn't know was that the K Organization had very few men in the field. There were four men working in Latvia, Estonia; one Treasury agent operating in the Balkans; 12 vice-counsels in North Africa, and two "representatives" in Mexico City. All that changed, however, after Pearl Harbor.

As America entered the war, the British began to share its intelligence discoveries with COI. For example, they told Donovan they cracked the German Enigma codes and that they had rounded up all German spies operating there. They signed an agreement to share all intelligence information. To that end, Donovan sent George Bowden to England as liaison to Stewart Menzies, head of British intelligence group, ISOS.

COI's first operational orders came shortly after Pearl Harbor. FDR gave Donovan instructions personally to ensure that war between the U.S. and Vichy France did not break out, in the event of an allied invasion of North Africa (Operation Torch), and to protect the French fleet from the Germans. It was important that Spain remain neutral in the war. To that end, Donovan sent his first COI agents to the Iberian Peninsula to establish an arms network, infiltrate suspected fascist groups, set up direct communication links with his various agents in Spain and Portugal, and halt German infiltration of these countries by any means necessary.

The COI was replaced by the Office of Strategic Services (OSS) on June 13, 1942.

(*See Also*: Donovan, William; Fleming, Ian; Stephenson, William; K Organization)

Cairncross, John

In the lore of espionage, John Cairncross has the distinction of being "the Fifth Man." He was part of the infamous Cambridge Spy ring.

John Cairncross was born to Scottish parents. Unlike the other members of the group, he did not come from a privileged family, his father was an ironworker and his mother a teacher. He worked his way up the educational ladder, attending Glasgow University, and the Sorbonne where he earned degrees in French and German. From the Sorbonne, Cairncross attended Cambridge where he became the fifth member of the Cambridge Five.

In 1936, he took the difficult Home Office and Foreign Office examinations, and received the highest scores in the history of the tests. He was immediately hired as a member of the British Foreign Service. In his first assignment, he and Donald MacLean became instant friends. Soon both were spying for the Russians, Cairncross delivering secret information on

British strategy for Nazi Germany.

His next assignment was at the super-secret Government Code and Cipher School (GCCS) located in Bletchley Park. At Bletchley, British and American code breakers cracked German codes intercepted from listening posts in allied countries across the world.

After his stint at GCCS, he was given a choice assignment, working for MI-6 in London. He pilfered countless documents and handed them over to his Soviet contacts, including the British plans for Yugoslavia after the war. In later years, Cairncross would reveal that he began spying for the Soviets way back in 1932. After the war ended, he went back to the Foreign Office and continued his spying.

Cairncross's undoing was Burgess and MacLean's escape to the Soviet Union. Police searched their apartment and found Treasury documents in Cairncross's handwriting. He was fired, and ended up at the United Nations working on economic development projects in Africa.

In 1967, British intelligence made known to him that he was being investigated as a spy. Cairncross agreed to cooperate with the authorities and told them he had stopped spying years earlier. He went to Italy to live in peace, but it wasn't until 1981 that his spying activities during the war were publicly revealed. He was never prosecuted, and returned to England in 1995. He died the same year.

(*See Also*: Cambridge Spies)

Cambridge Spies

The most important of all the Soviet spy rings to operate in the years before and during World War II was comprised of highly idealistic and educated British students at Cambridge University, commonly known in intelligence history as the "Cambridge Five" or "Cambridge Spies." The principals were: Guy Burgess; Anthony Blunt; Donald MacLean; Harold "Kim" Philby; and John Cairncross.

One thing these men had in common, besides Marxism, was Cambridge University during the 1930s. It was during this period that the Russian NKVD devised a master plan to infiltrate British intelligence—MI-5—and MI-6, the counterintelligence department (comparable to our CIA). They set their sights on Cambridge University because it was a hotbed of British intellectualism. Their plan was to recruit bright, young men and plant them in the British Foreign Service and intelligence agencies.

At Cambridge, Anthony Blunt and Guy Burgess were members of a society called "The Cambridge Apostles," as well as lovers. The Apostles' members believed in Marxist philosophy and were amenable to recruitment. According to Yuri Modin, the Soviet "handler" for the Cambridge Spies,

Burgess was the one who enrolled Blunt. In time, both Philby and MacLean were added to the group.

Anthony Blunt was one of the most cultured men in Britain. He was the grandson of an Anglican bishop and son of an Anglican vicar. Blunt served in MI-5 during the war and used his position to spy for the Soviets. After the war, he was hired as the Director of the Courtauld Institute of Art, and became one of the most knowledgeable art historians of his day. As his reputation grew, he was appointed as the art advisor to the Royal Family of England and knighted in 1956. In 1979, it was revealed that Blunt was a spy for the Soviets, and Prime Minister Margaret Thatcher withdrew his royal recognition. Blunt died in 1983.

Guy Burgess came from a naval family, and attended Eton. After a hushed up scandal involving homosexuality, he arrived at Cambridge and continued his secret life. He met the men who would occupy most of his adult life.

Burgess eventually went to work for MI-5 and from there pulled Kim Philby into the Cambridge Ring. He accompanied Philby to Washington where they both assumed positions in British intelligence, working closely with the American CIA, befriending top men in the American intelligence apparatus, while giving Soviet handlers all the information at their disposal. In time though, the British were able to learn of both Burgess and MacLean's treachery, and both men fled to Russia to live out their lives.

Donald MacLean, an aristocrat, attended Cambridge but was not in the inner circle of his spy compatriots. At one time, he served British Prime Minister Stanley Baldwin, and was later posted to the British Embassy in Washington from 1944 to 1948. During this time, MacLean passed information concerning the private communications that went on between Churchill and Roosevelt to Russia, and later on, Churchill and President Truman. He also sent information on the top-secret Manhattan Project that led to the development of the atomic bomb. The information MacLean gave to the Russians, paved the way for the development of the Soviet's first atomic bomb.

Adrian "Kim" Philby was one of the 20th century's most stellar spies. He was named Kim by his father, famed Arabist St. John Philby, after the character in Kipling's *Jungle Book*. It has been written that young Kim took on his father's anti-British hatred and embraced the Cambridge Spy Ring. He was a man who could be anything he wanted to be, and did not let any one know of his real identity. The popularly accepted story is that Philby was recruited into the spy ring in 1934 by Arnold Deutsch of the KGB and by Edith Tudor-Hart, a British communist. Philby said that he in turn, brought in Burgess and MacLean. Philby married four times. The last was a Russian woman, after his defection.

Philby was a stutterer, but that didn't prevent his being an influential member of British intelligence. Unknown to his colleagues, Philby revealed that the British had broken the German Enigma codes. Along with spying, he instructed new recruits to the British secret service. After the war, Philby was posted to Washington where he served as the liaison between MI-6 and the CIA. He was privy to files provided him by the FBI, and mixed socially with members of the counterintelligence staff of the CIA, then headed by James Angleton. It was even rumored that Philby was being groomed to take over the entire Secret Intelligence Service. He defected to the Soviet Union in 1963.

The lasting effect of the Cambridge Spies' activities was a deep distrust between the intelligence services of America and England. Cooperation between the FBI and the CIA diminished significantly. As far as the British were concerned, they never dreamt that Blunt, Burgess, Philby, and MacLean, all prime candidates for blackmail because of homosexual leanings, would ever betray their own country.

(*See Also*: Philby, Kim; Burgess, Guy; MacLean, Donald; Cairncross, John)

Camp X

In war, myth and reality often combine to make perfect theater, no more so than in the case of the allied training facility located in Canada called Camp X. There are different interpretations of what took place at Camp X— who was there and what role it played in the war.

The story of Camp X was right out of a James Bond novel, with spies running amok, underwater training facilities, miniature submarines operating in a deep lake, parachutists infiltrating Europe, trainees learning silent kill techniques, and countless other lethal skills. While the historical record is correct in that some or all of these activities took place at Camp X, the reality is much different than reported.

Camp X was formed when it seemed the Nazis were about to conquer Europe. With Great Britain on the ropes, it was decided by the top members of British intelligence that a safe, yet highly secret training camp had to be established out of harm's way, with the facilities to train a large group of men for future missions inside Europe. They wanted the place to be near the United States for its communication capabilities. They selected a desolate spot about an hour from Niagara Falls, New York, the town of Whitby.

Two major Canadian cities lay in a direct route to Camp X; Toronto was 30 miles west, and Montreal was some 300 miles to the east. The actual site of the base was between the towns of Whitby and Oshawa, bordered by the tracks of the Canadian National Railroad. The main bodies of water _surrounding Camp X were Corbett's Creek, a heavily wooded area, and

CAMP X

Thickson's Point. Forty miles of water guarded the place, as well as hundreds of miles of dense woods. According to William Stephenson, author of *A Man Called Intrepid*, the Camp X land had been bought in small lots until a huge base was created.

British Security Coordination used the site to operate Special Training School No. 103. STS 103 trained allied agents in the techniques of secret warfare for the Special Operations Executive (SOE) branch of the British Intelligence Service. Hydra was another operation, a network that communicated vital messages between Canada, the United States, and Britain.

Camp X was run under the direct supervision of Stephenson's BSC in New York. Charles Vining and Tommy Drew-Brook were direct emissaries of Bill Stephenson. Drew-Brook was the head of the Canadian British Security Coordination team, and Vining was the first head of the department.

The action arm of the operation was directed from there, and the administrative from Toronto in an office building that housed the Canadian Bank of Commerce. Other Canadian governmental organizations to oversee Camp X were the Royal Canadian Mounted Police (RCMP) and the military. The Prime Minister's office was kept informed, and kept its secret close to the vest.

One important section of Camp X was not physically on site. It was a secret group called "Station M," based in Toronto. The men of "Station M" forged papers and documents for use by the men who trained at Camp X, and went into Nazi-occupied Europe.

As the camp began its deadly business, agents were sent there from all over the world. Men from the FBI came to learn new skills and report back to J. Edgar Hoover, who kept an eye on things from his post in Washington. On numerous occasions, William Stephenson came to Camp X to see how his recruits were doing and Bill Donovan, the head of the OSS, and then secret agent, Ian Fleming. It was rumored that Fleming took part in various training courses, but his prowess left much to be desired.

One of the most important aspects of Camp X was its communications buildings. It was from here that female operators sent and received coded and decoded messages to and from allied listening posts across the world. The nerve center of this communications hub was an area designated as "Hydra." Hydra was a short-wave transmitter/receiver with a huge Rhombic Antenna. This link with the outside world was made possible by a covert relationship with the Canadian Broadcasting Company, which supplied much of the material needed to build the network.

As demand for information on everyday life in Europe grew, all kinds of people were "invited" to Camp X to deliver their expertise. Besides agents in training, sea captains just in from North American ports revealed information overheard in passenger conversations (mostly German). Agents spirited away garment bags, clothing, and other personal items from unsuspecting travelers in order to duplicate them for the men who would live behind enemy lines.

David Stafford dispels myths concerning events said to have occurred at Camp X in his book, *Camp X, OSS, "Intrepid" and the Allies North American Training Camp for Secret Agents, 1941-1945*. One of which was that Camp X agents assassinated Nazi killer Reinhard Heydrich, the "Protector" of Bohemia and Monrovia. Stafford points out that the BSC had no operational responsibility in Europe. Another myth is that Camp X trainees destroyed the heavy-water plant at Vemok in Norway.

In the war against Germany, this location in the wilds of Canada proved to be one of history's successful secret training grounds for allied agents in history.

(*See Also*: Stephenson, William; Donovan, William; Hoover, J. Edgar; OSS)

Canaris, Wilhelm

One of the enduring questions of World War II is whether or not Admiral Wilhelm Canaris, head of the German Abwehr, was working for the British Secret Service during its last years.

Canaris served in the German military during World War I, dabbling in espionage. He was in the submarine and surface fleets, and set up a spy network in French-occupied Morocco. Using a false passport he arrived in New York in 1916 to sabotage American armaments factories.

In April 1915, Canaris's ship, the *Dresden*, was sunk near the Chilean coast. Her entire crew was captured and put in chains. Canaris somehow managed to escape, and walked across the snow-capped Andes toward Argentina with forged papers.

He boarded a ship bound for Holland via Falmouth, England and landed in Berlin in October 1916. He immediately reported to the German military. They saw great potential in Canaris and sent him off to Spain. Using the code name "Reed-Rosas," Canaris then made contact with anti-Spanish, North African tribesmen whom he tried to entice into revolt.

British intelligence agents in Spain were watching Canaris. It has been written that British Army Captain Steward Menzies vetoed plans to assassinate Canaris, proposed in 1943 by none other than British agent Kim Philby. In later years, when speaking about this incident, Stewart Menzies admitted, "…he did give me assistance. I liked and admired him. He was damned brave."

In 1920, Canaris took part in a plot to overthrow the German government organized by Wolfgang Kapp. Its goal was to return Germany to her pre-World War I status. Canaris served a brief time in jail after the unsuccessful coup.

While he was working as a military intelligence officer for the Third Reich, Canaris was mistrustful of Hitler's leadership and, more importantly, his conduct in war. While it has not been totally confirmed, it's widely believed that Canaris met with representatives of British intelligence during hostilities.

Canaris was playing a dangerous game of double-dealing against his superior officers. On one occasion, Heinrich Himmler sent him to Spain to persuade Francisco Franco to cooperate in taking over the British rock of Gibraltar. Instead, Canaris got the Spanish dictator to refuse to allow German troops on Spanish soil and to bar Spanish participation in any attack on the "Rock." The Abwehr chief also tipped off Franco to the impending German attack on the Soviet Union.

After the war, Ramon Serrano Suner, Spain's foreign minister, and Franco's brother-in-law, revealed "how amazed he was that, despite the dramatic Nazi march to victory, Canaris kept insisting…that Germany would lose the war in the end."

Canaris was also playing with fire with his most ardent foe, Reinhard Heydrich. Both men knew each other from their navy days but a rather hostile relationship formed when they were vying for the top spot in German intelligence circles. Canaris had a secret file on Heydrich consisting of rumors that Heydrich had Jewish bloodlines.

What is known about Canaris's clandestine meetings with the British SIS is that he gave intelligence information via a Switzerland contact. Her name was Madame Szymanska, a Polish national who had a relationship with the SIS.

In February 1944, Hitler, even more distrustful of Canaris, dismissed him from his post. By July, Canaris was arrested and sent to a concentration camp for activities against the state. He was tried for treason, and hanged in April 1945, just before the war ended.

(*See Also*: Dulles, Allen; Menzies, Stewart; Popov, Dusan)

Casey, William

When Ronald Reagan was elected president in 1980, one of his first appointments was that of his old friend and campaign director, William Casey, as head of the CIA. This was a political appointment, to be sure, but a fact that was omitted, or forgotten, was Casey's experience in espionage rooted in the early days of the OSS, under William Donovan.

Bill Casey grew up in Queens, New York. He attended Fordham University, married, and began his career as a lawyer. His family's politics were that of Roosevelt's New Deal but soon young Bill gravitated to the

Republican Party. He campaigned for Wendell Willkie, who ran opposite President Roosevelt.

As the war spread in Europe, the United States prepared to enter the conflict. Casey was offered a position in a think tank called the Research Institute of America by his friend Leo Cherne. Casey and his fellow workers wrote a book on America's preparedness. It was published as *The Business and Defense Coordinator.*

Soon, Bill Casey and the rest of America would be caught up in the war. On June 15, 1943, he was commissioned as a lieutenant junior grade in the U.S. Navy. His first assignment was with the Office of Naval Procurement in Washington, where his unit was responsible for naval landing craft. Casey decided he wanted to see action, and called Jerry Doran, whom he knew to be involved in undercover work. Casey was passed through many channels before meeting a man named Colonel Vanderblue, a recruiter for the OSS. The men talked for hours, and he was accepted into the OSS two weeks later.

Casey worked with other men in a section that handled cables from OSS agents across the world. It was their job to filter each piece of information, catalogue it into priority sections, and decide which piece to send to Donovan's desk. Of Donovan in those early years Casey said, "I was just a boy from Long Island. Sure, I had worked with high-level government officials, generals, and admirals. But never had I been in personal contact with a man of Donovan's candlepower. He was bigger than life. I reveled in my association with that man. We all glowed in his presence."

Casey was given the job of manufacturing cogent reports out of the information that came flooding into London OSS headquarters. His reports were sent to Washington for top members of the Roosevelt administration. It was at Casey's hand that operation policy evolved. His work was noticed and in time earned him an important position in the London OSS. It also made him a favorite of Bill Donovan. Casey traveled to the beaches at Normandy after the invasion, to Algiers, and many other significant battlegrounds.

In time, he was promoted to Chief of the OSS Secretariat in the European Theater of Operations. He wrote an important policy paper on German operations called "An OSS Program against Germany." It detailed OSS covert operations in the German army. One of his jobs, as the war neared its end, was to recruit agents among all categories of people; communists, prisoners of war, etc. Casey oversaw their training, and was on hand when they were sent behind the lines.

The war's end brought the closure of the OSS and shut down Bill Casey's spy career. He returned to civilian life and described his time as an OSS agent as, "…the greatest experience of my life."

Chambers, Whittaker

The name Whittaker Chambers is synonymous with one of the most notorious spy scandals of World War II, which eventually brought on the post-war Red Scare. His name will be forever linked with that of Alger Hiss, a top-level State Department official, who Chambers unmasked as an agent of the NKVD.

Whittaker Chambers was born Jay Vivian Chambers in Philadelphia to a dysfunctional family. In their Long Island, New York home Whittaker's father would cruise for male partners, ignoring his wife for days; his grandmother would wander their home hallucinating. His young brother took to alcohol and would eventually commit suicide.

Whittaker's passport out of this home was his keen intellect. He was accepted into Columbia University in New York where he took on the unkempt look of the times, an outcast among the intellectual elite on campus. At Columbia, Chambers soon gravitated to the world of American communism, espousing Marxist ideology.

He was a brilliant poet but was forced out of the university after writing a "blasphemous" play. He went to work for the New York Public Library but was fired, accused of stealing books. In 1925, he joined the Communist Party and worked for two of their most important publications, the *Daily Worker* and the *New Masses*.

Chambers moved to Baltimore in 1934 and acted as a courier for Soviet intelligence operating inside the United States. He gave them low-level documents gathered from various U.S. government agencies.

By 1932, Chambers had grown disillusioned with Joseph Stalin and began to break away from the party. He developed deep Christian beliefs, and would eventually become fervently anti-communist. Chambers was pushed out of Soviet orbit for good when Stalin and Hitler signed a non-aggression pact in August of 1939, at which point he decided to share his knowledge of Soviet espionage operations on American territory with the FBI.

He was introduced to Assistant Secretary of State Adolf Berle in September 1939 by friend and anti-communist journalist, Isaac Don Levine. Chambers told Berle that Russian spies had infiltrated U.S. government agencies. He accused Alger Hiss, one of the most prominent figures in Washington.

On August 3, 1948 Chambers testified before the House Un-American Activities Committee. At first, Chambers's story was not the political bombshell Berle expected. Some committee members asked that no further hearings be carried out. However, an ambitious young California congressman named Richard Nixon called a private meeting to discuss Chambers's charges, and the committee agreed to full hearings.

In one of the most dramatic political confrontations of the decade, Hiss and Chambers confronted each other at the House Un-American Activities Committee hearing. Chambers appeared on the radio show *Meet the Press*, in which he publicly accused Hiss of being a communist. Hiss responded with a $75,000 libel suit against Chambers.

In court, Chambers produced 75 confidential State Department documents given to him by Hiss in the 1930s. Hiss was indicted by a grand jury on two counts of perjury, having lied about passing classified State Department documents to unauthorized recipients.

In a melodramatic court case that began on May 31, 1949, Chambers confessed his leftist leanings but never wavered in his allegation of Hiss's spying. On July 7, 1949, the jurors deadlocked at 8-4 for a conviction. A second trial was held on November 17, 1949, and Hiss was found guilty. He wrote his memoirs in prison.

Whittaker Chambers wrote *Witness*, an account of his ordeal. He died on July 9, 1961.

(*See Also*: Hiss, Alger)

Churchill, Peter

Peter Churchill (no relation to the Prime Minister) was one of the ablest agents sent into the field by the British Special Operations Executive (SOE). He was born in Amsterdam, Holland, and grew up in the shadow of his father, a British diplomat. Churchill graduated from Cambridge and joined the army in 1939.

When the war began, he joined the SOE. Fluent in French, he was sent undercover to Paris to start SOE's first spy network. In France, Peter Churchill took the code name "Raoul" and contacted a large French resistance movement. He trained the resistance fighters in secret codes and radio operations, setting up his headquarters on the posh French Riviera, from which he sent coded messages to London.

Churchill recruited a Frenchman named Andre Giraud, an artist who operated a resistance group out of Corsica. Odette Sansom, a beautiful radio operator at the SOE, was sent to France to link up with the French underground under the code name "Lise." But she would be the first victim in Churchill's spy network, when she was contacted by Hugo Bleicher, a known Abwehr agent.

A member of Churchill's team, Jean Marsac, was arrested by Bleicher and sent back into Churchill's ring to spy. Marsac's captors claimed to be part of an anti-Hitler group and demanded to be put in touch with certain British agents. He gave them Odette Sansom.

Churchill and Sansom were arrested before they had a chance to flee.

They were tortured by the Gestapo but told their captors that they were married, and related to Winston Churchill. Their lives were spared for that reason alone. Both were sent to POW camps and released after the war.

Cohen, Lona and Morris

Morris and Lona Cohen were Soviet spies whose work spanned the decades of World War II and early days of the Cold War. Their espionage work involved the Russian attempt to steal America's atomic secrets. They were associated with the Rosenberg spy ring, as well as Russian Colonel Rudolf Abel.

Morris Cohen was born in New York in 1910, the son of Russian immigrants, and at one point worked as a substitute teacher in the New York City school system. He became a member of the Communist Party in 1935 and volunteered to fight for the Republican side in the Abraham Lincoln brigade. He was recruited into the Soviet intelligence services after being wounded in battle.

Morris worked in a defense plant during the war and was able to gather information for his Soviet controllers. Besides his affiliation with the KGB, Morris Cohen worked for the Soviet trading company Amtorg, a Soviet cover for industrial spying.

In 1941, he married Lona Petra, herself an American communist who became a courier for the KGB. What we know of the Cohens's activities is due in part to the collapse of the old Soviet Union and subsequent release of its top-secret documents. New information based on the Soviet files on Morris and Lona Cohen was revealed in the book *Venona: Decoding Soviet Espionage in America* by John Earl Haynes and Harvey Klehr (Yale University Press, 1999). According to Colonel Vladimir Chikov, a press officer in Russian intelligence, the Cohens were an integral part of the Rosenberg atomic bomb spy case.

During their active espionage career, they were known as "Peter and Helen Kroger." According to Chikov, Morris also used the alias "Louis" and employed an unnamed scientist who played a key role in developing the Manhattan Project.

In the meantime, Morris was inducted into the U.S. Army in 1942 and ceased his espionage until the war's end. However, Lona worked as a courier for the Soviets in the United States during the war and made several trips to New Mexico, site of the Manhattan Project. On one of these trips, she received top-secret material from a source inside the project, code-named "Perseus." Authors Klehr and Haynes say that Lona Cohen ran an espionage network made up of defense plant workers.

After the arrest of the Rosenbergs, Lona and Morris fled to New Zealand. In 1954, again using the "Kroger" alias, they moved to London where they opened up a bookshop as their cover.

They met a Canadian named Gordon Lonsdale there. He spied for Russia, and the British had both him and the Cohens' under close surveillance. Lonsdale was finally arrested in January, 1961. The police searched the Cohen's home and found a spy apparatus belonging to Lonsdale.

They were arrested for espionage and given a 20-year prison term. They had served only eight when they were exchanged in a spy swap on October 24, 1969. Lona died in Moscow in 1992, and Morris died three years later.

Colby, William

William Colby, future Director of Central Intelligence, was born in St. Paul, Minnesota on January 4, 1920. He attended Princeton University, graduating in 1941. After Princeton, he attended Columbia Law School.

Drafted after the United States entered the war, Colby became a second lieutenant, assigned to airborne and artillery units. He took airborne training at Fort Benning, Georgia, but was reassigned after a jumping accident. In time, he was chosen for the Office of Strategic Services—America's first spy organization—whose job was to take the war directly to the enemy. He took part in commando training in Scotland and England. Commandos parachuted into enemy territory where they blew up bridges and power plants, as well as supplying resistance groups with desperately needed supplies.

Colby also joined a secret team called the Jedburgh Operation in which teams of three were sent into France after D-Day, on June 6, 1944. It was their job to meet up with the local French resistance and pave the way into France. Colby served well and was returned to London after a few months in the field.

After returning, he took command of a unit called the OSS Operational Group. Its purpose was to send agents into Norway to sabotage German industrial and military installations. Colby and his OSS agents spent many months evading German patrols. By the end of the conflict, Colby had earned the rank of major and had been awarded the Silver and Bronze Stars for bravery.

He returned to Columbia for his law degree and joined a Wall Street law firm headed by William Donovan. His first work was with the Legal Aid Society and the American Civil Liberties Union. He moved on to the National Labor Relations Board in Washington.

In June 1950, Colby joined the newly created CIA. It sent him to Sweden and Italy. From 1959-62, he served as CIA Station Chief in America's new international hot spot, South Vietnam. Working his way up in the CIA, Colby was appointed Deputy Director for Operations in 1973. In the same year, President Nixon appointed him Director.

It was during Colby's tumultuous term that a number of scandals rocked the agency. *New York Times* reporter Seymour Hersh revealed a secret CIA operation called "Operation Chaos," an illegal mail-opening scheme aimed at certain America citizens. When questioned by the Congress, Colby said it was an essential counterintelligence operation. Colby blamed the debacle on his chief of counterintelligence, James Jesus Angleton. Colby then fired Angleton, a highly secretive man, amidst intense pressure from the public and Congress.

Colby left public service in 1976 and wrote a book called *Honorable Men: My Life in the CIA*. William Colby died in a tragic canoe accident on the Chesapeake Bay in May 1996.

Coon, Carleton

If Hollywood decided to make a movie about World War II's most forgotten agent, it would be about Carleton Coon.

Coon was born on June 23, 1904, in Wakefield, Massachusetts and graduated with honors followed by a doctorate from Harvard. Like Indiana Jones, Coon traveled to North Africa, the Balkans, the ancient lands of Ethiopia and the Middle East doing anthropological work. After his fantastic trip, he joined the faculty of Harvard. Unknown to Coon, his work at ancient digs in North Africa would bring him back during the war, as a secret agent for the OSS.

As America became entangled in the war, Coon joined the Office of Strategic Services and was commissioned with the rank of major. He was given the job of operations officer and returned to North Africa as recruiter to the nomadic Riff tribesman of Morocco before allied forces landed there, during Operation Torch.

Coon worked along with his OSS partner, Gordon Browne, as the main agents to the Moroccan tribes. In fact, Coon and Browne wrote a proclamation to those in the path of the allied landings, urging them to revolt and fight off their Nazi captors. As the war progressed, Coon was put in charge of a group called *Corps Franc d'Afrique*, which consisted of newly freed Algerians of French descent headquartered near Algiers.

Coon's Corps was involved with one of the most controversial activities of the war; the assassination of French Admiral Jean Darlan in December 1942. It is still not known who killed the renegade French admiral, but circumstantial evidence pointed to Coon and his OSS allies. He was in Algiers at the Palais d' Eté, the site of the Darlan assassination on the afternoon of the murder.

Later in the war, Coon joined the British espionage unit Special Operations Executive (SOE), whose members were not above assassinating someone to complete their job. At SOE, Coon took on the identity of a

British major named Captain Ritinitis. Coon himself believed in the art of political assassinations in wartime. He wrote, "...Therefore, some other power, some third class of individuals aside from the leaders and the scholars must exist, and this third class must have the task of thwarting mistakes, diagnosing areas of potential world disequilibrium, and nipping the causes of potential disturbances in the bud. There must be a body of men whose task it is to throw out the rotten apples as soon as the first spots of decay appear."

Toward the end of the war, Coon was sent to head a group of commandos in Corsic, and took charge of Operation Audry, intended to infiltrate Yugoslavia to supply the resistance movement. He died on June 6, 1981.

Coplon, Judith

The release of the Venona intercepts has been a windfall for students of espionage history. One of the names revealed was that of a Soviet spy during World War II named Judith Coplon.

She was born in Brooklyn, New York. Her father was a successful toy manufacturer, who gave very generously to the poor children of the neighborhood. She attended Barnard College and took courses in Russian studies. The more she studied Russian culture, the more she became enamored of the Soviet system and soon became active in the communist student group. It was from these roots that Judith would grow into a Russian spy.

In 1943, she got a job with the Department of Justice. Although a background check was required, they failed to notice her Russian political leanings. She worked in the Foreign Agents Registration section of the Justice Department and had access to FBI files.

Friend, fellow communist, and KGB spy Floria Wovschin pointed out Coplon's potential to ringleader Pavel Mikhailovich Fitin, the Soviet Union's top spymaster working in America. In 1944, the New York KGB office gave permission to take on Coplon. Vladimir Pravdin, a KGB agent working undercover for the Soviet news service *PRAVDA*, said Coplon, "...was a serious person...politically well developed...there is no doubt of her sincere desire to help us. She has no doubts for whom she is working."

The Venona tapes on Coplon applaud her work but did not permit her to steal top level documents until she was firmly established in her Justice Department job. Coplon warned the KGB of FBI counterintelligence operations directed against them.

As part of her job in the Foreign Agents Section, Coplon had knowledge of all foreign agents operating inside the United States. These people had to register with her section thus the FBI knew all potential spies inside the United States. Coplon was able to accumulate a large dossier of names, which she used to her advantage.

Coplon had her own Soviet KGB contact/agent, Valentine Gubitchev. On trips to New York, she passed along FBI materials to him. By now, the FBI knew that its most guarded secrets were finding their way to the Soviet government, and traced the leak to Judith Coplon. She was put under surveillance and subsequently arrested in 1949 in the process of passing counterintelligence files to Gubitchev.

Gubitchev claimed diplomatic immunity and was returned to Russia. Coplon was sentenced to 75 years. However, she never had to spend a day in jail, as her case was appealed on the grounds that the FBI had used an unauthorized wiretap while gathering evidence against her.

Corvo, Max

Max Corvo's name is well known among the survivors of the old OSS. Corvo was born in 1920 and is still alive at this writing. Unlike many of his counterparts in the wartime OSS, he entered the service as a private. After extensive training, he was assigned to the OSS Secret Intelligence Branch (SIB).

The SIB was an outgrowth of the original Coordinator of Information led by William Donovan. Its assignment was to collect intelligence information by any means necessary. SIB agents worked in hot spots such as the Middle East, Africa, and Europe. Max Corvo acted in such a capacity in Italy, working with local resistance groups, and labored along with the troops after the invasion of Europe. One of his jobs was to recruit Italian-Americans to operate in North Africa, Italy and Sicily.

As the invasion of Europe progressed, director William Donovan put a large-scale operation underway that would galvanize Italian partisan groups under OSS control. In discussions with allied and partisan leaders, it was decided the United States would abide by a request from the Committee of National Liberation that the OSS provide a top officer to keep them informed. The mission was code-named "Operation Chrysler," and sought to, "...guide and control developments [in northern Italy], and create a unified partisan command."

To that end, Major William Holohan took on the responsibility of liason. Holohan was a graduate of Manhattan College, and Harvard Law School but his most agreeable trait was an ability to interact with the odd types with whom he came in contact during the Chrysler mission.

Max Corvo, as Company D's chief of intelligence, did not take kindly to Holohan's appointment.

Major Holohan was captured and killed—the only one of an entire unit—during a rendezvous with partisan leaders. In order to clear up the mystery surrounding the death, William Donovan ordered Max Corvo to investigate. A wireless operator in Holohan's unit confessed to his murder, but his confession made little sense.

After the war, Corvo returned to his home in Middletown, Connecticut, to start a newspaper. Holohan's murder case was never really solved.

(*See Also*: Holohan, William)

D

D-Day Deception

On June 6, 1944, 175,000 British, American, Canadian, and other allied troops making up the largest air and sea armada ever assembled crossed the English Channel bound for France.

An espionage strategy integral to the invasion of Normandy was the Super-secret Double Cross System that turned captured German spies into agents for the British and sent false information back to Berlin. There were false radio and communication signals, the breaking of the German cipher *Enigma*, and the Ultra System, which allowed British intelligence to read every German war message to and from diplomatic posts and military base.

The British "turned" a number of captured German spies into double agents. Daily reports of preparations for a landing at the Pas de Calais were systematically fed to Hitler's top staff, keeping thousands of German troops and tanks away from the prime landing zone—Normandy.

The British and Americans created phantom armies, complete with call and radio signals, which were broadcast back to Germany. Dummy warplanes, tanks, and troop carriers were all reported in the double agents' false messages. But Eisenhower's biggest espionage gamble was a report on the eve of D-Day that a German spy was working for the British; code-named "Garbo."

Garbo sent a message to the Germans giving the precise details of the "Overlord," the cover name for D-Day. Garbo sent another message saying that the Normandy invasion was feigned and that the real objective was Pas de Calais. Hitler had to make the most important decision of the war. He canceled an order that would have sent a *Panzer* (tank) division to Normandy. Thus, the use of spies and deception saved the D-Day operation, making way for an eventual victory.

Dansey, Claude

Most historians of espionage agree that the man most disliked among the shady professionals who inhabited the spy world was Claude Dansey.

Dansey was born on October 21, 1876 in London. His father was an army officer who sent Claude off to boarding school in Belgium in order to set him on the right track. However, the school's headmaster read the students' mail, and found Claude's letter to a 24-year-old man named Robbie Ross, with whom Claude had had an affair. He was sent packing to South Africa to complete his education.

Dansey's work experience included scouting for the South African Light Horse Battalion and in the jungles of Borneo. He went to Somalia where he headed British intelligence and reported back on information he gathered from his agents in the bush.

As World War II began, Dansey was thrown right into the thick of the spy game. He was sent to neutral Switzerland, a hotbed of intrigue where spies of all the warring nations operated. However, he refused to cooperate with OSS, whose agents had also set up shop there.

When an anti-Hitler German named Fritz Kolbe, a mole high in the German Foreign Office, offered to supply Dansey with top-secret German dispatches and other information he was rebuked by Dansey. Claude did little to endear himself to his bosses in the SIS, and his operatives produced little valuable information as a result.

As Vice Chief of the British SIS (Secret Intelligence Service) during World War II, Dansey proved himself a ruthless soldier who sent men to their deaths without blinking an eye. He controlled thousands of spies in Europe during the war. Many years later Dansey met Stewart Menzies, who would describe his new colleague as "a man that would commit murder easily, so long as he was not caught—in short, a man capable of anything." Menzies disliked Dansey yet put up with his outlandish behavior because he was one of the best espionage minds in history.

In London, Dansey was put in charge of operation "Z." The "Z" organization was run parallel with SIS, with neither knowing the other existed. Dansey's "Z" agents were to roam the battlefields of Europe working their deadly business, led by Claude from his headquarters at Bush House in the Strand in London.

After the demise of the "Z" network, Dansey tried to offer himself up as the new "C" but Stewart Menzies preempted the position. He came away with the title of assistant chief of the secret service instead.

Claude Dansey's only legacy, said one contemporary, was to give spying a bad name.

(*See Also*: Menzies, Stewart)

43

Darlan, Jean

"Operation Torch" was an attack planned against Nazi strongholds in French North Africa in 1942, with landings in Algeria, Morocco and Tunisia meant to create a front in the heart of Europe. However, before "Operation Torch" could be put into action, certain events would lead to the assassination of French admiral Jean Darlan, that had British intelligence's fingerprints all over it.

When Hitler's troops entered Paris, all resistance from the regular French army broke down. Hitler proceeded to carve the country into two sections. The Free French, who tried to sabotage operations against the Germans, nominally occupied one. The Vichy French, who were actually puppets of the Germans, occupied the other.

Admiral Jean Darlan was the French naval commander under the Vichy puppet government. As time went on, Darlan would serve as its vice president. He was hated by military and civilian leaders in Washington and London, and had been implicated in the destruction of the French fleet at the battle of Mers-el-Kebir in June 1940. He also helped German General Erwin Rommel secure military supplies via French ships. Darlan went so far as to jail U.S. counsel-general Robert Murphy.

Under pressure from allied countries, Darlan agreed to turn over his forces to the side of the invaders but he was still extremely suspect. Something had to be done about him, but what? The question was violently answered on December 24, 1942, when a young Frenchman named Bournier de la Chapelle entered Darlan's headquarters and executed him. Chapelle was tried secretly and put to death. But the story does not end there.

Chapelle had been training at a secret British espionage unit called Special Operations Executive (SOE), which was responsible for assassination and sabotage operations across Europe. He served in a paramilitary unit called the Corps Franc d' Afrique, whose members wore British military uniforms and were linked to secret operations of the OSS/SOE. In another bit of coincidence, the head of the British Secret Service, Stewart Menzies, was in Algiers when Darlan was shot. Equally suspicious was the Algiers presence of OSS agent Max Corvo. To this day the assassination of Jean Darlan remains officially unexplained.

(See Also: Corvo, Max)

Davis, William Rhodes

In the pre-war years many influential Americans were sympathetic to Hitler. Some of them were household names like Henry Ford and Charles Lindbergh. William Rhodes Davis was such a man. An oil industrialist and advisor to many important Washington insiders, he was also an agent for Germany with the code-name Agent "C-80."

Davis was born in Montgomery, Alabama, in 1889. As a young man, he moved to Oklahoma where he worked on the railroads heading west. During the 1913 boom in the oil business, Davis organized his own oil company in Muskogee, Oklahoma, and became one of the country's richest men.

Davis had established an oil company called Crusader Oil with distribution in Texas, Louisiana and Mexico. He also branched out of the country and established holdings in Germany, Sweden and other Scandinavian countries. He had homes in Houston and Scarsdale; his New York headquarters was in Rockefeller Center (along with Bill Stephenson's BSC).

During the late 1930s, Davis proposed a deal with the German navy to use blocked German assets stored in the vaults of the First National Bank in Boston to build a refinery in Germany. His processed oil would then be bartered for industrial tools and other goods.

Davis met with Dr. Hjalmar Schacht, the president of the national bank of Germany, with his proposal. However, Schact turned him down. He then went to Adolf Hitler, who agreed. Davis's oil factory, Eurotank, was built in Hamburg and supplied the German navy with all the fuel it could use.

Davis was not content to limit himself to Germany. He wanted to expand into Mexico, and persuaded the German treasury to help finance his scheme. In a bizarre twist, the influential American labor leader John L. Lewis pleaded Davis's case with the Mexican government. Lewis contacted Alejandro Carillio, a deputy to the minister of the Confederation of Mexican Workers. He said Davis was "absolutely all right" and soon thereafter, the Mexican government agreed to allow Davis to establish a refinery on their soil. Davis's company provided Mexican oil to Germany, while the Germans paid by sending vital industrial goods to Mexico. All this activity by an American citizen did not go unnoticed by the FBI, who kept a close watch on Davis.

Once war began in 1939, Davis tried to get his oil shipments from Mexico to Germany through the British naval blockade but eventually had to cut his losses and end all trade between the countries. Davis recognized that his only hope of getting his oil business back on track was the end of the war. Davis came up with his own peace plan. It involved President Roosevelt mediating between Western powers and Germany to end the fighting. Davis contacted Hitler's most trusted colleague, Herman Goering. Goering told Davis to proceed to Washington and gave him a cover name and code, "C-80."

Advisor Adolf Berle and FDR listened attentively to what Davis had to say. The president, however, neither endorsed nor rejected the oil tycoon's peace offer from Goering. Goering told Davis to return to Washington and continue pursuing his peace initiative. When Davis requested another meeting with the president, he was rebuffed. Davis's attitudes toward Hitler were well known to the State Department, and it had a file on him. Roosevelt had read the FBI reports on Davis and knew he was an active Nazi agent. So ended the one and only meeting between an American president and a known German spy during the war.

Donovan, William, "Wild Bill"

William J. Donovan was born in Buffalo, New York, on January 1, 1883. The Donovan family had little money and young Bill had worked his way through Columbia University. He received a law degree in 1907 and returned to Buffalo to his first law practice. While in Buffalo, Donovan organized an army cavalry troop, which eventually became part of the National Guard.

His first job was U.S. District Attorney for the Western District of New York. He was also active in local Buffalo Republican politics, and ran unsuccessfully for the Republican nominations for Governor and lieutenant governor of New York in 1922 and 1932. In 1929, Donovan founded the Wall Street law firm that would bear his name: Donovan, Leisure, Newton and Lumbard.

Donovan used his copious political connections to break into intelligence for the United States. In 1919, while honeymooning in Japan, Donovan detoured to Siberia on behalf of the United States government. His mission was to report the activities of the anti-Bolshevik, White Russian forces under the command of Admiral Alexander Kolchak.

He also went to Europe at the behest of the Rockefeller Foundation to set up a supply line of vital supplies for relief victims of the war. In Poland he organized a lifeline for displaced persons. He made his way to England where he met with high-ranking officers and was informed that because of the German blockade of the oceans, most, if not all of the Rockefeller relief supplies would not get through.

In later years, Donovan would say that this 1916 meeting with William Stephenson, later head of the British BSC, gave him his calling in the intelligence field. In that pivotal European sojourn, Donovan traveled to Belgium under the guise of relief work activity. He was actually gathering information on German military supplies and funneling it to the British.

In 1939, he went to Ethiopia to report on the Italian-Ethiopian war for America. He also made trips to observe the Spanish Civil War, to the Balkans, and Italy. When the Germans attacked Poland, President Roosevelt asked Donovan to report on England's ability to wage war. During his trip, Donovan made contacts with many in British intelligence.

Besides his trip to Britain, Donovan made forays to Mediterranean areas to analyze the military situation for Washington. Donovan reported that the British would be able to beat back the Nazis as long as they were well supplied.

William Stephenson called Donovan to get the United States to aid his country against Germany. FDR approved of the plan and sent Donovan to London. There, he met with the highest-ranking officials of the British government, including King George VI, Prime Minister Winston Churchill, and Stewart Menzies.

Menzies took the extraordinary risk of telling Donovan, a private citizen, about the British breaking German Ultra codes and other information. Donovan promised to do all he could to gain U.S. military aid to England. It was during this trip that British intelligence agents approached Donovan with the idea of a centralized American intelligence agency. Donovan presented it to FDR, but military leaders met it with hostility. General Sherman Miles, the head of army intelligence, such as it was, claimed such an agency would be "very disadvantageous" to the nation.

Another powerful Washington figure who did not take kindly to Donovan's plan was the head of the FBI, J. Edgar Hoover. Hoover saw it as a challenge to his control over counterespionage in the United States. He lobbied FDR hard to stop Donovan's plan but the president limited the FBI's jurisdiction to the Western Hemisphere. Donovan had a valuable ally in President Roosevelt, a firm believer in a national intelligence agency.

Donovan saw himself as the head of a newly created, peacetime espionage agency, carrying on where the OSS left off. But the sudden death of President Roosevelt and the ending of the war changed those plans. The new president, Harry Truman, disbanded the OSS, and opted for pre-war intelligence methods. Donovan left the government a wiser but sadder man.

After retirement he served for a time at the Nuremberg war crimes tribunal. After the war, he became Ambassador to Thailand from 1953 to 1954, where he called for containment of the new Soviet threat brought on by the Cold War.

Bill Donovan's lasting legacy is found today in Langley, Virginia, home of the Central Intelligence Agency. In 1959, the year he died, his portrait was hung at CIA headquarters as a memorial to his single-handed responsibility for the modern American espionage establishment.

(*See Also*: COI; Hoover, J. Edgar; Stephenson, William; OSS)

Double Cross System

One of the most important British counterespionage operations of World War II was the "Double Cross System," run by the agency responsible for counterespionage activities.

The British had been able to read German military secrets from a variety of electronic sources. One of them was code-named Ultra. The other invaluable intelligence coup was the capturing of the German Enigma machine in which the British were able to decipher German codes and ciphers emanating from Berlin and elsewhere in Germany. The combination of Ultra and Enigma proved to be the difference between victory and defeat.

One of the men most responsible for the success of the Double Cross System was the noted historian, Hugh Trevor-Roper. Trevor-Roper worked for an organization called MI 8-C, which monitored German wireless traffic. All the information gathered by Roper was turned over to the huge decoding branch of British intelligence called GCHQ, the Government Communications Headquarters responsible for Enigma intercepts.

Trevor-Roper was able to deduce that German spies entering Britain would be carrying codebooks. He was able to break the German code via a popular book of the time titled *Our Hearts Were Young And Gay*, as the source of the code. Dick White and J.C. Masterman were other noted intelligence operatives who worked with Trevor-Roper, and played important roles in British intelligence.

Using Double Cross, the British were able to learn the identities of each covert German agent who landed on their soil. They were arrested upon arrival and given two options; cooperate with the British or be shot. Most of them chose the first. The group that ran the Double Cross System was called XX (Twenty Committee).

A wave of German agents arrived in Britain in preparation for a German invasion of the British Isles called "Operation Sea Lion," which never materialized. Most of them were "persuaded" to work for the Brits. Using these genuine German agents, the Double Cross men were able to feed false information back to Germany.

The most important "double" infiltrating England was a German agent named Wulf Schmidt, code-named Tate. Tate gave false information concerning the landing areas for the German V-2 rockets attacking England from bases in Germany and conquered territories.

The Germans awarded Tate the Iron Cross for his sterling performance, but he never returned to collect it.

(*See Also*: D-Day Deception; Masterman, John)

Dulles, Allen

Allen Dulles came from a distinguished and politically well-connected New York family. His maternal grandfather, John W. Foster, was Secretary of State under President Benjamin Harrison. His great uncle, John Welsh, was the U.S. Ambassador to London in the 1870s. He graduated from Princeton University in 1914 and taught school in India. The young Allen Dulles began his diplomatic career in May 1916 when he was appointed the third secretary in the American Embassy in Vienna, Austria.

One day at the embassy he received a call from a revolutionary Russian figure named Vladimir Lenin. Lenin wanted to meet with someone in the U.S. Embassy. Dulles refused the meeting, saying that he had a date and could not cancel it. In later years, Dulles would never forget that nearly fateful encounter with one of the most important figures of the 20th century.

After the United States entered the war in 1941, Dulles began a career in intelligence that would last the rest of his life. He joined the newly created Office of the Coordinator of Information, the predecessor of the OSS, and ran its New York office. Dulles's agents specialized in the collection of information from German émigrés to America.

With the advent of the OSS, the U.S. needed an espionage outpost in the heart of Europe. Dulles was asked to establish a spy operation in Bern, Switzerland. He was forced to travel across Europe; finally bucking the regime in occupied France who tried to refuse him entry into Switzerland. He was finally allowed to enter the country and took up his post as the "Special Representative of the President of the United States." However, everyone in Bern knew why Dulles had come and stayed away from him.

He assembled a network of anti-Hitler German military officers whose common aim was to see the Führer removed. His number one German contact was a diplomat named Fritz Kolbe, code-named "George Wood." When Kolbe first contacted British intelligence they thought he was a German spy and told him his services were not needed. He next reached out to Dulles whom he found to be more amenable.

Kolbe was a member of the anti-Hitler group called the *Schwarze Kapelle*, or Black Orchestra, whose members worked for the German high command, but who made contact with American intelligence in order to end the war.

Over the next several months, Kolbe provided Dulles with thousands of pages of diplomatic material from the German foreign ministry. The British never trusted the information provided by Kolbe and expressed their misgivings to the Americans. One of the men who made derogatory comments to Bill Donovan, head of the OSS, was the Russian double agent Kim Philby.

Because of Kolbe, Dulles was able to achieve an intelligence bonanza: anti-Hitler activities in Bern. He had contact with anti-Nazi generals during their unsuccessful assassination attempt on Hitler, reports on the German development of the destructive V-2 rocket that destroyed much of London, and the successful penetration of the Abwehr in Bern by two of his most trusted agents, Hans Gisevius and Fritz Molden.

Dulles served as OSS Station Chief in Bern during the war. In 1953, Dulles would become head of the CIA, appointed by newly elected President Dwight Eisenhower. He served during the entire Eisenhower administration and headed many of the most controversial operations carried out by the CIA during the Cold War; the overthrow of the Shah of Iran, the coup in Guatemala, the U-2 incident and the CIA-Mafia attempts to kill Fidel Castro of Cuba.

(*See Also*: Kolbe, Fritz; Canaris, Wilhelm; Black Orchestra; OSS)

E

Earhart, Amelia

By the 1920s, America's foreign policy was clearly focused on Japanese military moves in the Pacific. This particular region was the seat of one of the most intriguing mysteries of the day.

Amelia Earhart and her navigator Fred Noonan left New Guinea on July 2, 1937, on a 2500-mile flight to Howland Island in the central Pacific. Somewhere along the way, their plane went down and neither was heard from again. But is there more to the Earhart story than meets the eye? The book *Lost Star: The Search for Amelia Earhart* by Randall Brink (W.W. Norton, 1994) suggests the possibility of espionage in connection with the flight.

Earhart flew a modified Electra airplane mounted with onboard cameras and a 1,400-mile fuel reserve. The plane contained a hidden navigational device that emitted a signal detectable by any number of navy ships along her flight path. In fact, the coast guard cutter *Itasca* was waiting in the waters off Howland Island to pick up her signal.

Mr. Brink writes that the route Amelia originally planned to fly was not the one she carried out. It is a fact that the United States was interested in any potential Japanese military moves in that region of the world, four years earlier than the Pearl Harbor attack. There has been speculation that Amelia Earhart and Fred Noonan were taken prisoner by the Japanese and that the United States government knew in advance the actual purpose of her flight. The most convincing proof lies in the files of the U.S. Navy's wartime OP-20G and OP-16 ONI (Office of Naval Intelligence) only recently released to the public.

A tantalizing piece of evidence lies in a letter from Secretary of the Treasury Henry Morgenthau to Eleanor Roosevelt's personal secretary, Malvina Scheider. It reads in part "...this letter that Mrs. Roosevelt wrote me about trying to get the report on Amelia Earhart. Now, I've been given a verbal report. If we're going to release this, it's just going to smear the whole reputation of Amelia Earhart."

No one knows in what context this letter was written or what its implications are. Whether or not Amelia Earhart was on some sort of pre-Pearl Harbor intelligence mission for the United States is still debatable. One thing is certain; her story is far more intriguing than we're led to believe.

Earle, George III

That city of mystery, intrigue and sex, Istanbul, was a hotbed of espionage during World War II. By 1943, intelligence agents from England, Germany, the United States, and Japan flocked to the city to check out each other, take in the sites, and occasionally eliminate an enemy who was doing too much snooping for its own good.

Into this mix came an American who made no secret of his disdain for the Nazi regime. He thought nothing of using his lovely girlfriend to fool the Germans, and proudly served as the personal representative of President Roosevelt. He was George Earle III, a Lieutenant Commander in the armed forces, and the former Governor of Pennsylvania (1935-1939).

George Earle had been serving in the diplomatic corps as U.S. Minister to Bulgaria, when he was assigned a secret mission in Turkey. He also served from 1933 to 1934 as the American envoy to Austria. Earle had a powerful backer in the person of King Boris of Bulgaria who liked the straightforward American and his anti-Hitler views. This coupled with counting FDR among his long-time confidantes made George Earle cocky.

But Earle's outspoken opposition to Hitler was not well received by the brass in the State Department. He was called back to the United States and Secretary of State Cordell Hull lobbied FDR to give him a less important—lower profile—diplomatic assignment. Franklin Roosevelt had other plans for George Earle.

Ever since 1942, the president had heard from intelligence chiefs that anti-Hitler German officers were planning to overthrow the Führer. Roosevelt wanted someone he trusted to oversee the coup. He sent George Earle to Istanbul to link up with these Germans and report back on what he found. He would be the personal representative of the President of the United States. In reality, Earle was FDR's personal spy.

Before he could take on his duties, a matter of the heart had to be addressed. He sent a telegram to a beautiful Hungarian girl named Adrienne Molnar asking her to join him in Istanbul. She didn't have a visa, so she turned to a journalist named Louis Matzhold for help. Adrienne didn't realize that Matzhold was a German agent in Admiral Canaris' Abwehr. Matzhold knew the real reason George Earle had been sent to Istanbul and figured if he played his cards right, Adrienne Molnar would be a conduit.

There was one flaw in Matzhold's plan. Earle knew who he was. Nevertheless, he met with the German spy and offered information, some false, some true. Earle said the allies were planning to land troops in 34 places when the invasion of Europe took place. Matzhold fell for the bait and reported back to the Abwehr. The false information fooled the Germans into diverting their troops when the allies invaded Sicily.

George Earle eventually penetrated anti-Hitler organizers in Turkey and met with German Ambassador Franz von Papen, their leader. Ironically, Louis Matzhold asked Adrienne Molnar, by that time one of the most desired women in the city, to help him defect.

Eddy, William

William Eddy was one of the most trusted OSS officers under the direction of Bill Donovan. He was given responsibility for a number of highly important areas of conflict for which the OSS was responsible, including operations in Italy, France, and parts of Spain, Tunisia, and Spanish Morocco.

Bill Eddy was born on March 9, 1896, in Sidon, Syria to American missionaries. Young Bill got to see the world and developed a taste for adventure. He graduated from Princeton University in 1917 and immediately joined the marines, where he was made lieutenant. During World War I, Eddy personally built a wooden leg to replace one lost in the war.

In 1942, shortly after the U.S. entered the war, Eddy was assigned to the Office of the Coordinator of Information, an agency headed by Donovan. Fluent in Arabic, he was assigned to French North Africa under the cover of the naval attaché to Robert Murphy in Tangier, Morocco. Eddy was put in charge of formulating plans for an American invasion of southern Europe, and forging relationships with members of the Free French intelligence services. But his work got off to a bad start when one of his secretaries, a Spanish woman named Francesca Pinto, was found to be working for the Germans.

As chief of OSS Algiers, Eddy was always in the field, making friends with the various Arabs he recruited. With the approval of the Joint Chiefs of Staff and General Eisenhower, Eddy "was to command all secret intelligence, special operations, and counterespionage from French West Africa to and including Libya, southern and southwestern Europe, including the Iberian Peninsula and southern France to the Atlantic coast of Italy. The area included Italy, Sicily, Sardinia, Corsica, France, the Canaries, the Cape Verdes, the Azores, the Madeiras, Spanish Morocco, Rio de Oro and Tangier."

With a payroll of millions of dollars and a staff of 450, Eddy established a network of agents in North Africa, Tangier, Casablanca, Oran, and Tunis.

His agents set up a clandestine radio network across thousands of miles, which reported on the progress of German armies advancing or retreating across the vast Arabian Desert. They stole German cable traffic; broke into the Spanish consulate in French Morocco to retrieve coded messages and gave false information to the Germans regarding allied invasion plans for North Africa. In one of his most important disinformation missions, he was able to divert German naval ships to Dakar, leaving the actual invasion site in North Africa undefended.

In 1944, Eddy was transferred to Saudi Arabia as an envoy and stayed there until 1946. He returned to the United States where he worked in the State Department as chief of the Department's Interim Research and Intelligence Service. Among his wartime decorations were the Distinguished Service Cross, the Navy Heart and two Purple Hearts.

He died in 1962.

Eifler, Carl

On December 7, 1943, two years after the United States entered the war, Bill Donovan made a dangerous and controversial trip to the jungles of Burma. Donovan knew the risks; if the Japanese captured him, there was no telling how many of America's most important secrets would be revealed.

Donovan's trip coincided with the inauguration of a rough-and-ready fighting force called Detachment 101, ordered by President Roosevelt personally. Donovan wanted to make sure the unit was secure before taking hostile action against the Japanese, who were then in almost complete control of Burma and Southeast Asia.

The man in charge of Detachment 101 was a former cop named Carl Eifler. He joined the Los Angeles Police force as a young man and later the U.S. Border Patrol along the rugged Mexican border. By 1941, Carl Eifler was working in Hawaii as the deputy director of the U.S. Customs Service in the islands. Eifler was a licensed pilot and a fighting man, who loved the rugged outdoors.

Donovan tapped Eifler to head Detachment 101, a unit that would take the war to the Japanese in the jungles of Burma, using stealth and subversion. The original idea of forming Detachment 101 came from Millard Preston Goodfellow, a New York newspaper publisher affiliated with the Boy Scouts of America. Goodfellow proposed the idea of a guerrilla force to Bill Donovan, who sent Goodfellow to see Joseph Stilwell. When Stilwell heard about Goodfellow's idea, he commented, "...if sent out to blow up a bridge, [he] would blow up a windmill instead and come back with an excuse."

Seeing trouble brewing, Donovan sent Captain Duncan Lee as a representative to Eifler's camp to investigate the now-tense situation.

Accompanied by Eric Sevareid, Lee wrote to Donovan that "the criticism of Eifler's SI (Secret Intelligence) is well founded." He also found Eifler's men to be improperly trained for their mission.

Arriving at Eifler's base camp at Nazira, Donovan and Eifler got down to business. In a risky move, Eifler dared Donovan to accompany him and his men into the Japanese occupied jungles to judge their work. The next day they boarded a Gypsy Moth light plane and flew to Knothead, an OSS base, some 275 miles behind Japanese lines. Donovan met the rugged Kachin tribesmen being trained by OSS men to fight the Japanese. The Kachins asked for shotguns instead of the machine guns OSS units normally used. Soon, 500 Springfield muzzle-loaders were airlifted into the dense jungle. Donovan had been so impressed; he would've given Detachment 101 anything they asked for.

Eifler's Detachment 101 rescued more than 200 allied airmen whose planes either crashed or were shot down over the Burmese jungles. At the height of the war, Detachment 101 had 500 U.S. personnel and 10,000 Kachins. It was responsible for killing more than 5,000 of the enemy.

Carl Eifler's Detachment 101 was the first U.S. paramilitary unit to operate during wartime. His men successfully created havoc behind Japanese lines in Burma by blowing up bridges, cutting communications lines, and ambushing Japanese patrols, paving the way for retaking Burma.

After the war ended, Eifler returned to divinity school and became a minister in California.

Enigma machine

Two German engineers, Arthur Scerbius and Boris Hagelin invented the first Enigma machine in 1923 for strictly commercial use. It was officially called "The Glow-lamp Ciphering and Deciphering Machine Enigma."

The Enigma machine was an electrical enciphering machine about the size of an old portable typewriter. Once the typist wrote his letter or message in plain text, a series of illuminated keys built into the machine would light up. This would allow a typist on the other end to read the encrypted message from the sender and retype the message.

Each letter was enciphered through an intricate series of plug board connections and rotors. For example, the letter A on the keyboard could become B; B could become C, or any other version that the sender wanted to set up. The plugs were inserted in any number of combinations. Key settings were changed once a day after the war broke out. What the Germans loved about the original Enigma machine was the fact that a potential enemy had to have the exact key settings on their own machine in order to break their code.

An early type of Enigma machine used by the Germans was a

ENIGMA MACHINE

Geheimschreiber. This apparatus had 10 to 12 motors and was hard to break. This was only installed in vitally important communications centers.

Soon though, the idea of this powerful espionage tool was noticed by the military of most of the industrial nations, and they began building prototypes of their own. The U.S. Army bought its first machine in 1928 for less than $150. In 1939, the year Germany invaded Poland, there were 20,000 machines in use by the German military.

One of the most powerful espionage tools the German military used during the war, it was a highly complex electronic instrument that sent secret military codes throughout the various branches of the German military establishment. It was, however, the one vital link broken by the British, which ultimately shortened the war and guaranteed victory. By the end of the war, British and American codebreakers were able to decipher and read almost all of the German and Japanese enciphered messages sent to military installations around the world.

In 1932, the Polish government broke into the German Enigma code with the help of French codebreakers. A French agent by the name of Hans-Thilo Schmidt, code-named "Asche," stole parts of the German Enigma. By 1938, Polish codebreakers were reading the daily reports sent from the German army and air force. When Poland fell, a number of its top scientists with knowledge of Enigma defected to the West. They helped their new allies break Enigma.

Working with a rough version of a computer, "Colossus," both American and British codebreakers finally "broke" the German Enigma with long hours and years of hard work. Turing was able to use a machine called "Bombes" to crack Enigma. He added 25 electrical relays to speed up the process in which these messages were read.

Another person primarily responsible for the breaking of Enigma was a British scientist named Gordon Welchman. Through hard and tireless work, Welchman came up with the concept of traffic analysis, which broke down messages coming in from German military units into the organizations who sent them, i.e., army, navy, air force. The German Naval Enigma was broken between 1941 and 1945. By the end of the war, Bletchley Park codebreakers were able to read 48,000 German army and air force messages on a monthly basis.

Without the extraordinary work done by the Americans and British at Bletchley Park in breaking Enigma, the war would have lasted longer and more blood would have been shed.

(*See Also*: Bletchley Park)

F

Federal Bureau of Investigation (FBI)

In the years before America's entry into World War II, there was no centralized intelligence organization that conducted foreign espionage activities. There were small intelligence units belonging to the armed services, mostly the army and the navy. The one quasi-intelligence service in operation was J. Edgar Hoover's Federal Bureau of Investigation.

Hoover was the first and only director the agency had ever had, and he ran his domain with an iron fist. As war threatened, Hoover knew the United States would become involved in the conflict sooner or later. He suggested to President Roosevelt that the FBI be the sole U.S. intelligence-gathering organization. But the president had other plans.

What Hoover and the rest of the country didn't know was that President Roosevelt and Prime Minister Winston Churchill had struck a deal to share intelligence information long before the December 1941 Japanese attack on Pearl Harbor. This information had to be kept top secret, for if the public or FDR's political enemies got wind of the deal, his political future would be in great jeopardy. Throughout the war, Hoover's FBI took a back seat to Donovan's OSS.

The first act in the American-British intelligence alliance began innocently enough in 1940 with Hamish Mitchell, special assistant to the director of the British Purchasing Commission. Mr. Mitchell arrived in Washington and met with an FBI official, offering to share his agents' information with the FBI. Adolf Berle, FDR's unofficial collector of intelligence information, immediately sent this proposal to J. Edgar Hoover.

Berle wrote a memo saying in part, "I feel we should discourage activities of this kind. If we are to have a combined counterespionage and secret intelligence unit, it should be our own....But I do think that this suggests a more expeditious way of getting information from these people into the hands of our own agencies, so that if there is thought of German or Russian espionage or sabotage we can deal with it promptly…."

FDR approved of Churchill's intelligence sharing initiative and sanctioned a trip by Churchill's personal envoy, William Stephenson. Stephenson was the head of the British Security Coordination. From there Stephenson would run all of Britain's counterespionage operations in the Western Hemisphere.

Stephenson was introduced to Hoover by Gene Tunney, a former heavyweight boxer. Hoover insisted on keeping the meeting from the State Department. The historical record is unclear about much of what went on, but it is clear that they first met in March 1942. In *Wild Bill And Intrepid: Donovan, Stephenson, and the Origin of CIA,* by Thomas Troy, a much earlier meeting between Hoover and Stephenson is described.

Troy claims that on January 29, 1940, both men were part of a British, American and Canadian symposium at FBI headquarters, called the "Hemisphere Intelligence Conference." In July 1941, British intelligence agents in America were sending secret messages to London via FBI radio.

Robert Sherwood, a speechwriter and personal friend of FDR, provides another indication of a close British-FBI relationship. He writes, "By the spring of 1941, six months before the United States entered the war, there was, by Roosevelt's order and despite State Department qualms…close cooperation between J. Edgar Hoover and British security services under the direction of a quiet Canadian, William Stephenson. The purpose of this cooperation was the detection…of espionage and sabotage activities in the Western Hemisphere by agents of Germany, Italy and Japan, and also Vichy France. It produced some remarkable results."

With Bill Donovan in charge of the OSS and its agents responsible for military and paramilitary activities in Europe, FDR gave Hoover's FBI *carte blanche* to operate in South America. To this end, Hoover established the Special Intelligence Service as part of the FBI. SIS agents were sent to South and Latin America posing as businessmen. Their job was to gather as much information as possible on the increasing number of Germans who made their way south of the border.

FBI agents were sent to many U.S. embassies in the region as "legal attachés." One of the most successful operations busted a plot by pro-German agents in Bolivia to overthrow the government.

The FBI was highly successful in tracking down a number of German Abwehr agents who set up shop in the United States. One of the German agents captured by Hoover's G-Men was William Sebold, a German-American recruited by the Abwehr to operate a spy ring in New York.

Sebold was "turned" by German intelligence while traveling to his native country and sent back to America as their number-one spy. But, unknown to the Germans, Sebold told the FBI about his German relationship. He sent back real and bogus information to Berlin. Operating out of his Long Island home, Sebold's activities were monitored by the FBI and in June 1940, the bureau captured 33 Abwehr agents controlled or known by Sebold.

In a major intelligence coup, the FBI arrested four German saboteurs as they were put ashore by a U-boat off the coast of Long Island, New York. An alert coast guardsman spotted them on a nearby beach. After a short man-hunt, they were all caught.

Another team of German agents landed off the coast of Maine at Frenchman's Bay. William Colepaugh and Erich Gimpel were arrested, and Colepaugh spilled the beans. He told them that they were trained at an Abwehr spy school under the command of Nicholas Ritter, the chief of espionage directed at the United States.

The FBI's biggest failure was in the case of a flamboyant Yugoslavian named Dusan "Dusko" Popov. Upon arriving in the United States on August 12, 1941, Popov, who had recently worked for the Abwehr, tried to make contact with the FBI. After waiting a week, he was finally contacted by Assistant Director Percy Foxworth. Popov told Foxworth that he had been working secretly for the Germans in London but so disliked the German regime that he began working for the British as a double agent, using the code name "Tricycle." He further stated that he had been sent to the U.S. to resurrect the now-defunct Sebold Spy Ring, but wanted to spy for the U.S. instead. He also stunned Director Foxworth by stating that he was ordered by the Abwehr to supply answers to a questionnaire given him by the Japanese, concerning the defenses of the U.S. Naval base at Pearl Harbor, Hawaii.

J. Edgar Hoover did not trust Popov, accusing him of being employed by the Germans still. He discounted Popov's Pearl Harbor material as German disinformation. Without FBI cooperation, Popov left the United States and returned to Britain in July 1943, two years after the surprise Japanese attack on the Hawaiian base.

(*See Also*: Hoover, J. Edgar; Popov, Dusan; Operation Pastorius)

Fleming, Ian

Ian Fleming led a secret life of his own. It was out of his wartime experiences that the *007* novels were born.

Shortly before Britain entered the war, Ian Fleming worked as a reporter for the *London Times*. A superb writer with more than his share of contacts, he traveled to the Soviet Union to cover the Metro-Vickers trial in which three British citizens were arrested by the OPGU (secret police) on trumped-up charges. His reports on the trial earned him a wide following, and his name became known in the right places.

FLEMING

After a stint as a London stockbroker, Fleming began a career in military intelligence working for (then) head of British Naval Intelligence, Admiral John Godfrey. He started working on a part-time basis in Naval Intelligence with the rank of lieutenant but was soon promoted to commander.

He soon joined full time and worked out of Room 39, the nerve center of naval intelligence. His first assignment was to collect information on German naval operations, under the code number 17F.

One of Fleming's teachers was an Australian pilot named Sydney Cotton, who flew a dangerous mission over the North German ports. Cotton mounted aerial cameras on the wings and photographed a large portion of the German fleet at anchor. Both men met often to work out new, untested gadgets for intelligence gathering.

As time went on, Fleming represented Admiral Godfrey in secret meetings with members of the Special Operations Executive (SOE), which was responsible for the secret war against Germany. Fleming's first field assignment sent him to France as a liaison between British intelligence and Vichy French admiral, Jean Darlan. He was later sent undercover to Tangier to monitor British naval intelligence operations near the vital Suez Canal.

In 1941, Fleming went on his most delicate mission yet. Bill Donovan was touring the Mediterranean, checking the status of Britain's strategies against Hitler. Among his stops were Madrid and Lisbon. Fleming was instructed by Admiral Godfrey to travel to Gibraltar to meet with Donovan.

In their meetings with Donovan, British officials told him their military secrets. "Operation Golden Eye" was a Naval Intelligence Division (NID) plan to carry out sabotage operations and retain communication links with London should Germany invade Spain. In the end, Operation Goldeneye was never implemented, but years later Fleming's James Bond movie *Goldeneye* was big box-office material.

With the cooperation of the NID and the SIS (Special Intelligence Service), Fleming set up a clandestine Golden Eye liaison office in Gibraltar, with its own radio network. But Fleming's most important contribution to Naval Intelligence was his command of "Number 30 Assault Unit" or AU-30. Fleming's "Red Indians" trained at a secret base outside London. They were all civilians, a sort of "dirty dozen"—men of questionable character not assigned to any regular army unit. During the D-Day invasion of France, Fleming's men secured vital information on German U-boat pens along the coast. In a daring mission, 12 of AU-30's men captured 300 German troops and destroyed docked U-boats at the port of Cherbourg.

In June 1941, Fleming and Admiral Godfrey arrived in the United States, where they met with FBI Director J. Edgar Hoover. Hoover took an immediate dislike to his two visitors, feeling they were interfering on his own intelligence turf.

In Fleming's final fitness report, his superiors wrote that he was not a really outstanding officer but had some rather ingenious plans that were never carried out. His alter ego, James Bond, fared slightly better. (*See Also*: Godfrey, John)

Foote, Alexander

At the outbreak of hostilities in Europe, neutral Switzerland became the focal point of espionage between the warring parties. Espionage agents from England, France, Germany, the United States, and Poland, used Swiss territory to spy on each other without any penalties from its government. One of the most important intelligence operations of the war took place in Switzerland, involving a spy that reported to the Russians on German military war plans.

The main character in the drama was Alexander Foote, who, unknown to the Soviets, was a British double agent. He was recruited into the GRU, Soviet military intelligence in 1938, and sent to Switzerland as its top spy.

Foote worked with three vital Soviet intelligence rings in Switzerland. The man who ran the largest of these groups was Sandor Rado, code-named Dora. Otto Puenter (Pakbo) and Rachel Dubendorfer (Sissy) operated the other two.

Through the close-knit family of Switzerland-based spies, British intelligence learned the identities of Foote and his partners. Foote distrusted the Russians and agreed to be a double agent for the British Government.

It was the job of the British to keep the Russians in the war, and they had to share their most vital intelligence secrets with Stalin to accomplish the task. He never really trusted Churchill or FDR And with good reason.

What he didn't know was that the British had been reading every German military and diplomatic message with the use of the Ultra eavesdropping program. The challenge was getting the Ultra information to Stalin without raising suspicions. A man named Rudolf Roessler, code-named Lucy, solved the problem.

By 1944, when the end of the war was in sight, the Swiss government closed down the three groups led by Foote and his fellow agents. Foote was arrested and served a short prison term. Roessler was also apprehended after the war ended and was subsequently released. He died in 1953.

Foote continued working for the GRU (who still did not know of his links to British Intelligence) and finally defected to London. (*See Also*: Roessler, Rudolf; Werther)

Franklin D. Roosevelt's Map

By 1941, the war in Europe had been raging for two years. President Franklin D. Roosevelt's sympathy was deeply rooted with the allies—Britain and France. But France had fallen, and England was being rocked by a series of military defeats. When pressed by critics at home, the president said publicly that he wanted the United States to be neutral in the war, but privately gave all the aid he could to the allies.

In October 1941, the president told a news conference he had obtained information showing German designs on the countries of Latin America. FDR stated that he possessed a map showing how Germany intended to carve up the free states into "five vassal states." When a reporter questioned where the map had been obtained to test its authenticity, the president said it was given to him by a "reliable source," and that it was indeed genuine. When asked further if he would give a copy of the map to the press, he demurred. Its authenticity is in doubt to this day.

FDR told the press about this map to gather American public opinion for the undeclared war by the U.S. Navy against German submarines sinking allied cargo ships on a daily basis off the Eastern seaboard of America. Another, and possibly more important, reason was that the president was terribly worried about any German penetration of the "soft underbelly" of the U.S.

In later years, the British military historian, H. Montgomery Hyde, in his book, *Room 3608,* stated the chart was taken from a German courier in Argentina by British agents. The courier had met with an "accident." The map came from Gottfried Sandstede, who worked as an attaché in the German Embassy in Argentina. According to the story, the British gave the map to its master spy in the United States, William Stephenson, head of the BSC.

According to Stephenson's account of the incident, "Sandstede paid for his bungling with his life. His identity…found its way back to the German Gestapo agents in Buenos Aires. They had Sandstede killed in yet another of the many 'accidents' that marked this secret battle."

But here, the "official" story is disputed. In their article, *FDR and The Secret Map,* John F. Bratzel and Leslie B. Rout Jr. say that Sandstede, head of the Nazi overseas organization *Auslandsorganisiation* in Argentina, was actually in Germany at that time. He was subsequently killed in action on March 9, 1944, on the Russian front.

What most historians do not dispute is the fact that the map was intercepted by Stephenson's BSC. It is possible that the contents of the map were taken to BSC's technical laboratory "Station M" in Canada, where an elaborate forgery department doctored German intercepts by the British.

Whether or not the contents of FDR's secret map were true, it proved the lengths to which the president would go to ensure that German interests in South America would be contained.

French Resistance Movements

When war broke out in 1939, the British government believed that the mighty French army would provide a barrier to any German conquest of Europe. However, they were shocked by a sudden and total collapse of the French armed forces. With Hitler in control of Paris, military resistance to the invading Germans ended immediately.

In British intelligence circles the fall of France posed another problem; how to mount a successful covert resistance movement against the Nazi occupiers. They were in a perilous position, as Special Operations Executive (SOE) "did not possess one single agent between the Balkans and the English Channel." Immediately after the fall of France, both SIS and SOE set up sections dealing with the unorganized French resistance groups still operating.

In the aftermath of the German seizure of the country, France was divided into three sections: an occupied German area; unoccupied zone; and a north coastal exclusion area. By the end of 1940, however, organized resistance to German authority began to grow in the occupied areas. They comprised about 80 separate resistance groups. These groups would, over the course of the war, make up a large-scale counter-resistance movement involving the OSS and elements of the British intelligence services.
(*See Also*: Maquis, The)

Fuchs, Klaus

The key Soviet atomic spy during the latter part of World War II was a brilliant native of Germany, Klaus Fuchs. He and another exceptional scientist, Theodore Hall of the Manhattan Project, passed the formula for extracting bomb-grade uranium to Soviet agents. The Soviet Union developed its own atomic bomb because of it.

Klaus Fuchs, born in Russelheim, Germany in 1911, was the son of a Lutheran pastor. As a youth, Klaus took on his father's anti-Hitler stance but was attracted to communism, joining the party while attending the University of Kiel. He later studied in England, where he received his Ph.D.

Early on, he made a reputation as a brilliant physicist, a fact not unnoticed by the Soviets. When the war broke out, he was arrested as a suspected German agent and spent a year in an internment camp in Canada. It was there that Soviet agents contacted him, hiring him to supply information.

He returned to England, moved to Glasgow, and was hired by the British to work on The Tube Alloy Projject, which was England's name for the development of its own atomic bomb.

How British intelligence did not notice, or chose to ignore Fuchs's communist background, is hard to imagine. To be sure, Fuchs was one of the most exceptional scientists in England. At that time, the Soviet Union was still an ally of the British, and any enemy of the Führer couldn't be too bad.

In 1942, he became a British subject and began working with the

Soviets. During that year, he contacted Semion Kremer, the secretary to the military attaché in the Soviet Embassy in London. His job was to provide information on the atomic bomb project.

The GRU (military intelligence) didn't know how lucky they were when Fuchs was sent to the United States in December 1943 to continue scientific experiments relating to the atomic bomb. Once in the United States, Fuchs came under the control of the NKGB intelligence section. Fuchs was transferred to the Manhattan Project in the deserts of New Mexico.

On January 27, 1950, while being questioned by British intelligence officers, Fuchs broke down and confessed to being a Russian spy. He revealed the scope of the Russian atomic spy operation and the names of its members: Harry Gold, Julius and Ethel Rosenberg, and David Greenglass, among others.

He was tried and convicted of violating the Official Secrets Act, rather than treason. He served nine years, and lived out his remaining time in East Germany. Klaus Fuchs died in 1979.

(*See Also*: Manhattan Project; Greenglass, David; Gold, Harry; Venona; Rosenberg, Julius & Ethel)

G

Garcia, Juan Pujol aka "Garbo"

The British recruited a flamboyant Spaniard named Juan Pujol Garcia, better known in espionage lore as "Garbo." Garbo was the most successful agent in the British Double Cross program.

Juan Garcia was an anti-Republican Spaniard who believed that Franco would lead Spain to ruin. He knew that he had to work against the regime and decided the best way to go about this was to offer his services as a spy for the British. He was unsuccessful and turned to the Germans where he was accepted by the Abwehr.

He left Madrid in July 1941, telling his new German employers that he was heading for London to set up a secret spy network. Instead, he headed for Lisbon, Portugal where, once again, he asked the British to let him spy for them.

For nine months, Garbo lived in Lisbon and sent reports back to Germany. For a man who had never been to England before, Garbo did a fantastic job fooling the Abwehr into accepting his bogus information.

Garbo said that he had recruited five agents for his network, dubbing them "J-1" to "J-5." He gave them false identities such as a Portugese named "Carvalo," a Swiss named "Gerbers," and an unnamed man from Venezuela. Another man "recruited" by Garbo was "Fred" who came from Gibraltar. This came to be known in the spy business as creating "Notional Agents," identities created to transmit fabricated information.

Garbo's false data was so good that he received this cable from the Abwehr, "Your activity and that of your information gave us a perfect idea of what is taking place over there; these reports, as you can imagine, have an incalculable value, and for that reason I beg of you to proceed with the greatest care so as not to endanger in these momentous times, either yourself or your organization."

In January 1944, Garbo received a letter from Germany telling him that the Abwehr had received word of a major allied offensive from Europe. Could he please watch for any unusual ship, air, or ground movements and report on them immediately?

What the Germans were referring to was D-Day. Garbo's most important disinformation operation began. At midnight on June 5th, 1944, he radioed Madrid asking that the channel be kept clear, as he had vital information to send. But German radio operators on the other end did not reply.

On June 6, 1944, Garbo began sending a message that lasted 129 minutes. He reported that he had located the whereabouts of an allied force called "Army Gruppe Patton," in the eastern part of England. He further said that the allied push at the Normandy beaches was only a diversion and that the real invasion would take place at the Pas de Calais.

Garbo's vital message was forwarded to Hitler's command center in Berchtesgaden. Using Ultra, British code breakers learned that the Germans bought Garbo's story. In reality, "Army Gruppe Patton" was a phantom army complete with false radio signals.

In response to Garbo's warning, Hitler ordered the Fifteenth Army, composed of tank and infantry units, be diverted from Normandy. Garbo's bogus information was indispensable in the allies' successful invasion of Normandy on June 6, 1944.

By August 1944, German radio warned that Garbo's cover was about to be blown. Compromised, Garbo went underground. All in all, the Germans paid Garbo and his phantom network almost $340,000. They even awarded him the Iron Cross. Ironically, Garbo was the best agent they ever had.

German Flying Bombs (Operation Crossbow)

By 1944, the war had entered a new phase. The Germans were on the run but sought to inflict as much destruction on Great Britain as possible. Some of the new, deadly weapons unleashed against the British were the V-1 unpiloted rockets launched from bases in German occupied France against civilian targets in London. These "flying bombs" were part of the blitz on London in the summer of 1944.

To counter attacks on British cities, the intelligence agencies came up with a highly sophisticated deception program using Garbo to pass misleading information back to the Abwehr. The departments charged with that responsibility were the Air Ministry and, of course, the SIS.

As V-1 attacks on London and other British cities began, the plan went into effect. After an attack on targets in Northwest London, Garbo reported back that the bombs had hit in Southeast London. Their reports to Germany told of bombs falling short of targets, and coordinates that would hit less populated areas.

Garbo cabled to Abwehr headquarters, "It has also occurred to me that I might take on the work of making daily observations and let you have by radio an exact report on objectives hit so that you will be able to correct any possible errors of fire...."

As the date for the invasion of Normandy neared, and with a massive army poised to strike the heart of the European continent, the V-1 raids were abandoned. Once again, the actions of one of Britain's spies helped save London from unnecessary death and destruction.

German Intelligence Operations in the United States

At FBI headquarters, J. Edgar Hoover was following the developments in Germany very closely. In a speech to the chiefs of police in San Francisco, Hoover told his startled audience that the FBI's job of going after bootleggers, car thieves, and criminals like John Dillinger and "Pretty Boy" Floyd were coming to an end. Their new job was to address German espionage or sabotage operations aimed at the United States. With the blessing of President Roosevelt, Hoover got down to the business of capturing Nazi spies in America.

Fortunately for Hoover, he did not have far to go. In pre-war America, the command post for German espionage operations in the United States was the German Embassy, only a few miles from the White House. The man in charge of spying on America was Dr. Hans Thomsen, the *Chargé d'affaires*. Thomsen organized a group of 47 V men across the country, whose job it was to gather as much information on America as possible. Thomsen also put on his payroll a number of newspaper reporters from neutral countries. One such agent, a close associate of U.S. Attorney General Homer Cummings, provided Berlin with the minutes of meetings between FDR and his cabinet.

Unknown to Thomsen, the German SD Chief Reinhard Heydrich, planted a spy inside the embassy to keep an eye on him. This agent was "Baron" Ulrich von Gienanth, the second secretary of the embassy. Von Gienanth was a popular member of the Washington social set and got information from party goers.

His main job was to cultivate as many important Americans as possible whose political sympathies leaned toward Hitler. His first recruit was Laura Ingalls, a successful woman flyer who flew her plane over the White House, dropping peace leaflets over the president's mansion. Working secretly with Baron von Gienanth, Laura Ingalls spoke against Roosevelt at pro-German rallies around the country.

By 1938, the most valuable German agent in New York was Guenther Rumrich. Rumrich was born in Chicago, Illinois, in 1911, and moved to

Vienna where his father worked as a secretary in the Austria-Hungarian consulate. He was later transferred to Bremen, Germany. In 1929, Guenther returned to the United States and joined the army. He deserted but could not survive and gave himself up to military authorities. After four months of a court martial he was reinstated. He was then promoted to sergeant the next year. It was from his New York base that Guenther Rumrich would begin his career as a German agent.

A German-American, Kurt Ludwig, headed another German spy ring in America. Ludwig took over the group after its original head, an Abwehr agent, was killed in a car accident in New York's Times Square.

Ludwig had powerful connections inside the German military establishment, including Gestapo chief, Heinrich Himmler. He had arrived in New York in 1940 under the guise of salesman, looking for information on the size of United States Army units, their equipment, morale, etc. He made contact with a number of people in the German-American community in New York who proved able and willing to act as spies. In time, the Ludwig group was sending back imformation to Germany. He also visited the bustling ports of New York harbor, keeping track of the large troop ships.

Ludwig recruited a beautiful young woman named Lucy Boehmler, an all-American girl who was active in the German-American Youth Society. Lucy served as Ludwig's secretary and possessed an exceptional memory for details.

Ludwig also had Walter and Helen Mayer, whose Brooklyn home served as a meeting place for members of the gang. In attendance at the Mayer home were people who worked for defense plants making aircraft parts. The Mayers picked the brains of the unsuspecting guests.

The beginning of the end of the Ludwig gang came when he sent a letter, using an alias, to "Lothar Frederick" (Reinhard Heydrich), chief of the Nazi police. British letter openers intercepted it.

The FBI received a second letter saying Ulrich von der Osten had been "removed from circulation." Ludwig tried to flee the country but was arrested in Seattle, Washington. He was sentenced to 20 years in jail.

The collapse of the Ludwig, and Rumrich spy rings ended any German espionage operations in the United States for the remainder of the war.

Gibraltar

In the James Bond film, *The Living Daylights*, agent 007 jumps from a Hercules airplane over the Gibraltar. In real life, "Gib" or the "Rock," as the rugged island was called, was a hotbed of spies, a springboard for British expansion into North Africa.

Gibraltar was a vital British base situated off the coast of Spain. In 1940, the British evacuated almost 17,000 troops believing that a German invasion via Spain was pending. At 1,408 feet, Gibraltar has a commanding ocean view, vital to the detection of German ships that approached the coast of North Africa. The Rock's airfield was used as a jumping off point for the invasion of North Africa in 1942.

On the eve of Operation Torch, the code name for the allied invasion of North Africa, General Eisenhower moved his headquarters to Gibraltar. A French commander, Henri Giraud wanted to direct Operation Torch, but Eisenhower turned him down. In one of the most spectacular episodes of the war, Ike arranged for Giraud's extradition from France.

During the war, Gibraltar saw its fair share of the fighting. At one point, Vichy French bombers dropped 600 tons of explosives on the fortress to revenge a British naval attack on French warships at Mers-el Kabir on July 3, 1940.

The British presence at Gibraltar couldn't be budged. Its strategic location made it ripe for intelligence gathering by both sides, and as the war went on, spies of all stripes made their way to the Rock. German sympathizers witnessed all naval traffic across the straits in Spain. While most of the local population was pro-British, some were loyal to the neo-fascist government of Spain.

As terrorist activities against naval targets mounted, the British SIS took action. The British recruited an unnamed lieutenant in the Spanish army to act as a double agent. From radio intercepts, it was ascertained that sabotage operations were being conducted at the port of Algeciras. One of the deadliest incidents was a February 1941 explosion in the North Tunnel of the island. Mines were found in the harbor attached to numerous ships. SIS agents got lucky and arrested a Gibraltar citizen named Jose Estrella Key, who was sent back to England, tried and executed.

British commanders at the Rock, made inquiries to the Franco regime. In August 1942, the British Ambassador to Spain staged a protest, which led to a crackdown on Abwehr locations at Tangier and Ceuta. However, this was done with a wink and a nod as the Spanish military kept a steady stream of naval reports available to the Germans.

The Portugese government also took a hand in putting a corral on German spy operations in their sphere of influence. At one point in the war, the Portugese authorities made espionage by foreigners on Portugese territory a criminal charge. All this action was just a prelude to the anticipated Nazi invasion of Spain, Gibraltar, North Africa, and eventually the Suez Canal. This invasion went by the cover name, Operation Felix.

This proposed action did not go over well with Spain's dictator for life, Francisco Franco. In order to stem any German invasion, Franco declared that Spain was in a state of "nonbelligerency." Two days later, Franco sent his troops to take over Tangier.

The British went so far as to send a personal representative to Franco in the person of Sir Samuel Hoare. It was Hoare's mission to prevent Franco from caving in to German pressure for military bases in that country. Hoare was somewhat successful—Franco pledged not to allow German troops to occupy Spain.

As preparations for Operation Felix began in earnest, Abwehr chief Canaris, along with members of his staff, including Hans Piekenbrock, Lieutenant Colonel Hans Mikosch, and Captain Hans-Jochen Rudloff, traveled to Spain. The crafty Canaris met secretly with a number of his old contacts in the Spanish military, including General Juan Vigon, chief of Spain's General Staff, and General Carlos Martinez Campos, head of Spanish intelligence. In these audiences, Canaris urged them to advise Franco not to give in to Hitler's entreaties. Canaris did all he could to undermine the Nazi regime.

In his reports to Hitler, Canaris said that he doubted an attack would take the island, that, in his opinion, the plan was too risky.

In a private meeting with the Spanish dictator, Canaris told Franco that if he made a military or political pact with Hitler, Spain would suffer in the end. Franco then met with the German Ambassador to Spain, Eberhard von Stoher. He told the ambassador that the only way he would make an alliance with the Führer would be if Germany promised to hand over Gibraltar as well as Morocco to Spain. His demands were rejected.

With Canaris's spies openly staking out the Rock, the unexpected happened. Hitler suddenly dropped plans for Operation Felix, saving Gibraltar for *007*.

Godfrey, John

Admiral John Godfrey inevitably spurs debates on the history of espionage during World War II. John Godfrey served as head of British Naval Intelligence until mid-1942. The controversy is in his relationship with the OSS, and his personal/business friendship with naval aide Cmdr. Ian Fleming.

Godfrey's first consideration to a high position in the British espionage establishment came with the death of Sir Hugh Sinclair, head of British Intelligence. Two possibilities to succeed Sinclair were Stewart Menzies, and Admiral John Godfrey. Menzies was high in the espionage pecking order, having served 25 years in intelligence.

Menzies also had major political connections throughout the British government and Foreign Service. Prime Minister Winston Churchill preferred a naval officer for the job, but after the "beer hall *putsch*," an attempt on Hitler's life in the form of a wine cellar explosion that wounded and killed many innocent people, Churchill learned the value of Menzies's intelligence experience and chose him for the job.

With the post out of his reach and the dismissal of his predecessor, Lieutenant Commander Norman Denning, Godfrey was named Director of Naval Intelligence. His job was to direct the powerful British navy in the protection of its far-flung empire.

While not directly in his bailiwick, Godfrey suffered his first defeat in the intelligence arena, when, on April 5, 1940, despite repeated warnings, the German army invaded and occupied Norway. Before the invasion, it was believed by many in the government that Hitler's next move would be either an attack on France or the Low Countries. No one thought Norway was the target.

In the aftermath of the Norwegian tragedy, Menzies documented the events leading up to the fiasco. His report claimed the Secret Intelligence Service had provided ample warning of a possible German attack on Norway, and laid the blame on the shoulders of Godfrey: "Godfrey in particular appeared to have been delinquent in not passing SIS reports upward on the grounds that he did not trust them."

Godfrey moved on, directing traffic from Naval headquarters, overseeing the routing of British warships and sending his spies across the globe to counter the Nazi invasion. With his workload expanding at an alarming pace, Godfrey needed an assistant. He chose a London stockbroker with a talent for writing, named Ian Fleming. Speaking about his new job at Naval Intelligence, Fleming boasted, "…the division is now the finest intelligence organization in the world." He called his boss, Admiral Godfrey, "a real warwinner."

With the German occupation of France reaching fruition by the summer of 1940, Admiral Godfrey sent Ian Fleming as his personal representative to assess the military situation. Fleming made his way to the French city of Tours, headquarters of the French Ministry of the Marines. His arrival came during a sensitive time between the allied services. Fleming attached himself to the staff of Admiral Jean Darlan where he could keep Godfrey up to date on the latest developments.

In 1940, on orders from President Roosevelt, William Donovan traveled to Britain to report on the war's progress. Donovan was royally treated while in England, meeting with representatives of military and political worlds. One of them was John Godfrey.

Donovan and Godfrey met for a period of two days with Godfrey opening his entire section to Donovan's perusal. Donovan told the Admiral he was going to recommend that a person be appointed as a "sensible ambassador" between the countries so that a loose alliance in intelligence gathering functions between the U.S. and Great Britain could be established. FDR liked the idea, and appointed Bill Donovan.

To that end, it was agreed that a high-level delegation should be sent to Washington to coordinate the countries' new intelligence relationship. Admiral John Godfrey and his aid, Ian Fleming, pioneered this difficult assignment.

The two men left London in May 1941. They stayed two nights in Estoril, where, as the story goes, both spent a profitable night at a gaming table, taking in a large sum from two Portugese card players. They also looked in on the British BSC's mail intercept station in Bermuda.

They arrived in New York on May 25, 1941, wearing civilian clothing so as not to attract attention. They signed their immigration papers as government employees, and settled in at the posh St. Regis Hotel near Central Park. They met with William Stephenson at his BSC headquarters in Rockefeller Center. Here, Stephenson described how his secret intelligence gathering operation functioned.

After their brief New York stay, they traveled to Washington where the most difficult part of their journey was to begin. Their first meeting was on June 6, with the irascible FBI Chief, J. Edgar Hoover. For 16 minutes, Godfrey and Fleming listened to Hoover's opinion of anyone foolish enough to usurp his intelligence domain. Fleming later wrote of that conference: "Hoover received us graciously, listened with close attention to our exposé of certain security problems, and expressed himself firmly but politely as being uninterested in our mission."

Getting nowhere with Hoover, Godfrey pulled strings in Washington, and with the help of Bill Stephenson and Arthur Hays Sulzberger, publisher of the *New York Times*, was able to arrange a meeting with Eleanor Roosevelt. The president listened in, and the result was the appointment of Bill Donovan as head of the Coordinator of Information (COI).

Much to Godfrey's shock, just days after being promoted to the rank of vice admiral, he was relieved of his duties as head of naval intelligence. He was sent to India as the Flag Officer Commanding Royal Indian Navy. No reason was given for his reassignment.

In 1969, noted intelligence writer Thomas Troy interviewed the 81-year-old Godfrey about his war experiences. About his part in FDR's appointment of Donovan as head of COI, the Admiral said: "...the late intervention, namely, an hour and a half with FDR, had had some effect, because...the COI was established within three weeks."

Commenting on William Stephenson, Admiral Godfrey said of the BSC chief: "he had a streak of ambition that caused him to think of himself as a kingmaker." Troy writes that Admiral Godfrey "was the only British admiral who received absolutely no recognition for his services."

In 1946, Godfrey was held responsible for a mutiny in the ranks of the Royal Indian Navy. Godfrey never complained of the way he was treated in the aftermath of that incident, but colleagues attest to his bitter disappointment.

(*See Also*: Fleming, Ian; Donovan, William)

Gold, Harry

Harry Gold (Golodnotsky) was born on December 10, 1912, in Bern, Switzerland. His mother was a revolutionary and moved to Switzerland from France because of her politics. His father left Russia in 1903 to avoid military service. The rest of the family emigrated to the United States when Harry was a young man, fleeing religious and political persecution.

Harry Gold was a courier and intelligence operative for the Soviet GRU (Military Intelligence) in the years prior to and during World War II. His name will be forever linked to the infamous Rosenberg spy ring that pilfered U.S. atomic secrets and gave them to the Soviet Union.

He earned a degree in chemistry at the University of Pennsylvania and began to dabble in left-wing politics, as did so many others of his generation. After graduation, Gold worked in a sugar factory in Pennsylvania. Among his early technical successes was the production of a dry ice.

By 1935, Harry Gold had become a dedicated communist and begun his spy career. Working in New York City, he was recruited by the Russians and gave the Soviets economic information about his company. A Soviet agent code-named "Black" described Harry Gold's early work as "absolutely trustworthy."

Eventually Gold met Alfred Slack, a "talent spotter" for the Russians. By 1942, still working as a chemical engineer, Gold started spying for $100 a month. Slack provided information from the Eastman Kodak Company on the recovery of silver from used film, as well as details of explosives developed at the Holston Ordinance Works in Kingsport, Tennessee.

Gold became quite enthusiastic about his espionage career. He tried to set up his own laboratory to work on the thermal diffusion of gases, but the Russians refused the $2,000 he needed to get started.

In the spring of 1944, Gold was given a new Soviet controller, Anatoly Yatskov, code name "Alexsey," because the FBI had put a 24-hour watch on Semyonov. Yatskov was listed with the State Department as the General Consul with the Soviet Legation. In reality, he was the GRU's agent in the United States. His main job was to obtain information on the still infant

U.S. atomic bomb project. Yatskov's ordered Gold to put him in contact with a brilliant British scientist researching the atomic bomb project. That man was Klaus Fuchs.

Fuchs had been working on the U.S. Manhattan Project to build an atomic bomb since 1943, when he came to the attention of the Soviet Union. He was taken on by the Russian intelligence and became their number-one source on the project. Gold was Fuchs's contact man, but neither knew the true identity of the other.

They first met on February 5, 1944—Fuchs carrying a tennis ball, and Gold a green-covered book as covert identification. Gold filed a lengthy report on their encounter. Fuchs told Gold details about the atomic bomb project, code-named Enormoz, that most of the work was being done at a secret location named "Camp Y" in New Mexico.

At their next meeting on February 25th, Fuchs turned over some of his notes concerning the Enormoz Project. They continued to meet on a regular basis until May of that year. Fuchs was then transferred to New Mexico, which put him squarely in the heart of Enormoz

With Fuchs under constant surveillance in New Mexico (as were all employees), other means of contacting him had to be arranged. On a trip to Chicago, Fuchs had his sister in Boston tell Gold when he would be in contact. When the Japanese surrendered in 1945. Fuchs met with Gold at a Santa Fe liquor store on the pretense of buying celebration supplies. At that meeting, which turned out to be their last, Fuchs handed over a treasure trove of material, including the results of the bombings of Hiroshima and Nagasaki.

Fuchs, it turned out, was not Gold's only atomic weapons contact. Other sources were Martin Sobel, a rocket scientist from the General Electric Laboratories, and David Greenglass, an army machinist (and brother of Ethel Rosenberg) at Los Alamos. In 1946, Fuchs was sent back to Britain and arrested by British authorities in 1949. Unfortunately for Gold, the FBI had learned of his spy activity and placed him under surveillance.

Harry Gold's downfall came, ironically, from Fuchs's own testimony. When questioned by the Russians about whom he'd worked with during the war, Fuchs claimed it was Gold—and Gold alone. Fuchs was shown two films of Gold. Gold was shown on an American city street and impressed Fuchs as a man in a state of nervous excitement being chased. After seeing the film, Fuchs didn't confess that he knew Gold. In the second film, Gold was already in prison. After seeing that, Fuchs identified Gold and gave testimony against him.

Harry Gold was found guilty, and served two-thirds of a 30-year prison term. He was paroled in 1965. He returned to Philadelphia and lived out his life a dispirited and destitute man.

(*See Also*: Rosenberg, Julius & Ethel; Greenglass, David; Venona; Manhattan Project)

Golos, Jacob

To the casual student of wartime espionage, the name Jacob Golos may not mean much. It has been learned from the Venona materials and the writing of authors Allen Weinstein and Alexander Vassiliev, authors of *The Haunted Wood: Soviet Espionage in America—The Stalin Era*. We now know the true extent of the role Jacob Golos played in Soviet espionage operations in this country.

Jacob Golos was born Jacob Raisen on April 30, 1890, in the Ukraine. Not much is known about his early life except that as a young man he was involved in radical political movements in the Ukraine and jailed in a Siberian labor camp. He managed to escape and immigrated to the United States, where his parents had already taken up residence.

Jacob joined the Socialist Party, precursor to the American Communist Party. When the party split, Golos became a member of the Communist Party of America—CPUSA. The other faction was the Communist Labor Party. To demonstrate solidarity with the new party, he changed his name to *Golos*, which is Russian for "voice."

He returned to the Soviet Union in 1919 and worked for the Bolshevik regime in a Siberian coal mine. It is also believed that during his stay in Russia, he joined the Cheka, or secret police.

In 1923, Golos became a writer for the magazine *Novy Mir*, a publication of the CPUSA's Russian language journals. He also worked as a party organizer in Detroit and Chicago. In 1927, Golos took on an assignment that would last until his death in 1943 and root him firmly in the United States. He was one of the founders of a Soviet front organization called World Tourists, a travel agency composed of workers who were members of the CPUSA.

World Tourists worked closely with the official Soviet travel agency, Intourist. Intourist functioned as a reputable agency, arranging trips across borders, handling the necessary paperwork, and shipping parcels back to Russia. A certain percentage of the profits from World Tourists went into the coffers of the CPUSA to fund their operations.

Another part of Golos's operation was faking U.S. passports. The names on these passports were taken from the files of the deceased, and persons who had permanently left the United States. In a federal investigation 16 people were exposed using fake credentials.

While World Tourists was busy arranging trips for its clients, the FBI kept a careful watch over their operations. As it became more obvious that World Tourists was working for the CPUSA, the federal government swooped down, charging them as an unauthorized agent of a foreign power. In a plea bargain, World Tourists pled guilty on the foreign agent charge and was fined a paltry

GOLOS

$500. Golos received a suspended sentence.

After a period of down time, Golos organized another cover business, calling it U.S. Service and Shipping Corporation. In charge was John Hazard Reynolds, a man of wealth and influence in the New York business community. Reynolds's wife was the heiress of the Fleischman Yeast Company. While Reynolds himself was never a member of the CPUSA, he lent his support to their activities. Reynolds did not take part in the daily operations of the company, leaving that job to Elizabeth Bentley, a beautiful woman who would play an integral part in Jacob Golos's life and in the CPUSA.

By the 1930s, Golos was working under the control of the GRU in New York. His main contact was Gaik Ovakimian, the Soviet Consul.

Golos and Elizabeth Bentley became lovers, but that posed a complicated situation for Golos. He was married, but in 1935, he sent his wife and son back to Russia. Soon, Bentley moved in with him. Bentley served as an intermediary between her many high-level contacts in Washington and Golos. In time, she would head the operation.

In November 1937, Golos went to the Soviet Union, where he met with Abram Slutsky, the head of Soviet intelligence. Slutsky told Golos that upon his return to the U.S. he was to continue his passport business, as well as recruiting sailors who shared their communist views. Golos soon had his agents in Canada, where his illegal passport concern flourished.

Soon, Bentley took on more important assignments for her lover. She serviced a number of mail drops for Golos, who received messages from his widespread contacts. Golos also sent Bentley to Washington, where she brought back sensitive data from his sources. Among Golos's Washington channels were Nathan Silvermaster and Harry Dexter White, who was the number-two official in the U.S. Treasury Department.

Ever since the fiasco with Golos's World Tourists, and his subsequent imprisonment, the FBI had been keeping a watch on his activities. In a deciphered letter concerning Golos's activities, the writer said: "If something happens to them (referring to other agents), much of what has been created will be reduced to ashes. Some operatives believe that Golos has become a virtual chief in the U.S. He provides people for different kinds of services and missions in every field of our work. Yet Golos is on the books of American counterintelligence as a major NKVD agent. Therefore, his presence in the station becomes dangerous for business."

There is also a fleeting connection between Golos and Julius Rosenberg. After Elizabeth Bentley defected to the FBI, she told them a man named Julius contacted Golos to offer the services of a number of unnamed engineers willing to work for the Soviet Union. Bentley did not know who this Julius was, but she was able to meet with him and provide the bureau with a description. The "Julius" who offered his services to the Golos network was Julius Rosenberg.

By 1942, the strains of operating his network took a terrible toll on Golos's health. After the Germans attacked Russia, once their ally, Golos even talked about returning to Russia to join the army. The final straw in Golos's relationship with the Russians came when they ordered him to turn over the web of American contacts that he had cultivated for so many years.

On November 25, 1943, Jacob Golos died of a heart attack. Elizabeth Bentley took over the reigns of his organization but within two years would become an informant for the FBI. The death of Jacob Golos and loss of Elizabeth Bentley deprived the Soviet Union of one of their most effective espionage rings operating in the United States.

(*See Also*: Bentley, Elizabeth; Rosenberg, Julius & Ethel)

Granville, Christine

One of the famous names in the resistance movements in Eastern Europe was a charming and talented woman named Christine Granville. She was born Krystyna Skarbek in Warsaw, Poland, 1915. Her father was an aristocrat named Count Jerzy Skarbek, and her mother a member of a wealthy Jewish family named Goldfeder.

Christine's father showered her with affection, and both father and daughter shared many pursuits. The elder Jerzy taught his child how to shoot. An expert shot, Christine claimed that during a hike in the forest, she'd gotten lost and cornered by a pack of hungry wolves. She managed to kill them all and return to safety.

After graduating from school, she married a Pole, Georg Gizycki, and moved to Kenya. But when Germany attacked Poland in 1939, her husband returned home and joined the army. The Polish army was no match for the Germans, and her husband was one of thousands killed at the beginning of the war. Granville got permission to leave Kenya and make her way to England. With her skill at languages and firearm ability, she applied to the Special Operations Executive and was accepted into its elite ranks. It was from this one interview that Christine Granville would become a legend in the underground resistance.

Granville went to Poland to rendezvous with underground groups. One of the first cloak-and-dagger leaders she met was Stanislaw Witkowski, a close ally of the SIS. With information from him, she made two hazardous trips back to London, at one point bluffing her way past German border guards who questioned her identity.

Her biggest accomplishment was the successful smuggling of Poles to London where they joined the free Polish resistance against Hitler. She also was able to get downed Allied airmen back to England.

Confronted by the Germans, and on the verge of capture, Granville showed great bravery and ingenuity. She talked her way out of jail twice by telling her captors she was related to Admiral Horthy, the Regent of Hungary. On another potentially fateful encounter, she persuaded German guards to let her go, by claiming to be the niece of British General Montgomery.

By 1944, Christine had assumed the code name "Pauline Armand" and embarked on her most dangerous mission. After spending some time in Cairo, Egypt, she parachuted into the Vercors region of France, where she linked up with the Maquis 1 (French clandestine organization). The man she reported to was the Maquis leader, Colonel Francois Cammaerts. Cammaerts's headquarters was in the Rhone Valley, where he commanded a large force of almost 10,000 men. She couriered messages over the Alps, consistently evading German patrols.

When two SOE agents, Xan Fielding and a French officer named Sorensen, were captured by the Germans and taken to Digne prison, Granville bluffed her way inside. Once inside, she demanded to see the warden. With a combination of threats, bluffs, and sheer luck, she secured the men's release.

After the war, Christine returned to London where she took on various jobs, including one as a stewardess on board the liner *Winchester Castle*, which made runs between England, South Africa and Australia.

On the *Winchester Castle*, Christine met one George Muldowney. Suffering from mental problems, Muldowney stalked her, making unwanted advances. George Muldowney attacked Christine in her hotel and killed her with a knife. He was arrested on the spot and hanged on September 30, 1952.

Greenglass, David

David Greenglass was a key cog in the atomic espionage case revolving around his sister and brother-in-law, Ethel and Julius Rosenberg. His evidence in their treason trial helped convict the couple in one of the most dramatic espionage trials of the century. Even today, some 50 years after the execution of the Rosenbergs for stealing American atomic secrets, the case is argued by historians.

David Greenglass was born in 1922 in New York City of Russian Jewish parents. He and his sister Ethel had a normal upbringing for any child of the crowded Lower East Side. As a teenager, he joined the Young Communist League, admiring its emphasis on the rights of the worker. It was at one of these meetings that David met his future wife, 19-year-old Ruth Printz. While both were members of the Young Communist League, neither would officially join the Party.

David went to school at the Polytechnic Institute of Brooklyn but failed the majority of his courses. He later transferred to New York's Pratt Institute. In 1943, two years after the United States entered the war, he joined the army. He took basic training at Aberdeen, Maryland, writing letters to Ruth, sprinkled with Socialist thoughts. "I am content," he wrote, "without so long as there is a vital battle to be fought with a cruel, ruthless foe. Victory shall be ours and the future is socialism's."

After graduating from basic training, David was transferred to Fort Ord, California, where he was schooled as a machinist, repairing tanks. He was soon sent to Jackson, Mississippi, in the spring of 1944, where he worked as a machinist at the Mississippi Ordnance Plant. In another letter to Ruth, David expanded on his political philosophy, "Darling, I have been reading a lot of books on the Soviet Union. Dear, I can see how far-sighted and intelligent those leaders are. They are really geniuses every one of them. Having found out all the truth about the Soviets…I have come to a stronger and more resolute faith…in the principles of Socialism and Communism."

In July of 1944, the army asked that six men from the Jackson facility be transferred to the Manhattan Engineer District, the code name for the project at Oak Ridge, Tennessee, developing the atomic bomb. After one of the men on the original list went AWOL, the military substituted David Greenglass's name instead. His activities there would ultimately seal his fate.

According to testimony by Elizabeth Bentley, Julius was the head of that branch. Julius Rosenberg's original assignment from the Russians was to recruit engineers among his friends and colleagues. David knew that Julius's "friends" were Russians, and since they both shared the ideals of communism, David was a willing participant in his brother-in-law's secret activities.

In later years, David Greenglass would tell an interviewer that he was first brought into Julius Rosenberg's life as a spy in 1943, at the Capitol Theater in New York. David claimed to have told Julius that he would "work" with him after the war, but "I suspected espionage. I suspected going into business as the background for espionage."

David's posting to Oak Ridge was an intelligence coup of the first degree. This secret installation was not noted on any map, and was the perfect place to undertake confidential experiments. "The MED was building a vast gaseous-diffusion plant and a series of electromagnetic isotope-separation units to enrich uranium for atomic bombs."

Much to Greenglass's surprise, he was reassigned to another facility that needed his expertise as a machinist in Los Alamos, New Mexico. He began working with high-speed cameras but had no idea that it was part of the overall plan to build the atomic bomb. As time went on, his task was to work on high-explosive lenses related to the bomb project. One of the top men at Los

Alamos who examined the work of his unit was British scientist and Soviet spy, Klaus Fuchs.

When it became obvious to Greenglass what he was working on, he contacted Julius telling him in a cryptic letter, "I am worried about whether you understand what my telegram is about? I really shouldn't because I know that you are intelligent and will understand. I most certainly will be glad to be part of the community project that Julius and his friends have in mind. Count me in, or should I say it has my vote."

Julius asked his brother-in-law for information on the Manhattan Project. In November 1944, Ruth joined her husband while he was in New Mexico on leave. She confirmed that he was working on the atomic bomb project. During that meeting, Ruth passed along requests for information given to her by Julius, including the layout of Los Alamos, how many people worked there, and any data he could get on the top men at Los Alamos, including Robert Oppenheimer.

By now, the Soviets made their presence known in the person of Anatoli Yakovlev, the controller of the Rosenberg spy ring. The Russian spymaster sent Harry Gold to meet with Greenglass in New Mexico. Greenglass had found, among other things, different types of lens molds; a picture of the bomb to be dropped on Nagasaki; and the amount of plutonium used in the making of the bomb.

Greenglass provided Gold with as much classified information on the atomic bomb as he could get. This material was given to Rosenberg and ultimately, the Soviets. David Greenglass left the army after the war in 1946 and briefly went to work for Julius. After many heated arguments concerning future spying for the Soviets, Greenglass said he'd had enough of the secret life.

The end came for all of them when the British arrested Klaus Fuchs. Fuchs implicated Gold, who then named Greenglass as his conduit. On June 15, 1950, FBI agents arrested David Greenglass in his lower Manhattan apartment. On July 17, 1950, Julius Rosenberg was arrested on espionage charges, and his wife was taken into custody one month later. Ruth Greenglass was not indicted but implicated her sister-in-law.

At the trial of the Rosenbergs, Greenglass testified against them, sealing their fate. Greenglass made a deal with the FBI, pleading guilty to conspiracy to commit espionage and made damaging statements to the jury. He was sentenced to 15 years but only served 10.

David Greenglass lived out his life in obscurity. The same, however, cannot be said of his sister and brother-in-law; they were put to death in the electric chair at New York's Sing Sing Prison on June 19, 1953.

Supporters of the Rosenbergs still believe Greenglass lied in order to save the lives of himself and his wife.

Griffith, Sanford

Despite modern media's obsessive use of polling to gauge the mood of the public, it is not only a modern-day tool. During the war, the British Security Coordination used this technique to persuade many pro-isolationists of the United States Congress to pass legislation that would aid Great Britain in the war against Germany. One of the men most responsible for this propaganda operation was a British intelligence agent named Sanford "Sandy" Griffith.

Lieutenant Commander Sandy Griffith had ties to the Special Operations Executive and the Secret Intelligence Service, two of England's key security agencies. As the war progressed, Griffith, along with two of his most trusted colleagues, Francis Henson and Christopher Emmet, operated a public opinion company run in conjunction with William Stephenson's BSC called Market Analysts Inc. Unknown to the public, they were highly successful in tracing British propaganda in their battle against the Germans.

Sandy Griffith attended Heidelberg University. When World War I broke out, he served in three different nations armed forces: Belgium, France, and the United States. One of his tasks during the war was to interrogate the thousands of German soldiers captured by American forces.

After the war, Sandy Griffith worked as part of the Armistice Commission, and later as a reporter for the *New York Herald Tribune*, and the *Wall Street Journal*. In the 1930s, he spent some time working for various stockbrokers including the major house, Dillon, Read.

In 1939, Griffith, now back in the United States, founded the company that would play a major portion in his covert life, Market Analysts. His office was located on the grounds of the 1939 New York World's Fair. His job was to promote some of the companies who had booths at the fair.

It was during this time, under circumstances that are still murky, that Sandy Griffith came into contact with British intelligence in the person of Dick Ellis. Ellis's background in the intelligence pecking order was suspect. He was a member of the British MI-6 as an assistant to Bill Stephenson, and was a major player in running William Donovan's Coordinator of Information Office. He was also seen as a double agent for both the Soviets and the Germans.

It is believed that Sandy Griffith first joined British Intelligence around 1938, working in Section D of MI-6—the dirty tricks department. This unit was part and parcel of the BSC organization. In a secret deal worked out by the BSC and Sandy Griffith, the Market Analysts would work with British intelligence as their official polling organization and dispenser of propaganda activities in the United States.

Working with Griffith was Christopher Emmet, an affluent businessman from Westchester County, whose ancestors served in the American Revolution. Christopher Emmet was also linked by marriage to the wealthy Morgan and Aldrich banking families. He was a Harvard graduate and during the late 1930s, worked for a number of organizations that were anti-Nazi and pro-British. In 1940, both Emmet and Sandy Griffith founded a pro-independence corporation called "France Forever."

Chris Emmet's ties to British intelligence were cemented in 1940 when he became treasurer of a front group called the Committee for American-Irish Defense. This group was located in the same building as Griffith's Market Analysts. After the war, Emmet served with MI-6 and also aided the CIA in its anti-Russian activities.

Many years later, Henson would write of his duties at Market Analysts, "My job was to use the results of polls taken among their constituents, to convince congressmen and senators on the fence that they should favor more aid to Britain." That they did.

Griffith's Market Analysts success came at the 1940 Republican National Convention where some 60 percent of the delegates polled said they favored more aid to Great Britain. Using questions like: "If Germany wins a decisive victory over France and Britain, do you think that we will be endangered in the U.S.? Yes—60%. No.—37.6%." And: "If you think we are endangered, do you favor our helping the allies with everything (check as many as necessary) short of war? 64.4%."

They repeated their accomplishment at the Democratic National Convention that summer. Eighty-five percent of the delegates polled said that a British defeat would be dangerous in the long run for the United States, and 65 percent said Germany was already menacing the security of this country.

Griffith got help from other important sources like the *Chicago Daily News* and *New York Times*, who wrote articles and editorials expounding the pro-British cause. They even lobbied Democratic delegates. Market Analysts wrote material supportive of the leader of the Free French, Charles de Gaulle.

Another poll run by Griffith was directed toward the powerful American Legion convention gathering on September 15, 1941. Bypassing the leaders of the organization, Market Analysts asked the members questions relating to America's attitude toward Germany. Over 40 percent of those polled felt the United States should join the war (a full two months before Pearl Harbor).

The results of the Legion poll were well publicized in the *Chicago Daily News,* a pro-British paper. Another national correspondent who played up Legion results was *New York Times* reporter Arthur Krock. Krock told his readers that the poll was a "stunning reversal, for the Legion has long argued against another war adventure abroad." As Griffith knew, most of his polls were not scientific. In fact, many of them used false information from poll-takers' leading questions.

Sandy Griffith's Market Analysts, working in conjunction with the BSC, was a major, subtle espionage tool used by the United States to add to the climate that would culminate in war on December 7, 1941.

H

Hall, Theodore

Theodore "Ted" Hall was one of the lesser-known names among the circle of Soviet spies operating inside America's secret wartime endeavor, the Manhattan Project. What would not be fully revealed until almost 50 years later was that another Soviet atomic spy passed equally important secrets to Russia.

Theodore Hall was born in 1926, the son of a furrier. His father, Barnett Holtzberg, brought his growing family to New York and thrived in the fur business. He was able to buy an expensive home on Long Island's South Shore. Ted attended PS 173, and he skipped many grades due to a superior intellect.

At home, he was exposed to such leftist publications as the "Communist Manifesto" and other literature that was less than traditional for a young boy. Before age 12, Ted took a step that most youngsters his age would never imagine; he and his brother Edward changed their name to Hall, because of anti-Semitism they were facing on a daily basis.

He joined the Young Communist League and later attended Harvard University. A brilliant physicist, he worked for the government out of college. Like so many young thinkers of the era, he felt communism was his political calling and joined many left-leaning groups.

What we now know that Ted Hall's role in the New Mexican atomic espionage ring during and after the war is based on the Venona files. They provide a vivid picture of Hall's relationship with the primary players in the drama: Klaus Fuchs and the Rosenbergs.

A personal account of Ted Hall, provided by Sergi Kurnakov, code-named "Beck," reveals a tall, slender, pale man, pimply-faced and carelessly dressed. His boots appear unclean over limp socks: "...[H]is English is highly cultured and rich. He answers quickly and very fluently, especially to scientific questions. Perhaps because of premature mental development, he is witty and somewhat sarcastic but without a shadow of undue familiarity and cynicism."

The Soviets recruited Ted Hall at 18, right out of Harvard. Like the other American members of a Soviet atomic ring who ended up at Los Alamos, Hall's communist political philosophy was either ignored or never investigated by the FBI during background checks. Ted Hall, at 18, was now the youngest Soviet agent sent inside the Manhattan Project. Scientists recruited along with Hall from Harvard included Ray Glauber, Kenneth Case, and Frederick Dehoffmann. The Russians dubbed him "Mlad."

He was sent to Camp 2 in Santa Fe, New Mexico, where he was put in charge of a small group of scientists, and worked on nuclear implosion techniques in the Experimental Physics Division. This process was instrumental in how the bomb exploded.

In time, Ted Hall gave the Soviets a detailed report on the "Fat Man" plutonium bomb, the one later dropped on the Japanese city of Nagasaki. The "Fat Man" bomb was also tested in the New Mexican desert outside of Los Alamos. One of the scientists who worked with Hall in the G (Gadgets) section in Los Alamos was an undercover Soviet operative named Klaus Fuchs.

At Los Alamos, Hall and his Harvard team were made "white badge workers," which gave them complete access to the complex. They were able to talk freely with scientists in other disciplines.

At Los Alamos, Hall met and was befriended by another scientist who shared his political views, Niels Bohr. Both men believed that the work going on at Los Alamos should be shared with the leading scientific minds of the day. Since that ruled out the Germans, according to Bohr and Hall, the only other recipient available were the Soviets.

Hall's state of mind regarding transferring atomic research to the Soviet Union is again displayed in a memo written by Sergi Kurnakov "He told me that a new secret weapon represents an 'atomic bomb' with a colossally destructive impact. I interrupted. Do you understand what you are doing? Why do you think it is necessary to disclose U.S. secrets for the sake of the Soviet Union? He answered: There is no country except for the Soviet Union that could be entrusted with such a terrible thing."

The minutes of this meeting were taken in New York when Hall was on a two-week leave from Los Alamos. At that time, he made a detailed arrangement with Kurnakov to deliver his secret material to him. The man chosen as intermediary was his former Harvard roommate, and close friend, Saville Sax.

Saville Sax came from the same Eastern European Jewish heritage as Ted Hall. His father, Boris Sax, fled the Ukraine for America in 1914. The elder

Sax caught the attention of the secret police when he began to criticize the Czar. Once safely in New York, Boris began to prosper in the upholstery business.

"Savy" Sax graduated from De Witt Clinton High School in New York and attended Harvard at age 18. He had a handicap in his left hand, deformed at birth. At Harvard, Sax soon graduated to communist teachings and joined the John Reed Society. During his stint at Harvard, Sax and Ted Hall would become roommates of like minds, beguiled by Marxist thought.

While Hall excelled in Harvard, Sax did not. After failing the army physical due to his hand, Sax's grades dropped, he cut classes and was eventually expelled. He went back to New York and worked two jobs for steel companies.

He began a new and exciting phase, not only in the Soviet cause but in his personal life, that of courier to Ted Hall. The jury is still out on why the Russians chose a person with no espionage training to be Ted Hall's personal courier. Susan Sax, Savy's wife summed up her husband's role perfectly. "Savy was a very unlikely spy." The most likely scenario is that Ted Hall pulled strings for "Savy" Sax. The Russians went along to avoid alienating their agent in Los Alamos.

"Savy" Sax needed a cover. He went to Albuquerque in the fall of 1944 as a prospective student in anthropology at the University of New Mexico. Both men would meet in Albuquerque, and Ted Hall gave his college roommate the secrets that would enable the Soviets to build the plutonium bomb. Both Hall and Sax invented their own code when passing information, based on verses from Walt Whitman's book, *Leaves of Grass.*

In 1944, Ted Hall was inducted into the army. He immediately contacted his bosses at Los Alamos. Now in the uniform of an enlisted man, he returned to his old work immensely relieved. In January 1945, Sax was able to complete his Harvard education. The next year saw both men teaching at the University of Chicago. While at the University, Hall met his future wife, Joan Krakover.

By the early 1950s, with the Red Scare dominating the headlines, the FBI had been investigating Hall for two years. An FBI memo on Hall read: "Hall has been identified as a Soviet espionage agent while at Los Alamos." Former FBI agent Robert Lamphere, leader of the Hall investigation, claimed the bureau got its first hint of a spy inside the Los Alamos facility from the Venona operation.

The Venona files reveal that the FBI was looking into an "unknown subject," also a soldier at the Los Alamos. Soon, the bureau turned its attention to David Greenglass, as it did not have a concrete case against Hall. No charges were ever filed.

An FBI memo written by the Chicago field office stated that although the FBI doubted Hall's guilt as the "unknown subject," both Sax and Hall were still "associating with known Communists." The memo also said that they doubted Hall was still working for the Soviets.

In a January 18, 1952, FBI report the bureau recommended, "Hall's name be removed from the special section of the security index and placed in the regular section." Hall left the University of Chicago and got a job at the Sloan-Kettering Institute in New York working on new X-ray techniques. By 1962, Hall and his family moved to England where he got a job at Cambridge University's Cavendish laboratory, again working on biological X rays.

The complete story of Ted Hall's secret life as a Soviet spy came out in 1995. Hall and Sax were identified as Soviet agents in a Soviet cable. In 1996, Hall gave an interview with a reporter from the *Washington Post* in which he refused to answer questions regarding his alleged wartime intelligence activities. "These events or supposed events happened 50 years ago. If they are made public, there will be a certain amount of interest, but it will die down. To help prevent…[U.S. control over the atomic bomb], I contemplated a brief encounter with a Soviet agent, just to inform them of the existence of the A-bomb project. I anticipated a very limited contact.…"

Important information concerning the actions of Ted Hall comes from authors Joseph Albright and Marcia Kunstel. In *Bombshell: The Secret Story of America's Unknown Atomic Spy* (Times Books, 1997), the authors reveal that in 1952, long after the war's end, Hall stopped working on the atomic bomb but continued meeting with the Soviets on an infrequent basis in New York. Hall's Soviet contact was identified as "Jimmy Stevens." They would meet in the Bronx and Coney Island to ascertain whether the FBI was following Hall.

Another valuable item concerns the Rosenbergs and Ted Hall. Hall was grief stricken concerning the Rosenbergs and at one point asked his Soviet handlers if he could take part of the blame off their shoulders. "You know, if it comes to that," said Hall, "perhaps I should give myself up and say, don't pin it all on the Rosenbergs because I was more responsible than they were."

Theodore Hall died at the age of 74 on November 1, 1999, in Cambridge, England.

Hall, Virginia

When William Donovan began recruiting for the OSS, he looked for the best people America could offer. One of the most competent female agents he hired was a Baltimore native named Virginia Hall. By the war's end, Virginia would be responsible for a vast underground network of French resistance fighters, totaling some 300 people.

Virginia Hall was born in Baltimore, Maryland, on April 6, 1906. She grew up in a well-to-do family, and attended the Roland Park Country Day

School. Her father, Edwin, owned a number of movie houses in Baltimore, and young "Dindy" loved the movies. In college, she mastered such foreign languages as Italian, French and German, and edited the school paper. After graduating from college, she continued her education in Austria and Switzerland. She concluded her studies at George Washington University in Washington, D.C.

In July 1931, she clerked in the American Embassy in Warsaw and traveled throughout Europe. Her next posting was Turkey, where she dropped her gun during a hunting trip. It went off, injuring her left foot. She was rushed to a hospital in Istanbul, and even though the doctors were able to save her life, gangrene had set in, and they had to amputate half the leg.

When the war broke out, Hall drove for the French Ambulance Service in Paris, until it fell to the Germans. She was able to escape to Spain, where she got a job as a code clerk to the military attaché in the U.S. Embassy. Eventually people in important posts noticed her talent. In 1940, Virginia Hall was offered a job in the British espionage agency. She was hired by Maurice Buckmaster, head of the French Section.

After extensive training, Hall was sent to Vichy, France. She held the distinction of being the first woman in the country to head a guerrilla force, claiming to be a reporter for the *New York Post* as her cover. She did indeed write many articles detailing the everyday life of the people, government corruption, and the plight of the poor.

With her role as newspaper reporter intact, Virginia traveled to Lyon, where she set up her secret Special Operations Executive (SOE) operation. Working with a number of the contacts she'd cultivated, she was able to safely return many downed pilots to England, as well as escaped POWs. She also set up a number of safe houses and arranged for supplies to be air dropped by the French resistance.

When it became too dangerous to stay in Vichy, she managed to get as far as Spain, but was arrested trying to cross the border. She soon was able to escape captivity and fled to Madrid. Under a new cover, reporter for the *Chicago Times,* she worked as a courier for the local resistance but asked for and was granted a transfer to SOE, France.

In November 1943, while in London, Virginia Hall changed employers. She joined the American OSS and quickly became a crack radio/wireless operator. One of her OSS colleagues said of her: "She was just back from Spain for SOE debriefings. She sometimes carried her detachable brass foot in a pack or leg bag. I have always had the greatest respect for that lady. Her courage knew no bounds."

Arriving back in France by sea, she linked up with a clandestine network called "Heckler," whose most important associate was Peter Harratt. They established themselves in the towns of Cher, Nievre, and Creuse, preparing for the invasion of France. Ms. Hall took on a new identity; she posed as a local named Marcelle Montagne.

As invasion day neared, German military activity increased. Both Hall and Harratt had to move quickly and often to escape detection. Soon though, she was ordered to the *Haute-Loir* district in southern France to organize a new resistance group. She set up her secret radio in the farmhouse of a local woman, and made daily transmissions to London. She traveled the countryside incognito, reporting on German troop movements.

After the successful breakout at Normandy, Hall's resistance campaign received a much-needed shot in the arm. A team made up of two Americans and one French officer who went by the name of Jedburg brought supplies and a powerful radio. The Jedburghs were run by a combined team of the British and OSS.

With their logistical help, Hall was able to organize three battalions of Free French soldiers successful in countering German activity in the area. By the time the Germans retreated, Hall's guerrillas had killed over 150 and captured hundreds more. She soon returned to a newly liberated Paris and a joyous reunion with her fellow resistance fighters.

Virginia Hall received the Distinguished Service Cross, the highest medal given to a civilian by the military. In the 1950s, she worked for the newly created CIA, married Paul Goillot, and after leaving the agency, retired to her Maryland home.

Virginia Hall died in 1982 in Rockville, Maryland, having never revealed her secret life to friends.

The Harvard Project

One of the most important tools that Bill Donovan used in his secret war against the Germans was psychological and propaganda warfare to cripple the morale of the German people and front line troops. Such techniques were not new, but those who participated in its various, subtle techniques, literally wrote the book for future practitioners.

The department that was responsible for "psy ops" was the MO or Moral Operations Branch. The MO Branch conducted two types of psychological warfare: "Black" and "White." White propaganda is conduct or information that comes from an open source and is attributable to the government it represents. "Black" propaganda, however, must disguise its source and its consequences. It is non-attributable to any national entity.

The OSS's MO Branch, established January 3, 1943, came under the direction of the Joint Chiefs of Staff. In early 1942, an OSS officer was sent to England to study its massive propaganda apparatus. Other areas in which the MO Branch was detailed to carry out were subversion, sabotage, and espionage. The MO charter claimed it had charge of "conduct of special operations not assigned to other government agencies." That dictate covered a lot of ground and when the U.S. entered the war, the MO Branch flourished.

One of the most important operations run by MO out of its Washington office was the Harvard Project. The Harvard Project aimed for German businessmen, convincing them that the top members of the German government would be detrimental to the war effort and their own well-being. It also promised local businessmen that American industry would help rebuild factories destroyed in the war.

The vehicle for this propaganda onslaught was a newspaper edited in Washington by OSS officers, called *Handel and Wandel*. This newspaper reported that the top brass in Berlin had special assault teams in every major German company, whose job it was to destroy industry, thereby removing it from enemy hands. It urged business owners to set up "counter groups" to protect their factories.

Following a sudden German attack on Russia, the paper claimed that Hitler made a secret deal with the Russians to keep the Nazi elite in office. Leaders of these companies were urged to change their operating policies to the Western Capitalist system.

The falsehoods and Black operations emanating from the Harvard Project were actually cleared by the U.S. State Department, demonstrating how predominant silent warfare had become.

Heisenberg, Werner

Werner Heisenberg was born on December 5, 1901, in Wurzburg, Germany and attended the University of Munich. He had a brilliant mind and began the study of physics under a celebrated professor named Sommerfeld. After graduating from the university, Heisenberg won his doctoral degree and wrote his dissertation in 1923 on the subject of turbulence in fluid streams. He studied under scientist Niels Bohr, who later participated in development of the American atomic bomb.

Heisenberg's area of expertise was nuclear and particle physics, and quantum mechanics. When his research into the laws of atomic reactions and nuclear physics caught the attention of the German government, he was put to work developing the nascent German bomb.

The OSS became alarmed at what they perceived as a race between the United States and Germany to build the atomic bomb. A decision was made in the highest levels of the United States government to kill Heisenberg. The operation started in October 1942 and ended in December 1944, when it was no longer prudent to continue, but then a second scheme was hatched. Hans Berthe, who helped build the atomic bomb in New Mexico, tried to persuade British intelligence to abduct Heisenberg from Germany, fly him to Switzerland and drop him by parachute over the Mediterranean to a waiting submarine. Luckily for Heisenberg, they refused.

The Heisenberg operation was reactivated in the summer of 1944. By December, Morris "Moe" Berg, had taken on the assignment for the OSS. He met with OSS officer William Casey at the posh Claridge Hotel, and after a week of briefing by intelligence agents Major Tony Clavert and Samuel Goudsmit, he entered Switzerland under the cover of technical expert to monitor Heisenberg's behavior.

Heisenberg was in Zurich, Switzerland, speaking at the Federal Technical College. Moe Berg was to observe the German scientist, determine if Germany was planning an atomic bomb, and if so, kill him. Berg met with Heisenberg and decided that there was no overt effort by Germany to build a bomb.

In *Heisenberg's War*, author Thomas Powers writes, "Heisenberg was quite right when he insisted that a massive effort would be required to build a bomb. But in Germany the first prerequisite for success was missing—desire for victory. No sense of danger, no optimism for the effort was ever pressed on authorities by Heisenberg or any other leading German scientist. But Heisenberg did not simply withhold himself...let the project die. He killed it."

Moe Berg and Bill Donovan were in Paris when they both learned of the sudden death of President Roosevelt, and Donovan admitted that the late president had been given full disclosure about the plot against Werner Heisenberg.

Werner Heisenberg was awarded the Nobel Prize in 1932 for his exceptional work in physics. He passed away on February 1, 1976, in Munich. (*See Also*: Berg, Moe)

Hemingway, Ernest

To his legions of faithful readers, Ernest Hemingway will be forever remembered as the author of *The Old Man and The Sea*, *For Whom the Bell Tolls*, and *The Snows of Kilimanjaro*. But what is not known to a majority of the American people is that Ernest Hemingway was an undercover agent for the United States during World War II, operating an amateur spy circle in Cuba called the "Crook Factory."

Ernest Hemingway had moved to Cuba to start another book around the time the United States entered World War II. He wished to become a secret agent for Uncle Sam. He had always fancied himself a man of action and in the spring of 1941, six months prior to the Japanese attack on Pearl Harbor, he met in Washington, D.C., with Marine Corps Colonel John Thomason, Jr. of the Office of Naval Intelligence.

Hemingway told Thomason that he would like to do his part for the country. He reminded the marine that he'd covered the Spanish Civil War and passed along his observations to his superiors. Colonel Thomason agreed to take on the famous writer as a cover agent for the United States.

Although Colonel Thomason forgot about his deal with Hemingway, he passed along the notes of his meeting to the FBI and the newly created Office of Strategic Services. It was from this brief encounter that J. Edgar Hoover and William Donovan would create a voluminous file on Hemingway.

Hemingway and his then-wife, the writer Martha Gelhorn, were living in Cuba at their home, *Finca Vigia*, in San Francisco de Paula, about 14 miles east of Havana. While Martha worked for *Colliers* magazine, Ernest began to organize his spy apparatus.

In February 1942, the OSS showed an interest in working with Hemingway. A letter from Lieutenant Commander Turner McBaine of the Office of Naval Intelligence to Whitney Shepardson of the OSS reveals the following:

> It is understood that Winston Guest is being considered. During the past year, he has been with Ernest Hemingway who is running a show in Cuba. Provided that he has completed his work in Cuba, it is suggested that you and 109 (unnamed agent) may consider approaching Hemingway. I know him intimately and can vouch for his integrity and loyalty one hundred percent. He is experienced in our business, is brilliant and fearless. We are not entirely clear whether he is recommending Guest or Hemingway for our show, and the clear text of the original does not make it clearer. I think, however, that he must mean Hemingway, and that we are safe in proceeding on that assumption.

There is a contradictory OSS document written by Robert Joyce, the second secretary in the American Embassy in Cuba, regarding Hemingway:

> I have been thinking ever since I entered the organization that Ernest Hemingway might be a very valuable addition to our ranks. He is, as you know, an authority on Spain, and his intimate acquaintanceship of non-Franco circles is perhaps more extensive than that of any American. He actually ran an intelligence show in Madrid during the siege, and his knowledge of guerilla warfare, and special operations in general, as well as the ins and outs of intelligence work is first hand and extensive.

The latter part of this memo by Robert Joyce reveals that, "Hemingway is a highly controversial figure. My personal conviction is that he is very much an individual who had never been particularly deferential to persons in high places. It occurs to me that he might be extremely useful in conjunction with operations in Spain or Italy."

In the end, though, the OSS offered nothing, and Hemingway went to work for the FBI, which did not want him as a spy but felt it could not afford to anger him. Hoover distrusted Hemingway because of his communist connections and his anti-FBI stand, but did not discourage Hemingway because of his personal relationship with President Roosevelt and his wife, Eleanor.

The FBI was responsible for all espionage and counterespionage in Latin America, the Caribbean and South America. FBI Special Agent Raymond Leddy was the bureau's liaison at the embassy and sent a steady stream of memos on Hemingway to J. Edgar Hoover.

Working from his secluded *finca* in the mountains of Cuba, Hemingway recruited a motley crew for his espionage purposes. The men who made up his "Papa Crook Factory," as he whimsically called it, were all friends; some were influential, and some merely pimps, bartenders in the Havana hotels, gamblers and playboys with too much time on their hands.

According to FBI files, U.S. Ambassador to Cuba Spruel Braden wanted Hemingway to gather information on the connection of certain Cuban government officials with the Spanish Falange movement and the involvement of Cuban political leaders with local graft and corruption inside the country. Hemingway's informants, according to the files, were not known to the FBI.

Hemingway convinced Ambassador Braden to allow him to use the writer's own 40-foot fishing boat, the *Pilar*, to scout the waters off the Cuban coast in search of German U-boats. As a cover for his U-boat hunt, Hemingway used his part-time work on behalf of the Museum of Natural History to study the "migration of marlin" off the Cuban coast. He told the ambassador that he did not want to get paid for his services but insisted that his "crew members be recognized as war casualties for purposes of indemnification in the event of any loss of life...from this operation." The FBI files report that Hemingway had four men working on a full-time basis, 14 men on a part-time basis. He received a $500 per month expense account.

For days on end, the *Pilar* plied the calm Cuban waters in search of German submarines to no avail. At one point a German U-boat was sighted on the horizon, and the *Pilar's* 50-caliber machine gun was readied for action. Unfortunately, by the time the yacht was positioned to fire, the U-boat headed for the depths. It was the most auspicious event in the amateur spying operation of Ernest Hemingway.

After a stint covering the D-Day landings in Europe, he moved back to the States to continue writing his book, *The Old Man and the Sea*, which he'd started onboard the *Pilar*.

In 1961, Ernest Hemingway committed suicide in his home in Idaho. The legacy of "Papa Crook's Factory" impacted American espionage operations only by inspiring the rule that amateurs would never again be allowed to take part in cloak-and-dagger missions.

Hess, Rudolf

The surprise arrival of the deputy leader of Germany, Rudolf Hess, in England has intrigued historians and writers. There has been speculation that the man who parachuted onto the Scottish Highlands was not Rudolf Hess but an impersonator. Another question concerning the Hess mission is the extent to which Adolf Hitler understood the course of action his deputy was about to take.

On the night of May 10, 1941, British air controllers operating out of the Royal Air Base at Turhouse, sent planes in search of a German *Messerchmidt* 110 seen crossing into Scotland. However, the nimble RAF pilots lost their target. Not wanting to be shot down, the pilot of the German plane had climbed to 6,500 feet, opened the cockpit, and dropped from the sky onto British soil. He landed near his intended destination, the Dungavel estate of the Duke of Hamilton.

The airman was wearing a Luftwaffe uniform, so there was no mistaking him for a German spy. A local man named Duncan MacLean found the pilot and called the local constabulary. In custody, the pilot identified himself as Captain Alfred Horn and claimed he was on a special mission. During interrogation Horn asked to see the Duke of Hamilton, David Douglas-Hamilton. Douglas-Hamilton was well known in Britain as the first man to fly over Mt. Everest and a Conservative member of the British Parliament. He was also known for his pre-war conciliatory attitude toward the German government. Alfred Horn confessed to Hamilton that his true identity was Rudolf Hess.

Hess claimed a mutual friend named Albrecht Haushofer had referred him, that he was on a mission of mercy, and that Hitler wanted to see an end to the fighting. Hess asked the Duke if he would be able to arrange a meeting for peace talks with some of the leading political leaders in the country. One part of his peace proposal was an agreement that England and Germany never go to war again. He also wanted the king to grant him a pardon because he'd come on a mission of peace.

The mutual friend to whom Hess referred happened to be directly connected to anti-Hitler groups. Albrecht Haushofer broke with the Nazis after the persecution of his family, because of a half-Jewish mother. He also had ties to a large Russian spy network in Europe called the Red Orchestra.

Albrecht Haushofer's father, Karl, had been Hess's teacher and was one of the most influential German political theorists of the day. Hess told Karl Haushofer he believed that if Germany made a deal with England an invasion could be avoided.

Haushofer told his son about his meeting with Hess and urged him to lend his name to Hess's plan. Haushofer gave Hess the names of British politicians who might be able to work out a deal with like-minded Germans if Hitler was deposed. Along with the Duke of Hamilton, he'd suggested Sir Samuel Hoare, the UK's Ambassador to Spain.

Two days after Hess's flight to England, the Gestapo arrested Albert for resistance activities. Many high-ranking German military and intelligence officers, including SD Chief Walter Schellenberg, believed Hess was "influenced by agents of the British Secret Service and their German collaborators, and they played a large part in his decision to fly to Scotland."

Another important member of the Nazi high command who had inklings of the Hess-Haushofer connection was Reichführer Henrich Himmler. Himmler was the chief of the German police, and his spies informed him of every move which the anti-Hitler resistance planned, including the actions of Hess and Albrecht Haushofer. Himmler himself had contacts with foreign representatives of anti-Hitler groups, including the representative of the Swiss Red Cross, Carl Burckhardt. Himmler was keeping all his options open in case the war went badly, and plans for Hitler's removal were effectuated.

In his meetings with the Duke of Hamilton after his capture, Hess insisted Hitler knew nothing of his trip and that Germany did not want to continue the war with Britain. He said Germany would eventually win the war and that if England made a separate peace, they'd be given lenient treatment after the conflict was over. Hamilton said that he couldn't make such agreements and turned Hess over to British intelligence.

Hess was taking a very serious chance if Hitler did in fact know about his flight to England. Hess was one of the few individuals in the government privy to Germany's plan to attack Russia.

Hess's secretary Ingeborg Sperr said that her boss never told the Führer about his upcoming flight and that Hess did it, "in his fantastic love for the Fatherland. He wanted to make the greatest sacrifice of which he was capable for Adolf Hitler, to leave nothing undone to bring the German people the desired peace with England."

Chief of Staff General Franz Halder said that the "Führer was taken completely by surprise by Hess's flight." Walter Schellenberg, a leading figure in the German espionage establishment, said Hitler was in such a state of shock upon hearing about what Hess had done that he could not speak.

Soviet documents released by the former NKVD in November 1990, tell of Stalin's paranoid reaction to the Hess mission. Stalin believed Hess's flight was a plan concocted by the Germans and the British intelligence services at the expense of the Soviet Union. Soviet spies told Stalin, "Hess had been lured to Britain as a result of an MI-6 plot." Kim Philby, one of the Soviet Union's wartime spies, said Hitler had given his approval to Hess in order to undertake peace initiatives with Churchill.

After the war, Hess was tried and convicted as a war criminal and sentenced to life in jail at Spandau Prison, where he would eventually be the last inmate. On August 17, 1987, he was found hanging in his cell.

Over the years there have been many conflicting theories about Rudolf Hess and his mission to England. Some have Hess killed by his jump, and replaced by a double—the so-called Doppelgänger premise. A doctor named Hugh Thomas, associated with the Royal Army Medical Corps who attended to Hess in Spandau, said he believed the man he cared for was not the real Hess.

Was Hess's mission a real "peace flight," undertaken on his own initiative, or did he act on behalf of the German nation? The answer might be in unreleased Russian and English files.

Heydrich, Reinhard

In a nation torn asunder by hatred, one of its most despised figures was Reinhard Heydrich, also known as "The Hangman." Heydrich was born on May 7, 1904, in Halle, Germany, his mother an opera singer and his father a composer. They named their son after a character in Wagner's *Tristan und Isolde*. One of his closest secrets was that his mother was Jewish. After graduating from high school, he joined a Nazi group called the Free Corps. In 1922, he became a navy cadet and bonded with a major figure in the German espionage establishment, Wilhelm Canaris.

Heydrich was a typical Aryan, with blond hair, a handsome face and blue eyes. In 1926, he was appointed to the rank of sub-lieutenant and sent for training to the Naval Signal School. After being promoted to full lieutenant, he was given his first assignment on the ship *Schleswing-Holstein*, where he dominated his men, handing out harsh punishments for infractions.

In 1930, the young Lieutenant Heydrich was in serious trouble. After an affair with a beautiful, young woman, Heydrich was charged with conduct unbecoming an officer when he impregnated and then refused to marry the young lady. The girl's father was an executive of one of Germany's key industries, I.G. Farben, and tried to pressure his friend, Admiral Erich Raeder, to punish Heydrich, but Admiral Raeder merely reprimanded him.

A year later, he married a woman named Lina Mathilde von Osten, an acquaintance of Henrich Himmler. Mathilde introduced her new husband to the powerful Himmler. After a few hours of talk, Himmler saw an anti-Semitic philosophy in Heydrich that ran parallel with his, and decided to appoint Heydrich chief of the SD, or *Sicherheitsdienst*, an intelligence-gathering component of the SS.

Heydrich moved swiftly to cement his position. He was involved in the purge of SA boss Ernst Roehm and moved up to the position of Brigadier

General. Heydrich became good friends with Himmler, who appointed him commander of the Gestapo in 1936. Heydrich was now one of the most authoritative figures in the German military and he immediately set about oppressing Germany's Jews.

One of his first major acts was to give the orders for *Kristallnacht*, or Crystal Night, in which the government physically and mentally assaulted Germany's Jewish population. On his orders, Jewish stores were destroyed and their owners arrested. The rampage laid the groundwork for the holocaust.

Heydrich got rid of a number of anti-Hitler generals, including General Werner von Blomberg and General Werner Freiherr. In 1939, Heydrich fabricated an incident along the Polish-German border in which Polish soldiers "invaded" a German military post. The "soldiers" were actually SS men. This incident incited World War II.

Heydrich was also responsible for planning the mass killing of Poland's Jewish population. When the war began, Hitler appointed Heydrich to design the "final solution." He was given the title of Deputy Reich Protector of Bohemia and Moravia—the western part of Czechoslovakia.

Czech resistance groups proclaimed themselves a separate state within Bohemia and Moravia, and an anti-German guerrilla organization took root. Heydrich appointed four SS police units to hunt down these armed dissidents, declaring martial law and crushing any opposition.

The British Secret Intelligence Services had been watching Heydrich's tactics and suffered a huge setback when Heydrich's SS killed a highly placed British agent code-named A54, who had been organizing local resistance. In the wake of A54's death, a secret meeting was held in London, chaired by Stewart Menzies, head of the SIS. He drew up a plan to assassinate Heydrich and Colonel Frantiscek Moravec, head of the Czech secret service in England.

By 1942, a number of hand picked Czech partisans were taking part in the Heydrich assassination plot. They were trained at an isolated base called Cholmondeley Castle and Park in Malpass, Cheshire. Three teams were sneaked into Czechoslovakia to organize the Heydrich hit.

The men who took part in the assassination plan were Lieutenant Adolf Opalka, Sergeant Josef Valcik, Sergeant Jan Kubis and Sergeant Josef Gabchik. They parachuted under the cover of darkness near the Czech town of Lidice, where they linked up with the local resistance.

Heydrich took the same route every day. The assassins planned to hit him when his car drove on the Rude Armady V11 Kobylisky near the Vltava River. The assassins would be positioned along the route to ambush Heydrich's convoy. A worker repairing an antique clock in Heydrich's office threw a schedule of Heydrich's activities into a wastebasket, where it was found by a cleaning woman, Maria Rasnerova. She smuggled the schedule to two of the hit team, Kubis and Gabchik. On the morning of the 27th, when Heydrich's car slowed down, the two men pulled out machine guns, which jammed. They threw hand grenades under the car and fled. Heydrich's spleen was badly damaged in the attack. In the hospital, he contracted blood poisoning and died on June 24, 1942. It has been suspected that the hit team was supplied with an experimental biological toxin given by the Britain's MI-6.

The four conspirators made their way to the Church of St. Cyril, where they received sanctuary from the local priest. Someone betrayed them, however, because the SS stormed the church. The four men killed themselves rather than being taken alive.

In reprisal for the assassination of Heydrich, the Germans destroyed the city of Lidice, killing all the men and boys, and sentencing the women to concentration camps.

Himmler, Heinrich

If Reinhard Heydrich was the epitome of the ruthless, sadistic German, then Heinrich Himmler could have been his twin. Himmler was the second-most powerful person under Hitler, in charge of the "Final Solution." As leader of the Nazi secret police, he used his power ruthlessly to eliminate political enemies as well as millions of fellow countrymen who did not live up to his Aryan ideal.

Heinrich Himmler was born on October 7, 1900 in Munich, Germany. During a stint in the army, he tried to enter the German equivalent of Officers Candidate School but was rejected. In 1919, he got a degree in agronomy from the Munich Technological College and found a job in a poultry farm.

Four years later, Himmler went to a Nationalist Socialist Workers Party meeting in which the guest speaker was Adolf Hitler. Dazzled, Himmler immediately joined the Nazi organization and became one of Hitler's most trusted lieutenants.

He took part with Hitler in the Munich Beer Hall Putsch, for which Hitler was arrested and later released. In the wake of the Beer Hall incident, with both Hitler and Roehm under arrest, Himmler went to work for Nazi leader Gregor Strasser.

Himmler began publicly speaking out against Jews, communists, and any other group the party chose. The harsher Himmler spoke, the more he drew to his cause. When Hitler took over the government, he appointed Himmler chief of the secret police, and Himmler set up one of the first concentration camps: *Dachau*.

In 1934, Himmler orchestrated a violent purge of Ernst Roehm's secret army, called the "Night of the Long Knives." In the wake of Roehm's demise, Himmler's SS, or *Schutzstaffel*, became the preeminent security force in the country. His SS troops were put in charge of security at the growing number of concentration camps in Germany.

Hitler further named Himmler as the Commissioner for Consolidation of German Nationhood. This title gave him complete control over the physical elimination of Germany's Jewish population as well as any other ethnic group deemed inferior. Himmler took to his new job like a fish to water. Among the horrors he created were "stud farms," where virgin girls of pure German blood were given to German soldiers to breed an Aryan race. He also oversaw the eviction of hundreds of thousands of Poles from their ancestral homes to make room for Germans.

Himmler oversaw the slaughter at Auschwitz and administrated the killings during the Warsaw Ghetto uprising. He was responsible for ghastly medical experiments conducted on children, the very old, the sick, and the mentally handicapped. His chief advisor in these terrible experiments was The Angel of Death, Dr. Joseph Mengele.

As the war progressed, Himmler transformed a large number of his SS police units into armed soldiers. He named these troops the Waffen SS. Himmler took over all foreign espionage and counterespionage operations when Admiral Canaris was fired after the unsuccessful assassination attempt on Hitler. Now he not only controlled the domestic police but Germany's spies on the continent.

As Germany's prospects grew bleak, Himmler hoped to depose Hitler and take over the government. Himmler desperately needed to know whether or not the allies would make a separate peace treaty with Germany once Hitler was thrown out. To that end, he conducted third-party negotiations with Allen Dulles, head of the OSS in Switzerland.

In 1943, Allen Dulles had a secret meeting with an old German acquaintance named Prince Max-Egon von Hohenlohe, concerning America's postwar attitude toward Germany. Another man who joined in the talks was "Mr. Bull," an international banker named Royall Tyler. They discussed the war and its related issues in Geneva for about three months. A memo in the National Archives recorded the gathering: "In [Dulles's] view, a peace had to be made in Europe in which all of the parties would be interested. We cannot allow it to be a peace based on a policy of winners and losers; never again must nations like Germany be driven through need and unfairness to experiment with crazy heroics. The German state must remain in a peace settlement as an intact institution...division of Germany or a separation of Austria cannot be an issue."

The details of the Dulles-Prince Max discussions were sent to Himmler and from what Dulles had to say, Himmler might have believed that he had a friend in the OSS officer. However, no separate deal was made with anti-Hitler elements during the war.

In April 1945, with allied troops inside Berlin, Hitler saw the imminent destruction of his "thousand years" Reich, and turned the military over to Himmler. Himmler disguised himself as a policeman named Heinrich Hitzinger and tried to flee the country but was captured by British troops. While being attended by a doctor in his jail cell, Himmler took a poison pill and died within minutes.

Hiss, Alger

Alger Hiss was one of this country's most respected diplomats, serving in Washington since the 1930s. For members of that generation, the name Alger Hiss invokes memories of a time when the communist threat seemed to be just around the corner.

The fallout from the Hiss case pitted liberals and conservatives against each other. Now, almost 60 years after the espionage trial of Alger Hiss, new revelations may put to rest the question of whether Hiss was an agent for the Soviet Union during and after World War II.

Hiss was a graduate of the prestigious Johns Hopkins University and Harvard Law School. He was a protégé of Felix Frankfurter (future Supreme Court Justice) and worked as a law clerk for Associate Justice Oliver Wendell Holmes. In 1933, Hiss joined the new administration of Franklin Roosevelt and worked in the Agricultural Adjustment Administration, the Justice Department, and the State Department. His work in the State Department was surrounded with controversy.

In the summer of 1944, Hiss was a member of the Dumbarton Oaks Conference, the organization that created the United Nations. As a trusted member of the Department of State, Hiss went to Yalta for the meeting of FDR, Stalin, and Churchill. The Yalta Conference divided post-war Europe into spheres of influence between the Western powers and the Soviet Union. Hiss was appointed temporary secretary general of the newly founded United Nations, a post where he would have worldwide political power. By 1947, with a strong UN, Hiss was appointed president by John Foster Dulles, Chairman of the Board of Trustees of the Carnegie Endowment for International Peace. According to Whittaker Chambers, Hiss was a member of the Soviet secret service during this time.

Whittaker Chambers brought the communist/espionage charges against Alger Hiss. Chambers had gravitated to the world of American communism at Columbia, espousing Marxist ideology. By 1937, however, Chambers had grown disillusioned with Stalin and had broken away from the party. He became a devout Christian and fervent anti-communist.

By 1947, a federal grand jury for New York was hearing testimony from undercover FBI agents on allegations that members of the federal government secretly belonged to the Communist Party. However, no solid cases of espionage could be proved and the probe seemed futile. At FBI headquarters, J. Edgar Hoover wanted to place blame and leaked information to Congress to restart the case. Hoover sent one of his most trusted agents, Assistant Director Louis Nichols ("Hoover's ghost") to Capitol Hill to give confidential FBI information to Congress on supposed communists in government.

One of the Senators to be given this FBI intelligence was Homer Ferguson, a Republican of Michigan who considered Hoover's material a blessing. He was a member of the Senate Investigations Subcommittee who would play along with Hoover's every request. He turned this material over to his counterpart in the House of Representatives whose House Un-American Activities Committee (HUAC) would lead the hearings on agent Nichols's charges. The main accuser was Whittaker Chambers.

The initial charges against Hiss did not come from Chambers, however. In 1945, a cipher clerk in the Soviet Embassy in Ottawa named Igor Gouzenko, defected to the West. He brought hundreds of documents supporting the fact that the Soviets had been spying for years on Canadian soil. The Canadians immediately brought this information to the FBI. One of the most important pieces of data revealed an American who was an assistant to the Secretary of State was a Soviet agent. Gouzenko's charge was corroborated by American courier, Elizabeth Bentley. The man was Alger Hiss.

It was now Chambers's turn in the national spotlight, and he relished his new status. He told the HUAC committee that Hiss was a secret member of the Ware group, a Soviet network based in Washington, headed by Harold Ware. Chambers did not accuse Hiss of being a spy, only a communist. Hiss publicly denied Chambers's charges and even denied knowing him. At first, the press believed Hiss's denials, but eventually his story wore thin.

One of the members of HUAC who did not believe anything Hiss had to say was Congressman Richard Nixon of California. Nixon had been privy to Hoover's leaked material, and he persuaded the rest of the committee to investigate Hiss's relationship to Chambers.

The scene now shifted to New York, where HUAC was in special session. Chambers testified to Congress that Hiss's wife, Priscilla, was a communist, and the Hiss family knew him by the alias "Carl." Chambers said that Hiss donated his old Ford to the Communist Party. But there were segments of Chambers's testimony that were not correct concerning Hiss. He said erroneously that Hiss did not drink, that Hiss was shorter than he actually was, and deaf in one ear.

On August 16, the committee brought in Alger Hiss to respond to

Chambers's allegations. When shown a picture of Chambers, Hiss said he "had a certain familiarity." Hiss further testified that he had known a man matching Chambers's description as an acquaintance who went by the name of "George Crosley." Hiss said that at one time he sublet his apartment to "Crosley" and that he was an unkempt man who sometimes wrote articles for magazines (Chambers was a freelance writer). Hiss said that he gave the old Ford to Crosley and was given an oriental rug in return. At an August 25th hearing, Nixon brought Chambers and Hiss face to face. Hiss said that Chambers was really "George Crosley."

Responding to Hiss' charges, Chambers appeared on the *Meet The Press* radio program and said "Alger Hiss was a Communist and may be now." A month later, Hiss filed a lawsuit against Chambers for his comments. Chambers said in kind, "I do not minimize the ferocity or the ingenuity of the forces that are working through him."

At the trial, Chambers promised to bring forth evidence that would confirm Hiss's espionage. Chambers said he kept documents made up of 65 pages of typewritten copies of secret material, four pieces of paper with Hiss's handwriting on them, two strips of developed microfilm of State Department documents, three rolls of undeveloped microfilm, and other papers.

In what was to become the most controversial part of the case, Chambers turned over the microfilm that he had hidden at his Maryland farm, in what became known as the "pumpkin papers," because he hid them in a hollowed-out pumpkin on his property.

A grand jury indicted Hiss for perjury on December 15, 1948, for denying giving Chambers secret information from the State Department. He was never charged with espionage.

The trial began in New York Federal Court on May 31, 1949, and lasted for six weeks. The state based much of its evidence on an old Woodstock typewriter owned by Hiss and his wife, reportedly used to type State Department materials.

The defense responded by saying that Chambers lied about hiding film in 1938. Eastman Kodak, who manufactured the film, said it had been manufactured in 1948. After an angry call from Congressman Nixon to Kodak headquarters, the company quickly altered their story and said that the film was indeed made in 1938. The trial ended in a hung jury. Another trial was set for November 17, 1949, at which time Hiss was found guilty and given a 44-month prison term.

A number of cables implicated Hiss, who went by the code name "Ales." According to a March 30, 1945, message from Washington to Moscow concerning agent "Ales": "Ales is probably famed State Department official, Alger Hiss." The Venona files also report a meeting between a KGB officer and a

GRU (Soviet military intelligence) officer whose source in Washington was "Ales." Another file linking Hiss to Soviet intelligence comes from a cable to Moscow from its agent "Vadim"—who was in reality, Antoli Gromov, the station chief of the NKVD (the forerunner of the KGB), in which he reports a conversation between agent "A" and "Ales."

The Venona files say that "A" was Iskahk Akhmerov, one of the most important Soviet spies in the United States during the war. This same intercept states that "Ales" had been working for the Soviets since 1935. Hiss continued to work for the Russians even after Chambers left the party in 1938. The files buttress the Hiss/Russian relationship in that "Ales functioned as the leader of a small group of neighbors probationers, for the most part consisting of his relations." In the Venona transcripts, "Neighbors" refers to members of the American Communist Party. The tapes also say that "Ales" went on a separate trip to Moscow after the Big Four meeting in Yalta. The record proves that Hiss went to the Soviet capital on the plane carrying U.S. Secretary of State Edward Stettinius, along with two other career diplomats.

With the release of the Venona files, it now seems that historians finally have answered the riddle of what role Alger Hiss played during World War II and the Cold War. However, partisans on both sides of the political spectrum will interpret the newly released files looking for vindication for their own views.

(*See Also*: Chambers, Whittaker)

Hitler's Gold

On the morning of February 3, 1945, a massive air raid comprised of 1,000 bombers from the 5th U.S. Army Air Force attacked Berlin. As the unsuspecting American bombardiers let loose their powerful explosives, neither they nor anyone else could have known that their actions that winter day would set in motion a dangerous game of espionage, corruption, and theft, concerning high-ranking members of Hitler's government, allied soldiers, and American counterintelligence agents.

The prime target of the air raid was the Tempelhof marshaling yards in Berlin, where what was left of the German armaments were stored. Other important targets were the Reichstag, the Reich Chancellery, Goering's Air Ministry, and the Reichbank—the depository of the German government. The Reichbank took 21 direct hits, but amazingly, the 5,000 employees who huddled in the basement survived.

The Reichbank was the leading bank in Germany, holding vast amounts of gold and currencies belonging to Germany and other conquered nations. With it in flames and allied troops on the edge of Berlin, the president of the bank, Dr. Walter Funk, knew he had to take drastic action to save his precious reserves. At a meeting in Hitler's bunker, it was decided to take as much of the Reich gold out of the city as possible to a safe location in the Bavarian Alps. They removed 450 sacks of paper marks but left 550 sacks buried in an abandoned mine shaft in the city of Merkers. This was the first of two trips that would be made to hide Hitler's gold.

On March 22, 1945, the U.S. Third Army led by Lieutenant General George Patton crossed the Rhine. By April 6, military police from Patton's command received information from two displaced women that gold was hidden in the Kaiser's mine.

A half-mile below ground Patton's men found 550 sacks of German paper currency totaling about a billion Reichmarks stacked along the walls of the main passageway. General Dwight Eisenhower decided that the gold had to be moved to a safer place. On April 14, 1945, the treasury of the Third Reich was taken to the Reichbank in Frankfurt, which was now in American hands.

But not all the gold was removed, and in that dark pit, a half-mile below ground level, the great Reichbank robbery began.

Unknown to the Americans, Frederich Rausch, Hitler's personal security officer, was charged with removing the rest of the gold. Rausch concealed the gold in Hitler's own hideout, deep in the Alpine forest of Berghof. The gold and currency were to ship south in two separate convoys to protect it from falling into the hands of the Americans.

Two trains, code-named "Adler" and "Dohle" were loaded on April 13th and 14th, bound for Munich. After a hazardous journey over war-torn Germany, the gold finally arrived at the small town of Mittenwald in the Bavarian Alps. The man in charge of the Reichbank evacuation, Director Hans Alfred von Rosenberg-Lipinski, took 25 bags of bullion for himself.

The job of burying the remaining gold fell to the hands of Colonel Franz Pfeiffer, the commander of the famous Mountain Infantry School in Mittenwald. It was up to Colonel Pfeiffer to move the $15-million worth of foreign notes and gold, and he did it with pure professional efficiency.

He had the gold taken up into the mountains, two miles north of Mittenwald to the Forest House owned by Hans Neuhauser Sr., Chief Forester of Walchensee. When the job was finished, seven caches of Reichbank currency as well as ammunition and gold were buried in at least three separate holes. As the U.S. 10th Armored Division reached Germash, the closest town to the buried gold, Colonel Pfeiffer surrendered.

But the Americans, in the confusion of occupying the area, forgot about Colonel Pfeiffer and his fortune in gold. A local American undercover agent had discovered Colonel Pfeiffer's cache, and an investigative team was sent up the mountain, where they found guns but no trace of money.

It was now up to the Americans to mount a full-scale investigation. English officer Michael Waring was chosen. Waring arrested Friedrich Will and Captain Heinze Ruger, two Reichbank officials. Ruger broke under questioning and on June 6, took the Americans and Waring up the mountain, where they found 364 bags with a total of 728 bars of gold, valued at $10 million.

A theft of great proportions did take place, but it didn't concern the 728 bars that have been described. Diverted by the Americans, the money disappeared into thin air, and nobody was ever arrested.

After hiding for several weeks, Colonel Pfeiffer finally surrendered and led his captors once again up to his mountain redoubt, where he exhumed a small portion of his hidden assets. He turned the money over to the army who, shockingly, refused to accept it. Instead, the money was given to the German Military Government.

The process of counting the gold now lay with the Foreign Exchange Division. Of the 89 bags of foreign currency dug up, only 72 had been retrieved. Where did the other 17 bags go? To answer these questions, Brigadier Waring turned to a man who would play a large role in the gold mystery, Captain Fred Neuman.

Neuman was General Patton's interpreter, an intelligence officer and a German Jew. He met with the principals of the Reichbank robbery, including Colonel Pfeiffer who handed over $400,000 to Captain Neuman. Immediately after signing for the money, Captain Neuman got into his car and was never heard from again.

In what was beginning to look like an endless cycle, the matter was handed over to the U.S. Army's Criminal Investigation Division. But one more curious dimension was added to the growing confusion. What made the American zone different from the other allied areas of conquered Germany was the dense criminal activity that occurred there. It was like the old West, replete with drugs, prostitution and black-market racketeering.

The man who finally blew the lid on the Reichbank robbery was Guenther Reinhardt. Reinhardt was a member of the CIC (Counter Intelligence Corps) in Bavaria who had made the right contacts wherever he went. During his travels, Reinhardt met two newspaper reporters, Ed Hartich and Tom Agoston, whose articles on the Reichbank robbery had been suppressed by the military censors.

When Reinhardt's superiors discovered that he had met with the two reporters and was ready to talk, they quickly ordered him to stop his inquiry and threatened to have him arrested. Reinhardt sailed home and wrote a 55-page report detailing the lost gold from the bombing of the Reichbank to its mysterious disappearance in the Bavarian Alps. The famous Reinhardt

Memorandum was about to put an end to theories about the Reichbank robbery.

As the Christmas season of 1947 came and went, Washington learned of systematic corruption and conspiracy in the American zone of Germany. General Clay put the cover-up into high gear and appointed Orville Taylor, Special Assistant to the Secretary of the Army, to file a report on Reinhardt's charges. The Taylor report rebutted Reinhardt's memorandum, calling it the work of an overly imaginative writer with no solid facts.

That was the end of the investigation. Nobody in Washington ever looked into the missing gold and currency allegedly stolen from the Reichbank. Nobody looked into the massive corruption in the American zone of Germany, and more importantly, no one was ever prosecuted for one of the crimes that took place during the war.

Holohan, William

In the latter part of 1945, the OSS mounted a plan in Italy called Operation Chrysler to "act as a liaison with partisan commanders, attempt to guide and control developments in northern Italy, and create a unified partisan command under the direction of the supreme allied commander." This simple enough sounding order started one of the most controversial and mysterious events to come out of the war, leading to a congressional investigation.

The Chrysler mission was laid out by William Donovan and Colonel William Suhling, the Chief of Special Operations in Italy. Throughout the war, the OSS had been supplying the various anti-German, Italian resistance groups, including some of the communist factions, with military and communications equipment. Towards the end of the war, it was decided by the OSS to suspend these airdrops because of intense quarreling among groups. However, other items like food, clothing and medicine were parachuted in for the rebels.

Donovan and Suhling decided to have an American team sent into Italy to sort out conflicts between various segments of the resistance. They wanted a non-Italian officer to conduct the mission, one who would not be unduly influenced by them. The man chosen to lead the Chrysler Mission was Major William Holohan. Bill Holohan was a Roman Catholic, a graduate of Manhattan College in New York and later Harvard Law School. Prior to the war, he had worked as a lawyer for the Securities and Exchange Commission. When Bill Donovan approached Bill Holohan about taking over the mission, he immediately volunteered his services.

The units responsible for running Operation Chrysler were the Fifteenth Army Group under the command of General Alexander and the National Committee of Liberation Headquarters in Milan. During the height of the war, the Po Valley, where this mission was to take place, was under the control of the Germans. Now, in 1945, the various resistance groups were in charge, vying with each other for superiority. It was the job of Major Holohan and his team to make certain that the groups took orders from the Fifteenth Army Group.

Originally, the OSS's mandate was to develop and train guerrilla fighters in the Po Valley whose job it was to attack German troops. A Lieutenant Giannino commanded the original operation but the two missions were combined under Major Holohan.

Holohan's team was dropped behind the lines on September 26, 1944. Their jumping-off point was at the Maison Blanche Airport in Algiers, and their destination was an area near Lake Orta, north of Milan. The unit was comprised of the following people: Major Holohan; Lieutenant Aldo Icardi, the intelligence officer; Sergeant Carl Lo Dolce, the wireless operator; Tullio Lussi, an Italian secret agent; and two others, Sergeant Giarmicoli and Sergeant Ciaramicola. Three weeks after landing, Giarmicoli and Ciaramicola left the party to meet up with other resistance groups.

Lieutenant Aldo Icardi, 23, Major Holohan's immediate deputy, was a graduate of the University of Pittsburgh, taking a degree in political science. He was a professional intelligence agent whose job it was to oversee the dangerous crossing of Americans into enemy-held territory. He also was in charge of a Special Intelligence Training school in southeastern Italy. He was fluent in Italian (Major Holohan did not speak the language).

Upon landing, the Americans were met by members of the resistance and were taken to their camp. They spent the next month hiding from German patrols in the town of Coiromonte. At one point, the Germans sent out scouting parties after the Chrysler team.

As part of their mission, Major Holohan carried a certain sum of money that was to be used to finance espionage operations headed by "Georgi," whose name was Aminta Magliari, the head of a partisan group called SIMNI, or Military Information Service of the Partisan Forces in Northern Italy. He was also head of security for the Chrysler mission. A woman named Marina Duelli was also assigned as a courier to Major Holohan. One secret mission funded by Holohan's money was called Salem and run out of the headquarters of the National Committee for Liberation in Milan.

Before leaving Algiers, Major Holohan was given funds by Tullio Lussi, a partisan leader code-named "Captain Landi." Captain Landi belonged to the Di Dio resistance organization. A high school teacher in Milan, Landi joined the OSS in Bari, Italy, and was assigned to the Chrysler mission. He gave both Major Holohan and Lieutenant Icardi gold coins, comprising 100 marengos to each roll, for a total of 2,100 marengos. They also carried $16,000 U.S. and $10,000 in Italian lira. The disposition of the money would play a part in the tragic events that followed.

HOLOHAN

Major Holohan used some of this money to pay the expenses of Georgi's men, until it was decided that they wouldn't be able to carry the heavy gold bars with them. Georgi made a deal with Major Holohan to sell the gold at market prices and return the cash to him. A business deal was worked out between Georgi, Lieutenant Icardi, and a few local Catholic priests in the Lake Orta area. The money, about $15,000, would be used to finance the purchase of buildings, machinery and land to be used after the war.

In the third week of November 1944, the Chrysler team captured four men in civilian clothes who were operating in their area. They turned out to be three German soldiers and a Swiss citizen. On them were detailed scale maps of the area, as well as direction-finding equipment.

Shortly before this incident, the Chrysler team suffered its first major setback. A large airdrop of guns, ammunition and supplies, code-named Pineapple 1, headed for the Di-Dio-Christian Partisan Brigade was intercepted. The supplies were taken by a communist group called the Sixth Nello Brigade. After all was divided, the Di-Dio group got one third of the supplies, while the communists claimed two-thirds.

The question was how the communists knew of the airdrop. Was there a traitor in the Chrysler group or among their allies? Major Holohan met with the leader of the communist group in that part of Italy, Vincenzo Moscatelli, to clear the air. The major told Moscatelli that there would be no further airdrops unless or until his men agreed to work directly under American supervision and stop the internal fighting.

For some time, the Chrysler team had been holed up at the town of Villa Castelnuovo. Sympathetic locals told them that a fascist patrol was looking for them. The major decided to leave the area, and as the team made their way through the dense, cold forest, a number of shots broke out. Men scattered for cover. In the ensuing battle Major Holohan was killed.

When Bill Donovan learned of the death, he ordered Captain Landi to mount an investigation. While rumors abounded that the communists or the Germans killed the major in order to get control of the supplies, Captain Landi startled Donovan by saying that one of Operation Chrysler's men was the actual killer.

Intercepted German signal traffic in the area of Villa Castelnuovo reported no mention of the capture or death of Major Holohan. OSS radio officers did, however, learn from their intercepts that the Germans mentioned the disappearance of an "officer" not an "agent."

Lieutenant Icardi took over command of the Chrysler team and was awarded the Legion of Merit. In February 1945, Carlo Lo Dolce suffered a nervous breakdown and was sent to Switzerland to recover. But the case was still not closed.

After the war, the Army's Criminal Investigation Division investigated the death of Major Holohan. The lead investigator was Agent Frederick Gardella. After a long and difficult process, Agent Gardella found out many incriminating facts, including the following:

> Icardi and Lo Dolce made many statements about wanting to "get rid of the Major"; Icardi was organizing business deals for the future and not letting his superiors know about it; any new information provided by the partisans was to be given only to Icardi, not Major Holohan; the disappearance of Major Holohan was a political move started by the Communists headed by Moscatelli; and "…both Icardi and Lo Dolce did not cooperate with Major Holohan…Icardi was more interested in personal affairs, and of elevating his position with the mission than carrying out his required duties." In the ensuing years, Major Holohan's body was found floating in the cold waters of Lake Orta, wrapped in a sleeping bag, with two bullets in his head.

In 1950, the investigation was turned over to the Italian police. They chose Lieutenant Elio Albieri to investigate the case. Among the people Albieri interviewed were Giuseppe Mannini and Gualtiero Tozzini. During the war, they had served as Major Holohan's bodyguards. Both men confessed that they, along with Icardi and Lo Dolce, murdered Major Holohan on the night of December 6, 1944, by putting cyanide in the officer's soup. Lo Dolce then shot the major and dumped his body into the lake.

Under orders from General George Marshall, Lo Dolce was taken in for questioning at a Rochester, New York, police station. He confessed, and wrote a report on the fateful night. He backed up the Mannini-Tozzini story, saying Mannini poisoned the major and then killed Major Holohan with his Beretta.

Aldo Icardi was called before a congressional committee looking into the Holohan affair. Icardi said that upon hearing shots from the Villa Castelnuovo, he fired blindly.

In the end, the U.S. government took no action against Icardi and Lo Dolce. Since the Italians couldn't get jurisdiction over the two Americans, they were both convicted for murder *in absentia*. Mannini and Tozzini were acquitted.

Hoover, John Edgar

J. Edgar Hoover's name is synonymous with the Federal Bureau of Investigation. Until his death in 1972, he was the only director the FBI ever had, controlling his fiefdom with an iron fist, creating one of the world's preeminent police forces.

That indeed was the face that Hoover wanted an adoring public of the

1930s through 1960s to see. To thousands of youngsters during those years, the ultimate compliment was to be a "G-Man." Director Hoover kept America safe from gangsters, conmen and thieves. But what the public did not know was that there was a deeper, calculating J. Edgar Hoover, who consorted with the same mobsters he was publicly trying to put away.

John Edgar Hoover was born on January 1, 1895, in Washington, D.C. (Hoover would live out his entire life in the District of Columbia). He was the youngest of three children, from a family who read the bible every day, and had little time for friends or socializing after school. While attending George Washington University, Hoover worked part time in the Library of Congress to help pay for his education. He graduated in 1916 with a degree in law and joined the Department of Justice the next year for $900 per year. His first assignment was special assistant to Attorney General Thomas Gregory, checking for spies among the new German immigrants to the United States. He was promoted to head of the Enemy Alien Registration section, deciding whom to watch.

In 1919, he was put in charge of a newly created branch called the General Intelligence Division, where he was to check on the actions of radical groups operating in the United States. The next year, he was given the prestigious position of assistant director of the Bureau of Investigation, later to become the FBI.

Hoover's tenure in his new post coincided with the "Red Scare" in America, following the end of the first World War. The Red Scare was provoked by the toppling of the Czar in Russia, and the coming to power of the Bolsheviks under Lenin. The height of the scare came on June 2, 1919, when a bomb was placed near the front door of Attorney General A. Mitchell Palmer's home.

The bomb throwers were killed when their explosive went off prematurely. Following the bombings, the Attorney General ordered hundreds of arrests. Hoover played a direct role in the prosecution of these suspects, and it was out of the "Red Scare" mentality that his hatred of communism, fascism, and other un-American philosophies took root.

Attorney General Palmer gave Hoover the job of writing a paper dealing with these incidents, and he reported a well-organized plot by anarchists to take over the United States. The report brought on another series of mass arrests and deportations.

During his tenure at the Bureau of Investigation, Hoover made a name for himself by cleaning up corruption within the agency. He discovered that the Director, William Burns, was in league with a number of business executives, in a scandal that would later be called the Teapot Dome Affair. Looking for a person who could provide squeaky-clean leadership to the Bureau of Investigation, President Calvin Coolidge's new Attorney General, Harlan

Stone, appointed J. Edgar Hoover as the next director. The agency was given a new name, the Federal Bureau of Investigation. For the next 48 years, the FBI was to become J. Edgar Hoover's wife, mistress, and life.

During the 1930s, Hoover expanded the FBI, including the establishment of a state-of-the-art fingerprint division that kept records of millions of Americans. The 1930s also saw the FBI going after the big names of the criminal underworld in America. Among the targets of Hoover's G-Men were Al Capone, John Dillinger, and Charles Arthur "Pretty Boy" Floyd. His concentration on domestic crime changed on December 7, 1941, when Japanese bombs hit Pearl Harbor.

Almost immediately after the attack, the FBI drafted a list of Japanese to be placed in internment camps. FBI agents also went on guard at all Japanese diplomatic and government buildings.

The day after the attack, Hoover sent President Roosevelt a tape from a Japanese person named Mori in Hawaii. The communication mentioned the weather, the location of the Pacific fleet at Pearl Harbor, and other military information. Part of the conversation concerned flowers native to the islands. Hoover felt the reference to flowers might be a code for "...a prelude to the proposed bombing of the Hawaiian islands...."

Hoover sought to distance himself from the attack and made many references to the president regarding the Mori dispatch. He told FDR that the Special Agent in Charge (SAC) in Hawaii told army and navy intelligence that the flowers message referred to the Hawaiian Islands, and that Naval Intelligence scoffed at the idea.

Further covering his bureau, Hoover told the president that the military had intercepted a message concerning plans for the air raid 10 days prior to the assault at Pearl Harbor. Hoover told FDR that it "contained...the complete plans for the attack on Pearl Harbor as it was subsequently carried out." He ended his memo by saying that "...At this time, it is impossible to determine whether there was a breakdown in the military radio and a failure in the messages to reach their destination, or whether the messages were delivered but not acted on by the military authorities."

What Hoover was referring to was the "Winds Message" present in the days and months after the attack. On November 26, 1941, the Navy intercepted a message from Tokyo to the Japanese Embassy in Washington that it should listen for certain phrases in shortwave broadcasts from Japan if ordinary communications with Japan were stopped. If certain words concerning the weather were repeated five times, that would be a signal to burn all codebooks and secret documents at the embassy.

In the wake of the attack, FDR ordered Supreme Court Chief Justice Owen Roberts to look into the circumstances surrounding the surprise attack. Back in Washington, an anonymous letter reached top-government officials criticizing Hoover's bureau. The author of the note asked Justice Roberts to look "into the adequacy of the FBI, the agency directed by the President and supposed by the public and Congress to deal with the Fifth Column in our own territory."

Hoover was personally attacked by John O'Donnell in the *Washington Times-Herald* of December 29, 1941. It reads in part, "The nation's super Dick Tracy, FBI Director J. Edgar Hoover, is directly under the gun. The preliminary report places the Pearl Harbor Fifth Column blame directly in Hoover's lap. By order of the president, this has become Hoover's direct responsibility. Long-time Capitol Hill foes have been whetting up their snickering, itching to take a crack at the detective hero as far back as the days of kidnappers and gangsters. Leaders are holding them back with the promise that the report of the Roberts Board of Inquiry will provide the ammunition for an all-out drive to oust Hoover from his seat of tremendous power." Needless to say, this never happened.

On December 8, 1941, FDR put Hoover in charge of all news censorship. He undertook this job for two weeks before handing it over to Byron Price of the Associated Press. In a clandestine move, FBI agents broke into the Japanese consulate where they obtained the names of all Japanese spies operating in the United States. It was a highly illegal action, which crippled Japanese espionage operations.

Hoover's FBI took on an expanded role in intelligence collection when England's Bill Stephenson opened up his clandestine intelligence-gathering organization called British Security Coordination in New York. BSC officers taught selected FBI agents the techniques of mail opening and other secret arts. Mail from German and Japanese diplomats was opened in the Main Post Office in Washington and taken to FBI headquarters, where it was returned to the mails. This was called "Z-Coverage" and was expanded to include mail openings of supposedly neutral consulates and embassies in New York and Washington.

One of Hoover's greatest triumphs during the war was the capture of a number of German spies who came ashore by submarine off Amagansett, Long Island (See Operation Pastorius). A lone coast guardsman named John Cullen spotted five men on the Amagansett beach.

Hoover ordered a massive manhunt for the spies and imposed a news blackout. He got lucky when one, George Dasch, turned himself in to the FBI. Traveling to the capital, Dasch had an extraordinary personal audience with Hoover in his office.

Hoover's number-one adversary was not a German or Japanese spy, but his counterpart in the American espionage establishment, William Donovan.

Donovan wanted responsibility for America's intelligence operations in North America, but FDR opted to go with Hoover's FBI. After much wrangling, the heads of both the Military Intelligence Division and the Office of Naval Intelligence sided with Hoover in this bureaucratic showdown. A directive by Attorney General Francis Biddle said that OSS agents could operate in the Western Hemisphere but only out of the continental United States and that they must inform the FBI.

Donovan made Hoover bristle when his OSS agents broke into the Spanish Embassy in Washington. They came back again in a nighttime raid, but this time two FBI cars stood nearby with their sirens blasting, and the OSS agents fled.

Regarding the incident and the conduct of the FBI, Bill Donovan said, "the Abwehr gets better treatment from the FBI than we do." He sent his own spies into the FBI to make a secret inquiry into the allegations that Hoover was having a homosexual relationship with his long-time partner and friend, Assistant FBI Director Clyde Tolson.

As the war progressed, Hoover set up an organization within the bureau called SIS (Special Intelligence Service). SIS agents penetrated South America, reporting on the large German communities in such places as Argentina. They expanded their duties as they rounded up German spies and helped friendly countries in the area to stop German sabotage of their economic and military plants.

One such incident took place in Bolivia, where SIS and British agents broke up a possible coup against the government. By the end of the war, the FBI had arrested 250 enemy agents, broken up numerous secret radio transmissions and helped arrest countless German couriers. They excised numerous plans to disrupt allied shipping along the Panama Canal.

After the war, Hoover lobbied to expand the FBI overseas but was turned down by President Harry Truman. Instead a new, worldwide U.S. espionage authority was established and named the Central Intelligence Agency.

J. Edgar Hoover continued his reign over the FBI until his death in 1972. His successors carried out institutional changes to make the FBI less subject to one-man rule, opening up the bureau to minorities and women, utilizing the most modern computer techniques. Hoover's legacy continues to this day with an FBI building in Washington erected in his name.

Hyde, Henry

On April 8, 1997, an obituary appeared in the *Washington Post* announcing the death of Henry Hyde at age 81. To the casual reader, the name would probably not register. But to those who served in the OSS during World War II, the name of Henry Hyde was well known. For it was Henry

HYDE

Hyde who was responsible for one of the most highly successful espionage missions of the war, the so-called "Penny Farthing" operation that sent clandestine agents into France in the months preceding the Normandy invasion.

Henry Hyde was born in 1916 in Paris, and spent his formative years in Versailles, France. His father, James Hazen Hyde, was an influential man who boasted Cole Porter as a personal friend. Another acquaintance was a British spy named Biffie Dunderdale who, if one is to believe rumor, inspired Ian Fleming's agent James Bond. The elder Hyde lived in France for 42 years, and his son grew up a passionate defender and lover of everything France had to offer.

Henry spoke many languages, including German, French, and English. He attended schools in France, Switzerland, England, and Germany. He also attended Harvard Law School and graduated in 1939.

William Donovan learned of Henry Hyde's vast experience and brilliant mind and lured him into the OSS. With preparations growing steadily for the invasion of Europe, Donovan and his brain trust desperately wanted someone to oversee the secret operation of sending allied agents into southern France to establish a clandestine radio network and monitor the moves of the Germans.

In due course, the OSS made a deal with the Free French intelligence leaders wherein the French would provide submarine transportation for agents, as well as their training by the OSS. The Americans would also pay the French $70,000 and provide parachute and radio training for its agents. The man Donovan chose to lead this endeavor was Lieutenant Colonel W. Arthur Roseborough, chief of secret intelligence in Algiers. Instead, Lieutenant Colonel Roseborough became entangled in a head-to-head quarrel with some of General Eisenhower's top aids and was sacked. The man chosen to replace him was Henry Hyde.

What Hyde didn't know, as he took command of this secret band, was that he was about to become embroiled in a gigantic dispute between two of Britain's most powerful intelligence agencies. He would also create one of the most successful communications networks of the war.

Hyde began his work in 1943 and was given the title of chief of Special Intelligence for France. He had no special training in the clandestine arts save for a crash course at an OSS school in Washington, D.C. There, he learned the art of secret writing, ciphers, and basic tradecraft. He also received help from the Polish Secret Service and the British SOE. In 1943, he was allowed to recruit his first three French agents who would subsequently be dropped behind German lines in France for the invasion of Europe.

Chosen by Hyde was a man named Truc, his radio operator. Before being hired by Donovan, Truc told the OSS chief that his men had been working behind the scenes in France for some time and were willing to work for the Americans.

After a quick training course, the men traveled via sea and land to France and Spain, where they were to link up with an agent named Bollo. French police working for the Germans in Toulon subsequently captured Bollo. After leading them to an allied wireless station, he was shot. Truc and his assistants were captured by the Germans but managed to talk their way out of jail. In the aftermath of the Truc disaster, Hyde wrote to Bill Donovan that, "it does not pay, humanly or practically, to send off agents who are not completely prepared."

The disaster of the Truc agents at the hands of the enemy only made Hyde more determined to set up a covert American presence in France. In time, his Penny Farthing became the first large scale OSS penetration of Europe.

In May 1943, the French gave Hyde his first four agents to be trained in the Penny Farthing program. Hyde envisioned a series of agents and radio operators who would take up positions in the Rhone Valley from Marseilles to Bordeaux, Lyon, to the French-Italian border. Two of the men Hyde took on were Jean de Roquefort, known as "Jacques," and Mario Marret, called "Toto."

As head of Special Intelligence (SI) in Algiers, Hyde had ultimate control over his agents but could do nothing concerning their transportation to France. Hyde asked the U.S. Air Force for permission to drop his agents in France but they refused, saying they couldn't spare any planes. Hyde told Donovan of his troubles, and the OSS leader put Hyde in touch with General Curtis of the army air force in Tunis. Hyde pleaded his case to Curtis, who gave in and allowed Hyde five of his B-17s for his team's traveling needs.

After training, Hyde and his team made their way to England dressed in civilian clothes. It was here that the Penny Farthing unit would get caught up in a vicious bureaucratic fight between the Special Operations Executive and the Secret Intelligence Services, who tried in vain to prevent Hyde's men from using British soil for their training and operations. Hyde met personally with Claude Dansey, the SIS's second in command in London to iron out their problems.

He promised to share any and all intelligence obtained by his agents with the British, and told Dansey bluntly that the British networks were far from secure. What Hyde did not realize was that under an agreement between the OSS and SIS, the Americans were not allowed to conduct "any independent unilateral operations in Europe from British soil." The OSS was allowed only to work with British teams in any covert operations.

Hyde then met with Stewart Menzies, head of British intelligence, claiming his work was not an OSS-London operation, but an OSS-Algeria operation. "We only want to use England as a launch pad," said Hyde to Menzies, "and only because OSS-Algeria suffers from a complete scarcity of methods of transportation. The only thing that concerns us is the possibility of an American disembarkation in the South of France. The American military staff wants to have its own sources of information, in addition to those of the British and of the French."

Hyde's mission to "C" proved successful and four days after their meeting, the British gave the go-ahead for the Penny Farthing team to use their country for missions into France.

Over the next several weeks, Hyde and his team took every precaution, building covers for Jacques and Toto. They were to become Frenchmen from Lyon, complete with false identities, papers, and businesses. They left on July 16, 1943, from Tempsford airfield on board a Halifax aircraft, thus becoming the first OSS agents to be sent into Nazi-occupied France.

Jacques and Toto established themselves in Lyon, then under Nazi occupation. One of the first people recruited by Jacques was a Jesuit Priest named Father Chaine. Father Chaine had taught Jacques years earlier, and he arranged for them to use his home as a hiding place. He was able to find a number of men to join their cause, and used his father-in-law, a local doctor in Lyon, to recruit agents.

The father-in-law took on a number of criminals in Lyon, who acted as couriers and provided news of German troops in the area. These men, in turn, obtained local prostitutes trained by Hyde and his team. They were given information kits on how to identify local German units. These girls of the street were a vital link to Hyde and his agents in Lyon.

On April 11, 1944, disaster struck. Mario Marret (Toto) was captured by the Germans and taken into custody by the Gestapo. If Marret broke under interrogation, the entire Penny Farthing program would fail. Luckily for Marret, he was put under the watch of two Abwehr officers, Franz Oehler and Ako von Czernin. Marret convinced them he was an important OSS officer, and cajoled his jailers to allow him to send a coded radio message of their choice on the BBC.

Marret learned the two Abwehr officers believed Germany would lose the war and proposed a deal, his life for theirs. The two Germans insisted on the condition that they not be prosecuted for war crimes. Marret contacted Jean de Rocquefort, who told Henry Hyde of the unusual deal. It is still not clear if any discussions were ever held between the OSS and the two Germans, but all three found their freedom.

Over the course of many months, Hyde's men were able to set up at least eight radio locations, moving frequently to avoid capture. Jacques hired 300 subagents, who covered German military posts in Bordeaux, Clermont, Ferrand and Grenoble. Sixteen wireless stations provided news. With the increased coverage, it was inevitable the Germans would locate some of their hiding places, and three of Hyde's teams were captured.

One of Hyde's most important intelligence coups was the identification of a large contingent of German trains. Hyde sent word to Force 163 in Algiers. Allied bombers struck at these railheads, inflicting great damage. The raids took place in the weeks preceding the Normandy invasion, saving countless lives.

Another major intelligence bonanza from the Penny Farthing organization was due to Captain Jean Lescanne, a former French army officer. He was able to locate the formidable SS Das Reich Division along the French National Routes 20 and 126. Headquarters sent the following message back to him, "Your message 67 the best ever received here. You do your country a great service."

Hyde's Penny Farthing operation proved a brilliant success in the allied campaigns, code-named Neptune and Dragon, which were related to the allied invasion of North Africa. Henry Hyde received the Bronze Star and a personal citation by President Roosevelt for his work in the OSS's North African campaign.

I

U.S.S. Indianapolis

Of all the war tragedies, none was greater than the sinking of the *U.S.S. Indianapolis* on July 29, 1945, which killed almost 800 crewmen. What's worth noting about the *Indianapolis* is that prior to its sinking, it was on a dangerous mission that would have a profound effect on the outcome of the war.

By July 1945, the Germans had surrendered, making Japan the enemy. By now, it was a foregone conclusion that the allies were going to win the war against Japan, too, but the Japanese emperor refused to sign a peace treaty, hoping against hope that the fortunes of the military campaign could be reversed.

The Japanese didn't know that the new American president, Harry Truman (FDR died that April), had ordered the use of an atomic bomb to end the war, thus saving hundreds of thousands of casualties in an American invasion of the Japanese mainland. It was under these circumstances that the *U.S.S. Indianapolis* played a significant role in the ensuing drama.

On July 16, 1945, the ship left berth at the Mare Island Naval Shipyard in California bound for Tinian Island in the Marianas. The vessel carried critical parts for the atomic bomb that would be dropped on Hiroshima and Nagasaki. The *U.S.S. Indianapolis* had previously seen action in several campaigns, including the "Great Marianas Turkey Shoot" and at the battles of Iwo Jima and Okinawa.

The captain of the *Indianapolis* was a distinguished naval officer named Charles Butler McVay. Charles McVay was a 1920 graduate of the U.S. Naval Academy at Annapolis. He rose in the ranks and served as a naval aide to President Franklin Roosevelt before the war. In November 1944, Charles McVay was given command of the *U.S.S. Indianapolis*. Only McVay knew that his actions would cause a navy scandal, eventually leading to his death.

On July 26, 1945, after reaching Tinian with their secret cargo, the

Indianapolis shoved off. A Japanese submarine attacked three days later while cruising in an open ocean approximately 600 miles west of Guam. At five minutes to midnight, the first torpedoes slammed the ship, destroying the communications area, hindering contact with the engine room. The vessel was listing heavily. Reluctantly, Captain McVay gave the abandon ship order.

The surviving crewmen spent five days in lifeboats bobbing about in shark-invested waters. Running out of food and water, enduring a ruthless Pacific sun and ever-present sharks that preyed on the dying. Three hundred and sixteen men out of 1,196 survived. One was Captain Charles McVay.

In December 1945, after the war ended, Captain McVay went on trial for dereliction of duty. The charges brought against him by the Naval Court Martial were, "inefficiency in failing to issue and ensure the execution of orders for the abandonment of the *U.S.S. Indianapolis*," and "negligence in Suffering a Vessel of the Navy to be Hazarded by neglecting and failing to cause a zig zag course."

The prosecution charged that Captain McVay violated rules of engagement by not running a zig zag course to outrun Japanese submarines that might be in the area. The government brought Commander Mochitsura Hashimoto, the officer in charge of the Japanese sub that sunk the *Indianapolis*, to testify that in his opinion, he would have sunk the ship even with a zig zag run.

The Court Martial Board found Captain McVay innocent of the abandoning ship order but guilty of negligence. No charges were brought against him for the loss of the ship. Captain McVay was demoted, but the court urged clemency due to his exceptional wartime record. In time, charges against him were dropped.

Captain McVay retired from the navy in 1949 as a Rear Admiral. However, the damage done by the circumstances surrounding the destruction of the ship and the accusations against him were never repaired. In 1968, Charles McVay turned a gun on himself, the last, tragic casualty of the U.S.S. *Indianapolis*.

Iron Cross (Operation)

During the war, the OSS used many foreigners as agents or field soldiers for secret missions in Europe. Among those recruited into clandestine operations were members of the French resistance, Italian partisans, and even captured anti-Hitler Germans. One of the OSS's boldest missions involved the use of German POWs from internment camps for capturing German military leaders. The code name for this mission was Iron Cross.

Iron Cross was put into effect in the last days of the war when the German army was on the ropes and defeat was only a matter of time. As allied armies converged on Germany, Hitler ordered a large number of troops to retreat to a redoubt, high in the alpine forests. Here, Hitler envisioned a last-ditch guerrilla campaign against advancing armies. It was from this heavily forested arena that the Nazi leader hoped his Third Reich would be revitalized.

The American in charge of Operation Iron Cross was Aaron Bank of the OSS's Special Operations (SO) branch. SO was the clandestine brainchild of Donovan's OSS, specializing in guerrilla warfare, sabotage, and paramilitary operations.

Forty-one-year-old Bank made the army his career. He sought adventure —the more dangerous the better. He was a superb swimmer, and a playboy who traveled the world from Miami Beach to the Bahamas and other exotic ports of call. At the Bay of Biscay, Bank worked as the chief of lifeguards at the Hotel Miramar for five years. In 1932, Bank changed occupations and dabbled as a real-estate agent. Unfortunately for Bank, the worldwide depression bankrupted him, and he joined the army. With his knowledge of French and German, he was transferred to the OSS, a perfect fit.

For most of the war, the SO branch worked closely with the French resistance movement in German-occupied France, leaving German secret operations to the specialized Secret Intelligence (SI) Branch. The man in charge of OSS SO London was Gerald Miller, a civilian banker. Miller had frequent confrontations with Bill Casey concerning the disposition of both SO and SI operations on the continent. After much discussion among the top OSS factions, Bank's SO team was given permission to mount Iron Cross.

The plan was to use about 175 German POWs, most of them communist, who would be persuaded to fight against their homeland. Their job was to parachute into the Inn Valley, near the towns of Kufstein and Innsbruck, where they were to conduct sabotage operations, attempt to garner defections from the German units in the area, and finally, attempt to kidnap German military leaders. At the top of their list was Adolf Hitler.

Four Americans were assigned to Iron Cross. Bank was their commanding officer, also supervising the training of this motley crew. Among the men picked for Iron Cross, Bank assigned two Germans, Klaus and Horst, as aides. Their training took place outside of Paris, where they learned how to use different rifles, as well as demolition tactics and how to parachute from low buildings. By the time the men were ready for assignment, there were only 100 of the original 175 left.

Aaron Bank took on a cover in order to merge successfully with the local population. He was given a false identity, of a man from French-occupied Martinique, Henri Marchand. "Marchand" left Martinique after the war began and moved to France in order to find work. He labored for two years and then decided to join the German army.

As the training for the Iron Cross team neared its end, William Donovan made a trip to Paris to meet with SO leaders. In a sudden move, Donovan ordered that the mission of Bank's irregulars be changed. Instead of conducting sabotage missions, he instructed them to capture the top Nazi leadership consisting of Goebbels, Goering, and Hitler.

That April, Bank, one of his American radio operators, Klaus and Horst arrived in the city of Dijon to prepare for the raid. They and the rest of the team were to land in the town of Schwaz, near the Inn River Valley. This location was close to Hitler's mountain-top hideaway, Berchtesgaden. Soon thereafter, the remainder of the team arrived at Dijon.

It was on the eve of what was to be one of the most daring missions of the war that everything fell apart. The top leadership of the OSS, including Gerald Miller, London SO chief, decided that Iron Cross was no longer militarily or politically feasible. With the war nearing its conclusion, it was decided to scrub the raid.

It was left to Aaron Bank to tell his men the bad news. All their planning and work were for naught. After the hostilities ended, Bank's German POWs returned to their former lives.

Italian Patriot Bands

Of all the countries on the European continent from which the OSS mounted secret operations, none was more important than Italy. The use of Italian landscape in military operations against the Germans was extensive, exploiting many different political parties for the common end.

The decision to use Italy as a jumping-off point for American raids was opposed in Washington by the Joint Chiefs of Staff. The Chiefs wanted as much control over military policy as possible, and they distrusted the use of clandestine operations over force.

After the Quebec Conference of August 1943, where American policy for the invasion of Europe was formulated, President Roosevelt decided to use Italy as a base for OSS operations. American military planners decreed that an invasion of Italy would begin from Sicily. The main obstacle was the lack of spy networks in Italy. In order to utilize it as a funnel into Germany, underground groups had to be organized.

The officer in command of American forces in Italy was Col. Edward Glavin, the OSS commander of the central Mediterranean theater of operations. As Glavin took over the Italian operations, he was to find that there were two competing OSS intelligence services operating in Italy. The first was the Italian SI (Secret Intelligence) led by Vincent Scamporino, and the second, the OSS SI detachment associated with the U.S. Fifth Army. As the two groups began operations it became obvious there would be no cooperation between them. Each wanted its own share of the intelligence pie, causing confusion and bitter differences between them.

The teams sent both SI divisions into the field with mixed results. Those attached to the Fifth Army often clashed, not only with the enemy but also with the Italian navy and British intelligence agents working in Italy.

Soon some of Scamporino's men became bogged down in internal Italian politics, especially among partisan groups. In order to get a firmer hand on the Italian operations, Edward Glavin moved his headquarters from Algiers to Caserta, Italy.

In late 1943, the allies captured Naples and set in motion a large allied/Italian partisan resistance alliance. OSS teams made contact with many different partisans, including communists and socialists. One of the main allied military units to run covert teams was Company D of the 2677th Regiment. Colonel William Schuling, who ran Company D, had no sooner taken over than he ran into problems with some of his communist agents. They wanted to use American radio transmitters to relay messages to communist cells, as well as instruct their men to disregard orders given by the OSS.

Throughout the war, the OSS had to work with numerous extremist patriot bands, whose goals were diametrically opposed to their own. Declassified OSS records show many of these partisans to have been cold-blooded killers and crooks.

Many individual bands constituted the National Committee of Liberation that brought about unification. They were the Partito D'Azione, Socialist Party, Communist Party, Democrazia del Lavoro, the Democratici Cristiani and the Partito Liberale.

The two most active resistance parties in Northern Italy were the Party of Action and the communists. Another important group was ORI, headed by a man named Raimondo Craveri, or "Mondo." Mondo's ORI worked closely with the OSS, having established a number of large courier systems in Northern Italy and a messenger system in Switzerland. At this time, the ORI was completely controlled by the OSS. OSS documents reveal that Mondo decided not to work with the British, but remain with the OSS, who provided his band with all necessary supplies. The ORI's job was to destroy all railroad stations in the Bologna and Florence areas.

Communists were very active in the area, vying with the ORI for supplies. Of the patriot band situation in the country, Colonel Glavin said, "There are disadvantages to our getting involved in this matter. OSS should not exclusively tie itself up with any one organization."

The OSS also had to deal with a man named General Ricciotti Garibaldi who wanted to raise his own militia to fight the Germans. Garibaldi came to Naples in 1944, crossing the zone at Cassino. He was a Republican in his politics, and came to Toulon to offer his services to Count Sforza in the assassination of the king of Italy. In 1926-27, Garibaldi was living as a political fugitive in Paris, where he contacted a Colonel Macia from Catalan, and promised to recruit volunteers among Italian anti-fascists for an expedition into Catalonia. But Garibaldi was providing the names of Italian volunteers to Mussolini's secret police. He was subsequently arrested by the French police and later released.

In March 1944, Garibaldi arrived in the town of Santa Maria and got in touch with a paper merchant named Inigi Verde, age 48. Verde was a violent anti-fascist who had been a defendant in a number of court cases. A deal was made between the two men in which Verde would set up a large volunteer force of 100,000 men, called "Young Italy," to fight the Germans.

Another person contacted by Garibaldi in his anti-fascist cause was Giacono Campoccia of Caltagirone, age 53. "Campoccia is a bad character… judging from his past behavior he is nothing but a common law breaker." He was a former army officer who had been relieved of his post.

OSS documents reveal a cautious relationship with Garibaldi. "For the time being we are not able to pass judgement as to the real aims of General Garibaldi. However, it appears that he has political ambitions and he bitterly criticized Count Sforza, asserting that the Count did not have the historical background which would qualify him for the presidency of the Italian Republic. The appearance of Campoccia in the Garibaldi propaganda picture justifies any suspicion which one may entertain."

Despite bitter political differences with various Italian patriot bands, as well as the unsavory nature of some of their leaders, the work done by these cliques helped ensure victory in the war.

(*See Also*: Holohan, William; Vessel Case)

J

Japanese Peace Feelers

For the first two years of the Pacific war, the Japanese military seemed impregnable. Their surprise attack against the U.S. Naval base at Pearl Harbor, Hawaii, on December 7, 1941, devastated much of the Pacific fleet and plunged the United States into war. Immediately following the Pearl Harbor attack, Japanese troops occupied the Philippines, attacked British bases in Southeast Asia, and assumed a dominant military position.

But American industrial and military strength grew, providing tanks, planes, guns, and bombs to the soldiers and airmen across the globe. The tide soon turned. By 1944, with the United States gaining tactical military victories over Japan in such battles as the Coral Sea and Midway, the end of the Japanese war machine was in sight.

The role played by American code breakers in translating military and diplomatic codes was hidden from the Japanese during the Pacific war. From listening posts in Hawaii, California, and other parts of the Pacific, navy cryptologists translated messages from Tokyo to their military and diplomatic embassies. The name for this secret endeavor was "Magic."

Magic was the combined work of the army and navy, with roots in prewar America. In 1939, the Japanese began using a code known as Purple, a complicated machine cipher that sent diplomatic and military messages. A brilliant army cryptanalyst named William Friedman broke Purple. By the end of World War I, he and his wife, Elizabeth Smith, were the premier codebreaking experts in America. Between wars, Friedman worked as the chief of the Signal Intelligence Service where he honed the cryptographic service into a fine machine. Through years of painstaking work, Friedman and his team built a replica of the Japanese Purple machine, and deciphered a steady stream of vital messages from Japan.

By 1945, with the war turning in America's favor, army and navy code breakers were able to read all signal traffic coming out of Tokyo. These messages were sent to the desk of General George Marshall, the Army's Chief of Staff, who drew up a list of the people in the Roosevelt administration permitted to see the Magic messages. The president and his advisors were seeing the beginnings of peace feelers from Tokyo.

One of the earliest Japanese peace feelers decoded by the Magic intercepts was a summary from the War Department's Office of Assistant Chief of Staff, G-2 (intelligence), dated March 25, 1943. The message was a March 19 letter to Tokyo from the Japanese Ambassador to Moscow, Sato. Part of the letter reads as follows:

> You [Morishima] informed me that there may be strong opposition to maintaining the status quo and that many advocate lashing out at the Soviet Union. Therefore, when this question comes in the Foreign Office, I want you to be present and take part in the deliberations and use every conceivable means at your command to drive home our arguments....

It is not entirely clear from the foregoing whether Sato thought the whole question of war or peace with Russia was to be debated in Tokyo in the near future, or whether the phrase "when this question comes up" was a reference to some narrower issue.

The message demonstrates how the Japanese viewed a military and political relationship with Germany. Sato continued:

> Since Stalingrad fell, I have entertained an ever deepening conviction that we cannot depend upon Germany's strength. But when the Germans unconditionally surrendered at Stalingrad on February 5th, I told myself that we could no longer extract much of Germany, and today I still say the same thing. Therefore, what are we Japanese going to do? I have thought that, if we could help the Germans and Russians make peace, it would be to our advantage and would tranquilize the northern area. I have also thought that it would be a good thing if we could get a perfect understanding with Russia and try to have her turn with us against a common enemy, the Anglo-Saxons. I still think so, but whether or not Germany and the Kremlin stop their bloodshed is not the question.
>
> Let us take a very large view of the war. We can now see that it is going against the Reich. Even if Germany continues her fight, I still think that from our point of view it would be better if she laid off Russia, withdrew from the Russian front and saved her strength.
>
> Nevertheless, supposing that fortunately Berlin and Moscow should make peace, and that Tokyo and Berlin should make a concerted attack on the United States and England, wouldn't we still have to fight this grim battle of the Orient alone and singlehanded? We

must face this reality.

Another War Department document in June 1945 concerns the role of the Vatican in peace talks. In a message of 3 June, Ken Harada, the Japanese Envoy at the Vatican, advises Tokyo that he has rejected the request of an unidentified American to discuss peace terms. Harada's report reads as follows:

Mgr. Vagnozzi, who was formerly a counselor of the Apostolic Delegation in the United States (1942-43) and is now in the Department of Foreign Affairs, paid a visit on the 27th to the priest Tomizawn, who is a non-career employee of our office. Vagnozzi made the following statement:

"An American, who has been in Rome several months, wants to get in contact with Japan in connection with the question of peace and has requested that I act as intermediary. I am not at liberty to reveal his position or name, but his father occupies a rather influential place in society, and he, himself, is a Catholic and a sincere person. He says that he has no official status and that if plans are made to carry on further discussions, it will naturally be necessary for someone with official standing to handle it."

Regarding the reasons behind such a move, Vagnozzi stated: "The European war is over, but Russia's attitude tends to bring an increasing deterioration in the political situation. A consideration of the state of affairs in the Far East suggests that Russia may enter the war in its final stage. As for Japan's position, one can already say that she has no prospect of victory."

In discussing the conditions that the United States would stipulate for an armistice, the American said that as a guess they might include the return of the occupied territories, the disarmament of the army and navy, and the occupation of Korea. He made no reference to the political structure of Japan and he said that he believed that Japan proper would not be occupied.

I let the matter ride for a while because the terms were patently absurd and because I had various suspicions concerning his objectives. Then Vagnozzi sent word that he would like some sort of an answer, so I requested Tomizawa to make the following brief reply: "At the present time I believe that Japan does not seek to hasten the coming of peace. Furthermore, it goes without saying that we cannot discuss such questions with a person whose official position and identity are unknown to us. Naturally, if it is established that he has an official standing and the United States has any wishes to convey, they can be taken under consideration. However, any proposals limited to so-called unconditional surrender are entirely out of the question."

A further Magic diplomatic summary of June 25, 1945, reports on

Japanese peace feelers with the government of Sweden. This document revolves around the Japanese Minister to Stockholm, Okamoto, accusing his Military Attaché, Major General Onodera, of secretly talking with "foreigners," including Eric Erickson, a Swedish oil man. The report also concerns conversations between Widar Bagge, the former Swedish Minister in Tokyo who had just returned to Sweden and met with Okamoto.

"According to what I heard," reported Bagge, "at the Swedish Foreign Ministry the day before yesterday, Major General Onodera has been trying to establish contact with the allies using one Eric Erickson as contact man, with the idea that it may be possible to obtain peace terms which would not involve too much…of the Japanese army and navy. Erickson passed the word on to Prince Carl, a younger brother of the Swedish King, and the Prince asked a person close to him to communicate with the Foreign Ministry. The matter was naturally out of the question for the Foreign Ministry and it flatly refused to become involved, saying that it could not handle back door scheming of that sort."

"In conclusion, Okamoto asked the Japanese Foreign Office to take steps at once to see that such activity as that of Onodera was prohibited regardless of whether or not Onodera was acting on orders from Army Headquarters. The Minister added that a duel diplomacy at the present time would be disastrous and I feel very strongly that the Foreign Office must take a firm attitude."

What is obvious from these Magic letters is that by 1945, the Japanese government was convinced victory was impossible and peace feelers from the Emperor were looking for the best terms available to Japan. The government leaders decided to fight to the end. This decision ultimately resulted in the dropping of two atomic bombs on Nagasaki and Hiroshima in August 1945.

(NOTE: Researchers can view all the "Magic" diplomatic summaries at the National Archives at College Park, Md. They contain not only the material quoted above, but all types of military, political and diplomatic messages beginning in 1941 and ending in 1945.)
(*See Also*: Magic; Quigley, Martin)

J.E. (Joan-Eleanor) Missions

By 1945, the OSS had become successful at penetrating enemy territory and establishing covert agents in both France and Italy to serve as a Fifth Column. These agents and networks conducted sabotage and guerrilla operations against certain military and industrial targets. After the D-Day invasion, it was more important than ever to gain a covert foothold in Germany. But that proved difficult.

Germany was still a nation under military and police rule despite the pounding inflicted upon its civilians and its military defeats. Many Germans still believed in Hitler's goals and were less likely than the French Maquis or the Italian partisans to cooperate with anti-government forces. The Gestapo and SD were in total control of everyday life, making resistance to Hitler dangerous. Still, the OSS devised an intricate plan to penetrate Germany with its agents and establish a safe communication system for them. This covert operation was dubbed J.E. or Joan-Eleanor.

Lieutenant Commander Simpson named his system the "Joan-Eleanor" for a major in the WAC (Woman's Army Corp) of whom he was fond, and "Eleanor," after De Witt Goddard's wife. The operation took shape in the fall of 1944, after the Battle of the Bulge. It ran out of a London station, organized by the SI Division. Men from France, Belgium and Poland were recruited and given intensive training in communications and military tactics.

The J.E. missions called for an agent on the ground to talk with a specially equipped plane flying 30,000 feet above. The radio carried by the agent was light, only four pounds. It was operated by a high-frequency, longlife battery with a vertical direction finding apparatus attached. This sophisticated device enabled the agent on the ground to communicate with the OSS officer on the plane, and receive precise information about military targets on the ground.

The most important element of the operation was that the man on the ground would be able to send and receive, in a short period of time—minutes, rather than days or weeks—the same amount of information that a regular W/T or radio would take.

To facilitate the airdrops of J.E. agents, the OSS turned to the Air Force, who gave a small number of its old B-24s for agent drops into enemy held territory. The detachment assigned to work with the OSS was the 492nd bombardment group, Eighth Air Force, operating out of Harrington Air Field near London. These missions were called "Carpetbagger flights."

Using modified B-24s, these specially built planes, equipped with highly sophisticated radio and communication devices, dropped agents into France and Belgium. In time, though, the planes were replaced by British Mosquitoes. These specially designed Mosquitoes had their tail sections remodeled to carry the J.E. operator and a sophisticated oxygen-supply system.

The man primarily responsible for the birth of the J.E. missions was a 37-year-old Texan, Lieutenant Commander Stephen Simpson. In the 1920s, Simpson had worked for the RCA Company doing radio transmission work. Now he was doing the same for the army. He and DeWitt Goddard at RCA built a receiver that fit in a suitcase for the man on the ground, as well as a larger one for the person flying above.

The first J.E. mission into Germany proper was called "Bobbie." The purpose of "Bobbie" was to insure an open route for OSS agents from Holland infiltrating Germany. It was undertaken by a Hollander named Anton Schrader, a 27-year-old engineer from the Dutch East Indies.

Schrader had studied at the University of Utrecht and fled to England after Holland was occupied by the Germans. He worked for Dutch intelligence and was accepted into the OSS. He had the distinction of being the first J.E. agent to set foot on German soil. He parachuted from a Liberator bomber near the town of Ulhrum, Holland, and set up an underground system that would bring dozens of OSS agents into Germany via Holland.

Over the next several months, "Bobbie" provided the OSS with tactical information on German military plans and troop movements near Arnhem. In February 1945, Schrader was captured by the Gestapo in a case of mistaken identity. He took a huge risk and told his captors he wanted to become a double agent. He sent false information back to the OSS, using language that tipped off his counterpart in the plane that he was in trouble.

In a bizarre ending to his captivity, the Germans sent him to London with a message for the OSS. They requested that certain OSS officers meet with a Gestapo representative, who would turn over all intelligence they had on Japan in return for their cutting off aid to Russia.

To further prove his worth to the Germans, Schrader warned of an impending invasion of Holland near the city of Friesland. Three Nazi paratroop divisions were sent to Friesland to await the invasion that never came. On May 1, 1945, he crossed German lines and escaped into allied territory.

Other successful J.E. missions included "Chauffeur," which saw two Belgian agents parachuting into Germany near Regensburg in March. These men started a large-scale wireless system originating from area farmhouses. They used local prostitutes to report information gleaned from German soldiers. One of the most important pieces of news reported by the girls was the location of the German General Staff in Regensburg—"the Hotel Du Parc, Maximillanstrasse, the street facing the station, first house on the left."

The most dangerous J.E. mission was dubbed "Hammer," which penetrated Berlin. The men chosen to be on the "Hammer" team were two natives of Berlin, Paul Land and Toni Ruh. Both were anti-Nazi communists living in England. The "Hammer" operation was one of the most well-planned OSS missions. It conducted four practice runs into Germany.

When Land and Ruh were safe in Berlin, they had three primary objectives: to make contact with an OSS-approved, anti-Nazi group called the Free German Committee; to send intelligence; and to pave the way for more OSS agents in Berlin.

In Berlin Paul Land's father gave them a place to hide. Posing as daily laborers, they sent back vital information on the state of the German military in the city, the condition of the industries (most operating despite intense allied bombing operations), as well as maps of German military formations.

The J.E. missions were just one of the vital cogs began by the OSS in its successful infiltration of Germany in the latter part of the war.

Jedburghs

The Jedburghs were created out of the need to supply an expanding French Maquis underground network in the months prior to the Normandy invasion. The leader of the Free French, General Charles de Gaulle, complained to Prime Minister Winston Churchill about the lack of military supplies to the Maquis from the allies. The British had a more efficient supply line to the French resistance, one that the OSS desperately wanted a hand in. Bill Donovan met with Secretary of State Cordell Hull in Washington to rectify the situation.

Hull met with army General George Marshall, who reported that most of the material to the French underground came from the United States. But General de Gaulle made a statement thanking the British for their help, and criticizing the United States for not doing enough. That statement inspired the concept of the Jedburghs.

The primary purpose of the Jedburghs was to parachute into France during and after the D-Day landings to link up with the French resistance and communicate with London via wireless, bringing the entire network under the responsibility of General Dwight Eisenhower.

Each Jedburgh team consisted of three OSS men, the British Special Operations Executive and a member of the French resistance. All three men wore their country's uniform upon landing so if captured they would be held as POWs instead of shot as spies. One of them was a radio operator who sent vital military knowledge to their superiors in London.

Most of the British Jedburgh recruits came from their tank corps, while the Americans primarily chose radio men and graduates from signal schools. In December 1943, a combined SOE-OSS recruiting team arrived in northwest Africa and took on more than 100 Frenchmen. Three-hundred Jedburghs were needed for fieldwork with another 300 recruited for Army Group headquarters on communications duty.

Jedburghs were trained at a location called Milton Hall, an estate near Peterborough, England. The enlistees were taught military skills like map reading, guerrilla tactics, radio communications, and aerial supply.

One American who participated in the Jedburghs was William Colby, who would later become Director of the Central Intelligence Agency. Colby said of his time in the Jedburghs, "We ate together, talked together, drank together. They encouraged us to form ourselves into teams. It was a courtship then a marriage sort of thing."

The Jedburgh teams first began parachute drops into Brittany, as well as the south of France in 1944. Their main job was to link up with the French resistance and confront the Germans using hit-and-run raids. At the height of their power, the Jedburgh nucleus had 101 three-man teams, of which 92 were sent into France. Also, one of the two men sent into a particular country was a native of that land. Consequently, more Frenchmen were assigned to Jedburgh duty.

On paper, their instructions were to, "A) Organize for guerrilla activity, B) Equip units with arms and stores, C) give instruction in the course of arms, D) provide radio communication and pass along orders received from London, E) Lead, giving technical advice or assist in operations against the enemy."

On the ground, working 40 miles behind the front lines, the Jedburghs attacked as many vital German military assets as possible, including railroad tracks, bridges, trains, and power stations, while conducting guerrilla raids against fortified German positions. The one area they were not supposed to touch was intelligence.

Jedburgh teams were most successful in confusing German-controlled rear areas directly after the Normandy Invasion. General George Patton, gave the Jedburghs his ultimate praise by saying that they "credited resistance with providing appreciable aid in the early days of my campaign."

Despite their small size, the three-man Jedburgh teams were one of the most effective fighting units sent into battle during the war.

(*See Also*: French Resistance Movement; Colby, William)

K

K Organization

When William Donovan was appointed by FDR as the new Coordinator of Information (predecessor to the OSS), he was traveling uncharted territory. The president's instructions were to build America's first coordinated intelligence agency from scratch, and Donovan asked for help from a wide variety of public and private officials.

At first, he concentrated on a Research and Analysis Branch to integrate information from foreign and domestic sources. He paid little attention to a Secret Service or counterespionage agency. That would come later.

Donovan had a chance meeting with a World War I army intelligence veteran named Wallace Banta Phillips. Phillips was a native of New York City, educated at the Sorbonne in Paris. In 1939, the year war broke out in Europe, Phillips was working for the Office of Naval Intelligence, one of the few U.S. intelligence-gathering agencies. Phillips headed a group called the "K Organization," which was responsible for running a clandestine network of spies in the Middle East, Europe, North Africa and Mexico.

In August of 1941, Bill Donovan met with Wallace Phillips, and the two men became instant friends. Phillips told the new COI chief about his responsibilities at ONI and then dropped an unexpected bombshell. His boss, Rear Admiral Walter Anderson, had asked him to speak to Donovan about the transfer of his K Organization to Donovan's. Donovan listened as Phillips explained how the K Organization came into being, under the command of a committee of representatives from the FBI, State, War and Navy departments. After checking Phillips's credentials, Donovan accepted the offer. With the acquisition of the K Organization, a new espionage agency was born.

Donovan made Phillips an associate by appointing him Director of Special Information Services on November 17, 1941. Phillips's responsibility was to "engage and supervise representatives of this agency for service abroad, in obtaining necessary information and data which may bear upon national security and be necessary in the interest of national defense." The K Organization was given a budget of $2,546,000 to fund its overseas operations.

The K Organization had few agents in the field and were disorganized. Among them were four agents operating under Soviet domination in Lithuania, Latvia, and Estonia. These men were run by the assistant naval attaché in Helsinki, Finland. "Their reports," wrote Phillips, "have been very fragmentary…nothing of any importance has come in for the past six weeks."

There was also one agent in Bulgaria who was trusted with all Balkan operations; 12 vice consuls in North Africa; the Assistant Curator of the Metropolitan Museum of Art in Iran; and the Foreign Editor of the *National Geographic Magazine* in Afghanistan. The K Organization also had a number of agents in Mexico, which stepped on FBI Director J. Edgar Hoover's toes and incited a feud.

The FBI had jurisdictional responsibility for intelligence-gathering missions in Latin America and Hoover viewed the transfer of Phillips's men to COI control as interference on his turf. The dispute was solved when agents were returned to navy control.

The K Organization inherited by Bill Donovan was the forerunner of the OSS's Secret Intelligence Branch, which would become integral to American covert operations during the war.

KG 200

The *Luftwaffe* was the German air arm during the Second World War. Its mission was to protect Germany from attack as well as conduct bombing campaigns against the enemy. But there was one secret unit in the *Luftwaffe*. Its operational name was Kampfgeschwader or Battle Wing 200. Most would know it by the name KG 200.

KG 200 was commanded by Colonel Werner Baumbach, a man decorated with the Knight's Cross for bravery. During the war, KG 200 flew airplanes like Junkeers and Heinkels, as well as captured British and American aircraft such as the B-24 Liberator and the Boeing B-17 Flying Fortress. At various times during the war, this covert air unit operated in conjunction with the German espionage agency, Abwehr.

KG 200 dates back to the period after World War I when the Abwehr used the Special Squadron Rowehl to fly reconnaissance missions over Poland. The man in charge of Special Squadron Rowehl was Colonel Theodor Rowehl, by now a civilian pilot, hired by the Abwehr to fly photographic assignments over Germany's adversaries.

Rowehl hand picked men for his sorties, and used *Luftwaffe* air bases for their operations. Their routes took them all over Europe, Africa, and the Soviet Union, making detailed maps of their targets.

When Germany entered World War II, the duties of KG 200 changed. By 1944, Captain Karl Gartenfeld had taken charge of the air unit, renaming it the 2nd Test Formation and expanding it into four squadrons. Its mission was to drop agents behind enemy lines. Later that year, KG 200 joined the 1st Test Formation under the command of Lieutenant Colonel Werner Baumbach. After intensive training, 32 different types of aircraft were ready for action. KG 200 had subdivisions of agent fieldwork, short- and long-range operations, and radar-jamming techniques.

Located in wooded areas, out of sight from planes overhead, clandestine air units flew missions that covered the Mediterranean, Africa, and Eastern Europe, especially the Soviet Union, as far afield as Ireland and Iceland. One of its most important sections was Detachment Olga, who landed agents in France. All KG 200 missions were flown under the cover of darkness.

With the loss of many aircraft due to the ferocious air campaign in Europe, KG 200 used a number of captured American and British planes as well as spare parts they'd accumulated. One of the planes was a B-17 called the *Phyllis Marie,* which was forced to make an emergency landing in Germany on March 8, 1944.

In July 1944, KG 200 was assigned one of the most audacious tasks of the war. The head of the SS intelligence service, Ernst Kaltenbrunner, devised a plan to kill Stalin using a KG 200 plane and a specially selected crew to fly to Moscow. The plan was code-named "Operation Zeppelin," and used an Arado Ar-232B, a four-engine aircraft that would carry a highly trained crew of assassins to the outskirts of Moscow. Their job was to penetrate the Kremlin and murder the Soviet leader. The plan ended in tragedy when the plane carrying the assassins crashed.

As the war progressed and Germany faced defeat, KG 200 was given the task of training a small cadre of suicide pilots. These men were to use gliders in training, but when they turned operational, were to fly on the dangerous V-1 buzz bombs, slamming into allied targets (they were modeled after the Japanese kamikaze pilots who crashed their planes into American ships in the Pacific).

As the Third Reich fell, many of pilots of KG 200 fled in order to save their lives. After the war persistent rumors cropped up reporting that KG 200 pilots were used to fly high ranking Germans to South America or other safe havens. The role of this secret German air arm, more of an intelligence gathering unit, rather than a traditional bombing platform, remains shrouded in secrecy.

Kennedy, John F.

Breaking German and Japanese codes helped to end World War II. In the early days of the war, code breakers in London and Washington, D.C. were able to translate important military and diplomatic communications and ciphers relating to the Axis war plans.

The Japanese navy began its cryptographic activities in 1925, well before their attack on Pearl Harbor. They had already established themselves as the new power in the Far East, having defeated the Russians in the Russo-Japanese War. The only country that stood in their way was the United States, and the Japanese directed all their attention to countering American influence.

Their code-breaking section, which was part of the Naval General Staff, was called *Tukumu Han* or Special Section. Operating out of the Navy Department, this fledgling unit comprised six men and modeled their ciphers on those used by the United States Department of State. The Tukumu Han was also able to decipher Chinese codes for use in attacks against them.

The Japanese Special Section was unable to break various codes used by the United States military, especially those of the navy. Fearing that their secret communications were being monitored, the United States changed their codes, ending any further chance of a Japanese penetration.

As the United States drew nearer to war, the navy established listening posts in the Far East and were able to intercept and decode all their radio traffic. American and Australian coastwatchers on hundreds of small islands across the Pacific monitored Japanese radio messages, as well as ship and troop maneuvers.

On August 2, 1943, Lieutenant Arthur Evans of the Royal Naval Volunteer Reserve, a part of the Australian coastwatchers unit, spotted a flame in the dark waters of Blackett Strait. It belonged to a U.S. Navy ship called P.T. 109, the patrol boat commanded by Lieutenant John F. Kennedy, which had been struck head on by the Japanese destroyer *Amagiri*.

Later that day, Lieutenant Evans heard from his Solomon Island network that there might be survivors. He was told what islands the escaping crew might be headed for.

Kennedy and his remaining personnel were on a small island called Plum Pudding, in the middle of a small Japanese garrison waiting to be rescued.

The Japanese took no action when a group of Solomon Islanders working for the Americans found Kennedy and his men on the island and relayed their planned escape route via the Ferguson Passage. The Japanese troops that surrounded the area picked up the signals coming from Lieutenant Evans and the Americans, but because of indifference or unwillingness to decipher the Australian code, no action was taken.

(*See Also*: Allied Intelligence Bureau)

Kennedy, Joseph P.

Joseph Patrick Kennedy (1915-1944) was the first child born to Joseph Patrick Kennedy and Rose Fitzgerald, parents of the future president of the

United States. He enlisted in the U.S. Navy in May 1941 and was assigned to Naval aviation. He trained at the Squantum Naval Air Facility in Quincy, Massachusetts. After completing his instruction, he was transferred to the naval air station in Jacksonville, Florida.

It was here that young Kennedy learned to fly the latest planes in the American arsenal. He graduated from flight school on May 6, 1942 and was posted to the Banana River field for his next assignment, where he honed his aviator skills. In time, he became a proficient pilot and was sent to Europe.

By March of 1944, Joe Kennedy had flown more than 20 successful missions against German targets in Europe. He wrote home to his parents saying that he would like to remain in Europe. It was at this time, two months prior to the D-Day landings at Normandy, that young Joe Kennedy would become involved in a secret mission called Operation Aphrodite. It would end in his death.

By the spring of 1944, Germany was losing the war. Hitler unleashed the Nazi's newest and most powerful weapons, V-1 buzz bombs, against London. These "vengeance weapons" were long range, able to carry an explosive charge up to 20 tons.

The Americans had bombed the German test site at Peenemunde, which housed the rocket-launching sites and inflicted considerable damage. But the Germans constructed concrete bunkers to house the V-1s and V-2s along the coast of France in a direct route to London. Shortly after the D-Day landings, the Germans began a concerted aerial blitz against civilian targets in London. German rockets were also fired from fortified sites along Belgian and Dutch coasts across the English Channel. Something had to be done to counter the slaughter in the sky, and the Americans came up with an ingenious, yet dangerous idea.

The genesis for Operation Aphrodite came from General Carl Spaatz, the commander of the U.S. Strategic Air Forces in Europe. A modified B-17 bomber would be stripped and transformed into a flying bomb. The pilot would carry thousands of pounds of high explosives, an unprecedented amount, in the cargo compartment. The modified B-17 was to fly to heavily fortified V-1 sites, followed by another plane intended to "guide" the lead aircraft to the target. Before reaching the target, the pilot of the B-17 would bail out over the English countryside leaving the plane to crash into it. Joe Kennedy volunteered for the job.

The crew consisted of Kennedy and fellow officer Bud Willy, accompanied by sixteen Mustangs for air cover. A Mosquito plane was sent along to take pictures. The photographer was Elliot Roosevelt, the son of the president. The date was August 12, 1944.

Their plane took off before dawn without complication. Then, tragedy struck. With only 10 minutes remaining before Kennedy was to bail out of his plane, the backup aircraft sent a signal for Kennedy to make a turn before exiting the aircraft. A huge explosion completely disintegrated the plane, killing both Kennedy and Willy instantly. A pilot in one of the back up planes was later to say about the death of Lieutenant Kennedy, "It was the biggest explosion I ever saw until the pictures of the atomic bomb." On the ground, 59 buildings in the path of the detonation were destroyed.

Ironically, when the allies finally made their way to the V-1 sites, they found them abandoned.

Kent, Tyler

In World War II literature, the name Tyler Kent is little known. But Tyler Kent, a code clerk of the American Embassy in London, was involved in one of the serious spy scandals of the day.

Tyler Kent was born on March 24, 1911, in Manchuria, where his father, Captain William Kent, was the U.S. Consul. As a young man, Tyler accompanied his father to diplomatic postings in Germany, Switzerland and Ireland. In 1926, Tyler attended St. Albans school in Washington, D.C. He was accepted by Princeton University and graduated in 1932 with a degree in history. He left Princeton to continue his studies at the Sorbonne (studying Russian), the University of Madrid, and George Washington University. He took the Foreign Service test and was sent to the U.S. Embassy in Moscow as a code clerk, working for William Bullit, the first American Ambassador to the Soviet Union.

Kent lived in a hotel in Moscow, away from most of the Americans who were assigned to the embassy. He was under surveillance by the NKVD, the Soviet intelligence service, which brought him in contact with one of their most attractive female agents. An affair ensued, and Kent was reprimanded by the ambassador for his extracurricular activities and for negligence in his embassy work. For a while, Kent straightened up, prompting the senior foreign service officer in the Moscow embassy to write to Ambassador Bullit that, "You will be glad to hear that although Kent is still keeping his nose firmly pointed to the North Star, his work has improved greatly."

While working in Moscow, Kent met a beautiful Russian woman named Titania Ilovaiskaya, a translator for the International News Service, and a full time employee of the NKVD. Titania did not withhold her connections to the NKVD, but that did not prevent Kent from pursuing a heated affair. Kent supposedly passed on information from the embassy to his lover. While in Moscow, Kent lived beyond his means. He owned a car and spent money lavishly, under the watchful eye of the Americans and the Russians.

In October 1939, Tyler Kent was transferred from Moscow to London as code clerk. The ambassador there was the wealthy, influential, Irish-American millionaire Joseph P. Kennedy, patriarch of the Kennedy clan. Ambassador Kennedy was adamantly opposed to President Roosevelt aiding Great Britain against Germany with operations such as Lend Lease, whereby American military aid was sent to the British. Ambassador Kennedy's objections to the president's policies hurt his standing with Washington.

The American Embassy in London in 1940 was a hotbed of U.S.-British diplomatic activity. Secret messages between President Roosevelt and Winston Churchill, then the First Lord of the Admiralty, passed through the embassy's code room regularly. Tyler Kent was privy to highly classified material from FDR to Churchill describing a stream of covert U.S. aid to Britain, despite the fact that America was still officially neutral in the war.

While in London, Kent met a woman named Ana Wolkoff and became her lover. Her parents owned a popular establishment in London where radicals came to discuss the issues of the day.

Over time, Ana influenced Kent with anti-Semitic, pro-Hitler views. She then tried to get information from Joan Miller, who worked in the British War Office, who promptly reported her. She was placed under a watchful eye by MI-5. The British Security Service learned of Kent's relationship with her, and that information, too, was sent to the American Embassy.

With little persuasion, Ana convinced Kent to give her documents that came in from Washington, including letters to and from FDR and Churchill. The Germans relayed the information to the Italians.

MI-5 agents told Ambassador Kennedy of the Kent-Wolkoff affair and the fact that they believed Kent was working for the Soviets. Kennedy canceled Kent's diplomatic status and sent the Special Branch police to his Gloucester Place home.

Police found more than a thousand documents in Kent's home. Among these were copies of Churchill's cables to Roosevelt and keys to the U.S. Embassy code room. His arrest sent shock waves through the U.S. State Department in Washington. Ambassador Kennedy was ordered to conduct an investigation on all the other code clerks under his employ, including their personal lives. The State Department suspected all of their codes and ciphers had been compromised, including the important Strip Cipher, the most secure method of communicating with Washington.

Tyler Kent's arrest was kept from the media on both sides of the Atlantic. His trial was conducted in a secret court in Britain. He was charged with stealing official government documents. During the proceedings, Kent admitted to stealing secret material while at the U.S. Embassy in Moscow.

Kent was kept in London until one month after the war ended and then deported to the United States. Kent never admitted to being a Soviet agent, and a FBI investigation never proved a connection.

Tyler Kent died in Texas in 1988.

"King" (Friedrich Kempter)

The depression years hurt Germany, like so many nations around the world, with severe economic hardships. German currency plummeted in value, and countless Germans left the country. Thousands flocked to Brazil, and a large refugee community developed. One of these people was Friedrich Kempter, then 19 years old.

When he stepped off the boat at the Brazilian port of Recife in 1923, he could never have guessed that by the end of the war, he would head one of the largest German espionage networks in South America.

Friedrich Kempter's first job in Recife was a year stint in a textile factory. He would later be employed as a bookkeeper and traveling salesman. In 1938, he began working for a company that collected commercial and industrial information for German businesses interested in Brazilian connections. One day, Kempter was told by his employer that he was going to get a letter from a German firm in Hamburg and that he should do as they said. The company was none other than the Abwehr. The German intelligence service was recruiting people to go undercover in Brazil. The letter offered him a small stipend to report on ship movements through Rio de Janeiro, as well as any information on British trade with South America. In time he learned the true identity of his employer and was given the code name "King."

In February 1940, with the approval of the Abwehr, he began his own commercial information company. He got the funding for the operation from a man named Heribert Mueller. Mueller had previously lived in Vienna and lived in Brazil for 10 years. They named their company Rapid Informer, Ltd., and code-named it "Rita."

Kempter soon told Mueller about his espionage activities and got Abwehr permission to bring in his partner. As time went on, the Abwehr dubbed the information coming in from Rapid Informer the "Message Center." Information was sent via air or cable to Germany. Most of the early work concerned allied shipping in Brazil and South America, as well as American military activities they could report on. As the quality of their work improved, the Abwehr sent Kempter to Buenos Aires, to enlist prospective agents.

He was referred to a man by the Abwehr, called Ottomar or "Otis," a displaced German known in the city for his radio program, the "German Hour." He was also an Abwehr agent.

Kempter also made contact with an Abwehr agent living in Ecuador named Walter Giese. Giese worked at the German legation in Quito, Ecuador, but was in reality a high-ranking Nazi party member (Giese went by the code name "Grief"). Giese's work revolved around allied shipping and spying on the American base at the Panama Canal. He reported home that the Americans were building a submarine base there.

Kempter set up a radio transmitter in Brazil. With the help of a German businessman named Beno Sobisch, who taught Kempter how to use this new technology, the fledgling radio net was in business. Kempter also turned to a German communications company named Siemens, who gave him access to their transmission center.

What Kempter did not realize was that the FBI was operating undercover in South America and had put his firm, Rapid Informer, on the Black List of companies forbidden to deal with U.S. firms.

Kempter and Ottomar set up a radio nest in Buenos Aires with the Abwehr's reluctant blessing. While they approved the deal, the German intelligence service in Hamburg was worried. Kempter had been using his real name when broadcasting to Hamburg, irresponsible behavior in the spy game. The Abwehr also cautioned Kempter and Otis not to broadcast too often, as the Argentine Congress had begun an investigation into Nazi activities in that country.

"Danger acute, acute," read one message from Hamburg to Kempter. "As long as danger is acute, restrict reception and discontinue transmission entirely." Soon, Otis was instructed to stop, and Kempter was told to cease contacting him.

One of most important duties performed by Kempter concerned General Rommel's military campaign in North Africa. Kempter was told to report on the shipment of military equipment from South American ports to British forces in North Africa. Kempter radioed that a British cargo ship, the *Rodney Star,* weighing 12,000 tons was sailing for England. German U-Boats followed the cargo ship and sunk her.

At the height of his spying activity, Friedrich Kempter ran one of the most efficient Abwehr networks in South America. Over the years, he had sent more than 400 radio messages to Germany on countless topics. For his valued service, he was awarded the War Service Cross first class.
(*See Also*: Latin American Espionage)

Kolbe, Fritz

It is every spymaster's dream to have a source whose information is beyond reproach. One such person walked into the office of Allen Dulles, the OSS Chief in 1943. His name was Fritz Kolbe, a highly placed German diplomat.

When Allen Dulles began his operations in Berne, he might as well have put a shingle in his door. Switzerland was the espionage capital of Europe, where spies kept tabs on each other. From his listening post in Berne, Dulles and his network of undercover agents had a powerful listening post for espionage activities in the Third Reich. Dulles soon had his first opportunity to recruit a German diplomat.

On August 23, 1943, a German physician named Fritz Kochertaler approached an official in the British intelligence service, MI-6, named Count Vanden Huyvel. The count wasn't interested, so Kochertaler went to see Gerald Mayer at the U.S. Office of War Information. He told Mayer that he represented a highly placed anti-Hitler German diplomat who wanted to work for the Americans. Could a discreet meeting be arranged with Dulles? That night, the German envoy met at Dulles's home at Herrengasse 23 to meet with the man, Fritz Kolbe.

At 42, Kolbe worked for the German diplomat, Karl Ritter. Ritter was one of the most important agents receiving intelligence from Berlin. It was Kolbe's job to read Ritter's missives and write reports on them for the ambassador. Kolbe saw all intelligence reports that came into the embassy.

Without solicitation from Dulles, Kolbe offered up the diplomatic information that crossed his desk. He carried a briefcase with 186 documents smuggled from Ambassador Ritter, known in OSS lore as the "Berne Report." The information concerned a plan to rescue a captured German agent in Dublin and, most important of all, the Germans' breaking of the U.S. cipher system.

The British checked Kolbe's information for authenticity using the Ultra system. Claude Dansey, second in command at MI-6, and Kim Philby, head of the Iberian Section of MI-6, told Dulles that Kolbe's material was fake. It wasn't, and Dansey had to reconcile himself to the fact that the British let go one of the most important double agents of the war. Dulles, meanwhile, accepted Kolbe's offer to commit treason against Germany. Dulles gave Kolbe the code name, "George Wood."

In a cable to OSS headquarters, Dulles wrote about Kolbe, "I now firmly believe in the good faith of Wood and I am ready to stake my reputation on the fact that these documents are genuine."

In subsequent visits to Dulles, Kolbe exposed Abwehr's secrets. Dulles sent the information, dubbed "Kappa," to London and Washington.

In March 1945, one month before the war ended, Kolbe was allowed to stay permanently in Switzerland. By the time his double agent work ended, Kolbe had given Dulles about 1,600 articles concerning Germany's top diplomatic and military secrets. After the war, he disappeared among the countless men and women determined to begin a new life.

(See Also: Dulles, Allen; "Cicero;" Ultra)

Kuhn, Bernard

A family of spies, known as the Kuhns, was committing espionage on behalf of the Japanese in the Hawaiian Islands prior to the attack on Pearl

Harbor.

The attack by Japanese forces on Pearl Harbor was not on impulse. Over a long period of time, the Japanese organized an elaborate undercover operation based in the Hawaiian consulate. The German Kuhns settled in Hawaii as "sleeper" agents, waiting to be called to duty.

The members of the Kuhn clan included the father, Bernard, his wife, Friedel, and their children, Ruth and Eberhard. All of them would perform espionage duties of one sort or another in the islands.

Bernard Kuhn was the most important member of the spy ring. He was born in 1895 in Germany, and enlisted in the navy at age 17 in 1912. After World War I, he gravitated to Hitler's Nazi party, believing in their hatred of Jews and non-Aryans. He joined the Nazi party, and his son worked for Dr. Joseph Goebbels, Hitler's propaganda minister. He was also a friend of Henrich Himmler, who appointed Bernard Kuhn to a position with the Gestapo. At one point, his son brought his beautiful sister Ruth to a party where she met Goebbels. Goebbels was smitten, and an affair began.

The Kuhns came to the attention of General Karl Haushofer of Berlin University. Haushofer maintained contact with Hitler's Japanese allies, who recruited caucasians for spy missions abroad. Haushofer offered the Japanese the Kuhn family.

They saw a chance for a new life outside of Germany, and happily headed to Tokyo for intelligence training. In 1934, the Kuhns were formally taken on by the Japanese intelligence service and paid $2,000 a month, with a $6,000 bonus, to be paid at the end of each year.

In Tokyo, the Kuhns worked closely with Kanji Ogawa, deputy chief of the Third Bureau, Japan's naval intelligence organization.

Using the money provided to them by the Japanese, the Kuhns bought a home on Honolulu and blended into the population, seeming to lead normal lives. Bernard opened a furniture store. Friedel got a job as a hairdresser near the large Kaneohe Marine Corps Air Station on Oahu. As Bernard's business prospered, he met many American military officers who shopped at his place, and befriended them to gain information about the base.

Ruth Kuhn, a beautiful young woman, soon dated a number of her American naval peers. The officers gave her vital news about the number of ships in Pearl Harbor, what types of vessels were in port, and the numbers of sailors at the base at any one time. Sometimes, their son Eberhard too accompanied his sister on dates. The unsuspecting sailors would take brother and sister on guided tours of the ships at dock, giving the young Kuhns intimate knowledge of the American fleet at anchor.

The Japanese paid the Kuhns through an account with the Deutsche Bank in Berlin under the name Roechling Steel Works. The money was dispensed by a man known only as "Dr. Homberg," Roechling's representative in Japan.

In 1939, Captain Ogawa was appointed to the post of Naval Attaché in Washington and visited the Kuhns on his way to the United States. Using Captain Ogawa's money, they purchased a second home overlooking the Pearl Harbor Naval Base, a perfect site in which to spy on the American fleet.

Captain Ogawa was not thrilled with his sleeper agent, thinking him ill equipped for such an assignment. However, Kuhn told his boss he had set up a short-wave radio system to relay information to waiting Japanese submarines outside of Pearl Harbor. Before departing for the United States, Captain Ogawa told Kuhn to "lay low until further notice."

The Kuhns came to the attention of the 14th Naval District's intelligence office, who kept track of foreign nationals in the islands. The fact that Bernard Kuhn was still spending money even after his furniture store went bankrupt, made the agents take a second look at him.

The FBI office in Hawaii was also interested in the Kuhns. But the rivalry between the intelligence agencies was so extreme that they let the Kuhns slip right through their collective fingers. Bernard Kuhn also had help from a professional spy operating out of the Japanese consulate, Takeo Yoshikawa, a Japanese naval officer who went by the name "Morimura."

As the date for the Pearl Harbor attack neared, the Japanese Consul General in Hawaii gave Kuhn new orders. He sent Kuhn to the vast Pearl Harbor naval base to pay special attention to where each ship was anchored. Kuhn made his first trip to the base on November 28, 1941. Two days later, Kuhn, with a map of the fleet in hand, he reported his findings to Consul Kita.

On December 1st, Kuhn designed a system to send a series of signals to the consulate describing ship movement at Pearl. He placed advertisements in the newspaper, lights on the Kalama and Lanikai beaches, and signalled from windows in their home.

All this information was sent in code from the consulate to Tokyo using a cipher system designated PA-K2. U.S. code breakers were able to crack this system, which led to the capture of the Kuhns.

The Special Signal Service intercepted a radiogram sent by the Japanese, which found its way into the RCA system. This report was given to Captain Irving Mayfield, the Hawaiian district intelligence officer. After decoding the message, Captain Mayfield notified the FBI, and they converged on the Kuhns's home.

In the early morning hours of December 7, 1941, the Kuhns began signaling the consulate. FBI agents also saw the signals and swooped down on the Kuhns. With a solid case of espionage looming against them, Bernard Kuhn confessed. He was put on trial before a military court and found guilty

KUHN

on February 21, 1942.

The Kuhn family was released after the war and disappeared from sight. Captain Ogawa's "sleeper agent" never had time to pose a real threat to the Pearl Harbor naval base. The powerful Japanese armada took care of it for him.

(*See Also*: Pearl Harbor Attack; Yoshikawa, Takeo)

L

Lamphere, Robert

Robert Lamphere was a highly placed FBI agent who took part in some spy cases during the war years. He went on to participate in the Cold War.

Robert Lamphere, born on February 14, 1918, in Wardner, Idaho, graduated from the University of Idaho in 1940 and got his law degree from the National Law School in Washington, D.C. Upon graduation, he joined the FBI. He was posted to bureau offices in Birmingham, Alabama, and New York City where he looked into Selective Service Act violations.

In 1945, the year the war ended, he began working in the FBI's Soviet Espionage Squad in New York. By 1947, he was promoted to a management position in the Espionage Section at FBI headquarters in Washington. His first assignment was to develop a counterintelligence operation against Soviet spies operating in the United States. It was from this work that Lamphere would take part in some of the most vital Russian espionage operations; the Venona files, and the cases of Klaus Fuchs and the Rosenbergs.

While working at FBI headquarters in 1948, Lamphere was given a number of KGB messages deciphered by the Army Security Agency. He asked to see the man in charge of this operation, Meredith Gardner. Gardner was most responsible for the cracking of the Venona files. Lamphere was given the translations of certain KGB messages obtained in 1944. How the FBI got these commercial texts from the Russians is not known, but it is possible that a black-bag job—when an agent illegally enters to copy documents—was carried out to steal them. These messages were sent between the Soviet consulate in New York and Soviet Intelligence in Moscow.

One of the messages centered on someone inside the U.S. Manhattan Project. Klaus Fuchs, a British scientist was supplying information on the breakdown of the uranium process. A full-scale investigation of Fuchs began, and MI-5 was informed.

Fuchs was picked up by the British in 1950 and Lamphere, along with FBI Assistant Director, Hugh Clegg, went to England to take part in his interrogation. Fuchs decided to cooperate, admitted his role as a spy in the Manhattan Project, and named a number of his accomplices, including Harry Gold and David Greenglass.

In 1949, Lamphere began working with the new MI-6 representative in the United States, Kim Philby. Philby was given access to the Venona material by the FBI, and he promptly told one of his fellow British double agents, Donald MacLean, to get out of the U.S.

As it became evident that the Soviets were conducting an espionage attack on the United States in the late 1940s, the FBI took active steps to counter these activities. They took photographs of everyone entering or leaving the Soviet Embassy in Washington, as well as their consulates in other American cities. One of the Soviets whom Lamphere tailed was Anatoli Yakovlev, whose real name was Yatskov, the chief of the KGB's New York office.

The FBI's investigation of Klaus Fuchs led to the arrest on espionage charges against Ethel and Julius Rosenberg. In later years, when speaking about the Rosenberg case, Robert Lamphere said that the FBI recommended the death sentence for Julius, but requested that Ethel be given a 30-year sentence.

Both were put to death at Sing Sing prison in New York on June 19, 1953.

In 1955, Lamphere resigned from the FBI and began working for the Veterans Administration as a deputy administrator. In 1961, he left government service altogether and took on a job in the private sector with the John Hancock Life Insurance Company.

(*See Also*: Fuchs, Klaus; Philby, Kim; Rosenbergs; Venona; MacLean, Donald)

Lanikai & The Isabel

On December 2, 1941, five days before the surprise Japanese attack on Pearl Harbor, President Roosevelt personally ordered one of the most controversial intelligence missions of World War II. The president dispatched the yacht *Lanikai,* and two other small ships, right into the middle of the oncoming Japanese fleet approaching the Hawaiian Islands.

This little-known mission has stirred considerable debate among historians and "revisionists" as to why FDR sent the ships to sea. Was he interested in keeping track of the Japanese fleet, or was the *Lanikai* to be used as "bait" for a Japanese attack against the United States in the Pacific?

On December 1, 1941, shortly after FDR returned to the White House from Warm Springs, Georgia, his presidential retreat, he sent a message to the Chief of Naval Operations. Both men had been communicating about the final objective of the Japanese fleet. U.S. Naval Intelligence reported that a force of 30,000 Japanese troops were aboard the fleet, which included 70 transport ships. Whether its destination was the Philippines or the Dutch East Indies, the president wanted to keep an eye on their movements.

British RAF pilots were flying aerial reconnaissance missions over a wide area of the Pacific and were joined by American squadrons as well. The *Isabel*, a converted dispatch ship of the Asiatic fleet, left for the waters off Indo-China on December 3, 1941. She was spotted two days later by a Japanese patrol plane, but no action against her was taken. She finally reached her duty station 22 miles off the coast of Indo-China and stayed there for five days before returning to Manila.

The *Lanikai*, skippered by Admiral Kemp Tolley, was moored in Manila Bay and left her berth early on the morning of December 7, 1941, just hours before the Japanese attack. Once she heard of the raid on Pearl Harbor, she returned to port. Shortly after being recalled back to Manila, the *Lanikai*, now flying the Dutch flag, began a harrowing 82-day cruise ending in Australia.

Why the *Lanikai* was sent to Australia flying the Dutch flag and not the American colors is still not known. Admiral Tolley believed that his ship was to be used as "bait" for a Japanese attack and said he could prove it. Unfortunately for history, he kept his silence.

(*See Also*: Pearl Harbor Attack)

Latin American Espionage

During the war, Latin America was the largest neutral area in the world. Refugees from all over Europe came there to escape the war. A large number were aliens from Japan and Germany, a potential Fifth Column to serve as possible enemy agents against the United States. The OSS took elaborate steps to counter any potential subversive actions south of our border.

When the war started, President Roosevelt gave intelligence jurisdiction over South and Latin America to the FBI. In order to circumvent this policy, the OSS had to keep one step ahead of the resident FBI agents who operated in Latin America, mostly out of U.S. Embassies.

Almost all of the countries in Latin America broke diplomatic relations with Germany and Japan when the war began. Still, the unstable political situation served as a springboard for espionage against the United States. Both Germany and Japan established an effective information and propaganda network aimed at America.

These included a large number of Axis sympathizers living in these nations and the diplomatic staffs of countries allied with the Axis. Another area of organized resistance against the U.S. was the prevalence of rumor in Latin America. According to the OSS report describing Nazi propaganda activities in Latin America in this regard, "...Rumor and gossip are the important channels in Latin America for passing on information among the influential urban groups. The grapevines are easily fed and easily tapped."

Emigrés in Latin American countries during the war came from Italy, Spain, Eastern Europe, Japan and China. Those, especially from Japan and East European lands, maintained allegiance to their homelands. These were possible recruits for the Axis governments.

On the other hand, according to the OSS, the exiled European immigrants tended to be anti-Axis and willingly revealed sensitive information. It optimistically reported, "[T]hese minorities and refugees offer the possibility of effective dissemination of a wide range of rumors, the preparation of plausible forgeries and black publications [publications containing false information detrimental to the Axis cause], and the operation of black radio with adequate cover. The last possibility would be of particular value for activity aimed at the Far East."

Despite the long distances between Latin American and Europe, the OSS was able to track radio and written communication by enemy agents. Censors monitored letters from Argentina to Japan via the Pacific, as well as mail carried on Argentine or Chilean ships to San Francisco or Seattle. U.S. agents read them before being loaded on Russian vessels bound for Vladivostok.

Shortwave radio transmitters between Latin America and Eastern Europe sent intelligence too. One way to counter these clandestine communications, says the OSS report was to "introduce the appropriate poison into Axis channels themselves or pass it along via simulated Axis channels."

The OSS used Buenos Aires as an avenue for counterespionage operations. The city was rife with potential recruits, as well as a gold mine for carrying out mail-drop operations. "The use of the black radio would be highly profitable against Japan because of the excellent cover provided by the Japanese colonies in Peru and the dearth of good bases of operations in other parts of the world." The OSS used rumors, forgeries, black publications (false stories in the local press), and undercover radio operations against German and Japanese targets.

The OSS dispatch described Argentina as the focal point of Axis espionage ventures in Latin America. "It is the center of all Axis activities in Latin America, the most direct channel of communications with the Axis countries and the most important one with Spain and other countries in the German orbit. Should Argentina break diplomatic relations with the Axis, open communications would cease but clandestine channels would continue to function with relatively little interference for a long time to come."

Buenos Aires was ripe for OSS entry, as the city was a mixture of openly pro-Axis people, as well as a large number of anti-fascist Germans, Italians, Hungarians, and other Europeans. An OSS counterespionage operation was directed against enemy activities in the city. As Argentina was the principal refugee center for escaping Germans, subversive rumors were planted by the OSS into these communities. OSS agents also planted false information using U.S. businessmen as fronts, while conducting legitimate commerce with their German customers.

Brazil was another high priority as far as the OSS was concerned. The country had more than 300,000 Japanese and some half a million Germans. Mexico, the nation that shared a common border with the United States, proved to be a particular problem in enemy espionage. Mexico had a large Fifth Column, and cooperation between German and Japanese espionage was strong. Here too anti-espionage strategies were employed.

According to OSS documents, Latin America was mainly used to counter Japanese expansion. With so large a Japanese population living in Brazil, Peru and Argentina, it was easy for American agents to plant false rumors and infiltrate Americans of Japanese descent into government and business. "The prospect of a longer war in the Pacific," reads part of the OSS document, "...in Europe provides time for ample development of Latin American bases of M.O. [Moral Operations] operations against Japan."

In the early years of the war, Latin America became one a highly developed area of German espionage, rivaling that of Spain, Switzerland or Sweden. The OSS pulled out all the stops to break the Nazi stranglehold using all the tools of the trade, including carrying out escapes of disaffected German officers, creating financial scandals in the marketplace, planting false and misleading documents in the diplomatic pouches of traveling German diplomats.

The OSS proved successful undercover operations against German and Japanese elements in Latin American could be done with a minimum of violence.

Lauwers, Barbara

Barbara Lauwers was one of the ablest and most daring OSS agents in the dangerous Italian operation. She was a liaison to German POWs in an OSS MO (Moral Operations) plan to plant misleading information behind German lines. The OSS code name for this enterprise was "Operation Sauerkraut."

Barbara Lauwers, nicknamed "Zuzka," served in the OSS Woman's Auxiliary Army Corps (WAACS) in the 2677th Regiment that was stationed in Bari, Rome, and Caserta, Italy. She was Czechoslovakian, and spoke English, German, Czech, Slovak, and French. Due to her language skills, she was chosen for an important OSS operation directed against German troops wavering in their allegiance to the Nazi cause.

She left for her assignment on July 21, 1944, under the cover of darkness. Accompanying her was Major William Dewart Jr., traveling to the town of Averso, Italy, which housed a large POW camp. They received operational permission from Colonel Edward Glavin, the head of OSS operations in Italy.

The "Sauerkraut" assignment came directly after the failed July 1944 assassination attempt on Hitler's life by a group of disaffected German military officers. Among them were Count Claus von Stauffenberg and Admiral Canaris, the head of the Abwehr.

Implementation of the plan was put in the hands of the OSS's Moral Operations Division, the psychological warfare contingent of OSS. The plan was to cripple the morale of the German military by planting false information emphasizing military defeats suffered by the German army, and telling misleading stories of discord among the military commanders in Berlin. The men who would carry out this deception operation were carefully selected German POWs being held in camps in Italy. It was Private Barbara Lauwers's job to select and help train these men.

OSS Rome was given the job of preparing the deception campaign. From its headquarters, agents created false newspapers, documents and leaflets, all written on German paper and set in German type. OSS MO agents also were able to find authentic German uniforms, complete with epaulets and insignias.

By July 22, she was able to recruit sixteen German POWs including, "Hans Tappert, a former naval officer from Brussels who was out for revenge; Karl Heiderich, nineteen year old resident of Canada, 'a boy scout type;' and Ernst Fichter, an auto mechanic from Innsbruck, Austria, who was an 'eager beaver.'"

Once all the men were picked, a convoy to Rome brought them to a place for new identities and cover stories. Will Williams adapted best to his new life. He was called Willi Haseneier. Willi was an accomplished artist, with little respect for military discipline. One of his talents was the forging of signatures. One of the false documents that Willi fabricated contained the signature of German Field Marshal Albert Kesselring.

The first group of German POWs, now OSS infiltrators, crept behind enemy lines by the Arno River. Once safely ashore, they began putting the tricks of their trade (leaflets, letters, etc.) on lampposts, trees, and on the sides of homes. The men, all dressed in the appropriate German garb, infiltrated many miles behind the lines, and even had some brief, yet scary encounters with actual Nazi troops.

All 16 men returned safely after completing a productive mission. They were also able to bring back intelligence having to do with the composition of military forces in the area.

With the successful completion of the first Sauerkraut mission, the U.S. Fifth Army Intelligence Branch expanded the program. Lauwers, and a group of 22 other OSS men worked in safe houses producing a multitude of faked papers, leaflets and other propaganda material. She was the only woman in the unit, but her work was exemplary. She was credited with inventing a propaganda device called "The League of Lonely War Women" which was directed toward the low-spirited German soldier. Propaganda indicated that any German soldier who was on leave in Italy, and wore a certain lapel on his jacket, would immediately find a beautiful woman who would have sex with him. Lauwers "League of Lonely War Women" deception plan was picked up by some stateside newspapers.

She also ran another successful propaganda operation aimed at Czech and Slovak troops who were assigned against their will to do menial tasks for the German front-line soldiers in Italy. Powerfully written missives were infiltrated to these units, emphasizing historically harsh treatment by the Germans against their country. In the end, hundreds of these men sneaked over to allied lines. For her participation in this operation, Barbara Lauwers was awarded the Bronze Star.

Following the end of the war, she left the OSS and worked with the Office of War Information. After returning to the United States, she joined the Voice of America. In later years, she married Joseph Coolidge. As of this writing, the couple are still alive.

(*See Also*: Italian Patriot Bands; Operation Sauerkraut)

Layton, Edwin

Edwin Layton was born on April 7, 1903, in Nauvoo, Illinois. He attended the U.S. Naval Academy and graduated in 1924. One of his first assignments was on navy surface ships where he learned the art of commanding a man of war. He was sent to Japan to serve at the American Embassy in Tokyo. It was here that he learned the Japanese language.

After a brief stint commanding a destroyer, Layton became an intelligence officer for the fleet commander at Pearl Harbor. What Lieutenant Commander Edwin Layton could not have known as he assumed his new position was that he would be part of the firestorm of acrimony and finger pointing that would follow the Japanese attack on December 7, 1941.

Lieutenant Commander Layton headed a group of code breakers out of Hawaii who were highly successful in breaking many Japanese naval codes.

They were able to track Japanese ship movements in the Pacific.

One of the first code systems that Layton worked on was the WE WE. The Japanese were building up their military forces in the Marshall Islands, including a large submarine force on the island of Kwajalein, an airfield at Palau, and a contingent of troops on Saipan. Layton passed this information along to Admiral Richardson who praised Layton for his fine work. Over time, Layton complained that the navy did not inform Washington that the Japanese were building up their forces in the Marshalls.

Even before the attack on Pearl Harbor, Layton had a running feud, accusing those in the intelligence loop of not sharing sufficient information with him regarding the whereabouts of the oncoming Japanese fleet.

Lieutenant Commander Layton was one of the people interviewed by a special commission that looked into the Pearl Harbor attack after the war. The person given the job of conducting an investigation independent of the congressional probe was Henry Clausen. In his interviews with Lieutenant Commander Layton, Henry Clausen found discrepancies and conflicting statements.

He tried to blame internal feuding within the Navy Department for the intelligence failure leading to Pearl Harbor. According to Clausen, Layton claimed to have an independent status in the intelligence pecking order in Hawaii. His liaison was Joseph Rochefort, head of the Combat Intelligence Unit, who reported to the Chief of Naval Operations in Washington.

He later said he was under the command of the Fourteenth Naval District in Hawaii, not the Pacific Fleet Command. Clausen saw disparities between his testimony and that of Colonel Edward Raley, the U.S. Army-Air Force intelligence liaison. Layton said that he had met numerous times with Colonel Raley three months before the attack, and passed along information concerning allied airfields in the Netherlands, East Indies and Australia. But Colonel Raley disputed Layton's alibi.

Clausen also reported that before the attack, Layton gave Raley, "top secret information from sources that had previously been found to be completely reliable." Layton insisted Raley promised not to make copies of the material or show it to his commanding officer before handing it over to General Martin, the head of Air Forces in Hawaii.

Layton told Raley the navy was listening to signals from Japan concerning "certain cryptic weather messages," the "Winds Message," which would break off diplomatic relations with the U.S. But he never informed Raley that the U.S. knew the Japanese were destroying their code machines in preparation for war. Clausen accused Layton of failing to carry out Admiral Kimmel's order to give the "war warning" message of November 27 to General Walter Short, the Army Commander in Hawaii.

In his investigation, Henry Clausen faults Layton for not briefing

Brigadier General Kendall Fielder, who was in charge of the army's intelligence branch in Hawaii. The Colonel wasn't cleared to receive Top Secret or Magic information and had to depend on Layton. Layton admitted that he had no formal liaison with Fielder and did not give him the same intelligence that he passed on to Colonel Raley.

According to Clausen, the reason Layton did not share intelligence with the army is that he was taking orders directly from the navy, and intelligence sharing between the navy and the army would have to come from some other source. He believed Layton was hiding behind Admiral Kimmel to save himself.

After the war, Layton established a Naval intelligence program, and briefly served as the U.S. Naval Attaché in Rio de Janeiro. He also served as assistant director of intelligence for the Joint Chiefs of Staff and assistant chief of staff for the Commander in Chief Pacific Fleet. He retired from active duty in 1959.

He published a book on his wartime experiences called *And I Was There*. It came out one year after his death in 1984.

(*See Also*: Hypo, Station; Pearl Harbor Attack; Rochefort, Joseph)

Lee, Duncan

When President Roosevelt ordered Bill Donovan to set up the Office of Strategic Services, Donovan set out to bring on board the best and the brightest men and women available. Many of these people were personally known to him, coming from good families, attending the best colleges and universities in America, the so called "Blue Bloods" of American society. What Donovan failed to realize was that among these intellectuals and highly patriotic individuals were a small number of spies working under cover for the NKVD, the Soviet intelligence service, which was operating in large numbers in the United States. One of the most important Soviet agents employed in the OSS was a man who was a descendant of Civil War General Robert E. Lee, Duncan Lee.

Duncan Lee was born in China of American missionary parents. He arrived in the United States as a teenager and attended the St. Albans preparatory school in Washington, D.C. Upon graduation, he was accepted at Yale University, where he played on the football team. He was a brilliant student and graduated first in his class in 1935. He then went to England where he studied at Oxford as a Rhodes Scholar. Upon returning to the United States, Duncan Lee returned to Yale where he received a law degree. In 1939, he accepted a job with aaw firm, Donovan, Leisure, Newton and Lombard. (The Donovan at the head of the law firm's letterhead was none other than Bill Donovan, the head of the OSS.)

Lee did well in the firm, and Bill Donovan took an instant liking to this bright, energetic young man. When Donovan was appointed by FDR as the head of the Coordinator of Information (COI), one of the first people he brought on board was Duncan Lee. Lee would later transfer to the OSS upon Donovan's appointment to that office.

Unknown to Donovan was that as a student at Oxford, Duncan Lee became a communist sympathizer. It was something he would keep under wraps throughout his tenure at OSS.

His first assignment for the OSS was in China, a country where he had resided for 12 years. When he returned to the United States with the rank of captain, he served for a short time as Donovan's assistant. It was at this time that Lee was recruited by the Soviets. Lee's Soviet contact was Jacob Golos, who ran one of the successful Soviet penetration operations in Washington. Working closely with Lee was the beautiful American, Elizabeth Bentley. Bentley became Golos's lover and served as his second in command.

A deciphered message from Golos to the NKVD regarding Lee reads as follows: "Lee works on issues of guerrilla movement, sabotage, and commando. Cables coming from the State Department go through his hands. He collects them and shows them to Donovan at his discretion. All the agent information from Europe comes through his hands....Thanks to his appointment, he was withdrawn from the party group and made an illegal member. He wants to work with us and pass to us information he is able to acquire."

For the Soviets, Duncan Lee was a gold mine. Lee, however, did not like to hand any documents over to his contacts, among them Mary Price and Elizabeth Bentley. Instead, both Price and Bentley had to listen to what Lee told them and later, in the privacy of their homes, transcribe from memory all of Lee's information. Among the material turned over by Lee was data on OSS operations in Europe, the details of OSS agents dropping behind the lines into Hungary and Yugoslavia, and secret peace feelers between the United States and some anti-Hitler elements.

Lee met with Bentley a number of times during a two-year period. He later told investigators that he knew Bentley only as "Helen," and that Golos was introduced to him as a friend of her's named "John." He was given the coded name "Koch."

Decoded KGB documents show the scope of classified material that Lee handed over to the Soviets during the war. Among them were OSS operations in China and France, and American diplomatic initiatives concerning Turkey and Romania, among others.

One of the valuable pieces of intelligence that Lee delivered to the Soviets was a list of the people considered by the OSS as being the most dangerous as far as U.S. security was concerned. They were listed in three categories: 1) "known Soviet agents," 2) "known Communists" and 3) "Communist sympathizers." One man listed as a "known Communist" was

Maurice Halpern, then the head of the Research Section of the OSS. Halpern was "put on ice" for a six-month period. The Venona intercepts confirm that there were names of people on this registry who were supplying information to the Soviets.

Toward the end of 1944, Lee was sent to China to set up a clandestine link into Japan via allied-occupied Korea. The Russians took an active interest in Lee's China sojourn. Bentley went so far as to arrange a meeting between Lee and a number of Soviet agents in China. Along the route, the plane carrying Lee crashed in the dense jungle of Burma, and he was slightly injured. Upon returning to the United States, Lee, according to a KGB memo, "...his wanderings in Burma's jungles frayed him very much, and one will need some time to draw him back into active work with us."

Lee played an important role in keeping the Soviets abreast of any pending internal OSS investigations of suspected spies in the agency. One of the men whom the OSS was vigorously investigating was Donald Wheeler. Wheeler attended Yale with Lee and was also a highly placed agent in the spy group headed by Victor Perlo. Wheeler's expertise was on German manpower and military strength, and the disposition of German forces in the field. Lee supplied a long record of vital information to the Soviets based on Wheeler's work.

By September 1944, Lee was promoted to the position of chief of the OSS Japanese section. Lee continued to provide the Russians with information concerning allied and enemy agents operating in China, Japan and Korea.

Shortly after becoming Japan Chief, Lee's domestic life came asunder. While married, he commenced an affair with his courier, Mary Price. After Mrs. Lee discovered the affair, Price ended her working relationship with Lee. By now, the OSS had been quietly looking into Lee's activities, and he slowly but surely lessened his spying activities. A KGB letter concerning Lee's lack of interest shows how much the Russians had lost faith in him. "...Lee needs special guidance—he is one of the weakest of the weak sisters, nervous and fearing his own shadow. This, as well as his personal troubles, considerably hamper working with him at present."

Depressed and fearing for both his mental and physical safety, Lee emphatically told his KGB handlers that he was quitting the double life he had been leading for so many years. The Russians accepted his decision, cutting their own losses. Soon thereafter, Elizabeth Bentley defected to the U.S. and blew the whistle on the Soviet espionage cells operating in the Washington area. Of all the double agents working under William Donovan, Lee's espionage was the most damaging, and for Bill Donovan, a personal tragedy. (*See Also*: Venona; Golos, Jacob; Bentley, Elizabeth)

Legendre, Gertrude

In October 1944, a highly placed woman OSS officer left on leave from her Paris home in what was supposed to be a short, five-day journey to the front lines. This unsuspecting trip by Gertrude Legendre almost cost her and her companion their lives, as well as being a possible intelligence disaster for the OSS.

Gertrude Legendre, a Virginian, went to the Foxcroft School in that state. When the war began, she entered the OSS and spent her first year in the headquarters Message Center and Cable Desk in Washington. After her training, she was sent to the OSS London office. At that time, Gertrude was married to a navy man, Lieutenant Commander Sydney Legrende who was stationed in the Pacific. Prior to her departure for London, Gertrude had become the head of the Washington Cable Center, a prestigious posting in the agency.

She arrived in London in September 1943 and was assigned to the Central Cable Desk. Her main duties were to handle the detailed intelligence traffic that came in from 13 London OSS divisions. Gertrude handled communications from agents in France, China, Ceylon, North Africa and Italy, all vitally important areas in which covert OSS operations were under way.

In September 1944, she was sent to the Paris OSS office, working in the communications section. She was a civilian who had to wear a WAAC (Woman's Army Corp) uniform. It was during one of her free times that found Gertrude at the bar of the Ritz Hotel talking with an old friend from OSS days, navy commander Robert Jennings. After getting reacquainted, both Legendre and Jennings decided that they wanted some excitement and made arrangements that would take them to the front lines. On September 23, 1944, they left Paris bound for Luxembourg, the start of what they planned as a short, yet lively adventure.

After one day on the road, their car broke down. As they were seeking help, they were found by another OSS officer, Major Maxwell Papurt. Papurt offered to take them to the town of Wallendorf where they could get help. Along the way, their car was ambushed by a German patrol. In the ensuing fire-fight, Major Papurt was severely wounded, and all three were captured. The wounded major was taken to a German field hospital while Gertrude Legendre and Robert Jennings were bound over for interrogation. Legendre, speaking in French, told her captors that she was assigned to the American Embassy in Paris as a clerk, and was then serving as an interpreter for Jennings. When asked why they were in a battle zone, they replied that they did not know the area was not safe for travelers.

They were transferred to a town called Trier, near the Hunsruck Mountains. It was here that another round of interrogations took place. Soon though, they were sent to another location, the town of Flammersheim. From here they were moved to the small town of Diez, where they were separated and put into cells in an old castle that was used as a jail.

Legendre's inquisitor accused her of being a spy, working with Major Papurt, and confronted her with certain documents that were taken from the major upon his capture. Gertrude Legendre was now faced with the prospect of being shot as a spy. After days of questioning, she steadfastly stuck to her story, denying all the charges being brought against her. She did, however, tell the German officer that she was close friends with a number of high-ranking U.S. diplomats and military officers, including U.S. Ambassador Winant and General George Patton.

Over time, Gertrude learned that her German investigator was named William Gosewisch. Gosewisch had lived in the United States for 18 years, married an American woman, and had two children. On a trip back to Germany, he was inducted into the army (he was still a German citizen).

Over a long period of time, William Gosewisch became friendly with Gertrude Legendre and vowed to help her escape. Before he could provide any further assistance, Gosewisch was transferred. Before leaving, he told Gertrude that Jennings was being sent to an officers' prison and would be safe. Gertrude, to her dismay, was sent to Berlin by train right to the heart of the German intelligence establishment; Gestapo headquarters.

She spent the next two months sticking to her story and was spared further harm. One day she was shifted to a mountain-top villa on the Rhine River, where she lived with over a hundred other prisoners, mostly French. In a stroke of luck, Gertrude was taken to live at the home of a wealthy man named Dr. Hans Grieme and his wife. Dr. Grieme had contacts with important people in the German foreign ministry, and pulled his considerable strings in order to get Gertrude released. Through the efforts of Dr. Grieme, Gertrude was able to get in touch with William Gosewisch, who made arrangements for her freedom.

One night she was taken to the German-Swiss border where she boarded a train at the station in Konstanz. At a prearranged place along the route, she saw a man waving a lantern and quickly dropped from the moving train. In a scene worthy of a mystery thriller, she ran as quickly as she could to the Swiss border and was able to cross to safety under the thumb of dozens of German border guards.

When the OSS found out that she had reached safety, measures were taken to bring her in. A personal representative of Allen Dulles took Gertrude to see Dulles in Berne. Dulles, relieved that she was secure, and that none of her secrets had fallen into the hands of the enemy, managed for her passage to Paris. Before leaving, Gertrude asked Dulles if arrangements had been made to rescue her. To her astonishment, Dulles said, "You were too hot. OSS did not dare to touch you, nor did the Embassy." Bill Donovan ordered that Gertrude be sent back to the United States immediately, mostly for security sake. She was reunited with her husband, and through her valiant efforts, was able to bring her savior, William Gosewisch and his family to America after the war.

Leiber, Father Robert

The Vatican was a hotbed of espionage activities during World War II, with agents from all sides seeking out information about each other. The OSS had its own sources of information inside the walls of the pope's palace, and these men passed on valuable tidbits of knowledge from their sources. One of the men whom the Americans used as a conduit was a Jesuit priest, Robert Leiber, a confidant of the Papal Nuncio to Germany, Cardinal Eugenio Pacelli (Pacelli would later become Pope Pius XII).

Father Leiber, Bavarian by origin, during the war was a teacher of theological studies at the University of Munich. Cardinal Pacelli knew of Leiber's work and had him in for an interview. He was so impressed with the young man that he asked him to become his private secretary. Father Leiber accepted the offer immediately and became privy to decisions relating to the outcome of the war. Father Leiber worked alongside Cardinal Pacelli, when the future pope held the position of Secretary of State at the Vatican. Like many men of the Catholic Church, Father Leiber was anti-Nazi, seeing in the Hitler regime as a country bent not only on destroying the Jews and other minorities, but in subverting religious freedom in Germany. He worked behind the scenes with a number of anti-Hitler plotters and was privy to their plans.

It is not clear how and when Father Leiber came to the attention of the OSS, but by August of 1944, he was having confidential meetings with Donovan's representatives.

Father Leiber left Germany in 1932 to move to Italy, but he still had unusual sources of information on the plans to kill Hitler. Between 1939 and 1943, Father Lieber's main contact with the German opposition was a Catholic lawyer named Joseph Muller. Muller worked in the Abwehr beginning in 1939 and soon became disenchanted with Hitler's Third Reich. Over time, Muller made contacts with men inside the Abwehr who took active steps in trying to eliminate Hitler. One of the men with whom Muller worked alongside in their anti-Hitler plotting was Hans Oster. Oster, an officer in German Military Intelligence, was one of the plotters inside the cabal seeking Hitler's removal. Another source of intelligence for Father Leiber was a Hans Bernd Gisevius. Gisevius worked at Abwehr headquarters and was also a leading member of the opposition group. Gisevius later operated out of Switzerland and was also a secret contact with Allen Dulles who was OSS station chief in Berne.

Throughout the behind the scenes plotting against Hitler, the conspirators kept Father Leiber up to date on all their plans. He also knew of the winter 1939-40 plot against Hitler led by General von Halder. It was hoped by these men that the German offensive against Norway would fail, thus, giving the opposition ammunition to supplant Hitler. To their dismay, the Norwegian campaign was a success, and the plan was called off.

Leiber was also knowledgeable concerning a plot that was scheduled to take place in September-October, 1943. He received fragmentary details of this proposed action by a colonel in the German Embassy in Rome. The attempt was to take place no later than October 15, but it was all contingent on the stabilization of the Russian front. Since the military situation was still fluid, the plot did not go off. In his discussions with OSS representatives in Rome, Father Leiber described the failure of the plots for the following reasons: first, many of the conspirators were not sincere in their efforts to topple Hitler, and secondly, they did not want to imperil the overall safety of the Reich.

Father Leiber also discussed religious matters then going on in Germany with his OSS listeners. He said that in his opinion, as long as Hitler governed, the Catholic youth of the country was lost. Once the war was over, the Church had to place its trust for religious renewal on the very young and the present, older generation.

(Research Note: There has been a long running controversy regarding the role played by Pope Pius XII during the war. His detractors say he didn't do enough to save the Jews, while his backers say he took concrete steps such as denouncing the criminal actions of Hitler, and taking actions to save numerous Jews from certain death. While the argument surrounding the actions taken by Pope Pius XII are not in the scope of this book, the reader can decide for himself in the voluminous literature concerning the pope's role during the war. One of the recommended tomes is *Hitler's Pope: The Secret History of Pius XII* by John Cornwell.)

Lisbon Embassy Burglary

Lisbon, Portugal, was a spy's heaven during the latter part of the war. Being technically neutral, the city teemed with agents from around the world. The OSS established one of its first offices in Lisbon, taking advantage of this critically important geographical location. Situated on the Iberian Peninsula, with Spain as it nearest neighbor, Lisbon was the jumping-off point for OSS missions in North Africa and into continental France. It was from Lisbon in May 1942, that an event occurred that had the potential of causing a devastating intelligence blunder for the OSS and possibly, the entire American espionage system.

In the background of this affair lay the concept of Magic, the American code name for the reading of the Japanese military codes that were so vital in tracking that nation's troop movements, and reading their secret intelligence. If somehow, Magic were to be compromised, then the U.S. would be at a great disadvantage as far as keeping one step ahead of the Japanese.

The action that almost put Magic into jeopardy was an OSS burglary of the office of the Japanese military attaché in Lisbon. This covert operation was carried out by two of Donovan's men who worked inside the Japanese Embassy, a messenger in the Naval Attaché's office, and an interpreter who worked in the Military Attaché's department. What the two men, both Portugese, were looking for were copies of cipher material used by the Japanese military attaché. In their haste to get out of the embassy before they were discovered, they ransacked the place, leaving every mark of an attempted burglary.

Shortly after the incident took place, General George Strong, a West Point graduate, and then chief of Military Intelligence, reported to General George C. Marshall, the Army Chief of Staff. What General Marshall received from General Strong was an exaggeration as to what actually happened in the Lisbon embassy. General Strong had a deep dislike for William Donovan and his OSS. Strong did not like the idea that a civilian spy agency was working alongside of his Army G-2. Strong also saw in Donovan a rival for his chances of becoming the new head of America's post-war intelligence service.

General Strong told General Marshall that the two burglars had stolen the most sensitive of the Japanese military ciphers, especially those having to do with the American's knowledge, our successful breaking of their critical Magic information. He told Marshall that the Japanese would surely realize that a break-in had taken place and would change their Magic codes. General Strong wrote to the Army Chief of Staff saying, "If that was so (the changing of the most sensitive codes) for months we will face a blank wall as far as Military and Naval Intelligence from the Japanese sources is concerned, and our present Magic summary would cease to exist, with the possibility of catastrophic results as far as the activities of State, War and Navy are concerned."

The fallout of the Lisbon burglary went straight up to the president who ordered the Joint Chiefs of Staff to undertake an investigation. What the Chiefs discovered was not what General Strong had laid out. The man put in charge of the affair was Colonel C.R. Peck, the executive secretary of the Joint Chiefs of Staff.

Donovan made a powerful case to Colonel Peck, discounting most of what General Strong alluded to. According to Donovan, the signals taken from the Japanese Embassy were copies of the Military Attaché papers found in the garbage. This material was sent for analysis to the Army Cryptanalysis Bureau, who, after studying the files, reported that it contained a low level of intelligence value. Donovan also sent the data in question to the Special Branch which handled all Magic intercepts, and they, too, found nothing that would be cause for alarm.

The final coup de gras, as far as Donovan was concerned, came when he confirmed that General Strong knew in advance of the burglary. Through documents in his possession, Donovan proved that General Strong, as well as the Joint Intelligence Committee, had given permission for the operation. (The State Department also had pre-knowledge and approved the mission.)

Donovan had won round one against his nemesis General Strong. In the end, Magic was not endangered and proved to be a vital intelligence tool in winning the war.

(*See Also*: Magic)

Lockheed Plane Affair

In war, as in life, there are many ironic twists that can change circumstances for better or worse. One such turn of fate concerned a British spy, a German general, and a specially equipped airplane.

In the years prior to the outbreak of war, the British, ever fearful that a rearmed Germany would start another round of warfare on the European continent, took measures to keep track of Germany's military strength. The leaders at Whitehall were primarily interested in the capacity of the German air force. To that end, they sent one of their agents to penetrate the high-est levels of the Nazi military establishment, 41-year-old Frederick Winterbotham. Winterbotham was then chief of the Air Section of the British Secret Intelligence Service. Disguised as a lawyer, Frederick Winterbotham arrived in Germany in the early 1930s and was soon hobnobbing with many leading figures in government: Hitler, Goering, along with many top officers. By 1938, however, the Germans were beginning to question Winterbotham's activities, and he was asked to leave the country.

With his access to military information in Germany temporarily on hold, the spymaster had to invent other ways of learning German secrets. With his knowledge of airplanes, Winterbotham requested a specially designed twin-engine Lockheed aircraft be sent for a special mission.

Changes were made in the Lockheed, the most important of which was the installation of a new type camera able to take high-quality pictures from an altitude of 22,000 feet. Winterbotham's immediate task was to find the right pilot to fly the plane. He picked Sydney Cotton as his man.

Cotton was given a crash course in the operation of the newly designed Lockheed, and its important element, the high-resolution German Leica cameras. On flight trials in which Winterbotham accompanied Cotton, the new cameras worked perfectly, even at high altitudes.

Their first operational mission took them over the North African coast, where they successfully photographed a large number of Italian ships docked along the Mediterranean. Their next flyover proved more challenging.

In late 1939, Cotton arrived in Germany under the pretense of beginning talks with German firms who were interested in developing their own color photography. Cotton had by no, become known in Berlin and in time, he began flying over other cities in Germany like Frankfurt and Hamburg. The only difference was that his newly installed spy cameras were taking pictures of vital military installations on the ground.

All his hard work seemed on the verge of collapse when he was approached by General Albert Kesselring, the commander of the Luftwaffe's Air Fleet Number 1. Kesselring asked Cotton for a ride in the Lockheed. The general, fascinated by the plane, asked pointed questions about its capacity. In an ironic twist of fate, General Kesselring worked its controls while the German-made Leicas took pictures of his country below.

(*See Also*: Double Cross System; Winterbotham, Frederick)

Ludwig, Kurt Frederick

In 1940, one year after Germany invaded Poland, setting off World War II, the Nazis mounted a concerted effort to infiltrate the United States. One of their first agents was an American citizen of German parentage named Kurt Frederick Ludwig.

Kurt Ludwig was born in Ohio in 1903. His parents had emigrated 50 years before their son's birth. They returned with their infant son to Germany. Kurt got his education, married, and began work there. In the 1920s and 1930s, Kurt returned to America for short periods of time, but he saw himself as a pure German with no real tie to the United States.

Kurt Ludwig operated a business in Munich, and through it came to know some influential men, among them Dr. Robert Ley, a powerful Nazi labor leader and Reichsführer Henrich Himmler of the dreaded SS. Ludwig dabbled in espionage until he was arrested in Austria photographing bridges near the Austrian-German border.

He came back to Germany shortly after Nazi troops occupied Austria. Intelligence services made a formal offer to him, and Ludwig went back to the United States to initiate a major German espionage ring.

His initial training in espionage took place at Abwehr headquarters in Berlin. Ludwig's back channel would be in Spain but arrangements were made for his reports to be sent directly to Heinrich Himmler. When sending his spy material to Himmler, Ludwig would use the name "Lothar Fredreich." Himmler served as Kurt Ludwig's case officer.

In Spain, Major von der Osten outlined Kurt Ludwig's mission. In New York, he contacted an active German-American Bund, "for the purpose of gathering and sending to Germany, via mail drops in Spain and Portugal, detailed information on the size, equipment...location and morale of United States Army units; on aircraft production, and on the routing of convoys, as well as the movement of single ships between the United States and England."

He was instructed to send his reports back to Germany via the transatlantic clipper, forwarded to a following fictitious couple. He was also told to operate a transmitter that could reach Hamburg.

Upon arriving in New York, Ludwig attended various gatherings of the German-American Bund, a collection of German immigrants loyal to the fatherland. They were more than willing to listen to what Ludwig had to say, and many of them gave him their support.

One of his first recruits was Paul Theodore Borchardt-Battua, a former German army officer, who told immigration officials that he was a Jew, seeking a new life in the United States. Ludwig told his new members that he was to be called "Joe" when they met to discuss their clandestine work.

Ludwig was the case officer for an American soldier he recruited named Rene Charles Froehlich. Froehlich was stationed at Fort Jay on Governor's Island, right in the middle of New York harbor. He was a clerk in the hospital and saw all the patient records. Froehlich gave this information to Ludwig, who was able to learn the dispositions of the G.I.s as they were reassigned. The Abwehr now knew where many U.S. Army units were stationed, as well as their weaknesses and strengths.

Another of his agents was a reluctant Carl Schroetter of Miami. Schroetter, a Swiss citizen, had two sisters who lived in Germany as hostages to the Third Reich. He was blackmailed into working for the Abwehr while traveling in Germany. Schroetter was a captain of a charter boat named the *Echo of the Past*. He relayed information on naval maneuvers in the Florida straits.

Karl Mueller, a naturalized American citizen from Austria, became one of Ludwig's most productive agents. The two men often worked as a team, penetrating American industrial plans, gaining access from German sympathizers. In one brazen foray, they walked right onto the U.S. Naval Academy at Annapolis, Maryland, photographed cadets doing push-ups, barracks and port facilities along the river.

One curious agent of Ludwig's was Dr. Paul Borchardt, or "the Professor." Dr. Borchardt was a major in the German army in 1915 and a military instructor in Munich. Dr. Borchardt was paid in cash and never connected with other members of his network. It turned out that he was working for the Abwehr, and reporting back to Germany on Ludwig's operation.

The demise of the Ludwig espionage operation came from a series of letters intercepted by British mail openers stationed in Bermuda. The British, under the auspice of the BSC, were operating a mail intercept station.

Alert readers discovered a number of cryptic letters from a "Joe K" to accommodation addresses in Spain and Portugal. The BSC staff in Bermuda knew German agents in the United States used the countries as transit points for information headed for Germany. Using invisible inks, the BSC people were able to read Joe K's letters. They reported that the British stationed 70,000 men in Iceland, and that the U.S. sent 20 B-17 bombers to Great Britain. The BSC quickly notified the FBI.

The FBI received unexpected help with the Ludwig gang, due to an accident in Times Square, New York, on March 18, 1941. A man was killed trying to cross the street. He carried a Spanish passport and a lot of cash. He was identified as Don Julio Lopez Lido. Police were called, but what they didn't know was that there was another man named "Lido" disappearing into the crowd. The real "Lido," it turned out, was Ulrich von der Osten.

The NYPD used the ID to trace him to the Taft Hotel in New York and searched his room. What they found left them speechless. Among the items in Lido's possession was a report on the defenses of the U.S. Army stationed at Pearl Harbor, Hawaii, and nearby Hickham Field. This blistering information was immediately turned over to the FBI.

In Bermuda, BSC interceptors read a letter from "Joe K" referring to the killing of "Phil" in Times Square. All this evidence pointed to someone high up in the German espionage agency working in New York.

FBI agents found Ludwig along the New York waterfront, spying on the large troop and cargo ships docked there. In the summer of 1941, Ludwig left New York and headed for Montana. He then took a bus to Seattle, Washington, probably making arrangements along the way for his eventual passage back to Germany. In Seattle, Kurt Ludwig was arrested by FBI agents and taken into custody.

Kurt Ludwig was put on trial in March 1942, and found guilty of espionage. He received a sentence of 20 years. His secretary, Lucy Boehmler, was

given five. The remaining members of the Ludwig gang were arrested, thus, closing down Hitler's principal espionage net in the United States.
(*See Also*: BSC; Hoover, J. Edgar)

M

MacLean, Donald

Donald MacLean was a member of the famous Cambridge Spy Ring. All these men were British citizens recruited at Cambridge University in the 1930s.

Donald MacLean was born in London in 1913, the son of a lawyer who became a member of the British parliament. He attended the Gresham School, where his young mind found adventure and excitement in the Russian Revolution. It was also during this formative time of his life that Donald MacLean began having sexual affairs with other boys at school.

Through his father's connections, young Donald was accepted into Cambridge University, where he met and bonded with the men who would forever change his life. In endless political conversations, they lamented the British concept of democracy as outdated. They believed the answer was communism.

MacLean graduated from Cambridge in 1932 and took the exam for the Foreign Service. He passed with flying colors and entered the world of British diplomacy. When queried by his potential employer about his belief in the communist system, he dismissed it as a youthful fling, but in truth he had been actively enrolled in the Soviet spy system and was about to start proving his worth.

His first assignment came in 1935 when he joined the Central Department of the Foreign Office, which had the job of supervising policy towards Germany, Belgium and France. In 1938, he was sent to the British Embassy in Paris where he met his future wife, Melinda Marling. They were married right before France was overrun by the Germans.

As a trusted member of the Foreign Office, MacLean was able to siphon large amounts of political information to his Soviet controllers in London. In

1944, he was transferred quite suddenly to the United States. He became the first secretary at the British Embassy in Washington. For the Soviets, MacLean's reassignment to Washington was a goldmine. MacLean would now be in a position to pass on some of the most valuable information shared by Washington and London.

He also doubled as an important aide to the British Ambassador, with access to everything that came from London. In time, Melinda MacLean came to join Donald in the United States but chose to live in New York, where her mother resided (Mrs. MacLean was an American). This arrangement was fine with Donald, giving him sound reasons to go to New York. When he visited his wife, MacLean also paid a call on his Soviet controller, Vladimir Pravdin. Paravdin was a KGB officer, working under cover as a journalist for the Soviet news service, *PRAVDA*. The KGB provided MacLean with the code name Homer.

Besides his work in the British Embassy in Washington, MacLean was also a member of the Combined Policy Committee on Arms Development. This highly secret organization worked closely with the Americans on nuclear policy and development. MacLean gave the Russians vital knowledge on U.S.-British atomic strategy during the post-war years. It was during this time that the United States began an accelerated campaign to build atomic weapons, in effect starting the nuclear arms race.

During his stint in Washington, MacLean provided the Russians with a wealth of classified material. For example, he relayed private telegrams between FDR and Winston Churchill, strategic plans for the various military campaigns against the Germans and the Japanese, and British strategy in dealing with the Greek resistance. One message from the KGB to Moscow regarding MacLean's Greek plan reads, "Homer hopes that we will take advantage of these circumstances to disrupt the plans of the British."

In 1948, MacLean was making more frequent trips to the American Atomic Energy Committee in his capacity as the British representative to that body. This attracted the attention of the newly created CIA. The latter informed the FBI, and MacLean was placed under surveillance.

Using the Venona intercepts, U.S. Army cryptanalysis were able to listen in on communications between the Soviet Embassy in New York and their agents in the United States. U.S. analysts were able to discover that in June 1944, a man named Homer was making frequent trips between Washington and New York. That man was Donald MacLean.

James Angleton, the head of counterintelligence at the CIA, feared that MacLean was Homer and gave this information to Britain's MI-5, but they did little about the allegations.

In time, the newly nominated head of Britain's spy agency, SIS, Maurice

Oldfield, informed Kim Philby, one of their key agents in the United States (as well as being a double agent) that in his opinion, there was a mole who had penetrated the British Embassy in the United States. Philby knew exactly whom Oldfield was talking about: Donald MacLean.

Despite the American warnings that MacLean might be working for the Russians, he was put in charge of the American Department of the Foreign Service. Philby told MacLean that he was under suspicion by the CIA, and MacLean began to drink heavily and continue his liaisons with young men. Philby, not being able to contact MacLean personally, asked Guy Burgess to inform him that immediate steps had to be taken in order to protect himself from arrest. Also informed about MacLean's predicament was Yuri Modin, the Soviet intelligence officer who handled MacLean. Modin began the intricate process of getting MacLean back to the Soviet Union.

On May 25, 1951, Donald MacLean and Guy Burgess left England. They had driven to the port of Southampton where they booked passage on a boat, the *SS Falaise,* en route to St. Malo, France. From St. Malo, they traveled by train to Paris, and then on to Bern, Switzerland. False passports were awaiting them, and for the next several days they continued on to Zurich, Stockholm, Prague, and finally, to the Soviet Union.

In 1953, Melinda MacLean and her children joined MacLean in Russia. In time, Melinda MacLean became sexually involved with Kim Philby. After the defections of Burgess and MacLean, Philby became a prime suspect, and he was asked to hand in his resignation from the SIS. In 1963, he too defected to the Soviet Union.

Donald MacLean became a famous person in Russia, writing a book called *British Foreign Policy Since Suez.* In 1956, the Soviet government, in a not so surprising statement, announced that both Guy Burgess and Donald MacLean had defected.

In the large game of espionage, Donald MacLean provided the Soviet Union with some of the most valued information coming from the U.S. and UK. He is mentioned in 12 of the Venona cables deciphered by the Arlington Hall examiners. He died of a heart attack in Moscow on March 6, 1983, age 69.

(*See Also*: Venona; Philby, Kim; Burgess, Guy; Cambridge Spies; Manhattan Project)

Magic

Magic was the highest-classified intelligence collection in the United States during World War II. It had its roots in the late 1930s and early 1940s, when American army and navy code breakers went to work on the Japanese military and diplomatic codes. The Japanese used what they called a "Purple machine" to encode top-secret intelligence sent to their embassies around the world. The United States designated all the information culled from Purple "Magic."

If not for the huge success of Magic, the war would have lasted longer than it did, resulting in even more casualties. The Magic intercepts were crucial to discovering how much the United States command structure knew at the time of the attack on Pearl Harbor.

The man largely responsible for the concept of Magic was William Friedman, a talented code breaker. During World War I, Friedman was sent to Germany to decipher codes. After the war, he returned to the United States to the army's Signal Intelligence Service.

Friedman's staff consisted only of one assistant. His original mandate was to prepare or revise the army's codes and ciphers. By 1934, the army doubled the manpower available to Friedman's SIS, to 19. By the time the United States entered the war in 1941, it had over 300 employees.

By 1936, William Friedman's SIS had broken the Japanese cipher machine system called Taipua A, or Cipher Machine A, used for diplomatic traffic. In 1938, the Japanese changed their coding system, and it took the SIS two years to replicate a machine that could read the Japanese Purple messages.

The success of Magic allowed the United States to follow Japan's route to war, keeping a detailed record of their every secret move. The British had their own code-breaking unit named Ultra.

By July 1940, with England fighting alone against Germany, the United States and Great Britain agreed to share intelligence: Ultra with the U.S., and Magic with the British. To the consternation of many high-ranking U.S. military officers, the Roosevelt administration ordered the military to give two Purple machines to the British. It is ironic that one of the Purple machines that went to the British was originally supposed to be given to the U.S. Navy at Pearl Harbor. That error in judgment, not appreciated at that time, would have horrific consequences, which culminated on the morning of December 7, 1941.

Another U.S. military organization doing cryptographic work that involved the Magic intercepts was the navy's code-breaking group called OP-20-G, led by Commander Lawrence Safford. Safford and the SIS did not share all their information with each other. To further complicate matters, it was decided in 1941 that both agencies would deliver their Magic to the White House on alternate months!

This attempt at coordinating the agencies came to an abrupt end when some Magic materials were found in the office of FDR's personal military aide, Edwin Watson. When the news of this fiasco reached the army, its G-2 (intelligence) made drastic changes in the way Magic intercepts were disseminated. They stopped delivering Magic to the White House, and gave it to the State Department instead. After the president found out that Magic wasn't being delivered to him, the practice was suspended.

The use of Magic also had a profound bearing on the events leading up to the Japanese attack on Pearl Harbor and the circumstances surrounding the raid. With 50 years of hindsight, it is clear that the military commanders in Hawaii, namely Admiral Husband Kimmel and army General Walter Short, did not have possession of all the relevant Magic intercepts regarding Japan's war plans against the United States.

The historical record is replete with information the U.S. government possessed regarding Japanese military plans. The cooling of diplomatic relations between the U.S. and Japan should have warned them. They knew Tokyo had asked their spies in Hawaii to provide information on the number of ships at the Pearl Harbor naval base.

There was a "deadline" document to the U.S. State Department, regarding the breaking off of diplomatic relations. There were also secret Japanese contacts between Hitler and Benito Mussolini, and most importantly, the orders given by Tokyo to its Washington embassy ordering the destruction of its codebooks one-day prior to the hostilities.

Brigadier General Leonard Gerow, then head of the Army's War Plans Division, read the daily Magic sent to him, but later testified that he did not receive all of it from the navy. General Gerow placed blame on the navy for not warning its own commanders in Hawaii that the Japanese were asking for a detailed layout of the Pearl Harbor fortifications.

Another man with access to Magic was Colonel Rufus Bratton, the Chief of the Far Eastern Section of G-2 (army intelligence). Colonel Bratton testified that he had been privy to Magic at least a year before the Pearl Harbor attack, and that by December 1941, the volume of traffic was so great that he had to ask permission for his aides to handle the material.

Bratton's staff sent the unevaluated intelligence up the chain of command to the following people: 1) George Marshall, the Chief of Staff, 2) Henry Stimson, the Secretary of War, 3) Cordell Hull, the Secretary of State, 4) Leonard Gerow, the head of the War Plans Division, 5) Sherman Miles, the Assistant Chief of Staff, G-2, and finally, President Roosevelt.

The problem with all these men getting Magic was that no one agreed on which information was important. Consequently, the information Kimmel and Short needed in Hawaii was not delivered quickly enough.

Perhaps the biggest failure of Magic was the "Winds Message." This was a November 27, 1941, message deciphered by U.S. code breakers in which the Japanese government set a deadline for signing a peace agreement with the United States. The army and navy brass at Pearl Harbor sent warnings regarding this dispatch to their commanders in Hawaii. Admiral Kimmel was sent this letter, starting with the following words, "This dispatch is to be considered a war warning." General Short also received this note.

In his testimony before the Navy Board of Inquiry, Kimmel said that he was certain that the War and Navy Departments had information that a Japanese attack on the U.S. was imminent. "It was known at least three or probably four hours before the attack. All this information was denied to General Short and me. I feel that we were entitled to it. Had we been furnished this information as little as two or three hours before the attack, which was easily feasible...much could have been done."

While it is evident that the pre-Pearl Harbor Magic was not used properly, it was still highly successful. Using the information from Magic, the United States military was able to post these battlefield victories. During the battle of Midway, the navy was able to cripple Japanese aircraft carriers. This decisive battle was the turning point in the battle for the Pacific. U.S. pilots shot down the plane carrying Japanese Admiral Isoruku Yamamoto, the Commander-in-chief of the Japanese navy. We learned that the Japanese government made a policy decision not to join Germany in their war against Russia. The U.S. also knew in advance of the sailing schedules of the important Japanese merchant fleet and mounted an effective submarine campaign against them.

In the long run, Magic and the intelligence it provided proved invaluable in defeating Japan.

(*See Also*: Pearl Harbor Attack; Hypo, Station; Yamamoto Assassination; Midway)

McCormack, Alfred

Immediately after the surprise Japanese attack on Pearl Harbor, the Roosevelt administration began an investigation into the greatest intelligence failure in American history. Military intelligence agencies, ONI, Army G-2, and copious Magic intercepts read in Washington were not able to predict an impending Japanese attack against the United States or its allies. FDR asked his Secretary of War, Henry Stimson, to select an investigation to probe the disaster. The man Secretary Stimson chose for this significant assignment was Alfred McCormack.

Henry Stimson himself was in a quandary as to his own previous beliefs on the need for a unified intelligence-gathering system in the United States. It was Stimson who closed down the groundbreaking intelligence work done by Herbert Yardley during and right after the First World War. Yardley was a code clerk in the State Department and, without any formal training, was able to crack the department's codes. During World War I, Yardley was put in charge of the army's MI-8 cryptological section of Military Intelligence.

This unit came to be known as the "Black Chamber," the first, highly successful American code-breaking venture by any military branch. By 1919, he had broken the Japanese codes, and his work was instrumental in the American negotiations with Japan at the Washington Conference on the Limitation of Armaments (1921-22). When Herbert Hoover was elected president, he appointed Henry Stimson as his Secretary of State. Stimson saw no need for Yardley's Black Chamber and shut down his group saying, "Gentlemen do not read each other's mail."

Now, after the Pearl Harbor intelligence fiasco, Stimson, whom FDR had appointed as Secretary of War, had a change of heart and saw the appointment of Alfred McCormack as essential to control any future damage.

Alfred McCormack's instructions from the Secretary of War were to "investigate and recommend new procedures for handling and disseminating information derived from breaking enemy codes." He had to "study the problem and to determine what had to be done in order to make certain that all possible useful intelligence was derived from this source." This was a daunting task, especially for one who had no previous military training.

McCormack was appointed special assistant to Stimson on January 19, 1942. He was a lawyer by profession, working in the prestigious law firm of Cravath, Swain and Moore. His hobby was reading books on military history, and he was now thrust right into the actual making of history.

McCormack was to work out of Secretary Stimson's purview as a civilian, taking his orders from the Secretary. His appointment did not go down well with the entrenched military intelligence commanders, believing that he was interfering with their operations. He was ordered to study all possible uses of intelligence that could be used for cryptanalytic purposes. He was to cull the raw intelligence that came in from such secret sources as Magic, and other intelligence collection methods, and turn them into simple, readable reports. In his memorandums to the Secretary, McCormack described what his actual task was. "The real job was to dig into the material, study it in the light of outside information, not related to attendant circumstances and given its proper value."

As McCormack's study began to cut loose the red tape that was at the heart of the army intelligence system, Colonel Carter Clarke's MIS section for cryptanalytic activities was incorporated into his office. Colonel Clarke was to serve as chief of the section but he did not like having to work with a civilian. Now, in an incident that baffled the many people who knew McCormack, he accepted the rank of colonel in the army. This designation infuriated Colonel Clarke and the other navy and army officers he had to work with.

After months of detailed analysis by his staff, going over the Magic information, and studying how the army and navy went about gathering and sharing its separate intelligence data, McCormack was able to pull all the divergent pieces of the intelligence puzzle together. No longer did the various services keep certain material in its own coffers, while passing on that which they thought was unnecessary, or material believed not pertinent to the overall big picture.

By the mid-1940s, McCormack's staff had a clear picture of how much shipping the Japanese merchant fleet was carrying, thus allowing U.S. submarines to track and sink them. In 1943, they were able to monitor radio communications coming from Berlin from eight to 10 hours per day.

In a brilliant move, specially trained intelligence officers from McCormack's staff were assigned tasks as action officers with the army corps, divisions, and army headquarters staff. These men taught the rudiments of intelligence collection and the necessity of protecting sources and methods.

In the spring of 1943, when the United States and England shared its intelligence collections, McCormack and a team were sent across the Atlantic. They were assigned to the cryptographic location called Government Code and Cipher School (GC&CS) located at Bletchley Park. It was from Bletchley Park that British code breakers worked on Ultra and were able to intercept thousands of communications dealing with German submarine and land forces.

Going along with McCormack were William Friedman, the noted code breaker, and Colonel Telford Taylor. Taylor would stay behind at Bletchley Park and concentrate on breaking the Japanese diplomatic codes.

McCormack and his men were shown the most sensitive Ultra material, which was sent back to the United States for use by our own analysts, while the U.S. shared its Magic with the British.

McCormack handpicked a number of men whom he knew from his law days and brought them in to handle the Magic traffic that was now flowing in a steady stream. Among them were men who would play front and center roles in the political and cultural life in post-war America. They were Inzer Wyatt, who would be appointed as a Federal judge, William Bundy, an assistant Secretary of State and the editor of the influential magazine, *Foreign Affairs*, Alfred Friendly, who would become the managing editor of the *Washington Post*, Lewis Powell, a future associate justice of the U.S. Supreme Court, and many others. Their main job was to read the Ultra messages and collate them into coherent form for the review of the major U.S. and British military commanders.

As the army took over more and more duties that once belonged to McCormack, his original position as the main arm of the Secretary of War waned. In the weeks before D-Day, McCormack's section was turned over to the German Military Reports Branch. The daily manuscripts sent to General of the Army Marshall were now called, "Magic European Summary."

The intelligence just prior to D-Day was nothing less than fantastic. U.S. military planners had in their possession, via McCormack's work, a daily European summary with a complex card index, two sets of Ultra signals coming from Bletchley Park, detailed lists of German units, complete with their location and strength, and the logistical facts on much of the German forces in Europe.

Alfred McCormack was responsible for a complete revision in the way American intelligence professionals studied secret information for the rest of the war. Even so, most military commanders still did not trust Ultra or Magic, believing that the role of intelligence in war was not of importance in modern day conflict. This little recognized patriot brought the military to the realization that without the proper use of intelligence, wars in the modern era could not be won.

(*See Also*: Bletchley Park; Magic; Pearl Harbor Attack; Ultra)

Malaga Incident

The city of Malaga is located along the southern coast of Spain, on the shores of the Mediterranean Sea. It is a stone's throw from the bustling port of Tangier in North Africa. During World War II, Tangier was one of the hotbeds of OSS espionage and home to an early OSS station. OSS agents penetrated North Africa from Tangier, keeping a watchful eye on German activity. It was also from Malaga that an OSS operation slated for Spain went awry. It was an embarrassment to Donovan's men. This event became known as the "Malaga Incident."

The crisis for the OSS concerned the arrest of three agents in Spain and Spanish Morocco in late 1943 and the spring of 1944. The original mission of the group dates back to a year before their arrest. Their objective was to facilitate the work of the allied forces in Spanish Morocco and Spain if it became necessary to go to war with that country. The American Fifth Army worked with the OSS in the mission and was kept abreast of its progress. In time, the men were turned over to the X-2 (counterintelligence) branch of OSS. Their job was to protect the rear of any armies that might invade the continent. Their marching orders were not to engage in any military activity, but to lie low and await further orders. According to OSS records these men were inactive for long periods of time. While awaiting a supply drop which never came they tried to borrow money from the local population. In turn, they were arrested.

The first man who was caught in Madrid was sent in at the end of August 1943. He was helped ashore by a Major Duncan of the Marine

Corps. No further word was heard from that agent (as of November 29, 1943). The radio operator sent in with the first agent was in regular contact until February 11, 1944, when he was also arrested in Malaga.

Another radio operator was sent to the Spanish city Mellila in May 1943, and had been operating there ever since. He was arrested on February 23, 1944, after killing a Spanish policeman. After the incident, Spanish police found Tommy guns and "suitcases" in the agent's possession. His replacement was sent in, and the British gave his identity to the Spanish authorities. This man had to be taken out of the country on short notice.

The documents relate that the first group of three men left Algiers on June 21, 1943, and were taken aboard a converted British trawler named the HMS *Prodigal*. These men landed along the coast between the towns of Nerja, Malaga and Motril. The subsequent team of four left during the third week of August, and were transported by a motor boat by the French DSM (spy agency). Of the eight men in Spain, three were captured, three were taken out of the country, and two were in Spain, whereabouts unknown.

OSS files report the names of the three men arrested: Corporal Francis Comuriel, Jose Lopez Iglesias, and Salvador Rodriguez Santana. They were arrested in Melilla and were sentenced to death on March 10, 1944 for being "members of an American Information Organization at Oujda and Algiers, under Colonel Eddy." (William Eddy worked in the OSS station in Tangier.)

A new twist was now thrust into the picture concerning the three arrested men. It seems that the OSS had a suspicion that two of the agents "appeared to be British agents." "The third, Rodriguez Santana, has been previously reported dead by our MA, Tangier, and confirmed by our people in Madrid." OSS internal communications asked if "a common program could be worked out so as to evacuate these people from Melilla and keep them from being shot."

It was agreed by OSS higher-ups to send a Colonel Rodrigo to investigate whether or not Rodriguez Santana was still alive, and to look into the possibilities of bribing Spanish police into releasing the agents.

In his report to the 2677th Headquarters Company, of which the OSS was attached, Colonel Rodrigo made the following information available regarding his investigation. The men who were captured were originally part of a radio net operation infiltrated into Spain in 1943. They were sent in at the request of a Colonel Miller of X-2, counterintelligence, of the Fifth Army. This was part of an overall mission called the "Medusa Project." Colonel Rodrigo stated that he received inadequate responses from Colonel Miller, and that he could verify that Spanish police killed one of the men. Colonel Rodrigo also said that all the other agents sent into Spain were ordered to make their way to France or North Africa as quickly as feasible.

He also made clear that only one of the three men belonged to the U.S., and that the other two were British.

The OSS denied running any further radio operations in Spain or North Africa, and said that it had nothing to do with the situation. The OSS said that it was their belief that the threat to execute the two remaining men was "a bluff on their part against the pressure now being exerted upon them by the State Department to remove Axis espionage agents from Tangier and Spanish Morocco. In other words, they are trying to prove that we are coming into court with unclean hands."

The U.S. Ambassador in Spain said that he believed these statements of further American arms shipments into that country was a reprisal against our demands that the Spanish government remove German and Japanese "fifth columnists" from its consular offices.

The Malaga incident begs a number of unanswered questions. What were British agents doing in what was supposed to be a purely OSS affair? Did the OSS know that there were British agents in their group, and if not, was there a breach of security?

(*See Also*: Eddy, William)

Man Who Never Was, The (Operation Mincemeat)

In a cemetery in the Spanish town of Huelva, Spain, lies a body under the tombstone of "William Martin." Anyone taking a glance at this final resting place of the deceased would probably pay no attention. But the grave of Major "William Martin" contained the remains of a man who would play one of the pivotal episodes in allied deception against the Germans.

By 1943, allied military commanders were preparing final plans for the liberation of Europe. They all agreed that the easiest avenue onto the continent was through Sicily, and then, overland, into the heart of Germany. (The code name for the invasion of Sicily was Husky.) In order to pull this off successfully, a massive deception operation had to be organized in order to fool the Germans into believing that an allied invasion was slated for another area. What they came up with was a plan called "Operation Mincemeat," or what modern day writers called "The Man Who Never Was."

The men responsible for Operation Mincemeat were two British officers, Lieutenant Commander Ewen Montagu and Squadron Leader Archibald Cholmondley. Ewen Montagu was a reservist in naval intelligence, and Archibald Cholmondley worked in the Air Ministry. Prior to the war, Ewen Montagu was a noted barrister, and after the war would later serve as the judge advocate of the fleet. Montagu concocted an ingenious scheme whereby a body of a British officer would be placed in a strategic location accessible to the Germans, indicating that an allied invasion of Greece was in the offing.

Lieutenant Commander Montagu discussed this plan with Sir Bernard

Spilsbury, a noted English pathologist. A search for an appropriate body was launched. It had to be of military age and was to have fluid in his lungs, linking him to death by drowning. Combing the London morgue, a body was found which met with their precise criteria. The family of the deceased was quietly contacted, and after being told that the body of their dead relative was needed for a matter of state, and promising that the true identity would never be revealed, they quietly agreed to give it up.

Now, an elaborate cover story had to be created to fool the Germans into believing they had found a genuine British military officer. They gave the man a new name, Major William Martin of the Royal Marines. Major Martin's last posting was on the staff of the Chief of Combined Operations, Vice Admiral Lord Louis Mountbatten. Placed in Major Martin's hands was a large briefcase containing vital military information, including a letter of introduction from Admiral Mountbatten to Admiral Sir Andrew Cunningham, numerous pages of a book on Combined Operations authored by Admiral Mountbatten, and a letter from the Vice Chief of the Imperial Staff, Lieutenant General Sir Archibald Nye, to General Alexander.

The contents of Major Martin's valise would be a godsend for the Germans. The papers contained plans of the allies to attack Greece at Kalamata and Cape Araxos. They also contained notes saying that the proposed invasion of Sicily was just a cover to trick the Germans. Papers carried by the major also called for an attack on the Balkans.

As preparations for the operation mounted, added details of Major Martin's personal life were supplied. On his body were placed theater ticket stubs from two West End plays, dated for April 22, pictures of his girlfriend, as well as love letters from her (the letters were written by a secretary in Montagu's office), coins, matches, keys, and other aspects of daily life. Major Martin was ready to go to war.

In a scene reminiscent of a good Hollywood spy thriller, the body of Major Martin was placed on board the submarine *Seraph*, at Holy Loch, Scotland, under darkness of April 19, 1943. The crew of the *Seraph* was sworn to secrecy, never being told the absolute truth about their extra passenger.

On the night of April 30, 1943, the *Seraph* surfaced near the shore of Huelva, Spain, and sent the body of Major Martin into the sea. Also put overboard was a capsized rubber dingy, making it look like Major Martin had died in a plane crash in the ocean. The tides did their work and soon, the body of Major Martin washed ashore at Huelva. Some local fishermen contacted the Spanish police. Soon, Abwehr officers were called in. The trap had been set.

Over the next several days, the Abwehr opened and read the contents of

Major Martin's briefcase. They fell completely for the ruse set up by Ewen Montagu and his partners in British intelligence. The British were able to keep track of the German reaction to their find via Ultra. Reports back to Berlin concerning the papers on Major Martin's body by Abwehr agents in Spain tell of them being "absolutely convincing" in nature. In the months following the discovery of the body in Huelva, the Germans beefed up their forces in the eastern Mediterranean, especially along the areas of Kalamata and Cape Araxos, the very spots described in Major Martin's briefcase. Troops were also sent to the areas around Sardinia and Corsica. They also transferred a panzer division to Greece from France.

While the Abwehr was going over their newly discovered treasure trove, the British consul in Madrid made countless demands that the contents of Major Martin's briefcase be returned, and that arrangements for burial should take place. Upon receipt of the documents, British officials recognized that the papers had been read and resealed.

In July 1943, allied troops waded ashore at Sicily and won a deceive victory over the lightly fortified German and Italian troops. One month later, General George Patton's Seventh Army, along with troops from British General Bernard Montgomery, took complete control of Sicily.

Local authorities in a cemetery in Huelva buried Major William Martin.

For his actions in conceiving Operation Mincemeat, Ewen Montagu was given the Military Order of the British Empire. In 1953, he wrote a book on his wartime experiences called aptly, *The Man Who Never Was*. The book was later made into a movie, starring Clifton Webb.

Fifty-three years after the death of Major William Martin, evidence has come to light as to the possible identification of this soldier of mystery. According to Roger Morgan, a town planning officer with the Kensington and Chelsea council, the man's name was Glyndwr Michael. Michael committed suicide in London. One Francisco Rodriguez, a worker in the cemetery at Huleva, said that an unidentified person put flowers on the grave of Major Martin for a number of years. That person has since stopped coming.

Manhattan Project, The

Of all the secrets of the Second World War, the greatest was the development of the atomic bomb by the United States and England. Working under the strictest conditions, allied scientists harnessed the atom and changed the art of warfare as we know it. In one of the ironies of the war, members of the industrious spy operation that infiltrated the Manhattan Project leaked the development of the atomic bomb to the Soviet Union. The fallout of this spy affair would be felt in the early days of the Cold War, and changed the way post-war presidents dealt with Joseph Stalin's Soviet Union.

The concept of developing an atomic bomb dates back to the years before the war began. The most eminent scientists of the day knew about the theoretical process of nuclear fusion and fission but lacked the tools to connect them. Two of the best minds of the era, Leo Szilard and Albert Einstein, drafted a letter to President Roosevelt, which explained the possible role of atomic weapons in wartime.

Their letter was sent on October 11, 1939, and hit a nerve in the White House. Ten days later, the president ordered an Advisory Committee on Uranium (also called the "Briggs Uranium Committee") to look into the matter of producing atomic weapons. Nothing was done, however, and in time, the United States turned to Great Britain for help.

In February 1940, two British scientists, Otto Frisch and Rudolf Peierls, made the first technological breakthroughs in the development of fission U-235. They designed a "roadmap" from which other men of science would use to successfully build an atomic as well as a hydrogen bomb,

Soon, American scientists like Philip Abelson, Glenn Seaborg and Arthur Wahl would make important discoveries in the enrichment of uranium, and the critical use of plutonium in building a bomb.

These developments were so productive that Prime Minister Winston Churchill, on September 3, 1941, ordered his Chiefs of Staff to begin development of an atomic bomb.

In the United States, work on a bomb was begun under the direction of an organization code-named S-1, headed by Arthur Compton. (S-1 would later be renamed The Manhattan Project.)

During this time period, President Roosevelt had a discussion with his science advisor, Vannevar Bush, in which Bush told him that a program then underway to develop atomic bombs was proceeding rapidly, and that it was now out of the laboratory stage and proceeding into the industrial phase.

By the summer of 1940, one year before Pearl Harbor, the United States and the United Kingdom began in earnest to share their atomic bomb research. Vannevar Bush held countless meetings with his counterparts in England, and while the United States feared that the British would use their knowledge to make their own bomb, the Roosevelt administration had no choice but to trust them.

On September 17, 1942, official work on the Manhattan Engineer District was under way. The man appointed to supervise the project was General Leslie Groves. General Groves had previously been responsible for the construction of the Pentagon outside of Washington, D.C. Under extreme secrecy, Groves purchased 1,250 tons of fine-grade uranium from the Belgian Congo, which was sent to its new facility at Oak Ridge, Tennessee. In time, other locations were established in which British and American scientists would labor to build the bomb. They were in Los

Alamos, New Mexico, and Hanford, Washington, on a site on the Columbia River. Work on the bomb project was conducted in such places as the University of Chicago, as well as labs at the Du Pont and Kellog Corporation.

On October 15, 1942, General Groves appointed J. Robert Oppenheimer as head of the Manhattan Project, or Project Y. Oppenheimer was sent to Los Alamos, New Mexico, where critical work on the bomb was taking place. Oppenheimer was a professor of physics at Berkeley and worked with other scientists on the S-1 program. His family was also linked to communist front organizations, and his wife was a former member of the Communist Party. (Over the years, it has been alleged that Oppenheimer might have been working for the Soviet Union during this time. However, no concrete evidence linking him to Soviet espionage at Los Alamos was found.)

By 1943, work on the production of plutonium and the enrichment of uranium accelerated at Oak Ridge and Hanford. That same year saw the introduction of a modified airplane, which would be able to deliver the finished bomb, as well as the training of a special crew for that purpose.

In 1944, the United States government put a huge amount of resources, both men and money, into the Manhattan Project. It now rivaled that of the largest privately owned company. It was decided by the Manhattan Project scientists to shelve plans for the construction of a proposed plutonium gun, and instead, concentrate on the implosion theory, a chain reaction of the fissionable material that made up the bomb. Working around the clock for months on end, the scientists at Los Alamos, Hanford, and Oak Ridge were able to make huge strides in the construction of the world's first atomic bomb. The first test of the new weapon was approved in October 1944, and scheduled for the Alamagordo Bombing Range in New Mexico that same year.

The last piece of the puzzle was in place with the successful introduction of the explosive lens used in the implosion bomb. In February 1945, the enriched plutonium arrived in Los Alamos from Hanford, and in a military decision, the island of Tinian was chosen as the loading point for the completed bomb.

It was now that another unexpected development in the story of the Manhattan Project began: the infiltration of a number of Soviet spies right in the middle of Los Alamos.

The Soviet Union received its first reports on U.S. atomic bomb research from John Cairncross, a member of the infamous Cambridge Spy Ring. Cairncross worked as a secretary for Lord Maurice Hankey, the chairman of the British governmental organization studying atomic bomb theory.

The Soviet's top nuclear spy right in the heart of the Los Alamos complex was a British subject named Klaus Fuchs. Fuchs came to Britain in 1933 from Germany. He was a brilliant physicist, and also a member of the German Communist Party.

After serving time in a Canadian jail for supposed Fifth Column activities, Fuchs came to England, where, despite his communist roots, he joined British scientists responsible for building the atomic bomb. In December 1943, Fuchs was sent to the United States with a large British delegation assigned to the bomb project. He worked at the Oak Ridge plant with other members of his team. Fuchs was put in contact with a Soviet agent whom he would pass his top-secret material. That man was called "Raymond." In reality, "Raymond" was Harry Gold, a courier for the Soviet Intelligence spy ring operating in the United States.

Gold passed along the high-grade intelligence concerning the bomb to his Soviet contacts in New York, who gave it to Moscow. By 1950, Fuchs had returned to England where he worked in developing that nation's own atomic bomb. That same year, Fuchs, after being interrogated by MI-5, broke down and confessed his role as a Russian spy. He turned in David Greenglass, a soldier who worked at Los Alamos, as well as Harry Gold. Their arrest led to charges being brought against Julius and Ethel Rosenberg for their activities in the atomic spy ring. Fuchs, Gold, Greenglass, and the Rosenbergs were the main players in the Soviet's atomic spy ring during the war.

Two other atomic spies were Allan Nunn May and Bruno Pontecorvo.

Allan Nunn May was a British nuclear physicist who spied for the Soviet Union in Canada. He was a secret communist and was recruited at Cambridge University, along with Kim Philby, Donald MacLean, and Guy Burgess. He joined the British-sponsored Tub Alloys project (the code name for Britain's bomb-making program) in 1942 and worked at Cambridge. While in Canada, he was recruited by Colonel Nikolai Zabotin, the military attaché at the Soviet Embassy. May detailed the fruitful test of the atomic bomb at Alamagordo, New Mexico, as well as handing over parts of the Uranium 235, a complex component of the bomb. May was arrested on March 4, 1946, by Scotland Yard officers after a long surveillance. He was released from jail in 1952.

Bruno Pontecorvo was an Italian scientist who worked closely with Klaus Fuchs on atomic research. He was educated at Rome and Pisa Universities, and later went to work with Enrico Fermi, one of the best minds in the field of science. In 1943, he worked with the Anglo-Canadian atomic research group at Chalk River in Ontario, Canada. It has been alleged, but never proved, that during the six years he worked at Chalk River, Pontecorvo provided the Soviet Union with documents relating to his duties. After the war, he returned to England where he was an important member of a scientific team at Harwell, the location of Great Britain's nuclear research facility. Because of his checkered past, British officials transferred Portecorvo to a teaching job at Liverpool University in January 1951. When Portecorvo failed to show up at Liverpool, many questions began to be asked. In 1955, he surfaced in Moscow, saying that he had defected to Russia three years before. For many years, he worked on the development of Russia's first atomic arsenal. He died in 1993.

In recent years, charges have been leveled against Robert Oppenheimer, Enrico Fermi, Niels Bohr, and Leo Szilard, as being factors in the Russian spy ring operating out of Los Alamos. The man making these allegations is Pavel Sudoplatov, in his book *Special Tasks: The Memoirs of an Unwanted Witness-A Soviet Spymaster.* Sudoplatov states that he saw documents linking these men as Soviet spies based on information he read when he was the intelligence director of the Special Committee on Atomic Problems from 1944 to 1946.

He further says that Oppenheimer and his wife met twice with Gregory Kheifetz, a Soviet resident (intelligence officer) in Berkeley, California, in December 1941. He also says that Bruno Portecorvo met with a Soviet agent in 1943 and said that Enrico Fermi was going to provide information on the workings at Los Alamos, as well as Oak Ridge.

Pavel Sudoplatov's detractors are many and they point out discrepancies in his account. Most of the atomic intelligence the Russians received came in 1945, not before. The information they did get prior to 1945 came almost exclusively from Klaus Fuchs, who had unlimited access to Los Alamos. Also, by the time (1945) when Sudoplatov claims these spies were hard at work, most of the Russian espionage nets in the United States had been shut down with the defection of Elizabeth Bentley.

On July 16, 1945, the first test of the atomic bomb was carried out at the Trinity site in the New Mexico desert.

On August 6, 1945, the 509th Composite Bomb Group commanded by Lieutenant Colonel Paul Tibbits, in his specially designed bomber, the *Enola Gay,* dropped the first atomic bomb on the Japanese city of Hiroshima. On August 9th, a second bomb destroyed Nagasaki. Days later, Japan surrendered, ending World War II. The top-secret work begun by FDR almost six years earlier was finally revealed.

(*See Also*: Cambridge Spies; Fuchs, Klaus; Gold, Harry; Greenglass, David; Rosenberg, Julius & Ethel; Bentley, Elizabeth; Philby, Kim; MacLean, Donald)

Maquis, The

The Maquis was the name of the underground civilian resistance group that helped the British and the Americans in resistance activities against the Germans in enemy-held Europe. Their efforts were indispensable in aiding the allied armies at the time of the D-Day invasion of France on June 6, 1944.

The origin of the name Maquis comes from the Corsican word for parcel of "wild, bushy land," prevalent in many parts of seaside France. The

Maquis took shape with the fall of France in June 1940, when German troops overran that country and set up a puppet government under the Vichy regime of Marshal Henri Petain. With the loss of more than 100,000 French troops, large numbers of men from all walks of life in France banded together in loose, untrained, and ill-equipped groups to wage a clandestine war against their German occupiers. They began to call themselves the Armée secrète, or underground army.

The Maquis gained in popularity when the Vichy government called for the forcible use of thousands of men to work in industry and other forms of local commerce. By February 1943, the Vichy government ordered that three yearly details of men were to be called up for mandatory service. In reply to this order, thousands of men failed to report for work and drifted off into the hills and valleys of France to resist the German occupation of their country.

Organized resistance groups were formed in the rugged French and Swiss Alps—the United Movements of Resistance in southern France, and the communist-ruled National Front. Despite their divergent political philosophies, they banded together to fight their common enemy. These resistance groups not only had to fight the highly trained German troops who hunted them down, but also Italian forces, and the hated Vichy police. By the fall of 1943, the Maquis began hit-and-run attacks against the collaborationist French Militia, as well as selected German military targets in France. The Maquis had by now gotten the attention of the British SOE (Special Operations Executive) and to a lesser extent, the American OSS. In both London and Washington, plans to aid the Maquis were put into effect.

By early 1944, the allies estimated that the Maquis numbered close to 50,000 highly motivated, yet untrained and ill-equipped men. In order to rectify the situation, the allies agreed to send "Special Inter-Allied Missions" to work on the ground with the Maquis. Their mission was to turn the Maquis into an efficient paramilitary force under the overall command of military officers in London. Working with these Special Inter-Allied Missions were agents from the SOE, the OSS, and the Free French Service.

They were to "be put at the disposal of the Allied High Command, London, for D-Day operations, a number of self-contained units, located in appropriate sub regions of the Maquis. Such units were comparable to military formations introduced into the country by parachute and hidden until the day when directed to cooperate with an invasion of the Continent by Allied military forces."

It was decided in London that the Maquis were to be broken up into separate regions, and subdivided further into divergent sections. They were all to be linked directly to the London controlling center and given different assignments once the D-Day landings took place.

As the importance of the Maquis grew, a turf war between the OSS and the SOE began as far as who would supply them. The British took the lead in providing large amounts of supplies to the resistance groups, even diverting a large number of cargo planes for that purpose. In the United States, a different view took hold. The Joint Chiefs of Staff were reluctant to provide large numbers of U.S. aircraft to the provisioning effort, deciding instead to use all available planes for bombing runs against German industrial and military targets. With constant pressure being applied by the Free French government in exile of Charles de Gaulle against the United States for not doing enough to provide aid for the Maquis, Bill Donovan sought out Secretary of State Cordell Hull. Hull, fearing a rupture in French-U.S. relations after the war, put pressure on the Joint Chiefs who reluctantly ordered General Eisenhower to furnish the necessary U.S. military equipment. By May 1944, 32 four-engine aircrafts were put in service to aid the Maquis. OSS airdrops sent thousands of rounds of ammunition, sub-machine guns, rifles, pistols, explosives of all sorts, as well as food, clothing and medicine to the Maquis. All this equipment would be needed for the invasion of France.

As D-Day neared, an intricate plan was devised to alert the Maquis to be ready for action. This operation was headed by General Pierre Koenig, the commander of Special Forces Headquarters (SFHQ) under the command of General Dwight Eisenhower The first of these personal messages were sent out over the airwaves on the evening of June 4, 1944, two days before the Normandy landings. The BBC broadcast a series of personal messages each night after the nine o'clock news. Each Maquis unit had its own code messages and they had to listen for their instructions to come in pairs. The first half of the message told each individual group to prepare to carry out their assignment. When they heard their next message, they would carry out their mission: blow up a bridge, attack a certain unit, or kill a certain person. The overall purpose of the Maquis was to disrupt as much as possible the transfer of German troops and tanks to the Normandy area. This was done to great effect as each unit was called up by zones, so as not to alert the ever-watchful Germans into thinking that an organized revolt by the underground was taking place.

In after-action reports to General Eisenhower, it was evident how successful the activities of the Maquis were in blunting the arrival of German troops to the beachhead area. The German 77th Infantry took 13 days to make an ordinary two-day run toward Normandy; the 165th Infantry Division left Lorient on June 6 but did not arrive at Normandy until 10 days later. Maquis fighters took on German divisions in all parts of France, freeing up the tens of thousands of allied troops to make an effective breakout from the Normandy beaches.

During the pre-invasion landings, the Maquis took part in the rescue of an American airman who would later play an historic role in the annals of American flight. On March 5, 1944, an American Flight Officer was shot down in his P-51 over the Bordeaux area of France while making his bombing run. The pilot bailed out and was later rescued by the Maquis. He was given shelter and soon made his way to freedom via Spain, Gibraltar and eventually, to London, three weeks after his crash. The name of the flyer was Charles Yeager. Yeager would be the first man to break the sound barrier as a test pilot in the 1950s.

The role the Maquis played in the pre-Overlord (D-Day) invasion helped ensure the allied victory that would take place less than a year later.

Maskelyne, Jasper

Jasper Maskelyne was an illusionist and a brilliant magician, whose work for British intelligence during World War II turned defeat into victory, single-handedly fooling the Germans by his stealth of hand.

He came from a family of London magicians, thrilling fans of all ages with tricks that left the viewer wondering at the sights being played out before them. His grandfather was John Nevil Maskelyne, a watchmaker by trade, who turned the famous Egyptian Theater in Piccadilly into "England's Home of Mystery." John taught his son Nevil all he knew, and soon the Maskelyne family was the leading magical dynasty in all of England. The family called their show the "Maskelyne Magical Mysteries," which put on illusions and disappearing acts for thousands of their ardent fans. During World War I, Nevil developed a paste that protected British naval gunners' hands from the blast from their guns. Upon Nevil's death in 1926, his son Jasper took on the family responsibilities. He was soon to use his considerable knowledge of magic to help defeat the Germans once war broke out.

He was 38 when the war began, and his age kept him from being accepted into the army. He tried to persuade the military officers he spoke to that illusions and tricks could successfully be perpetrated against the enemy, but they turned a cold shoulder with a firm no. He decided to join the Home Guard, but a long-time friend of his, H. Hendley Lenton, spoke to Prime Minister Churchill about Jasper and his bag of tricks. The Prime Minister asked that Jasper meet with his assistant for scientific affairs, Professor Frederick Lindemann. Over the course of their get together, Jasper persuaded Professor Lindemann that indeed, he could aid the British cause by keeping the enemy off guard by using his professional talent. He was accepted into the army and was sent off for training.

Home for the next few months was the town of Farnham in County Surrey, 40 minutes from London. Jasper joined the Royal Engineers

Camouflage Training and Development Center headed by Colonel Frederick Beddington. Beddington's chief trainer was Major Richard Buckley who turned his magicians into soldiers. In time, Maskelyne and his men would come to be known as the "Magic Gang."

"The Magic Gang" consisted of expert craftsmen in wood design, industrial production, and metal finishing, who could create images that were not there. Using the right shadows, the magicians were able to create figures that made things look different from what they originally were. The work that Maskelyne created was nothing less than imaginative.

His first assignment was to create camouflage for military equipment in the deserts of the Middle East. In order to hide tanks and trucks from the enemy, Jasper used mountains of camel dung, which was mixed with paint to get just the right color. Passing German reconnaissance planes were fooled into mistaking these vehicles from ordinary sand (they also were exempted from the smell).

He next turned his attention to the continued German bombing of Alexandria harbor. He flew a plane over the water to photograph the pattern of lights. He next worked at a nearby beach called Marion Bay, where his craftsmen recreated the light patterns of the harbor. They designed fake ships with sticks and lights creating the illusion of a large number of tall masted ships. He also built small bombs, that when exploded and seen from the air, would replicate explosions going off. During one German air raid, all the real lights at the harbor were turned off and Jasper's men began exploding the fake bombs creating the deception that explosions of unknown origin were taking place below. The German pilots, thinking that their bombs were causing the destruction, dropped their remaining bombs into the sea.

One of Maskelyne's biggest deception operations targeted German General Rommel's desert forces. It was called "The Key to Rebecca." The Magic Gang sought to fool the Germans into selecting routes in the desert that were inhospitable for tanks, trucks and other heavy vehicles. Maskelyne designed a fake map, using material that made it look hundreds of years old showing the various routes through the desert.

This fake map describing the "hard" sections of the desert was placed in the clothing of a British officer who was having an affair with a German woman spy. This unfortunate officer was killed in battle, but not before the Germans found the map on his body. During the battle of El Alamein, the Germans fell for Maskelyne's ruse and their heavy armor became bogged down in the soft sands, suffering severe losses.

Another one of his deception/magical operations concerned the vitally important Suez Canal.

In September 1941, Lieutenant Maskelyne met with an old friend from civilian days, movie set director Major Geoffery Barkas. Major Barkas said that he had a new job for him. He was to "hide" the Suez Canal! The Suez Canal ran one hundred miles in a north-south route right through Egypt. The canal connected the Mediterranean Sea with the Red Sea, saving a thousand miles of ocean from England

This was the most direct route in ferrying British troops to the Middle East. Security was paramount, and the Crown would do whatever it took to protect it from falling into the hands of the enemy. During a tour of the canal he came up with what he thought would be the ideal solution. This involved the use of hundreds of high-powered lights along the canals banks that would "hide" it from approaching German aircraft.

The Magic Gang came up with the idea of subdividing each searchlight into many beacons by using 24 tin reflectors that would fit around the searchlight lenses. These beams would then be sent high into the sky above the canal, making it impossible to be seen by any approaching plane. They further modified the design by creating a reflecting system by which the lights were sent gazing from above in a powerful show of rays.

For the next several weeks, German planes circled the Suez Canal but were unable to penetrate the brilliant light show that Jasper Maskelyne created. As his fame and resourcefulness became known in the enemy camp, an assassination plot was hatched to eliminate him.

After the war ended, Jasper Maskelyne moved to Kenya and joined the police force. He lived there for many years and died in 1973.

Masterman, John

John Masterman was head of the super-secret Twenty Committee of British intelligence during World War II. He also ran the highly successful Double Cross System, which was responsible for the capture and the "turning" of agents that were sent into England by the Germans. Masterman's Double Cross System fed mostly false intelligence (as well as some real information) back to the Abwehr in order to deceive them.

John Cecil Masterman was born in 1891 in England. He taught history at Oxford, was appointed a don, and later, provost at Worcester College. He later served as the vice-chancellor or administrative head of the University. He was a good cricket and tennis player.

In August 1914, he was in Berlin during World War I, as an exchange lecturer. Because of his British nationality, he spent the remainder of the war in an internment camp in Ruhleben. Following the armistice, he returned to England.

When England entered the war, Masterman joined MI-5 and was thrust into some of the most intriguing secret work he could imagine. He was appointed the head of the Double Cross System, a highly detailed operation that captured German agents and turned them into double agents working for British intelligence. It was meant to control information to the Abwehr, break German codes, learn what the enemy's military plans were, and finally, con the enemy with faux British counter plans.

The most important accomplishment of the Double Cross System was to confuse the Germans about the allied invasion of France at Normandy on June 6, 1944. The allies fooled the enemy into believing that the invasion was to take place at the Pas de Calais area of France by leaking false reports. Masterman's Double Cross System was shrouded in secrecy during the war, known only to those who participated in it.

After the war ended, Masterman sat down and wrote a memoir about his wartime experiences. One hundred and twenty five copies were printed. Upon completion, 100 copies of the manuscript were destroyed. Masterman kept one copy for himself, and the rest went to the branches of British intelligence and government ministries whose job it was to ferret out classified material that should not see the light of day. For over 20 years, MI-5, MI-6, and the other intelligence services agreed that Masterman's book should never be published—as there were too many secrets that shouldn't be revealed.

His case was taken to Roger Hollis, Director General of MI-5 (in 1970), as well as then Prime Minister Alex Douglas-Home. Once again, they turned Masterman down. Undeterred, John Masterman decided to offer his book to Yale University Press, who finally agreed to buy it. The book, *The Double Cross System in the War of 1939-1945*, soon became a nationwide bestseller.

As the book neared its publication date in the United States, the British government accused Masterman of violating the Official Secrets Act and threatened to sue. With heavy pressure from Masterman's publisher and other historians, they finally relented. In a compromise with the British government, Masterman agreed to delete 60 pages of text that the official censors thought highly classified material, some 30 years after the war.

Masterman's *Double Cross System in the War of 1939-45* was considered by historians of military intelligence to be the seminal work on the role of counterintelligence in warfare.

In his review of the book, the noted British military historian Hugh Trevor-Roper, himself a veteran of the British code-breaking operations during the war, wrote, "…many of us wondered in 1945, whether counterespionage is not the best method of espionage. For German spies were not only a means of deceiving the enemy about our intentions, they were also a means of discovering his own."

John Masterman died quietly at age 86 in 1977.

(*See Also*: Double Cross System; Twenty Committee)

Mayer, Fred

Fred Mayer was a sergeant in the U.S. Army who worked as an agent for the OSS in a highly dangerous mission called Operation Greenup. The purpose of Greenup was to penetrate Austria at Innsbruck, gather intelligence on German strength near the Brenner Pass and the possible use by the Nazis of a redoubt, high in the Alps.

The Mayers originally came from the German city of Freiburg. Fred's father served in the army in World War I but left for America in 1938, fearing that their Jewish heritage would be a detriment under the Nazis.

They settled in Brooklyn, New York, where Fred secured a job in a Ford Motor plant. When the United States entered the war, he was accepted into the army and soon transferred to the OSS due to his language skills and German background. He was sent to Bari, Italy, the home of a large OSS detachment, which had responsibility for operations in Italy and France. In time, Fred Mayer was teamed up with Hans Wynberg, a Dutch Jew. Together, they made up the Greenup Mission. A trainer from the OSS prepared them for the field.

Working with the Fifteenth Air Force, the OSS made a detailed plan using the Mayer-Wynberg team. They were to parachute into Innsbruck, near the Brenner Pass, and report on train movements, as well as the locations of German troops, and military supplies. Innsbruck was the jumping-off point for supplies going to German General Kesselring's troops in Italy.

Fred Mayer was head of the mission, while Hans Wynberg served as his radioman. Another man was added to the team, Franz Weber, a lieutenant who previously served in the Wehrmacht's Forty-Fifth Infantry Division, and who now resided in an American POW camp. Weber was from the Innsbruck area and knew the countryside well.

The trio took their training at a separated area of the OSS base at Bari. By February 1945, they had completed their preparations and were waiting for the go signal. For the Greeunup team, this was a most dangerous mission. Their OSS superiors explained to them that previous operations into Austria all ended in disaster. The first mission into Austria, called Orchid, resulted in the deaths of two of its agents. Other missions originating from Czechoslovakia likewise proved fatal. Mayer vowed that this time, things would be different.

Later that month, the Greenup team boarded a B-24 bomber headed for Austria. High over the Austrian Alps, they parachuted near a frozen lake at an altitude of 10,200 feet. Using a makeshift sled, along with their radios and supplies, they took a treacherous run down the mountain. After a grueling trip, they found shelter in a mountain inn used by skiers. Passing themselves off as lost German soldiers, they sought and received assistance from the locals, who helped them down the mountain.

They sought protection at the home of a relative of Franz Weber, while they made a reconnaissance of the area. Using information gleaned from local sympathizers, the Greenup team radioed back to Bari news of shortages in a plant that produced Messerschmitt airplanes. At this point in the mission, Franz Weber's role as their guide to the Innsbruck area ended, and he effectively left the mission. Fred Mayer would now go by himself to Innsbruck. Under the guise of a wounded lieutenant in the 106th High Alpine Troops, he arrived in the city. Mayer's first contact was with a local policeman named Alios Kuen. Kuen, while officially working for the German military, was anti-Nazi and clandestinely helped Mayer carry out his work. Kuen put Mayer in touch with resistance leaders who provided him with high-grade intelligence bearing on German train traffic, the number of fighter planes at the Innsbruck airfield, and more importantly, the fact that the Italian dictator Benito Mussolini was staying at a local hotel. Mayer also learned that Henrich Himmler had arrived in the city. All this was radioed back to London. In time, Mayer would have over a thousand resistance fighters in the surrounding area under his command.

Using the intelligence gleaned from Mayer's work, the U.S. Fifteenth Air Force pounded the rail line running across the Brenner Pass, destroying a fully loaded German convoy.

Fred Mayer, using false papers that listed him as a Frenchman, got a job as an electrician in a local radio factory. After months of living on the edge, Mayer's luck ran out. The Gestapo had arrested a black marketer named Leo. Under interrogation, he told of knowing a man who headed an allied spy ring. That man was Fred Mayer. Mayer knew Leo but paid little attention to him. Mayer was put under Gestapo interrogation but stuck to his story of being a French laborer. He was beaten and subjected to harsh treatment. Just when Mayer thought he had run out of time, an unexpected event turned everything around.

The man in charge of Mayer's interrogation was Franz Hofer, the Nazi party leader in charge of the Tirol-Vorarlberg province where Mayer was being held. Hofer reported directly to Martin Bormann, Hitler's deputy, as well as the Führer himself. Hofer was tired of the war and believed defeat was just around the corner. He approached Mayer about connecting with the OSS to secretly negotiate surrendering his region. Mayer accepted. Mayer was detained while he waited for word from the OSS.

On May 3, 1945, elements of the U.S. 103rd Infantry Division, Seventh Army, entered the outskirts of Innsbruck. Days later, Innsbruck surrendered, obviating Hofer's surrender offer. Hofer was picked up by a U.S. Army intelligence team, but fled before he could be interrogated.

Following the capture of the city, Fred Mayer and Hans Wynberg were reassigned. Both men were promoted to the rank of second lieutenant. For his bravery in Operation Greenup, Fred Mayer was recommended for the highest award the U.S. could give: the Congressional Medal of Honor.

Menzies, Stewart

Stewart Menzies was born on January 30, 1890, in London. His parents were John Graham Menzies and Susannah West. He attended the famous Sandhurst Military Academy and joined the army after graduation. He served in France during World War I as a member of the Grenadier Guards, attaining the rank of Captain. During the war he was picked to be head of counterintelligence for the British Expeditionary Force in France. It was during this time period that the young Captain Menzies took notice of one of his German counterparts, Captain Lieutenant Wilhelm Canaris. Canaris was then working as a spy in Spain. His job was to ferment revolution among the desert tribesmen of North Africa. Two decades later, both men were to head each country's intelligence services.

In the interwar years, Menzies stayed in the army as a member of the Life Guards from 1910 until 1939. In 1923, he was appointed as the deputy to Sir Hugh Sinclair, the head of MI-6 until the latter's death in 1939. That year, he was appointed as "C," the new head of that super-secret organization. Menzies worked closely with then British Prime Minister Chamberlain and later with Prime Minister Winston Churchill, who had an avid interest in anything relating to secret work.

One of Menzies's top priorities was the breaking of the German codes, and he took an active role in the development of the Government Code and Cipher School (GC&CS), which was located at Bletchley Park. It was from this location that British (and later American cryptographers) worked to break the German Enigma code which proved instrumental in the winning of the war.

In July 1940, William Donovan, then representing President Roosevelt, arrived in England for talks with members of the British intelligence community. For a number of months, both the United States and England made a secret agreement to share each other's intelligence pie. Donovan came to London to learn to run a world-class intelligence operation. One of the first men Donovan met with was Stewart Menzies, "C."

Menzies met Donovan at his office at 52 Broadway, right across from St.. James Park. The British had hundreds of years of experience in the spy business, having founded their secret service under the reign of Queen Elizabeth I in the 16th century. Menzies's SIS carried out two distinct functions: the gathering of information and counterespionage operations outside of England.

Menzies took Donovan under his wing, imparting to him all of England's most valuable secrets, including the operations at Bletchley Park and the existence of Ultra, the means by which the British broke and read most of the German military codes. Upon his return to Washington, Donovan reported to FDR on his successful trip. A few months later, Donovan would be promoted to head the United States's first national intelligence agency: the OSS, Office of Strategic Services.

Shortly after the U.S. entered the war, Stewart Menzies took unprecedented actions to share Britain's most important counterintelligence with Donovan's OSS. On the advise of William Stephenson, who served as the Passport Officer in the United States, Menzies allowed Donovan's representative to see what came to be known as "ISOS," Intelligence Service, Oliver Strachey. Strachey was the head of the enemy intelligence communication branch at Bletchley Park.

The man slated to be Donovan's voice was George Bowden, a tax lawyer before entering the OSS. Bowden met in London with Major Felix Cowgill, then head of the counterespionage section of the SIS. Bowden spent three months in London, being briefed on all ISOS missions, including reading the messages sent to Abwehr agents (and deciphered by Ultra), and instructions from the German SD, or Sicherheitisdienst. The ISOS material was an immense help in Donovan's efforts to start up his OSS.

In another effort to aid the Americans, Menzies, with Churchill's approval, allowed certain hand-picked OSS officers from their X-2 branch to see the ISOS's summaries, most of them coming from Section V, the counterespionage branch of the British SIS. These messages were sent to New York, where they were studied and filed. Menzies also provided OSS access to its highly secretive XX Committee, the branch that ran German double agents.

At the end of 1940, Menzies addressed his attention once more to establishing clandestine contacts with his opposite number in German intelligence, Admiral Canaris. Through his network of agents inside Germany and elsewhere, Menzies knew that Canaris, as well as a number of other highly placed military men were looking for a way out of the war. Menzies had a hand in running the double cross system and one of the men whom he personally recruited was a flamboyant Yugoslav playboy named Dusan "Dusko" Popov. Popov was sent by Canaris to set up an espionage unit in England, but he had a change of heart and reported his situation to an MI-6 officer in Belgrade. Popov offered to work for the British, and he was accepted into the fold.

According to the popular accounts, Menzies met with Popov in December 1940, at which time Menzies asked him if he could get information on Canaris, as well as on his senior officers. Writing later of his conference with Menzies, Popov related what happened. Menzies told the Yugoslav agent that "You have the makings of a very good spy, except that you don't obey orders. You had better learn or you will be a very dead spy." Menzies asked Popov to seek information about Canaris's top aides, Hans Dohnanyi and Hans Oster. Dohnanyi was an Abwehr officer. He was part of the secret network that plotted against Hitler. Hans Oster was deputy chief of the Abwehr.

Popov wrote that "Menzies was contemplating a dialogue with Canaris or those close to him with a view to ousting Hitler. All information you pick up is to come directly to me with no intermediary."

Popov was not the only link to Abwehr headquarters. Thanks to the codebreakers at Bletchley Park, ISOS was able to read all the traffic originating at Canaris's office, offering Menzies a foolproof look inside the Abwehr chief's state of mind.

In 1942, Canaris wanted desperately to arrange a secret meeting with Menzies. He sent feelers to Menzies asking if Portugal would be a good spot for a rendezvous. Menzies asked permission of Britain's Foreign Secretary, Anthony Eden, but his request was shot down. Eden said that if Stalin ever found out that the British were covertly meeting with Canaris, this would further anger the Russian leader into thinking that the British were trying to arrange a separate peace with Germany at the expense of Russia.

The historical record is ripe with tidbits of information leading up to a possible covert encounter between the two spy chiefs. Canaris was in Spain during the beginning of the war and "indicated a willingness to treat with us; he would even welcome a meeting with his opposite number, 'C' (Menzies)."

One possible answer as to why Eden refused to allow Menzies to meet with Canaris is the fact that Kim Philby, a double agent working for the Russians, and a top member of MI-6, objected to any such get-together.

Menzies remained in his post until the war ended. However, his stature as Britain's most respected intelligence head suffered a mighty blow with the post-war defections of Guy Burgess, Donald MacLean, and later, Kim Philby, to the Russians. He resigned following the incidents and retired. He died on May 29, 1968, at age 78.

(*See Also*: Abwehr; Donovan, William; Popov, Dusan; Canaris, Wilhelm; Philby, Kim)

Midway, Battle of

The Battle of Midway was the turning point in the war against the Japanese in the Pacific. The battle put an end to Japanese military dominance in the region and could not have been won save for the use of U.S. Navy cryptologists in breaking the Japanese codes.

The code that U.S. analysts broke was called Purple, a system that was first perfected in the late 1930s. Purple was a machine cipher, dubbed by the Japanese as "Alphabetical Typewriter 2597." The Purple machine changed over plain text into a code known only to the receiver. This information was then translated into the Japanese language.

U.S. Army cryptographers broke the Purple code mainly through the efforts of William Friedman of the army's Signal Intelligence Service and Frank Rowlett of the navy. Through arduous work, America built its first Purple machine in 1940. This enormous intelligence feat enabled U.S. military codebreakers to read all of the Japanese messages and get a head start on their strategy.

The genesis of the Japanese plans to attack Midway Island followed the successful raid on Pearl Harbor. In that assault, the Japanese failed to destroy the aircraft carriers that were out at sea. In order to control the entire Pacific area, the American carriers had to be dealt with. Their plan was to lure the American fleet out into the open Pacific and deal it a crippling blow. If Midway was taken, it would then be a springboard for further attacks against Hawaii, and eventually, the West Coast of the United States.

In order to carry out this plan, the Japanese military decided on a diversionary invasion of the Aleutian Islands. They believed that they had enough military assets to take on two large-scale operations and still be able to defeat the U.S. Navy. In that belief, they were wrong. The Japanese navy allotted eight of their main aircraft carriers to the Midway-Aleutian campaign. As the large assault force left their home ports in separate waves from May 25-28, 1942, U.S. intercept stations in Hawaii and other locations kept a steady watch on their progress across the Pacific. Station Hypo was able to record that almost all of the destroyers that made up the Combined Fleet were heading to the mid-Pacific-in a line towards Midway. U.S. intercepts also discovered that the Japanese Second Fleet were heading for anchorages at Saipan.

Joseph Rochefort, the head of the Code and Signal Section of the Office of Naval Intelligence, who had been in charge of monitoring the signals emanating from the Japanese fleet, came up with a potentially huge intercept. He deciphered a phrase in Japanese with the words, "koryaku butai." This meant "invasion force" and was followed by the geographic mark, "AF." But what was "AF"? Two further intercepts relating to "AF" were deciphered by Rochefort's team, going to the Japanese Second Fleet, air units. The first went to the "AF occupation force, which was ordered to proceed direct to the Saipan-Guam area and wait for the forthcoming campaign." The second message told another unit, "To load its base equipment and ground crews and advance to AF." Rochefort was convinced that the designator "AF' was Midway. He now had to convince his superiors in Washington that he was correct.

Rochefort did not have to persuade Admiral Chester Nimitz, the commander of U.S. forces in the Pacific that "AF" was Midway. However, his arguments met resistance among the top navy brass who believed that the attack would center on Johnston Island, which was given the designator of AG. Rochefort came into contention over "AF" with Commander John Redman, who worked in the navy's code breaking section called OP-20-G. Commander Redman accused Rochefort of getting into areas of information recovery which was outside his province.

The argument over "AF" was finally put to rest with a suggestion made by Commodore W. J. Holmes. Holmes suggested that the American commander at Midway send a message in an open channel which they, the Japanese, could monitor, reporting that the island's water-processing unit had broken down, and that fresh water was badly needed. Holmes's counsel was taken with decisive results.

As expected, the Japanese radio analysts picked up the Midway water account saying that there was a shortage of water at "AF." This was all that the listening American analysts needed to know.

With this badly needed information in hand, Admiral Nimitz began to position his navy forces to intercept the oncoming Japanese fleet. He sent three aircraft carriers, some 350 miles from Midway, to prepare for the attack. On June 4, 1942, the Japanese took the bait, losing four carriers and a cruiser to a watery grave, hit by U.S. torpedo planes. U.S. aircraft destroyed more than 250 Japanese planes, and severely damaged another carrier. Among the Japanese carriers that were fatally hit were the *Akagi*, *Kaga* and *Soryu*. The U.S. Navy lost one of its top-of-the-line carriers, the *Yorktown*.

The decisive American victory at Midway effectively ended Japanese hegemony in the Pacific, and paved the way for the retaking of the Philippines and other islands.

Without the efforts of the navy's cryptanalysis, the success of Midway would never have taken place.

(*See Also*: Pearl Harbor Attack; Hypo, Station; Rochefort, Joseph; Magic)

MIS-X

In addition to the Manhattan Project, America's most highly guarded secret was an organization responsible for the escape and evasion of the thousands of allied POWs held in German camps, MIS-X. MIS-X was so hidden under wraps that following the war, all records of its existence were destroyed. By the end of the war, MIS-X successfully enabled thousands of prisoners to escape from harsh, and sometimes brutal imprisonment, using the most ingenious means possible.

MIS-X

The United States's only intelligence arm that was in existence at the time of the Pearl Harbor attack was the Military Intelligence Division, a 200-man attaché network assigned to the various U.S. embassies around the world. With America's entry into the war, the responsibilities of MIS-Y were greatly expanded, including a special unit called the Prisoner of War Branch. The POW Branch was originally tasked to provide files on American POWs held by the enemy. One of its sub-branches was a little-known and highly classified group called Military Intelligence Service Y, or MIS-Y. Its main function was to administer POW camps in the United States, mostly for German prisoners who were transferred to this country for interrogation.

The man appointed to supervise MIS-Y was Colonel Russell Sweet. Sweet's boss was Colonel Catesby Jones, commander of the Prisoner of War Branch. Jones served in World War I and was a descendant of the commander of the Civil War frigate *Merrimack*. Jones approved Sweet's plans for MIS-Y and did all he could to break the red tape needed to organize the operation.

Sweet's first assignment was the recruitment of skilled linguists from the army who would be the backbone of the new department. His second need was to find a suitable location. After much painstaking research, a site was found near the Potomac River on 80 acres of land that had once served as a Civil War base. The name of the place was called Fort Hunt. Fort Hunt was used by the town of Alexandria, Virginia, as a popular hideout for campers and young couples. The land was owned by the Interior Department, but Sweet managed to get the fort transferred to the army's use. Fort Hunt would serve as the main compound for the interrogation of enemy prisoners and as a training location for the cadre of U.S. soldiers who were to be sent into the POW camps to retrieve allied captives.

Fort Hunt began its operations in March 1942 under the leadership of Colonel John Walker. Colonel Walker turned Fort Hunt into a bristling military outpost, ringed with barbed wire fences, and patrolling MPs. Among the subterranean sections inside Fort Hunt was a covert unit called MIS-X, the escape and evasion department of the army.

The American MIS-X took its roots from the highly successful British MI-9 escape and evasion organization whose job it was to produce escape devices and letter codes to help liberate British POWs. MI-9 used ordinary looking devices to hide weapons such as shaving foam, razor blades, soap, in hiding guns, small knives, local currency, which were clandestinely smuggled into POW camps by newly captured soldiers.

The man put in charge of Britain's Prisoner of War Branch was Brigadier Norman Crockatt. Crockatt met with U.S. Major General Carl Spaatz, commander of the Army Eighth Air Force. Brigadier Crockatt explained how

MI-9 worked, and General Spaatz soon recognized that the U.S. too needed such a capability. By 1942, MI-9 had established a sophisticated network of dummy humanitarian agencies supplying British POWs with the tools needed for their escape. Letter codes were in use between the RAF flyers and those internees. Before 1943, almost 750 downed airmen and others were success-fully liberated from enemy incarceration.

General Spaatz got word back to Washington concerning MI-9 and told General of the Army George Marshall about what he learned. General Marshall, however, took no stock in MI-9's success and shelved the project for the U.S. Spaatz, not to be deterred, sought an audience with Secretary of War Henry Stimson, who, after listening to what General Spaatz had to say, paved the way for what was to become MIS-X.

At Fort Hunt, the table of contents of what MIS-X would become was put in place. Its job was to 1) teach ground-force intelligence officers, who would in turn instruct air crews on evasion techniques in downed enemy ter-ritory, 2) the use of codes among downed airmen, 3) the proper behavior after one's capture, 4) to retrieve as much information as possible from newly freed U.S. POWs, 5) the carrying out of secret codes and instructions be-tween themselves and POWs, 6) liaison with members of MI-9, whenever possible.

Secretary Stimson ordered that no money allocated to MIS-X would be permitted to see the light of day and "that necessary funds for execution of the functions of this section be provided from sources under the control of the Secretary of War or from such other sources, other than routine channels, as may be available." A token payment of $25,000 from his department's funds was made available to start up MIS-X.

The officer appointed to be in overall command of MIS-X at Fort Hunt was Lieutenant Commander Robley Winfrey. Before the war began, Robley Winfrey was a professor of civil engineering at Iowa State University. For five months, Winfrey lived in England learning the craft of escape and evasion. By October 1942, he was ready to put MIS-X into active service.

In the recruitment of skilled craftsmen and officers into MIS-X, no men-tion of Fort Hunt was ever divulged. Anyone coming into the base identified it as "1142," the Post Office Box number in nearby Alexandria, Virginia, where all mail was to be sent. Another important center of activity at 1142 was "The Creamery." "The Creamery" was MIS-X's workshop where skilled craftsmen used ordinary daily devices to hide escape and evasion materials that were to be smuggled into POW camps.

According to the Geneva Conventions, POWs were allowed to receive humanitarian packages from the Red Cross, including food and other basic needs for survival. MIS-X did not allow the Red Cross to be its secret conduit into the POW camps. Instead, they organized covert humanitarian organizations run by the army such as the War Prisoners Benefit Foundation and Servicemen's Relief which were used to send in legitimate, as well as "loaded" items.

In "The Creamery," MIS-X artisans used Ping-Pong rackets in which maps were inserted . Small saws were put inside shaving-brush handles, maps were hidden in shoe brushes. Such popular board games as Monopoly contained counterfeit passports, visas, and forged German travel permits.

MIS-X also received the cooperation of some of the biggest American corporations to aid in this effort. For example, the R.J. Reynolds Tobacco Company loaded cigarette packs with maps, and Deutsche marks, the Gillette Company designed thousands of specially crafted razor handles in which escape related materials were hidden. The Scoville Company, located in Waterbury, Connecticut, made millions of hollow uniform buttons with tops that unscrewed to unveil small compasses. The U.S. Playing Card Company of Cincinnati put in false backs into cards which contained maps of escape routes across the country. (After the war, most of these companies destroyed all records of their secret work for MIS-X.)

MIS-X instructed all imprisoned soldiers to resist captivity as much as possible. No longer were they to be passive inhabitants, but were to take all necessary measures to escape and hinder their captors. This was accomplished to a certain extent with the arrival of new allied POWs. These men brought in with them the necessary tools to allow a POW to send coded messages inside their regular mail to loved ones in the United States. At the Creamery, thousands of letters were sent to the POWs, using different types of stationery which included coded instructions, enclosing information on how to organize escape routes, as well as instructions from home.

Certain pilots were designated as a CU or code user. If a CU was captured, he was to immediately contact the highest-ranking officer in the camp and tell him that he had the means to aid in their getaway. The CU would write an ordinary letter home, telling his family and friends of his condition. But hidden in the message was a coded statement telling about their plans for escape, and the health of the POWs. When these letters arrived in the U.S., they were rerouted to MIS-X headquarters, where the secret notations were read. This program worked so well that by the end of the war, 7,723 men were used as CUs, and they were able to communicate with POWs in every German internment camp. After reading these secret messages, the letters were resealed and put back into the U.S. mail system.

In order to fool the Gestapo which opened all packages and letters coming into the POW camps, workers at Fort Hood devised an ingenious plan to ensure the safety of the material being sent to prisoners. All the parcels were made up of different types of cardboard, using different glues, string, labels, and tape. MIS-X executive officers also met with Postmaster James Farley to get his approval for shipping "loaded" parcels with different post markings. All mailbags originating from MIS-X were stamped with a special tag and then placed in various locations in the U.S. for insertion into the mail system.

The POWs too had their own chain of command and responsibilities concerning possible escape and evasion. Prisoners were given certain jobs such as tunneling, codes, the handling of maps, and most important of all, the security of the radios that were smuggled in. Each team had no knowledge of what the other was doing. The captives also used the extra food and utensils legally brought into the camps to barter with their guards for extra food and other comforts.

MIS-X had its most ambitious escape operation at the infamous German POW camp called Stalag Luft 111. Stalag Luft 111 was located 80 miles from Berlin and housed primarily all allied air POWs. They were guarded by a detachment of Luftwaffe (German air corps) troops. The Wehrmacht (German infantry) would oversee all other allied POWs. By March 1942, Stalag Luft 111 was divided into two separate compounds: the East where 2,000 British POWs were located, and a North area, used to house American airmen, which was completed in January 1943.

Hundreds of parcels containing tunneling equipment were sent to the POWs. In time, three huge tunnels were secretly built in the North Compound, nicknamed "Tom, Dick and Harry." During the night of March 23-24, 1943, 76 POWs crawled 335 feet through "Harry" to freedom. Unfortunately, only three of them actually made it past German guards. In reprisal, 50 of the escapees were executed. The popular film, *The Great Escape*, was based on this incident.

In the analysis of secret warfare, MIS-X was a resounding success. From 1942 to the end of the war, more than 7,500 American POWs escaped from their internment camps.

With the ending of the war, the entire MIS-X organization was permanently closed down, its records destroyed, the buildings at Fort Hunt dismantled, its participants asked not to speak of what they had seen or done. MIS-X, hidden from the public throughout the war, made a huge contribution of saving the lives of hundreds of brave men who probably would have met a harsh fate.

(Research Note: Research materials concerning Stalag Luft 111, and photographs relating to certain aspects of MIS-X can be found at the Air Force Academy Library in Colorado Springs, as well as the Washington National Records Center in Suitland, Maryland.)

Montgomery's Double (Operation Cooperhead)

As the date for the D-Day invasion neared, it was imperative that the Germans did not learn the exact location or date of the strike. A series of elaborate deception operations were put in place to lead the Nazis off the right track. One of the most ingenious, and rather lighthearted schemes revolved around substituting a double to pose as Britain's General Bernard Montgomery.

The man chosen to act as General Montgomery's substitute was Lieutenant M.E. Clifton James, of the Royal Army Pay Corps. Lieutenant Clifton James had been a stage actor for 25 years before joining the army. He had no intelligence training, but he did have one startling advantage for his new role—he was a dead ringer for General Montgomery.

In the early spring of 1944, Lieutenant James received a phone call at his office in Leicester, England, from Colonel David Niven of the British Armies Kinematograph section (motion picture unit). (David Niven was a well-known film star.) Colonel Niven asked to see Lieutenant James, and he complied without hesitation. Colonel Niven told him a most incredible story. He said that MI-5, the army intelligence section, had a vitally important job for him. He was to play the double of General Montgomery.

Colonel Niven told Lieutenant James about the imminent D-Day invasion and said that in order to fool the Germans about where the invasion was to take place, it was necessary to put General Montgomery in another location, away from the real objective: Normandy.

For the next several days, Lieutenant James was assigned to Montgomery's staff, traveling with him as he made his daily inspection trips in preparation for the invasion. Lieutenant James observed the general up close, imitating his every move, anticipating what he would do next. He was given a private meeting with the general who explained what the impostor's role would be and wished him success.

On a bright May day, Lieutenant James, now masquerading as General Montgomery, left England by plane, bound for his first stop, Gibraltar. As he deplaned at the Rock, he was met by a Brigadier Haywood and Captain Moore, his two personal aides during the deception operation. He was driven to the governor's house along a route lined with cheering and flag waving residents of the Rock. There, he had a conference with the governor, Sir Ralph Eastwood, who greeted his "old friend" warmly.

Shortly thereafter, Sir Ralph and "General Montgomery" took a stroll in the gardens behind the mansion. There, they were to meet with two Spaniards posing as prospective buyers of ancient Moroccan carpets. In due course, the duo met, and spoke briefly with Governor Eastwood and the general. The two Spaniards, it turned out, were German agents, "made" by British intelligence and allowed access to the governor's residence. During Lieutenant James's short-term stay on Gibraltar, no less than four Abwehr agents followed him around the Rock. Within hours of their meeting with General Montgomery, news of his arrival at Gibraltar was at Abwehr headquarters in Madrid.

"Montgomery's" next stop was Algiers where the rumor mill was ablaze with leaks that an allied landing force would possibly be sent to southern France. Among the crowd waiting to see the general were a number of Vichy French agents, as well as two Italian spies, working for the Germans.

For the next several days, "Montgomery" held conferences, took in the local sites, and made himself accessible to as many people as he could, among them, a number of German spies.

Just days before the Normandy invasion, Lieutenant James was hustled out of Algiers and was returned to Cairo. There, he witnessed the final assault on Hitler's Europe, and put on his own lieutenant's uniform.

Lieutenant James's deception was a success, as General Rommel's armored divisions never made it to the Normandy beaches, thus allowing a successful landing.

Later, Clifton James was to learn that when news of "General Montgomery's" planned arrival in Algiers reached the German generals, orders were given to have his plane shot down. Other plans called for his assassination. In one of the ironies of the war, Adolf Hitler himself canceled the Montgomery assassination plan.

Morde, Theodore/von Papen, Franz

Theodore Morde was an OSS agent who devised a bold plan to meet with the German Ambassador to Turkey, Franz von Papen, in order to overthrow the regime of Hitler and end the war.

In July 1943, Theodore Morde was a 32-year-old OSS officer then serving in Cairo. He began his intelligence work with the U.S. Military Intelligence, the COI (Coordinator of Information, the forerunner of the OSS), and finally, the Office of War Information. He was a graduate of Brown University, an explorer and a journalist, then working for the *Readers Digest* in Cairo. It is not known under what capacity Morde took on his task, either as a freelance diplomat or under the direction of the OSS.

While in Cairo, Morde contacted Colonel Gustav Guenther, then OSS Station Chief in that old Egyptian city. What Morde broached to Colonel Guenther was nothing but spectacular. He wanted an introduction to the German Ambassador to Turkey, Franz von Papen. Morde would try to persuade the ambassador to aid the U.S. in overthrowing Adolf Hitler from power and end the war. Morde further said that if this plan succeeded, then Hitler and his top aides, Himmler, Goebbels, and Goering, would be handed over to the U.S. for trial.

Morde told Colonel Guenther that he had done a considerable amount of research on Franz von Papen and realized that he was not a Nazi sympathizer, but someone whom the allies could covertly work with.

Franz von Papen had once served as a member of the German General Staff and was a member of the Catholic Church. He worked for the Catholic Center Party in the old Prussian Parliament, and was appointed to the post of chancellor of Germany by President Paul von Hindenburg with the task of stopping a rising Adolf Hitler from taking over power in Germany. During Hitler's power struggle, von Papen was unable to organize an effective political resistance movement against Hitler, who ultimately seized the reigns of power in Berlin. Hitler had even planned von Papen's death, but he narrowly escaped due to warnings by his close allies inside the government.

Morde met with OSS Chief Gunther who pulled a lot of very important strings in order to get him across the normally closed borders from Cairo to Turkey. Morde even met with FDR's special representative to China, General Patrick Hurley. Hurley ordered that OSS Cairo cut the red tape and get Morde's traveling orders and special permits for his trip to Turkey.

Morde arrived in Istanbul in the first week of October 1943 by rail and was met there by OSS Ankara representative, Lanning McFarland. Reluctantly, McFarland agreed to put Morde in touch with another man who could introduce him to the ambassador, Archibald Coleman. Coleman did not trust Morde and demanded to know who sent him. When Morde said he was sent by the president and General Hurley, no further questions were asked. Coleman was further stunned by the terms of the proposed German surrender that Morde gave him. Coleman made contact with members of his underground chain of intermediaries who finally put him in touch with Alexander Rustow, an economist and friend of von Papen. Rustow was able to make the secret arrangements for Morde's audience with von Papen.

When the two men finally got down to business, Morde told von Papen that he was on a "highly secret and important mission from the United States." He said that he had no connections with the American Embassy, nor was he an intelligence agent (a lie). He did say that he had a proposal to discuss with him which he believed the ambassador might be interested in pursuing. Morde then gave von Papen a magnifying glass and a tiny piece of microfilm which the ambassador began to read. What Morde gave von Papen were surrender terms offered by the Americans.

Among them were, "Recognition of the principle that Germany shall dominate the politics, industry, and agriculture of Continental Europe, Germany, U.S.A., and Great Britain shall be the "Big Three Powers." Germany on Continental Europe, U.S.A. on the American Continent and in

China, Great Britain overseas generally in Africa, Germany NOT to interfere with allied action against Japan, Lend Lease and direct aid to Russia to cease, provided Germany does not help Japan against Russia or against allies, and U.S.A. and Great Britain to guarantee that Russia never will invade an inch of German territory, further, to aid Germany by force of arms if necessary in preventing Russia from interfering commercially, politically, or industrially in the new post-war Europe."

After von Papen digested this information, Morde went further. He said that the American people had no animosity toward the German people, but hated Hitler and his henchmen for what they had done in bringing ruin to their country. He further told von Papen that in order for the war to end, that Germany had to "clean their own house, to eliminate Hitler, Goebbels, Goering, and Himmler and the rest of the criminals who had brought Germany to the state she was now in."

He told the ambassador that if "he knew of any possible way to hasten the fall of Hitler, he could count on every assistance from America." Morde also related that the United States was interested in either the capture or death of Hitler." Morde then asked von Papen if he clearly understood to what he referred, and he said *yes*.

Von Papen said that in his opinion, the American air raids against Germany were counterproductive and would only hasten the advent of communism in Germany. He also warned Morde that someday America and England might find that the Nazis and Russia might sign a separate peace.

As Morde closed the meeting, von Papen said, "You cannot realize how seriously affected I am by this talk with you. A man in my position has a great weight to carry and many troubles. I will think of what you have said to me and will try to give you an answer to take back with you to America." They agreed to meet again the next day.

Their October 6, 1943, conference got off to another good start. Von Papen said he wanted a post-war Germany to be economically and politically viable, that the Polish borders should revert to the 1914 frontiers, and admitted that the majority of the German people knew the war was unwinnable.

Toward the end of their conference, Morde again got down to business. He told his guest that only if Hitler was removed would America consider discussing a peace with Germany. "I told him bluntly that I was there to ask that he bring this about."

Von Papen responded by saying that he was in a dangerous personal situation, that an attempt had recently been made on his life. He said that any overthrow of Hitler had to come from within, but that he thought it could be accomplished. Von Papen bluntly told Morde that if Hitler was overthrown that "he must have something to offer to those friends, something definite and solid and based on a sacred understanding." He wanted assurances from Morde, of which he couldn't approve, of something other than an unconditional surrender of Germany. Morde asked for another meeting in the near future but it never took place.

Morde returned to Cairo and then flew to Washington to report on his meetings with von Papen. He met with FDR's top assistant, Edwin "Pa" Watson, but never had a requested face-to-face meeting with the president. Robert E. Sherwood, one of Donovan's most trusted advisors, and a confidant of the president's, told the commander-in-chief that Morde's passport should be taken away and recommended that no further action should be taken regarding Morde's meeting with von Papen.

The Morde affair still had many unanswered questions. Did FDR have advanced knowledge of Morde's trip to see von Papen? Who cut the travel documents for Morde to make the long, dangerous journey from Cairo to Turkey, when "civilians" were restricted in making such private trips? Who gave OSS Cairo instructions to cooperate fully with Morde's advanced plans? Who gave Patrick Hurley, FDR's intimate, instructions to let Morde proceed? What role did William Donovan play, if any, in the affair?

The Morde-von Papen discussions never bore fruit, but it did show just how many high-ranking Germans were ready to end the war, and end the bloodshed being unleashed on their country.

Morros, Boris

During the 1930s, the Soviet Union ran a well-organized espionage operation in the United States, infiltrating both the American government, as well as some of its major industries. One man well connected with both worlds was Boris Morros, who was a double agent for the FBI.

Boris Morros was born in St. Petersburg, Russia in 1895. He left for America in 1922 and began a promising musical career. He made his way to Hollywood where, for the next 16 years, he would work as a producer and music director for Paramount Studios. Among the motion pictures to his credit were *Flying Deuces,* which starred Laurel and Hardy, and *Second Chorus* with Paulette Goddard and Fred Astaire.

The Russian intelligence services in America knew of Boris Morros, because of his popularity among the Hollywood set as well as his Russian background. In later years, Morros would relate that he began his work for the Soviet Union in order to ensure that his family back in Russia would be given the food packages he was sending to them.

Morros was officially recruited in 1934 at the Soviet consulate in New York. Morros's father was in the United States at that time, and his son sought help in aiding his father's return home. Morros sought the aid of Peter Gutzeit, a Soviet undercover agent, in using diplomatic means to get his father back to the Soviet Union.

The Soviet consulate agreed, but on one condition. Morros would use his considerable influence in Hollywood to introduce certain NKVD operatives in the movie industry. When Paramount Studios opened their Berlin office, Morros was instrumental in staffing the studio with a number of espionage agents.

One of Boris Morros's most important agents in the Berlin studio was a NKVD operative named Vassily Zarubin and his wife, Elizabeth. In order to bolster his resume with the Soviets, Morros told them that he had been appointed to the position of "director of the firm's entire production in Hollywood." The Russians believed their new star and asked if he could recruit more "illegals" at Paramount. Morros never took up the Soviet's request. Morros also used his secretary as the conduit for funneling money to Vassily Zarubin in Berlin.

In order to find out exactly what Morros was up to, the NKVD sent an agent code-named "Archimedes" to visit him. When "Archimedes" arrived in Hollywood, Morros refused to see him, claiming his workload was too heavy. Peter Gutziet, Morros's controller, wrote of that incident, "I felt he was not very pleased about my arrival."

When "Archimedes" finally met with Morros, he admitted that he lied about his position at Paramount and that Morros was "simply a director of the musical sub-department of the firm's production department."

The NKVD was equally chagrined when it learned that Morros's secretary was aware that her boss was sending tainted money to Vassily Zarubin in Berlin. Despite that fact, the NKVD kept Morros on their payroll and used his services for their illegal work. When Peter Gutzeit was relieved of his stewardship over Morros, he wrote that Morros "was a friend of the Soviet Union and is ready to render any help he can."

In October 1944, control of Morros transferred to Jack Soble—"Abraham." It was at this time that Morros proposed to the NKVD a high-risk, high-profile business venture that he wanted them to fund. He wanted to establish a music publishing house in the United States, which would also serve as a cover for Soviet "illegals." After checking with Moscow, it was decided that the Soviet government would have no part in the venture. However, Morros's proposal was handed over to a rich, Soviet-leaning millionaire, Alfred Stern.

The Soviet entry into the American musical market took root in September 1944. Stern put up $130,000, which Morros put immediately to use. Morros envisioned recruiting composers from South America, conducting talent contests to see whom he would hire. He purchased orchestra equipment and began to heavily promote his new company in Hollywood. The undercover name for the operation was "Chord." The NKVD even proposed that Jack Soble be a full partner with Morros in Chord but changed their mind due to possible FBI investigation of Soble.

By 1945, Chord was bankrupt, never becoming the worldwide success Morros envisioned. Alfred Stern asked the NKVD to replace Morros as head of the company, but they declined. To make matters worse, Morros pleaded with the Russians to invest another $150,000. They too, refused.

It was at this time that Boris Morros decided to switch sides and contacted the FBI. He became a double agent, reporting on the Soble-Zarubin-NKVD espionage network in the United States.

By 1951, as Morros worked for the FBI, Soviet interest in him began to wane. His one-time handler, Jack Soble, was called back to Moscow but reemerged in the U.S. where he was arrested, due to Morros's actions. He was then stripped of his U.S. citizenship and with his wife fled to Canada.

The Soviets, still not aware of Morros's duplicity, continued to cultivate him. The Russian Vienna station had planned to meet with Morros on April 6, 1955. Morros told the FBI, and they put out all stops to keep him out of harm's way. When Morros was in Munich in January 1957, the FBI sent him an urgent cable warning him that his life was in imminent danger. He came back to New York and almost instantly began testifying before a federal grand jury, telling about his involvement with Soviet intelligence.

He wrote a book on his experiences called *My Ten Years as a Counterspy*. Boris Morros died on January 8, 1963.

N

Nascimento, Tulio

Brazilian army Captain Tulio Nascimento was the unluckiest and most unprepared spy for the Abwehr in Brazil. He was a licensed pilot, the son of a colonel in the Brazilian armed forces, and by 1942, on leave from the army, served as a technical advisor for the Brazilian Nickel Company. At 42, he was still a captain, due to chronic psychological problems. The fact that he suffered from syphilis also kept him from promotion.

During the war years, Nascimento was pro-Axis, telling everyone whom he met that he was an ardent advocate of Hitler and hoping for a German victory. In his delusional behavior, he would tell anyone who would listen that a German submarine was about to come for him and whisk him to the fatherland, where he would "drop bombs on England." Yet, despite his odd behavior, he was picked by the Abwehr to become one of their most trusted spies.

In the early 1940s, Brazil broke diplomatic relations with Germany, but the country remained an important espionage base for German spies. Nascimento was recruited into the German cause by a Captain Bohny and the German Ambassador to Brazil, Prufer. After a clandestine meeting between Captain Bohny and Nascimento, the latter joined forces with the Third Reich.

His first job was to sign up fellow pro-Axis sympathizers who would serve as couriers between Rio de Janeiro and Buenos Aires. Nascimento was put in contact with a man who would play a crucial role in his spying career, Gerado Melo Mourao. Mourao was a journalist for a pro-German newspaper called *Guzeta de Noticias*. He was also an author, fluent in nine foreign languages. His pro-Nazi activities were well known to the local police, who kept him under surveillance.

Nascimento's contact with Gerado Mourao was through his cousin, Alexander Konder, who also worked at the *Guzeta de Notcias*. At their first meeting, Mourao agreed to work with Nascimento to establish an information service.

As far as Nascimento was concerned, he was about to embark on his first job for the Germans. He met with the military attaché at the American Embassy in Brazil to set up a plant for fire-control systems. He wanted to inspect American firms that made the same material.

Nascimento was sent on his way. All preparations were made, until one snag—American listening posts picked up a message originating from the Abwehr saying a "local captain in our service departs in two weeks on commission. On invitation of General Miller he will be active at Sperry (war plants), in arsenals and aircraft factories. I have approved the trip and a payment of $3,000.00. He received [secret] inks." The "local captain" was Nascimento, and his visa was canceled.

If Nascimento was temporarily stymied, Mourao wasn't. He came to Argentina as a courier for Nascimento, as well as the German *chargé d'affaires* in the Buenos Aires embassy for $400 per month. Mourao then headed a group of men who reported to him on ship movements along the docks. At one point, Nascimento himself flew over the port in a rented plane to make observations. Before they could get down to serious business, the police arrested a number of Mourao's men and more importantly, confiscated their powerful radio transmitter.

Nascimento's name was never mentioned by those arrested because they did not know their superior. He was able to continue his spying activities. His next venture was to install a successful mail-drop organization between Buenos Aires and Brazil using a cipher provided by Mourao and his cousin, Alexander Konder.

Buoyed by his own self-importance, Nascimento offered 6,000 American dollars to his handlers for a high-risk adventure. He wanted to destroy a German cargo ship that had been taken forcibly by the Brazilian government. The ship was anchored at the port of Ilha das Cobras and was not well guarded. He asked Mourao if he knew anyone willing to take on such a job, envisioning saboteurs who would plant bombs around the ship. In the end, nothing came of the venture.

Why the Abwehr trusted Nascimento with such important matters demonstrated either desperation, or an overestimation of his abilities. In the grand scheme of espionage, Tulio Nascimento was a small cog in a huge South American Nazi intelligence wheel.

(*See Also*: Latin American Espionage)

Navajo Code Talkers

As the United States began its repossession of the Pacific islands in the weeks after the Pearl Harbor attack, it became obvious to American military commanders that secure communications were essential. Like the Americans and the British, Japanese cryptographers had cracked American military transmissions and were able to read our proposed battle strategy. A new, invulnerable code system was needed.

To that end, the marines used a code known only to the Navajo Tribes of the American Southwest. The men who carried out this bold plan were called Navajo Code Talkers.

The man most responsible for the organization of the Navajo Code Talkers was Philip Johnston, a civil engineer who lived in Los Angeles. He served with the army in World War I in France but was too old for active duty in World War II, but he still wanted to serve his country and unveiled an ingenious new espionage tool.

As a young man, Philip Johnston lived on the Navajo Indian Reservation, where his parents worked as Protestant missionaries. He knew the Navajo tongue, a language of Native Americans in the Southwest. He came up with the idea of using the Navajo language as a new tool of war. But how could he persuade the military to listen to his idea?

In February 1942, Philip Johnston arrived at Camp Elliot near San Diego and had a private meeting with Lieutenant Colonel James Jones, the Marines Signal Corps Communications Officer. Johnston explained his idea to the skeptical officer, telling him that no one except the Navajo knew the "hidden language," and that it would be a perfect means by which codes and messages could be used in the war. Impressed, Lieutenant Colonel Jones asked for a demonstration. A few weeks later, Philip Johnston returned to the base with four Navajos who would present their case.

They were separated into pairs and told to send messages in their own tongue to the others a short distance away. In record time, their content was translated seamlessly into English.

After the success of the demonstration, Lieutenant Colonel Jones went up the chain of command and contacted Major General Clayton Vogel, the commandant of Camp Elliot, told him what he had seen, and asked him to contact Washington. To Major General Vogel's surprise, the Marine Corps high brass agreed to use the Navajos in combat situations.

In May 1942, the first 29 Navajo recruits entered the marines from reservations at Fort Wingate, Shiprock, New Mexico, and Fort Defiance in Arizona. Most of these young men had never been outside of the reservation and were sent into a foreign world.

They arrived at Camp Pendelton, California, near Oceanside, the main marine recruiting depot in the country. They made up the 382nd Platoon but were called "the Navajo School."

For the next few months, the Navajos were taught how to be soldiers.

NAVAJO CODE TALKERS

They learned weapons, military discipline, and how to interact with white men, with whom many of them had had little or no contact.

One of the original men to train the Navajos was a fellow Native American named Dooley Shorty. Shorty hailed from a reservation in Cornfields, Arizona. Shorty and his team had their work cut out for them. The Navajo language had no meaning for any military terms and they had to be invented.

The trainers devised a two-part code, the first consisting of a 26-letter phonetic alphabet. The second part contained a 211 word English vocabulary with the Navajo equivalents. The word for "fighter plane" would be translated into Navajo as "dah-he-tih-hi," "submarine" was "besh-lo," while "squad" turned into "debeh-lizine."

The Navajo code talkers used a highly intricate system. When the code talker received a message, he had to first translate the words into English. He then used only the first letter of the English equivalent in spelling an English word. For example, the English letter "A" was translated into such Navajo terms as "wol-la-chee" (ant), and "be-la-sana" (apple).

After a lengthy training process, the first Navajo soldiers were sent into the Pacific war in August 1942 to the command of Major General Alexander Vandegrift's First Marine Division at Guadalcanal. They performed so well that General Vandergrift asked that 83 more Navajos be sent to him.

By 1943, over 200 more Navajos joined training at Camp Pendelton. One of their teachers was the same Philip Johnston, now with the rank of Staff Sergeant, who began the program in the first place.

The Navajos were assigned to all the marine units, as well as their Raider and parachute contingents in the bloody Pacific campaigns, including Okinawa, the Solomon Islands, Bougainville, Iwo Jima, Peleliu, and the Marianas.

Huddled in the dense jungle, working in pairs, one Navajo received messages while the other listened to his radio and deciphered them. The Japanese listening posts in the Pacific were able to pick up these strange sounding transmissions but had no idea what was being said.

The Navajo Code Talkers worked at a feverish pace when the marines landed at Iwo Jima. Working with the Fifth Marine Division, the Native American spies sent and received more than 800 messages without a single error in transmission. Throughout the Pacific campaign, the code talkers remained brave and dedicated. It was to their credit that the Japanese never broke another code.

After the war, many of the code talkers went back to their lives at the reservations but could not cope with the drudgery of daily life after their whirlwind days in the war. Unlike other returning GIs, they were denied the benefits that the others were receiving. For some, life was just the way it was before defending America in war.

Their story of bravery in action was relegated to the back of the history books or neglected completely. However, in 1982, 37 years after the end of the war, President Reagan named August 14 Navajo Code Talkers' Day. On September 17, 1992, 35 of them were honored with a ceremony at the Pentagon, in which a Navajo code talker exhibit was unveiled. In the year 2000, Senator Jeff Bingaman of New Mexico proposed that the Senate of the United States further honor the living members by presenting gold medals to the original 29 marines, and silver medals to 370 others. The Navajo Code Talkers were the real unsung heroes of the war.

Neumann, Franz

The Soviet intelligence service, the NKVD, worked tirelessly before the war to penetrate all facets of the American government, including the OSS. Operating out of its Washington embassy and its New York City consulate, Soviet agents developed contacts in private industry, including a large number of branches of the federal government.

One of their earliest targets was the OSS, which was in its infancy. Bill Donovan and his recruiters did not have time to check every newcomer to the agency, and some people with questionable backgrounds, i.e., communists, were taken on. One such person was Franz Neumann, an economist by training, who worked in the OSS's German section.

Little is known of Franz Neumann's family background except to say that he fled Germany in the early 1930s and made his way to England. He studied at the London School of Economics, and then came to the United States in 1936. He became a naturalized American citizen and found employment with the OSS in February 1942. He also was the author of a book on the German economy.

He was assigned to work in the German section at the same time that he was employed as a double agent for the Russians. Neumann's Soviet case officer was Elizabeth Zarubina (code name "Vardo"), the wife of the Soviet station chief in New York, Vassily Zarubina.

At their initial meeting on April 3, 1943, Neumann promised to hand over as much information as crossed his hands. As far as Elizabeth Zarubina was concerned, Neumann was just what the Soviets were looking for. That day, Neumann gave her information from private discussions between Cardinal Francis Spellman of New York and the pope, in which the Cardinal tried to persuade him to act more favorably toward the allies. He also knew about clandestine meetings between certain Spanish parties and a number of anti-Hitler generals, as well as the possible recruitment of German immigrants coming from Mexico into the United States.

Elizabeth Zarubina was concerned when her attempts to contact Franz Neumann failed. For over a year, Neumann offered no information to the Soviets. He chose to seek them out when he had something of importance to hand over.

His self-imposed absence ended abruptly in July 1944, after the failed attempt on Hitler's life. At that time, Neumann provided the Soviets with detailed descriptions of talks held by the OSS in Switzerland, and German resistance organizations.

Unexpectedly, for Neumann, Elizabeth Zarubina was recalled to Moscow, and either by design or faulty planning on behalf of the Soviets, no other Russian agent made any further contact with him.

In 1945, shortly after the war ended, he took on another prestigious assignment. He went to work as part of the Nuremberg War Crimes tribunal for Robert Jackson, the United States's chief prosecutor. (Robert Jackson would later become a Justice of the U.S. Supreme Court.) Neumann had strong, unconventional beliefs regarding Hitler's Final Solution. He believed that the holocaust was "the spearhead for general oppression, the first step toward the real goal—the destruction of civil society."
(*See Also*: Lee, Duncan; Morros, Boris)

Normandie, The

On February 9, 1942, reports of a huge fire were reported to the New York City Fire Department. Billows of smoke rose into the air over New York originating from the docks along the Hudson River.

What rescuers encountered left them breathless. A fire had erupted inside the French passenger ship the *Normandie,* at 1,029 feet in length, one of the greatest ships to sail the Atlantic between Europe and the United States. The firefighters tried in vain to contain the flames, unaware that the *Normandie* was very likely the target of sabotage.

The *Normandie* was one of the fastest liners to cross the Atlantic, making better than 30 knots of speed. A Russian engineer named Vladimir Yourkevitch at St. Nazaire designed the ship. She was actually built at the port of Le Harve. Workmen dredged the water along the piers to hold the massive ship.

On October 29, 1935, a throng of 200,000 fascinated people lined the shores along the Loire to watch the giant ship slide into the river on her first test trials. Weighing in at 30,500 tons, the *Normandie* plowed through the river at 17 knots, and was afloat in a record-breaking seven seconds. For the next two years, she was refitted in dry dock in final preparations for her life as a queen of the seas.

She had a 188-foot-wide hull, three large oval funnels, a miracle of modern architecture. The inside of the ship was opulent, bathed in Art Deco design with rooms decked out in multi-colored tapestry. The main dining hall was 305 feet in length, 46 feet wide and 25 feet in height.

A dozen crystal fountains delighted guests. She had 11 desks, 23 elevators, a crew of 1,345, and could carry a maximum of 1,972 passengers. Seventy-six chefs prepared more than 4,000 meals per day. The *Normandie* was powered by the newest generation of turbo-electric turbines, and could plow through the sea at 32 knots.

Ready for her maiden voyage to New York, she left her berth at Le Harve on May 29, 1935. Over the next four years, the *Normandie* carried 133,000 people between Europe and the United States without incident. On August 23, 1939, the *Normandie* made her last trip to New York.

The heart of German espionage activities in the United States was centered in New York City, where ships of all warring nations were berthed. The ports along New York's docks were an especially intriguing target for German subversive activities. Frederick Jourbet Duquesne was a Nazi spy in the city. Then 62, he led the U.S. spy operation.

Duquesne used various jobs as a cover for his spying activities: journalist, scientist, botanist. He lived in an apartment in the Yorkville section of Manhattan, an area made up of German immigrants. He'd begun spying for the Germans during the Boer War (South Africa), and had taken on assignments in South America and England. He was now in New York on his most dangerous mission. As he made his covert trips around Manhattan, he paid particular attention to ships that were docked at New York's huge West Side piers. One ship in particular caught his attention; the luxurious *Normandie*.

The *Normandie* was scheduled to return to France in two days, but her return voyage was abruptly canceled. On the day she was due back in France, Germany invaded Poland, beginning World War II. The French government decided to keep the ship in New York.

To the enchantment of thousands of New Yorkers another huge passenger ship docked next to the French liner. The *Queen Mary* was in the process of being re-outfitted, and soon set sail for Sydney, Australia, as a troop ship.

With France now in the war, a number of the *Normandie*'s crew left New York for miliary service. Her captain, Etienne Payen de la Garanderie, and a large contingent departed for Montreal in a special train. A skeleton crew of only 113 stayed behind.

Frederick Duquesne received orders from Berlin regarding the *Normandie*. He was instructed to sabotage the vessel before it could be turned into a troop ship.

Masquerading as a longshoreman, Edmund Scott, a reporter from the New York newspaper *PM*, got a job on the docks and learned that the U.S. Navy had secretly taken over the *Normandie*, preparing to turn her into a troop transport and take her up to Boston.

What Scott did not know was that right after the U.S. entered the war, the navy would requisition the *Normandie* and rename it the *U.S.S. Lafayette*. A firm called the Robbins Dry Dock & Repair Company was hired to rip the ship to shreds, remaking her into a troop transport. The repairmen were lax in their work, leaving unsafe conditions all over the ship. Early in the morning of February 9, the first cry of "fire" was heard.

The giant liner was completely destroyed in less than 12 hours. Initial reports blamed it on a careless crew. Other accounts of the fire were attributed to the work of German agents in New York.

As the ship burned along the banks of the Hudson, the first spy trial against suspected German agents in the United States was going on in the Federal Courthouse across town. One of the most important documents presented by the prosecution was a paper written by a German agent named Kurt Ludwig about how easy it would be to firebomb the *Normandie,* due to its lack of security.

In an investigation by New York District Attorney Frank Hogan, the sabotage link was unproven. No conclusive proof was ever established to attribute the fire to the work of German nationals under the direction of Kurt Ludwig or Frederick Duquesne. But what is unmistakable is that the German spy network in New York had the means, motive and opportunity to destroy the *Normandie.*

(*See Also*: German Espionage Activities; Ludwig, Kurt; Sebold, William)

North Africa

In the grand scheme of OSS secret operations during World War II, one area of utmost importance was North Africa. North Africa was the jumping-off point for actions not only of the OSS but of the British Intelligence Services, SOE, and SIS. U.S. military and intelligence planners used that part of the world for missions into Spain, France, as well as the preparations for the most successful allied operations of the war: the D-Day, Normandy invasion. Algiers was the headquarters of the OSS in North Africa and hundreds of agents from all parts of the world (not exclusively American) came to ply their age's-old trade.

The importance of North Africa to the allied war effort got the attention of William Donovan even when he headed the COI, the Coordinator of Information operation. On October 10, 1941, two months before the United States was attacked by Japan, Donovan sent a plan for undercover operations in that part of the world to President Roosevelt, "as a concrete illustration of what can be done" in the gathering of intelligence. Two months later, Donovan again wrote the president stressing the importance of a good subversive, underground network, which would be allied with the Western powers. Donovan lobbied the Joint Chiefs of Staff who had overall command authority when it came to allocating American forces around the globe for a stake of the action in North Africa. In time, the JSC relented and Donovan's COI began to get a foothold on the African continent.

With the approval of the JSC in hand, Donovan got personal orders from President Roosevelt concerning North African operations. FDR instructed Donovan to devise an espionage operation in conjunction with the British. He was told by the president that the White House wanted data on the political and military facets concerning the French army and navy. He was also to establish a communications network across the Mediterranean.

The president also told Donovan that when allied forces landed on the African continent, it was his responsibility to see to it that French troops were neutralized and did not cross over to the German side. His last task was to ensure that Spain remain neutral. If this venue was not enough for Donovan, he was further ordered to carry out missions in Spain and Portugal, in relation to German military movements.

This plan was called "Arcadia," and the president awarded Donovan the vast sum of $5 million in gold coin that would be sent to Gibraltar to fund the operation, which would include France, Africa, and the Iberian Peninsula. The man chosen to be the money dispenser for Donovan's operation was Atherton Richards. Donovan and William Stephenson, the head of the BSC, met with Richards in New York's St. Regis Hotel on April 2, 1942. Richards was one of Donovan's earliest recruits into the OSS, and came from a wealthy family in Hawaii.

With money in the bank, and Richards safely encased on "The Rock," the first clandestine mission regarding Spain took root.

By the spring of 1942, both the United States and Great Britain began to have grave doubts regarding the continuing neutrality of Spain. It was learned from OSS sources that Ramon Serrano Suner, the Spanish Foreign Minister, was leaning toward the Nazis and that he was in the process of trying to persuade Spain's dictator, Francisco Franco, into joining the Axis. To counter any such move, the U.S. and Britain sent two of their ablest men to Madrid, Sir Samuel Hoare and Carlton Hayes. Samuel Hoare was a one-time foreign secretary, while the American, Hayes, was a former Captain in U.S. Military intelligence, as well as an accomplished historian. Together, they devised a scheme concentrating on pro-Allied Spanish Generals who would persuade Franco from joining the war against the allies.

Hoare and Hayes used two other men to further their needs. Picked were Colonel Robert Solborg, a personal representative from Bill Donovan, and Captain Allan Hillgarth, the head of the British Secret Service in the Iberian area. They used a third man to act as an intermediary with the Spanish officers, one Juan March. March was once a friend of Franco's, and was mostly responsible for providing the money needed for his rise to power in Spain.

On Solberg and Hillgarth's behalf, March met with 30 cooperative Spanish generals, passing out a king's ransom of $10 million to ensure their cooperation. As an added incentive, an extra $1 million was put in the pool for any other officers who might participate. The bribery scheme worked, as Spain remained neutral throughout the war.

Another covert operation directed against Spain took place in Washington, D.C., in the summer of 1942. During 1941, a number of successful break-ins of the Spanish Embassy in Washington, D.C., by the British Secret Service took place. These black-bag jobs were undertaken in order to keep abreast of the changes in the Spanish codes. This new information was forwarded to the British code-breaking unit at Bletchley Park. British analysts picked up signs through their intercepts signaling Spanish ships at sea that a possible war message involving Spain might be coming. The only way to verify this news was to intercept the diplomatic messages between Washington and Madrid. In order to do so, a break-in of the Spanish Embassy in Washington was set in motion.

Donovan selected Donald Downes, a confidant of his, a former school teacher, to be in charge of the break-in. Downes called a man who specialized in cracking safes and break-ins, a New Yorker named G.B. Cohen. Cohen agreed to take on the assignment for free and immediately went to Washington for training. Cohen got help from an agent placed inside the Embassy who "broke" the dial to the safe, allowing Cohen to come and "fix" it.

The break-in took place on the night of July 29, 1942, when Cohen and a team that included one of Downes's agents, Jose Aranda, entered the embassy. The intrusion was a success, allowing the men to copy over 3,400 documents that were handed over to the Ultra readers at Bletchley Park.

With a November 8, 1942, invasion date scheduled for Operation Torch, another incursion of the Spanish Embassy was planned. Unfortunately, this one had very different results. The FBI had been tipped off to Donovan's plan, and when Aranda and his men entered the embassy, the waiting FBI agents arrested them. James Murphy, later to head the OSS operations in North Africa, was dispatched by Donovan to FBI headquarters, where, after much haggling, the burglars were released. The arrest of the Spanish Embassy team left bitter feelings between Donovan and his rival in intelligence, J. Edgar Hoover.

Both the Germans and the Italians had a strong foothold in North Africa, especially when the Vichy French government broke diplomatic relations with the British. With the departure of British troops from North Africa, the Germans quickly came in and created a large, covert network in the region.

The United States however, did have diplomatic relations with the Vichy regime and maintained consular representation there. We also maintained extra-territorial rights in French Morocco via a treaty with the Sultan. The United States's position in North Africa was further strengthened by the culmination of the Weygand-Murphy Accord of February 1941. This pact allowed the United States to send non-military supplies to North Africa with the stipulation that it would not be transferred to the warring parties in Europe. In exchange, the United States would be permitted to post certain officials to make sure that the terms of the agreement were carried out.

This was a perfect cover for intelligence missions, and in the spring of 1941, 12 officers hand picked by the Army G-2, the State Department, and ONI (Office of Naval Intelligence), were chosen for assignment. By the summer of 1941, they were sent under cover as vice-consuls in Casablanca, Algiers, Oran, Tunis, and Rabat.

These covert officers did not report to the various ambassadors in their host countries but did answer to Robert Murphy who operated in Algiers. Murphy preceded the 12 vice-consuls to North Africa as the special representative of FDR Murphy kept the president up to date on the results of the vice-consuls' missions as they bore fruit. Later, Murphy worked closely with Colonel William Eddy of Donovan's COI, to prepare for guerrilla actions on behalf of the allies in advance of the Normandy invasion. As the war progressed, Murphy was eventually put in command of OSS operations in North Africa.

As the American presence in North Africa took shape, Donovan asked FDR for permission to place one man in charge of all undercover operations. This person's job would be to "unify the activities of the vice-consuls and stimulate their efforts"—clearly double-talk for espionage activities. The man recommended by Colonel Donovan was William Eddy of the Marine Corps.

Eddy had previously served in Cairo as the Naval Attaché. He served with distinction in World War I, had been president of Hobart College, and spoke fluent Arabic. Donovan spoke on Eddy's behalf to Secretary of War Henry Knox who approved Eddy's appointment. In December 1941, William Eddy was appointed as the Naval Attaché in Tangier.

Eddy's task was to curry favor with the local native chiefs, paying them off if necessary, keeping a close watch on guerrilla bands, and preparing for eventual American raids against enemy targets. Another important task of his was to work harmoniously with the two substantial British intelligence operations in North Africa, SOE and SIS.

Eddy arrived in Tangier in January 1942 and immediately got down to business. He was the collection point of all intelligence material gathered from all sources in North Africa. Eddy also got help from his British counterparts in Gibraltar and Tangier.

The fall of France in June 1940 further complicated the work of the OSS in North Africa. Pierre Laval, loyal to the Axis cause, was now in power in

Vichy France, and he made special arrangements with the Germans to give them free reign in the region. The American networks that had so patiently been organized, now withered. Donovan lobbied the JCS to increase supplies to these bands but he was turned down. Nothing happened until Washington decided to close the COI and turned it into the Office of Strategic Services. With the birth of the OSS, the North African campaign took on a much higher profile.

Jean Darlan Vichy vice-premier, a defender of the Germans, and one of the most hated men in France, created the first crisis faced by the OSS.

The Darlan affair showed just how fragile the relationship between the Americans and the Free French led by General Charles de Gaulle, who was the dominant political figure in the country after the German occupation of the country. From London, de Gaulle badgered the United States for more supplies for his resistance movement and started a running feud between the Americans and British secret services as to who would provide the most supplies. De Gaulle was furious with General Eisenhower and the United States when Ike decided to recognize (with Washington's approval) Darlan's role as the political and military leader in France.

In retaliation for the American recognition of Darlan, de Gaulle stopped all cooperation between the OSS and his own intelligence service. The fallout of the Darlan affair caused the British and the pro-allied French to rally around de Gaulle, leaving the United States, at least temporarily, out in the cold.

In the middle of all this political chicanery, Darlan took a step on his own that made all sides wince. In October 1942, Darlan went to the U.S. mission in Algiers warning them that the Germans had received information on the proposed U.S. attack on Dakar and Casablanca. He also said that he believed that if that event took place, then Germany would launch its own invasion of Spain, via France.

Darlan was almost captured by forces loyal to the Free French in Algiers but somehow escaped. At this point, Darlan agreed to aid the allies and was rewarded in this regard when the Americans gave him control over Vichy areas of North Africa. The Americans tried to put out the considerable fires brewing over Darlan's new position by saying that whatever political appointments made by the general were only temporary in nature.

How Darlan knew that the Germans had information regarding proposed allied strikes into Dakar or Casablanca is ripe with speculation. Did Darlan have his own sources of information inside the Nazi hierarchy?

Allied reactions to Darlan's activities reached a crescendo when, on November 22, 1942, Darlan announced that he was "taking military and administrative control over the French empire." One reaction to Darlan's public statement came swiftly from the French navy who scuttled 73 of its warships to prevent them from falling into the hands of the Germans (Darlan had previously said that he would turn these ships over to the Germans).

The point now came in high allied circles about the necessity to remove Darlan by force. Alexander Cadogan, permanent head of the British Foreign Office, wrote in his personal diary that, "The Americans and naval officers in Algiers are letting us in for a *pot* of trouble. We shall do no good until we've killed Darlan." He ended his notation by saying, "De G's (de Gaulle) one remedy is 'Get rid of Darlan.' My answer is 'Yes, but how?' No answer." Soon, though, a response was found.

That vexing problem was suddenly, and violently answered on December 24, 1942, when a young Frenchman named Bournier de la Chapelle entered Darlan's headquarters and shot him. Chapelle was tried in a secret court, found guilty, and was subsequently and unceremoniously executed. But the story does not end there.

It seems that Chapelle was taking training from the British espionage unit called SOE, which was responsible for assassination and sabotage operations all across Europe. Chapelle served in a paramilitary unit, the Corps Franc d'Afrique, whose members wore British military uniforms and were linked to operations of the OSS/SOE. In another suggestive bit of coincidence, the head of the British Secret Service, Sir Stewart Menzies, "C," was in Algiers, when Darlan was shot. The assassination of Jean Darlan eliminated one huge problem for the allies, but other vexing military dilemmas were just beginning.

Toward the end of 1943, President Roosevelt and Prime Minister Churchill decided on the course of future military operations in North Africa and France. At the Teheran Conference, an invasion of France code-named "Overlord" and an invasion of North Africa code-named "Torch" were put in motion. General Dwight D. Eisenhower was given command of the Supreme Headquarters Allied Expeditionary Force (SHAEF).

Leaving Algiers, Eisenhower went to London to run the operation. One of the first decisions affecting the OSS was a significant new role they would play in covert operations in Italy. Donovan traveled to Algiers in January 1944, where he met his British counterpart, Colonel Douglas Dodds-Parker. Dodds-Parker ran the British SOE mission in Algiers called Massingham, responsible for all operations in southern France. Ike assigned Colonel Edward Glavin to mobilize his OSS forces with Dodds-Parker's SOE. Also involved in the pre-invasion planning with SOE and OSS were intelligence units under the command of de Gaulle, the Direction Generale des Services Speciaux (DGSS).

The OSS's first major operation linked to the North African campaign was the preparation for Operation Anvil, which was scheduled to coincide with the Normandy landings. OSS Algiers ran the operation with a staff called Force 163. In the weeks before the Anvil landings, OSS Algiers provided information to both the Massingham operation and Force 163.

When Anvil commenced on August 15, 1944, Force 163 was taken over by General Alexander Patch's 7th Army. In the time period between May 1943 and September 1944, the OSS provided 8,000 intelligence reports to the allied high command, many relating to operations coming from Spain and the Pyrenees mountain areas.

Operation Torch, the allied invasion of North Africa, proved just how fragile the cooperation between the British and American secret services had become. Both the OSS and SOE had separate missions, and fierce competition erupted. The SOE's most important role was the establishment of secure radio communications among Gibraltar, the invasion forces, and the elements under Colonel William Eddy. SOE forces also came ashore with the Torch landings, dropping supplies by submarine and aircraft.

As the Torch landings got under way, a fierce turf battle erupted between the two most powerful British intelligence agencies: SOE and SIS. For example, the SIS director in Tangier, Colonel Toby Ellis, tried to hinder not only operations run by the OSS, but also the SOE. Carleton Coon, one of the most important OSS operatives in Algiers, had harsh words to say regarding some of his SIS colleagues. Referring to one officer in the AFHQ Psychological Warfare Board that, "he is our enemy who has tried on several occasions to upset our shows." SIS, continued Coon, "is an imperialistic organization which we have any reason to mistrust."

One of the underlining areas of friction between the SIS and SOE was the attitude of the British Ambassador to Spain, Sir Samuel Hoare. He sent a stern warning to London saying that he would not tolerate any SOE or SIS agent operating in Spain who would give Spain's dictator, Franco, any reason to make a deal with Hitler.

Prior to Torch, another feud developed between Donovan and the SIS regarding operations in Algiers. By late summer 1942, Donovan set up a separately run OSS mission in that city for "out of area" operations once the invasion took place. He pressed Washington for permission to run his own operation in Tangier without British interference. Donovan's approach was upheld by the Allied Command who ruled that SOE's role in any pre-Torch operations would be severely limited.

By December 1942, however, a truce had been arranged between the two agencies and responsibility as far as operations were concerned, were ironed out. It was decided that the British Massingham mission would be divided into two areas. The British would operate Massingham out of headquarters at the Club de Pins in Sidi Ferruch, while the OSS remained at its own offices in Algiers. It was also agreed that future operations into Europe would be done jointly.

Bill Donovan arrived in Algiers, where high-level discussions with British intelligence officials as well as General Eisenhower took place. Eisenhower ordered that OSS and SOE "work together 100 percent" in any future operations. The first result of this new cooperation was the release of some British air units to the OSS from their base at Gibraltar.

When allied forces began "Operation Torch" on November 8, 1942, OSS units were on hand to provide help to the invading troops. They passed out maps, guided troops to their destinations, made hit-and-run attacks against German-fortified positions at the landing sites, and further inland, blew up bridges, cut communications lines, and harassed the enemy. OSS units went ashore at the main landing spots, such as Algiers, Oran, Port Lyautey, Fedala, and Safi.

The Torch landings were a complete success, as the invading troops encountered no major opposition. Using false information provided by the Double Cross System, German navy units were as far away as Dakar, looking for a nonexistent enemy. When the allied forces arrived at the Straits of Gibraltar, they took the first steps in gaining complete control over the Mediterranean. Torch was the springboard for the eventual allied landings at Normandy, two years later.

(*See Also*: French Resistance Movements; Coon, Carleton; COI; Darlan, Jean; Donovan, William; Eddy, William; Gibraltar; Hyde, Henry; Maquis, The; OSS)

Office of Strategic Services (OSS)

The OSS was the first official wartime intelligence agency of the United States. It functioned from 1942 until 1945, after World War II ended. OSS agents operated nearly worldwide during the war. The only areas where the OSS did not see action was the Pacific and South America. After the fighting stopped, the new American president Harry Truman disbanded the OSS. In just a few years, President Truman created another permanent intelligence organization: the Central Intelligence Agency.

The man picked by President Roosevelt as espionage chief was a World War I hero, a talented New York lawyer with impeccable national credentials, William J. Donovan.

When World War II broke out in 1939, FDR gave Donovan a mission to perform. With the United States neutral, the president sent him to ascertain how the United States could aid Britain in its battle with Hitler's Germany. He met all the main political and military figures in London and was entrusted with much of England's highly guarded military secrets. Donovan informed the president that with a sufficient amount of American military and economic aid, the British could weather the storm.

The stepchild of the OSS was the office of the Coordinator of Information (COI) which Donovan was appointed to on July 11, 1941, by FDR His charter was to "collect and analyze all information which may bear upon national security, to correlate such information and data and make the same available to the president and so such departments and officials of the government."

The COI was allocated a mere 92 employees at conception, along with a small budget. Donovan recruited the cream of the crop of American thinkers and doers and in time created the roots of a vast intelligence organization that would operate throughout the war, and its aftermath.

The COI was divided into various departments, including Research and

Analysis, Special Activities, SA/B, the intelligence branch, as well as SA/G, the covert sabotage division. The COI ceased its existence on June 13, 1942, when FDR appointed William Donovan, the director of the OSS.

The impetus for the creation of the OSS was the surprise Japanese attack on Pearl Harbor. The attack was the biggest intelligence failure in United States history, and FDR was determined never to let our guard down again. FDR had a tough decision to make concerning whom to appoint as this country's new intelligence czar. He was lobbied hard by the tough FBI Director, J. Edgar Hoover, who believed that he alone was the person to control all of the nation's espionage matters. The president, however, chose Wall Street lawyer, William "Wild Bill" Donovan.

Donovan handpicked the most brilliant men and women whom he knew through his professional and social circles for his new team. Men and women from all disciplines, such as law, journalism, sports, banking, the military services, academia, all were took on the job of a lifetime. Among those chosen by Donovan for the OSS were: Arthur Schlesinger, Jr., a Harvard professor, and later a Special Assistant to President John F. Kennedy, Julia Child, today's acclaimed "French Chef," Arthur Goldberg, a future U.S. Supreme Court Judge, movie director John Ford, Michael Burke, a latter successful businessman, and president of the New York Yankees, among dozens of others. (Detractors of the OSS called the agency "Oh So Social.")

The OSS was divided into different sections, each with its own responsibility. Colonel G. Edward Buxton was the assistant director of the Administration section, which was responsible for the administrative staff, the office of the General Counsel, and security. James Donovan was the general counsel whose job it was to handle the secret funds needed to run covert operations across the globe, as well as compile information on war criminals which were subsequently used in the post-war Nuremberg War Crimes Trials. The Technical Services unit was responsible for the secure communications between agents in the field and OSS headquarters in Washington. An integral part of this section was the Special Fund Branch which provided covert agents the local currency in the country they were to work in. The branch also provided certain market money to be used for the trapping of enemy agents. The Research and Development Agency devised specialized weapons and equipment which agents carried with them in the field.

The Intelligence Service was a top priority as far as the OSS was concerned. The man put in command of this specialized agency was Brig. General John Magruder. This branch was responsible for the analysis, collection and circulation of both intelligence and counter-intelligence information throughout the agency. The Research and Analysis Branch was the preeminent body in which daily and weekly intelligence reports were written and studied by Donovan and his top men. The Secret Intelligence Branch carried out covert operations in the field and was the most dangerous of all OSS operations. The counterespionage branch carried out missions against German intelligence agencies like the SD or the Abwehr. The Foreign Nationalities Branch gathered information needed by the OSS from foreigners living in the United States who had expertise in various specialities. The Censorship and Documents Branch intercepted mail and phone conversations of people thought to be working for the axis in the United States.

The OSS Operations Section was under the control of M. Preston Goodfellow. Their main function was the use of covert activity, sabotage, psychological warfare, and other types of covert activities. A number of branches directed by Goodfellow were the Special Operations Branch which carried out sabotage in enemy territory, the Moral Operations Branch which developed "black propaganda" to be used against the enemy, the Maritime Unit which took agents by boat and submarine, the Operational Groups which worked closely with the various resistance groups in Europe, i.e., French and Italian bands, among others.

OSS troops were an important part of almost every major military campaign of the war. Among them were Operation Torch, the invasion of North Africa, as guides for the troops at Normandy on June 6, 1944, D-Day, running covert operations in the jungles of Burma (Detachment 101) ferrying supplies to agents in China, supplying the much needed military supplies to the French resistance groups (the Maquis) in Europe, running covert networks of spies in such important countries as Spain, Turkey, and Portugal. The OSS conducted one of its most ambitious operations in Switzerland, where Allen Dulles, the OSS chief in Berne, conducted clandestine meetings with a number of anti-Hitler generals as well as private citizens who tried to work out a separate peace between the allies and themselves.

OSS agents worked in close cooperation with the two important British intelligence agencies, the SOE and SIS. After bitter feuds relating to the makeup of clandestine activities in Europe were settled, OSS, SOE, and SIS were on the ground together on the continent, working on their common goal: the destruction of Nazi Germany.

Two areas of the world were off limits to the OSS: South America and the Far East. Intelligence operations in America's backyard (Latin and South America) were officially the responsibility of J. Edgar Hoover's FBI. (It was a well-known fact that a number of OSS men secretly operated in South America, which created a bitter dispute between Donovan and Hoover that lasted well after the war ended.) Intelligence operations in the Pacific Ocean area were run by Admiral Chester Nimitz. General Douglas MacArthur was in command of such activities in the Southwest Pacific, including the Allied

Intelligence Bureau, which was run in conjunction with the Australians and the New Zealanders.

OSS also received opposition from the established American military branches, especially the army. The army had its own spy network called G-2, which saw the OSS as a major obstacle to its functions. The navy too had its own set of intricate listening posts in various parts of the world, including the West Coast of the United States, the Hawaiian islands, and Dutch Harbor. The Joint Chiefs of Staff was at first hesitant to give its approval to the OSS, but as the war progressed and pressure was put on it by the president and Donovan, they grudgingly relented.

In a move that backfired on the OSS, Donovan sought a secret relationship with the Soviet intelligence arm, the NKVD). Donovan journeyed to Moscow in December 1943 to try to cement ties with the Russians. An agreement was reached between the two countries in the sharing of the intelligence pie. But what was unknown to Donovan was that the Soviets had established a large-scale intelligence penetration of the OSS operating out of its embassy in Washington, as well as its New York City consulate. A number of highly placed OSS employees working in its Washington headquarters, as well as a number of men and women employed in certain branches of the federal government, were passing secret information to the NKVD for a number of years. Confirmation of their treachery was only affirmed in recent years with the disclosure by the National Security Agency of the Venona intercepts.

In the final days of the war, Bill Donovan sought out President Roosevelt regarding the establishment of a new intelligence agency for the post-war world, based on the concept of OSS. Before Donovan received his answer, the president died of a massive stroke on April 12, 1945, at his summer residence at Warm Springs, Georgia. The new president, Harry Truman, had no interest in Donovan's intelligence plan and by his executive order of October 1, 1945, the OSS went out of business. By January 12, 1946, William Donovan resigned and the wartime agency that he so successfully built up was officially closed down.

The Research and Intelligence Branch was moved to the State Department, which was eventually merged into the State Department's Bureau of Intelligence and Research. The covert arm of the OSS, the Secret Intelligence Branch and the Counter-Espionage Branch were taken over by the War Department and renamed the Strategic Services Unit (SSU—the War Department was later renamed the Department of Defense). In 1946, the SSU was absorbed into the Central Intelligence Group (CIG), which was run by a combination of the army and navy. In 1947, the National Security Act was passed, which created the Central Intelligence Agency.

The OSS served a unique purpose as the central collection agency for all wartime intelligence operations. Its child, the CIA, learned mightily from its endeavors.

(*See Also*: Donovan, William; Casey, William; Stephenson, William; Hoover, J. Edgar; Venona; J.E. Missions; Morros, Boris; Dulles, Allen; North Africa; Coordinator of Information; French Resistance Movements; Italian Patriot Bands; and the various military operations named throughout this work)

OSS Burma

Long before the Japanese attacked Pearl Harbor on December 7, 1941, their armed forces had gained a strategic hold over Manchuria and by 1937 had occupied a number of significant port cities in China. This forced the nationalist government of Chaing Kai-shek to seek refuge from the oncoming Japanese, finally settling in Chungking, situated in the interior of the country. In order for Chaing to get his much needed supplies, he ordered that a large road be constructed from Kunming, China to Lashio, Burma. This mammoth, 681-mile road took a year and half and was built by thousands of Chinese workers. The road was finally ready for the ferrying of supplies in 1939. In a roundabout route, Chaing's provisions were sent by sea to Rangoon, Burma, by train to Lashio, and finally, by road to Kunming. This highway was called the Burma Road and served as the Chinese Nationalists' main avenue of supply for most of the war.

The Japanese also had major military successes in other areas of the Far East, including the Philippines, Singapore, and the Dutch East Indies. The United States was still in a catch-up mode after the Pearl Harbor attack, looking for anyway possible to blunt the Japanese onslaught in Asia.

The OSS was called into the picture, and it met the challenge by creating the first unit in the long history of the American armed forces that would be used especially for the purpose of paramilitary operations, including sabotage, assassinations, and hit-and-run raids. The name of this body was Detachment 101. By the time the war ended, Detachment 101 would rewrite the book on how paramilitary operations would be conducted.

The America military commander in the Far East was Major General Joseph "Vinegar Joe" Stilwell. It was Stilwell's job to counter the Japanese conquest of the region by any means at his disposal. In January 1942, Stilwell received a recommendation that a new contingent of troops trained in intelligence work and unconventional warfare be assigned to his command for the sole aim of conducting guerrilla operations behind the Japanese lines in Burma and China. The man who proposed this new unit was Preston Goodfellow, a confidant of Bill Donovan's OSS. General Stilwell agreed but asked that he be allowed to choose his own commander for the group. The man named to head Detachment 101 was Carl Eifler.

Eifler had previously served as a lieutenant under General Stilwell, and he knew him well. Eifler was stationed in Hawaii where he was promoted to captain and asked to take on the Detachment 101 assignment. Eifler was given carte blanche to pick his team, and he selected men who were fluent in such tasks as communications, engineering, spoke the languages of the Far Eastern countries, and who were, above all, physically able to endure the hardships of living and operating in a jungle environment.

The first two men selected by Carl Eifler were Captain John Coughlin and Captain William Peers. Captain Coughlin was a West Point graduate and would serve as Eifler's assistant. With these men in charge, the rest of the detachment was selected and trained.

With his men finally ready for deployment, Eifler chose as their base camp a plantation in the northeastern part of the Indian province of Assam, called Nazira. A cover for this operation was needed, and the one they chose was that of a center for research into malaria. (The real name of their establishment was the "U.S. Army Experimental Station.") Eifler picked 50 former members of the Burmese military who were anxious to fight the Japanese, and these men soon joined Detachment 101.

As their command center at Nazira grew, Eifler was able to establish secure radio communication with OSS headquarters in Washington, recruit hundreds of native Burmese to work as scouts, and train them in guerrilla warfare.

Eifler had his greatest success in gaining the cooperation of the native Kachin tribesmen who lived in the region. The Kachins, a rugged, simple people, were given arms and training, and they, too, undertook military operations against Japanese forces.

In February 1942, Captain William Wilkinson and a team of four men arrived in the Sumprabum area of Burma, where they linked up with the Kachins. Captain Wilkinson worked with the Kachins, who harassed the Japanese from an outbase called Ngumla. They were aided in their work by a Catholic priest named Father Dennis MacAllindon, who helped raise a sizeable army of native tribesmen.

The Kachins used tools of war that were known only to them in their fight against the Japanese. They used camouflaged, sharpened bamboo sticks that were buried in the ground. They were set off when a man stepped on them. (They were called pungyis.)

These men were soon joined in February 1943, by a 12-man contingent called "Group A," made up of soldiers from Burma and Great Britain, under the command of Captain Jack Barnard of the Burmese army. They were infiltrated into the Kaukkwe Valley of Burma and assigned the job of attacking the Mogaung-Katha Railroad. Their secondary mission was to build up a guerrilla force in the region called Myitkyina.

Myitkyina was an important target for Detachment 101, as it was the location for a large Japanese airfield. From there, Japanese planes attacked American aircraft flying over the "Hump," a large mountain range in the Himalayas located between China and Burma. This was the main route by which supplies were ferried to allied troops in Burma.

As the importance of Detachment 101 became more apparent, and their military successes grew, OSS was able, with the help of the army air corps, to send in more and more badly needed supplies. These provisions were airlifted into the jungle by C-47 cargo planes and B-25 bombers. In time, the OSS was able to provide Detachment 101 its own small fleet of reconnaissance planes, as well as a few boats for marine infiltration assignments.

In his only foray into enemy-held territory, Bill Donovan visited Detachment 101's headquarters in December 1943. In their jungle camp, Donovan made major changes in personnel. He appointed Colonel Peers in charge of 101, selected Colonel Coughlin to be in charge of OSS operations in the China-Burma-India theater, and, in a move that sent shock waves across the jungle canopy, reassigned Carl Eifler back to the United States.

With Colonel Peers now in charge of Detachment 101, major changes in their operational tactics were undertaken. General Stilwell ordered Peers to take on another 3,000 guerrillas, and work with a tough military unit called Merrill's Marauders in attacks against the Japanese.

By the beginning of 1945, Detachment 101's strength had grown to almost 11,000 and was now a formidable fighting force. As the war progressed, the tactics for 101 changed. They were now used primarily as support for front line army units, including those from Great Britain and China. They mostly provided these groups with intelligence on Japanese positions, as well as guiding them along the formidable jungle trails.

In recognition for its gallantry in battle, Detachment 101 was awarded the Presidential Distinguished Unit Citation. Army records record that Detachment 101 killed 5,428 Japanese soldiers, wounded almost 10,000, and captured 78 Japanese prisoners. They suffered 27 killed, as well as 300 Burmese and other native allies' deaths.

Detachment 101's wartime legacy can be seen in today's Army Special Forces and Navy Seal Teams.

(*See Also*: Eifler, Carl)

OSS Italy

Italy was the cornerstone of a myriad of OSS operations in Southern Europe, a proving ground for military forays into France and North Africa. The strategic position of Italy in the war was not lost on the allies when they were establishing their intelligence services.

Italy served as an important OSS bastion for covert missions in Europe.

From Italy, OSS men made contact with a number of Italian resistance movements, set up a clandestine radio communications network of agents reporting on German activities, infiltrated German lines using turned POWs, linked with anti-German emissaries in Switzerland, and provided needed supplies for the allied attacks in North Africa.

As America entered the war, it could count on a large number of newly arrived citizens of Italian descent who had immigrated to the United States in the early part of the century. Hundreds of thousands of these second generation Italian-Americans lived in the teeming cities of the Northeast, as well as in other parts of the United States, learning the customs of their adoptive country, yet never forgetting the families they left behind. When Italy entered the war, many of these Italian-Americans took up arms in defense of the United States, as well as seeing a chance to rid their homeland of the fascists who had taken power in Rome.

The first step in making contact with anti-Mussolini elements in the United States began in July 1942. The OSS sought out a number of Italian anti-fascist organizations and large labor groups. From this meager start, the OSS began a nationwide training program to enlist Italian-Americans into the service. The man the OSS turned to in this recruitment drive was Max Corvo.

Corvo was of Sicilian descent, picked by Donovan to run OSS's Sicily unit. Corvo in turn, tapped 12 Sicilian men and two lawyers to take on as many qualified Italians they could locate. These men were referred to as, "...tough little boys from New York and Chicago, with a few hoods mixed in."

"Their one desire was to get over to the old country and start throwing knives." Corvo also turned to a number of local Mafia gangs to broaden his staff. Many of these tough boys from the street however, did not meet up to OSS standards and had to be rejected.

The OSS was resourceful. It hired Luigi Antonini, the president of the International Ladies Garment Workers Union and Local 48, and Augusto Bellanca of the CIO Amalgamated Clothing Workers Union. It also went to notable university and college professors.

Once the enlistment program took root, new recruits were placed into the Special Intelligence Group (SI), and trained in paramilitary skills. Lieutenant Joseph Bonfiglio began testing the men for proficiency in the Italian language. Upon acceptance, these men were to be infiltrated behind the lines in Italy, mainly as liaisons with the separate resistance groups.

One of the OSS's initial schemes relating to the invasion of Sicily in 1943 was a relationship with the Mafia. In order to protect the New York docks from sabotage by enemy agents, the OSS turned to the mob. In what became known as "Operation Underworld," Assistant District Attorney

Murray Gurfein contacted one of the most dangerous mob chiefs of the day, Charles "Lucky" Luciano. Luciano cooperated with the ONI. If the OSS and ONI had any qualms about working with the mob, it was put on the back burner in favor of the war effort.

Using mob contacts in Sicily, they were able to provide both the ONI and the OSS with information on subversive activities in Sicily and aided American troops once they landed during the 1943 invasion. For his work for the government, Lucky Luciano won a petition for clemency from Thomas E. Dewey, because he'd "rendered a definite service to the war effort."

The Italian section of the OSS began operations in 1941, under the direction of David Bruce. Bruce was then chief of the SI Branch of the COI. Bruce asked his friend Earl Brennan, who once worked for the State Department, to take over the Italian SI. Brennan and his staff began intelligence collection preparations for the expected American invasion of Sicily, even before the event took place.

The SI Branch sent its own agents to the newly created OSS stations around the globe. Vincent Scamporino went to North Africa to work with Colonel William Eddy and would later play a role in the "Vessel case," a blown intelligence operation operating out of the Vatican.

In May 1943, Max Corvo was sent to Allied Force Headquarters to head up SI operations in Italy. Corvo and William Eddy began in earnest to prepare for Operation Husky, the attack against Sicily. Working with the British SOE, a number of marine craft were shipped over to the OSS for use in taking agents into Sardinia. The Sardinia operation was a joint OSS-SIS venture, code-named "Pt Ron 15." The first allied forces entered Italy on June 28, 1943.

For the OSS, Operation Husky was a model of success. This was the first time that they were able to use their expertise under wartime conditions. OSS teams provided General Patton's 7th Army with vital intelligence on German positions. The SI division made long-term contacts with local people who were willing to aid the American cause. Intelligence gathered in Husky was invaluable for the later invasion of Salerno, and more importantly, the OSS was finally recognized as a reputable fighting force.

In readiness for the invasion of North Africa (Operation Torch), the OSS designated Palermo its advance headquarters and sent a number of SI people to Morocco. In a shake-up of personnel, Donovan assigned Lieutenant Colonel Ellery Huntington to head the 5th Army unit and all the OSS men in the region. The 5th Army's job was tactical in nature, while the OSS base at Palermo was assigned the task of physically entering areas north of Rome. The OSS used the city of Brindisi as its jumping-off point for operations into northern Italy.

OSS received a shot in the arm with the surrender of Italy. The Italian army general staff moved its base of operations to Brindisi and immediately made contacts with the SI. Their intelligence agency, SIM, loaned a large contingent of its own men and resources for missions slated for northern Italy. The OSS also made deals with two large Italian resistance groups, the ORI (Organization for Italian Resistance), led by Raimondo Craveri, and CLNAI (Committee of National Liberation for Northern Italy).

In August 1944, Donovan made another personnel move, shaking up the Italian OSS. Colonel Edward Glavin replaced Colonel William Eddy. Glavin brought all OSS branches in Italy under one umbrella. Colonel Glavin moved his new military headquarters to Siena and then to Florence. OSS forces were also put under the command of Company D, 2677th Regiment, under the leadership of Captain William Shilling. Captain Shilling would head the OSS in Italy until the war ended.

In the history of OSS operations in Italy only one man, Second Lieutenant James Jesus Angleton, would be the catalyst for X-2, counterintelligence. Angleton would serve in the prestigious position as head of counterintelligence for the CIA and become involved in major espionage operations of the Cold War.

Angleton was first assigned to the London OSS station where he became a staff member. When a crisis erupted in the Rome OSS station, Angleton was given six weeks to turn the office around. He stayed in Rome for three years, rising from the position of chief of the X-2 unit, to chief of all OSS counterespionage in Italy.

By his 28th birthday, Angleton had risen to director of all secret operations, including intelligence and counterintelligence, for the Strategic Services Unit (SSU). In 1946, one year after the war, Angleton was put in charge of all intelligence units in Italy.

During the war, Angleton was responsible for four espionage enterprises with different outcomes. He was successful in making contact with a number of Italian secret service organizations, especially those of the Italian navy. Angleton learned his tradecraft from his father, Lieutenant Colonel James Hugh Angleton. The elder Angleton served from 1943 to the second half of 1944 as the X-2 representative to the Italian group, SIM. The elder Angleton had worked in Italy for the National Cash Register Company and as chairman of the American Chamber of Commerce.

The first operation the younger Angleton ran was called "Salty," which involved cooperation with Captain di Fregata Carlo Resio, the intelligence chief of the Italian navy. Resio offered Angleton the use of four radio operators for missions in northern Italy.

OSS ITALY

Project Ivy dealt with Prince Valerio Borghese, the head of the Italian navy's sabotage unit. This group had the job of shutting down German intelligence operations in the Florence area. Prince Borghese was an ardent follower of the Italian dictator Benito Mussolini, and it was rumored that he was still cooperating with the Germans. Angleton and Carlo Resio developed a joint operation to get into the Borghese organization (called Xmas). Also involved in IVY were elements of the Italian partisan group called Pubblica Sicurezza. In the end, it was not the OSS or Reiso's men who cracked the espionage ring led by Prince Borghese, but commands from the British and Italian secret services. With their help, Borghese surrendered to the OSS, worked briefly for them, and was finally held for trial in late 1945.

Using his connections with the Italian navy, Angleton was able to enlist the services of an undercover agent called JK1/8, aka, "Sailor," whose services were provided to the OSS by Carlo Resio, whom Angleton had come to trust. "Sailor" began working for the OSS during the summer of 1945 and helped with the Italian intelligence services rebuilding process after the war. "Sailor" held meetings with representatives of Soviet intelligence in Istanbul, Turkey, and told Angleton of the relationship between the Russians and some disparate elements of the Italian spy apparatus. "Sailor" told Angleton that certain members of the anti-communist groups in Albania had met with the Italian Royal Navy seeking funds and equipment in order to make an attempt to overthrow the government of President Enver Hoxha. The source also said that groups within the British SIS were working closely with the Italian monarchy, not the elected government. This penetration operation provided an intelligence bonanza for Angleton and X-2.

If "Sailor" was a winner, the last operation on which Angleton worked was a failure. This case was code-named Vessel and involved an OSS source inside the Vatican. The man receiving information on Vessel was Colonel Vincent Scamporino, director of the SI branch of the OSS in the Mediterranean. Scamporino had a source privy to developments in Vatican City. He was provided information on secrets emanating from the pope's palace. In time, Angleton also began receiving the same documentation from his own source, Fillippo Setaccioli, aka "Dusty." The provider for both the Scamporino and Setaccioli news was a journalist of some questionable character, Virgilio Scattolini. Angleton wanted to run Scattolini himself after it was learned that Scattolini had access to information coming from Myron Taylor, the U.S. representative to the Vatican. Scamporino turned down Angleton's appeal, deciding that Vessel would be the only intermediary delivering Vatican secrets. After reviewing the intelligence coming from the Vatican, it was clear that almost a third of the material provided by Setaccioli was false. The lessons learned by James Angleton in Italy were just the tip of the iceberg that would become his life's work in the CIA.

(*See Also*: Corvo, Max; Eddy, William; Italian Resistance Movements; North Africa; Vessel Case)

OSS London

The OSS London office served as the central base of operations for all U.S. covert activities throughout Europe. It was from there that all OSS missions on the continent, as well as in the Mediterranean, including North Africa, originated.

In 1942, a landmark agreement in intelligence sharing between the OSS and the British intelligence services, the SIS and SOE, was formulated. This was not an easy decision for the British to acknowledge, as they viewed the young upstart organization as not up to the challenge that they had been practicing for hundreds of years. The British did not want to share any of the intelligence pie with the OSS, believing that the Americans were interfering on their turf, i.e., conducting paramilitary missions in Europe.

OSS HQ was located one block away from Grosvenor Square, next to the American Embassy. Donovan staffed his office with the best people available. In the SO (Special Operations) area, he picked J. Gustav Guenther and Dick Heppner, along with Ellery Huntington, Whitney Shepardson and William Maddox for SI (Secret Intelligence), and William Phillips who was in command of the station.

While these men were the nucleus of the London operation, they still had to contend with the constraints put on them by their colleagues. SIS and SOE leadership tried to limit the means by which the OSS operated in theater Europe by controlling the means of transport for OSS men, stymieing OSS movements in Britain as far as training was concerned and limiting OSS contacts with the many exiled governments that called London home.

With the help of Donovan and the intervention of General Dwight Eisenhower, this hard-nosed British attitude toward the OSS gradually changed. Ike went to bat for the OSS, sending forceful messages to British intelligence officers, cajoling them into seeing the value of shared work by both parties. OSS London chief William Phillips met several times with Eisenhower, whereby it was agreed that Phillips would submit all projected operations. With pressure put on by Eisenhower, the SOE decided that it was easier to cooperate with the OSS than to combat them.

By 1942, OSS London was able to get their first breakthrough when the SOE agreed to make available to Donovan's men access to their agent chain from Spain to Gibraltar regarding escaped POWs. They also let the OSS have entree to their radio networks and to allow OSS men on the ground to use British radios for their own communications purposes.

The understanding worked out by OSS London and the Baker Street spies (Baker Street was the unofficial HQ for British intelligence, and the fictional address of Sherlock Holmes) let the OSS: 1) use Britain for military operations against France and other parts of Western Europe, 2) OSS cooperation with SOE missions throughout the region, 3) SO equipment, weapons and all needed supplies sent from Britain. Another meaningful accord agreed the OSS would be able to share in all SOE training and operational facilities for any action emanating from British soil. "The part of the accords pertaining to OSS London was intended to secure the sort of unprecedented access to SOE activities that would greatly accelerate the London station's ability to substantially contribute to military operations."

The man who did the most to make solid the new cooperation between OSS and SOE was Ellery Huntington. Huntington was promoted to the post of chief of worldwide special operations, and he arrived in London to view the scene firsthand. With his British companions in tow, Huntington toured SOE bases and worked out arrangements whereby OSS men were assigned to those units. OSS London established a large Geographic Desk which worked closely with their opposite numbers. This section was responsible for transport, operations and communications. OSS officers were also permitted to attend SOE training schools.

Huntington and Brigadier Colin Gubbins, a high-ranking officer in the SOE, set the stage for OSS operations in various parts of Europe. Gubbins arranged for OSS to mount operations in areas of France and Switzerland, where the British presence was the weakest. In return, OSS provided the necessary supplies to the SOE in France and the Low Countries, including planes, boats, and radio sets. SO units also were given assignments in Sweden and Finland via the penetration of agents into both of those countries.

One of London's most valuable sections was the R&A (Research and Analysis branch). R&A was responsible for writing reports on politics, European resistance movements, the role of the communists in the war effort, military intelligence matters, and post-war military and political concerns. One of the men who participated in the R&A section was Arthur Schlesinger, Jr., who worked on a publication called the *PW Weekly*. (The PW stood for psychological warfare.) The *PW Weekly* was culled from all sources within the OSS and its contents was sent to Washington for reading by the president and his top advisors (Arthur Schlesinger, Jr. would serve as a special assistant to President Kennedy during his administration.)

With SO now able to mount operations in Europe, the London base now turned its attention to getting SI into the act. In a major coup, Whitney Shepardson, who had been promoted to the post of chief of the secret intelligence section (SI), gained a British promise to let OSS London make covert contacts with many of the exiled governments then operating out of the British capital. Deals were made with the Dutch, Polish, Czech, Free French, and Belgians to share intelligence, as well as the latest political information they might want to pass on.

One of Shepardson's biggest coups in dealings with the exile community had to do with access to Charles de Gaulle's intelligence service the *Bureau Central de Renseignments*, or BRAC, which was steered by André Dewavrin. After a slow start, BRAC funneled major intelligence reports to SI London. In a fit of pique, Stewart Menzies, "C," tried to persuade Shepardson to curtail his relationship with BRAC, but he refused.

SI London also played a pivotal role in the planning for the Torch invasion. SI agents made extensive links with French groups, including the Free French, as well as some members of the Vichy government in North Africa. Their heaviest involvement centered around French Resistance Groups trained and equipped by the allies.

The OSS London station proved invaluable in intelligence collection throughout the war, a model to how an efficient organization of this magnitude should be run.

(*See Also*: Donovan, William; French Resistance Groups)

OSS Moral Operations Branch

The use of psychological warfare took center stage at OSS HQ once the United States entered the war. No longer was it primarily the use of massive force of arms that would defeat the enemy. Now, the subtle employment of nonlethal measures to compromise the civilian population, as well as the German armed forces, was put into effect. To that end, the OSS came up with detailed plans for the use of moral operations in continental Europe that would undermine the will of the enemy to stay the course.

The Moral Operations Branch worked closely with the SO arm when planning their operations. The training program of MO and that of SO were interchangeable. The MO Branch devised an overall plan for psychological warfare, as well as separate goals for most of the countries in Europe.

In preparing their outline for operations, the MO based all their assumptions on the fact that the Germans would make full use of the local population to hinder by any means the American progress across Europe. They would take such actions as blocking roads and promoting disorder and misinformation. The U.S. recognized this and took countermeasures to break the will of the masses. "It is the first function of the Moral Operations Branch of the OSS to employ secret radio, leaflets, and rumors and agents to sustain or to depress the civilian populations, and to use them or to keep them out of the way of the armed forces, as we are directed by the Theater Command."

"Before or during an invasion it may be desirable to create deception and to make feints or diversions at points other than those selected for serious attack. It is the third function of the MO Branch to use every psychological means to increase the effectiveness of such feints and diversions or to create deception by psychological means alone."

When devising their own MO manual, the OSS studied that of the British and decided that the United States could do better. The MO Division found what they considered many faults with British MO procedures and spelled them out to Bill Donovan. "Due to divided authority in secret moral operations, the British are considerably weaker in the particular field covered by the MO Branch of OSS than in any other. The British are naturally poor linguists and there are comparatively small foreign-language groups resident in Great Britain. Accordingly, they have had difficulty finding sufficient British recruits who both speak the continental languages and have the physical and mental qualifications for subversive operations in enemy occupied territory. The British press and Parliament have been bitterly antagonistic to every phase of the British political and psychological warfare and this has handicapped our ally in many phases of their development of manpower and equipment."

"When a successful invasion starts," continues the MO draft, "the people of Germany itself may be expected to be extremely apprehensive of what will be done to them both by the Russians and British troops and by the occupied peoples. Rightly or wrongly, the Germans believe that Americans will be more lenient and moderate. Under the circumstances, we should be prepared to play an unusually active part in weakening the morale of the German civilians and armed forces, even to the extent of being the chief spokesmen of the Allies for certain instructions, offers, threats, etc.

"The Germans are known to believe that Americans will be unusually ingenious and ruthless in every form of effort to create confusion and terror, to sabotage, to assassinate, etc. Thus, they may be expected to feel in advance some degree of the apprehension and respect for the unexpected things the enemy may do which is an essential ingredient of a nerve war." Prior to the actual invasion of enemy-held territory, the use of broadcasting and leaflets was the primary means of preparing and instructing the local population to play its part in psychological warfare. Once the invasion started, it would be the job of active agents on the ground to resist the enemy's expected actions. In order to counter German resistance once hostilities began, OSS MO agents were to be dropped behind enemy positions or infiltrated through the lines. Their job would be to take part in demolition and assassination operations.

Each American agent dropped behind the lines was expected to infiltrate a certain area and provide instructions to the local guerrilla bands encountered. These agents were also to deliver radio sets, as well as printed matter used for deception operations to these resistance bands. Fraudulent materials were to be "planted" on the enemy in order to lower his morale and create confusion on the ground. The United States Army Air Force and the British SOE aided MO agents in transport.

The MO Branch devised specific and detailed instructions for their agents once they landed in enemy territory. They were to make personal contacts with organized resistance groups, enlisting as many recruits as possible, giving them lessons on how to conduct MO plans. The use of intimidation of local officials, supplying these chains with their own radio sets, as well as other deception devices. OSS would try to enlist local people to act as guides, the use of friendly forces to destroy enemy installations, and the repairing of demolished infrastructure, drawing local maps for OSS use, placing diversionary signs to fool the enemy. Other MO devises would be the insertion into the local population of "black" leaflets—the use of outright lies to scare the enemy, threatening both military and civilians with death if they did not surrender, the threat of revenge if certain conditions stipulated by the OSS were not carried out, false reports to the enemy that people in the local community were armed and ready to retaliate against them, and threats of Fifth-column action against German troops.

This use of psychological warfare techniques was a vital part of the military strategy in the European Theater of Operations. The lessons learned from these early MO missions were expanded sometimes for better or worse by the CIA during the years of the Cold War.

OSS Special Activities

When the Coordinator of Information's Office was formed in 1941 under the direction of Bill Donovan, one of the first activities of the new spy apparatus that was put into effect was the "Special Activities-K and L Funds" section. This secret area was tasked with the job of handling all of COI's espionage, subversive activities (including sabotage) and guerrilla activities. When the COI was taken over by the OSS, this branch would play a major role in OSS operations across the globe.

The brainchild of what was to become the Special Activities branch came from Bill Donovan who envisioned a time when special troops would "soften up" the enemy, and prepare for the arrival on the battlefield of regular soldiers fighting a conventional war. He believed that these new SA men would be able to perform secret intelligence, infiltration, sabotage and subversive tactics and commando operations. Donovan asserted that both conventional and unconventional military operations could work side by side in battle.

Donovan met with FDR and a number of his trusted cabinet members in the summer of 1941 in Washington, where he outlined his new concept of warfare. FDR approved of what he heard and immediately thereafter christened the COI under Donovan's tutelage.

Donovan's first major hurdle in setting up his new bureau was the already existing intelligence operations then under the direction of the FBI, and the army and navy departments. These agencies were responsible for many aspects of intelligence work but none concentrating especially on subversive activities or paramilitary functions. This discrepancy was finally laid to rest when COI became operational.

With the United States now at war, the COI looked to North Africa as a potential staging ground for military engagements on a large scale. North Africa was also to be the initial hot spot where Donovan's concept of paramilitary activities would begin. With President Roosevelt's approval, COI secret missions on the African continent began.

The president told Donovan to contact British Prime Minister Churchill and discuss in detail the ideas generated concerning a cooperative relationship between COI and England's SOE. Prime Minister Churchill agreed on a U.S.-British plan of covert military involvement which would last throughout the war.

With Special Activities now on track, Donovan made his first personnel assignments. He picked Wallace Phillips and Lieutenant Colonel Robert Solborg. A latecomer to COI was Preston Goodfellow, who was brought on board in June 1942, when COI became the OSS. Wallace Phillips had earlier worked as the Special Assistant to the Director of ONI in the development of the navy's undercover program. Phillips brought along 13 of his most trusted agents for SA duty. These men were under State Department cover, a standard practice in such assignments.

Once the war began, the highest ranks decided to split Special Activities into Secret Intelligence and Special Operations. This was done on parallel with the two major British secret service branches: SOE and SIS.

Donovan and his men further decided that it would not be practical to have two British agencies dealing only with one American entity. "To meet this political necessity, and at the same time preserve the advantages of unified control and direction, Donovan separated Special Activities into a Secret Intelligence Branch and a Special Operations Branch in December (1942). Mr. David K.E. Bruce was appointed Chief of the Secret Intelligence Branch, designated SA/B (Special Activities/Bruce)."

In the overall structure of Special Activities, Secret Intelligence proved the most essential. SI's job was to create a covert agency whose primary task it was to obtain secret information outside the borders of the United States, chiefly through the work of undercover agents.

SI had two functions as it began its existence. First, to set up a network of agents in such neutral countries as Spain, Portugal, Switzerland, who would report on all political and military activities that they observed. Second, the formation of outposts in friendly countries such as Egypt, China and England, from which OSS missions against the enemy could be carried out.

In order to oversee the operations of the various components of SA, Geographic Desks were established, organized on a country by country basis. These desks developed intelligence projects for the entire SI branch. In all, nine Geographic Desks were set up, including that of Western Europe, Central Europe, the British Empire, Africa, the Near East, Far East, Northern Europe, Italy, and Eastern Europe. After the desks decided on the necessary covert missions, they were passed along to a Production Officer for approval. If the officer gave his ok, the project was sent up the ladder to William Donovan for disposal. When the proposed undertaking was given its final ratification, it was sent back to the various desks for its execution.

(*See Also*: COI; OSS; OSS Special Activities; OSS Special Projects Office; Donovan, William)

OSS Special Projects Office

The OSS Special Projects Office was established on December 31, 1943, in order to "carry out special assignments and missions as approved by the Director." The Special Projects Office was technical in nature and was primarily responsible for the development and acquisition of specialized intelligence, as well as weapons technology. All information gathered via Special Projects were sent directly to William Donovan.

The impetus for the SP Office grew out of a mission called Macgregor, which never saw the light of day but continued in another form. The initial purpose of Macgregor was to ferment insurrection in the Italian navy. Before this mission could get under way, Italy surrendered and the job was scrubbed.

The Macgregor mission dealt with the results of a test involving secret weapons technology, especially glider bombs. In order to learn more about this project, the OSS had to make contact with an Italian admiral, and an elaborate plan was put into effect to locate him. In order to do so, the OSS sent an agent from its base in Cairo to make contact with the officer via intermediaries in the Balkans. Working with agents from the Italian SI, a Macgregor member was sent into Sicily and taken by sea to an area near Rome. Contact with the admiral was thus arranged.

Besides the admiral, OSS Macgregor agents also met an Italian scientist who was knowledgeable in the area of electronics. These two people were then taken to the United States for debriefing.

While this was going on, another vital part of Macgregor was taking place. Agents were dispatched to the Torpedo Works in the city of Baia in order to salvage a barge loaded with experimental arms sunk in the harbor of Naples. These weapons were recovered and returned to the United States. What the OSS brought back was nothing less than the latest in undersea technology. The material was brought to the U.S. Naval Torpedo Station at Newport, Rhode Island. There, the technicians studied their treasure trove which consisted of literature on or the actual equipment which was made up of magnetic torpedo pistols, a new generation of guided torpedoes, winged aerial bombs, and a small, three-man submarine.

Another project taken on by SP was code-named Simmons, a plan to obtain information on secret weapons, especially that dealing with the HS-293 guided missile which the Germans had developed in late 1943. The OSS/SP learned of the HS-293 via an informant who had taken photographs of it on the island of Bornholm in September 1943. Before his capture, this agent was able to get the pictures into British hands.

Project Simmons actually started in April 1944, when the OSS learned where the Germans were keeping the HS-293. With the help of members of the French resistance, the Army Air Corps planned to attack the factory where the missile and its components were located. The plan was not carried out because of inclement weather.

If the proposed raid was a dismal failure, the OSS got lucky in their next attempt to control a HS-293. An SA man in Cairo made arrangements with a German officer who was willing to deal with the Americans in regard to the controlling mechanism of the missile. What the German officer offered were components to an ME-109 airplane located in Greece. The merchandise was successfully transferred to the United States.

SA took on another operation, Javaman (the original name for this plan was Campbell in January 1945). Javaman was a missile craft, which could be used to destroy enemy ships using remote control technology. "Javaman would operate by remote control radio from an aircraft and be aimed by the use of television." A test of the Javaman technology was successfully completed in August 1944 in the Gulf of Mexico. However, the powers that be at OSS/SA decided not to deploy it at that time.

It was then that General Douglas MacArthur learned about the Javaman program and made inquiries about its use in the Pacific. By June 1945, support personnel and equipment were sent to the Pacific for operational deployment, but before it could be put into effect, the war ended. The Special Projects Office paved the way for other modern intelligence/scientific organizations.

OSS Truth Drug Program

In the 1970s, the Congress of the United States conducted a wide ranging investigation of misdeeds of the Central Intelligence Agency, bringing to light many of the dark secrets that the agency had been responsible for during the decades of the 1950s to the 1970s. One of the revelations to come out of the hearings was the fact that the CIA had conducted a series of mind altering experiments using a battery of powerful drugs on unsuspecting human guinea pigs, some leading to their deaths.

The CIA, however, was not the original agency to experiment in the use of powerful substances on humans. Pouring over the records of the OSS, it seems that Bill Donovan's agency began a series of mind-altering tests during the war, although on a much smaller scale.

In September 1942, the OSS began looking for a drug that would work in coercing captured German U-boat crews or any other highly placed POWs into revealing information. The man the OSS turned to in this top-secret program was Dr. Stanley Lovell, the new project director investigating the search for a "truth drug."

Working in his lab, Dr. Lovell conducted trials with drugs such as "mescaline, various barbiturates, scopolamine, Benzedrine, marijuana, etc. The best results are obtained with the marijuana. A few minutes after the administering, the subject gradually becomes relaxed, and experiences a sensation of well-being. Whatever the individual is trying to withhold will be forced to the top of his subconscious mind."

These ingredients were put unknowingly into various foods of the person being tested, i.e., the dissolving of a colorless, odorless, liquefied form of marijuana into foods such as butter and mashed potatoes. After extensive experiments, the OSS was ready for field testing on human beings.

The first person to undergo this type of test was a known member of a New York Mafia gang, August "Little Augie" Del Gaizo. The experiment took place on May 25, 1943. "Little Augie" had been working with the OSS in the transporting of agents into German occupied Sicily. "Little Augie" had his own reputation to think of. He was known never to inform on any of his fellow mob members, a code of which he was very proud. The OSS provided him with two cigarettes that contained .14 grams of THC. After taking in the smoke, "Little Augie" becomes "obviously high and extremely garrulous." Quietly observing the session was Treasury Agent George White, who had previously arrested "Little Augie", during the course of his duty.

After the session ended, "Little Augie" "with no further encouragement," revealed the names of a host of New York City officials who were on the take, as well as information regarding the criminal networks of such Mafia dons as Meyer Lansky and Ben Siegel. Following the successful tryout on August Del Gaizo, the OSS would now identify the THC acetate as "TD" or "Truth Drug."

In 1944, OSS conducted other experiments using "TD" on an opera-

241

tional basis. According to Dr. Lovell, "Certain disclosures of the greatest value are in the possession of our military intelligence as a result of this treatment, which it is felt would otherwise not be known. Properly employed, it may be a national asset of incalculable importance." As secretly as the TD program began, it was quietly shut down before the war ended.

Oldfield, Maurice

Maurice Oldfield was the Director-general of the British Secret Intelligence Service (MI-6) from 1966 to 1978, aka "C."

Born in 1915, the son of a farmer, not the lineage one might expect for a person employing the highest position in British intelligence, Oldfield attended Manchester University and graduated in 1937. In 1941, he enlisted in the army and was attached to the South Staffordshire Contingent. He soon managed to glean another assignment more to his liking—that of an intelligence officer. He was then a corporal but in a brief period of time, was promoted to the rank of lieutenant in April of 1943. His first assignment was in the Middle East, where British intelligence had a large staff of covert operators stalking the large number of German spies that operated in that region. Maurice Oldfield worked in Military Intelligence throughout the war, and once the hostilities stopped, he headed back to London to a new job in the intelligence field.

In 1946, he began working for MI-6 or SIS. The mandate of the SIS was the gathering of foreign intelligence. He was assigned to its London headquarters, non-officially called "Broadway." He left London in 1950, and for the next three years served MI-6 undercover as a member of the staff of the British commissioner-general for Singapore. He was later transferred to the British Embassy in Washington in 1960. He remained in that position until 1964. It was here that Oldfield would act as the liaison with the FBI and the CIA. He also had a front-row seat in the subsequent defections of three of Britain's most notorious defectors: Kim Philby, Donald MacLean and Guy Burgess.

In his capacity as Britain's top intelligence officer in Washington, Oldfield had many conversations with Kim Philby. The two men discussed the ongoing investigation of an intelligence leak coming out of the embassy during the period 1944-45, as well as another emanating from the U.S. atomic laboratory in Los Alamos, New Mexico. What Oldfield did not know was that Philby was in the employ of the Russians and knew about the treachery of Klaus Fuchs, who was diverting top-secret nuclear information to the Soviet Union.

It has been hinted at over the years that Kim Philby may have known more about the penetration of the British intelligence services than just the perfidy of his two fellow spies, Burgess and MacLean. In an interview given by Oldfield to Philip Knightly who was working on a book on Kim Philby, Oldfield, commenting on Philby's own memoirs called, *My Silent War,* said "that the memoir was an accurate account of Philby's conduct as far as they go."

On October 13, 1975, an attempt was made on Oldfield's life by the Provisional wing of the Irish Republican Army who tried to kill him by planting a bomb in a London restaurant. It was spotted and removed minutes before "C" arrived to dine.

Oldfield resigned his intelligence post on October 2, 1979, and was appointed head of the British security setup in Northern Ireland.

Maurice Oldfield died on March 13, 1981, of cancer.

(*See Also*: Cambridge Spies; MacLean, Donald; Philby, Kim; Burgess, Guy)

Operation Bernhard

In order to finance their widespread intelligence operations across the world, the cash-short German government turned to an ingenious scheme to forge British currency. The plan was conceived at high levels of the Nazi Reich, and was put into production by concentration camp prisoners. The project was a success up to a point, and after its penetration by the British, disbanded in 1945, shortly before the war ended.

Operation Bernhard was the brainchild of the SD's Section F. Its original purpose was to undermine the value of English currency, but as the war progressed, an alternative plan to underwrite its operations, especially in the neutral countries as Turkey, Spain, Switzerland and Portugal, began.

The man who was originally tasked to implement the program was a German, Alfred Naujocks, an amateur boxer who joined the SS in 1931. He was also responsible for the fake "Polish" attack on the German radio station at Gleiwitz, close to the German-Polish border in which German soldiers, dressed as Poles "attacked" German territory, thus, justifying the eventual Nazi invasion of Poland on September 1, 1939. When the war started, Naujocks was in charge of the SD's document forging and special projects department headquartered in Berlin. After coming up with the counterfeiting idea, Naujocks took his plan up the chain of command to his ultimate boss, Reinhard Heydrich. Heydrich, in turn, sent the feeler to Adolf Hitler who gave his approval. Hitler sent Naujocks on his way but with one condition: under no circumstances would American money be copied.

The original name for the enterprise was dubbed Operation Andreas, a daunting task, no matter what it was called. First, the Germans had to duplicate higher denomination pound notes that had been in circulation since the mid 1850s. Secondly, the money then in use was printed "by letterpress from electrotypes." This would prove hardest in the duplication of the 5, 10, 20, and 50 pound notes. Other considerations that the Germans faced were getting the proper plates, paper, and ink.

The Germans obtained the linen type paper used by the Bank of England to produce the pound notes from two German paper mills. With engravers working around the clock in various parts of the country, Operation Bernhard was ready to begin testing in February 1941.

The original batch of 5 and 10 pound notes were sent to neutral countries where a strange request was made: the banks were asked to conduct tests to make sure that the money was real—it was.

Then, in a most unusual decision, the plan was put on hold due to infighting and political blackmail on the part of a number of highly placed German officers. Naujocks, who had made many powerful political enemies, was still a man who possessed a great amount of state secrets, was allowed to continue his counterfeiting.

After the political infighting was over, Walter Schellenberg, the head of the SD, or security police, found himself running the program. In another shake-up of operational personnel, a major named Bernard Kruger, once Naujocks's assistant, was given responsibility over the project (it was now renamed Operation Bernhard).

Major Kruger contacted a number of experts at the Reichsbank (Germany's national bank) as well as people at the Reich Printing Company for help in producing the counterfeit bills. In an act that was not common in an oppressive country like Germany, Kruger's requests were declined. Kruger next turned toward another venue where he could find skilled men to take on his secret task, prisoners in the Sachenhausen concentration camp. With a death sentence looming over them, the Germans found skilled craftsmen needed to work on forging British banknotes and, behind barbed-wire fences, the duplication process began. German printing firms were coerced into providing presses of the type used by the English. By 1942, almost 400,000 fake British bills were being sent into neutral countries, as well as used by the German regime to finance both overt and covert activities.

As the program progressed, a river of false bank notes were in circulation. A few trusted agents who sold them to German businessmen across Europe put the money into unsuspecting hands.

Many of the fake notes were sent to Italy and could readily be disseminated throughout Europe. The Germans used some of the money to buy back arms from the local resistance groups who had originally purchased their weapons from the allies.

In 1943, the British took their first concrete steps to stop Operation Bernhard. In a bit of dissembling to the general public, the Bank of England issued the following statement, in order "to provide an additional handicap to those who may contemplate breaches of exchange control and other regulations, the Bank of England would cease issuing notes above 5 pounds." By doing so, they would be able to trace any 5 pound notes that were bogus and take them out of circulation.

From the German point of view, Operation Bernhard was a success. While they did not fulfill their goal of wrecking the British economy, they were able to use the bogus money to their advantage.

In 1945, when the end of the war was near, Heinrich Himmler closed down the operation at the Sachsenhausen concentration camp and moved it in haste to the rugged mountains of Austria where, it was hoped, the final struggle against the allies would take place. Himmler ordered Major Kruger to burn all papers, printing presses, plates, anything to do with Operation Bernhard. Kruger obeyed, and much of the physical evidence was dropped into various lakes in the Austrian Alps.

Then, the allies hit paydirt. In May 1943, a German officer told his captors that he knew where forged British currency was located. Major George McNally operating out of Frankfurt was taken to the scene of the discovery. What he found startled him beyond imagination. After a thorough investigation by the Americans, it was discovered that more than nine million British notes, with a value of 140 million pounds were now in allied hands. They also found records of the forced laborers from the concentration camp who worked on the project.

Alfred Naujocks surrendered to the Americans in November 1944 and was jailed. Before he could stand trial, he escaped and was said to have made his way to South America. What is known is that he came back to Germany and lived in Hamburg until his death on April 4, 1960.

In one of the ironies of the war, a large amount of money coming out of Operation Bernhard wound up in the hands of a German spy named Elyeza Bazna, known as "Cicero." Bazna worked for the British Ambassador in Turkey during the war and was paid 300,000 pounds by his German bosses. Unfortunately for Bazna, he was arrested when he attempted to pass off his forged bank notes.

(*See Also*: Bazna, Elyeza; "Cicero")

Operation Bodyguard

In the pre-dawn hours of June 6, 1944, the largest armada ever sent into war came ashore on the coast of France at Normandy. A combined allied force comprised of more than 5,000 ships, 10,000 airplanes, and 200,000 men began the liberation of Europe, which culminated in the surrender of Germany almost one year later. Even as the allied troops waded ashore into Fortress Europe, the high command of the German military still believed that the invasion was just a feint, that the *real* invasion would come up the coast at the Pas de Calais, about 150 miles northeast of Normandy near the Straits of Dover. It was only after the allies broke through what little resistance the Germans put up and were on their way inland did Hitler's chief of staff, General Alfred Jodl, call their mistake in not fortifying the Normandy area Germany's "fatal strategic error."

Just how did the allies deceive the Germans into believing that Normandy was *not* the prime location for the Second Front in the European War? What actions did they take to convince Hitler that the invasion was to be elsewhere? The answers to that series of question lie in the massive deception campaign initiated by the allies in the months prior to the invasion, code-named Overlord. (The name for the overall deception plan was dubbed Operation Bodyguard.)

The man in charge of the Overlord operation was General Dwight Eisenhower, the Supreme Commander. Eisenhower had no illusions about the mammoth problem facing the allies, as he and his military advisors pondered what action was to be taken in preparing the invasion of Europe. The Germans were superior on the ground, with 59 divisions in France, while the allies had seven. The Americans had one advantage—a massive air force that could provide an air umbrella once the invasion began.

Eisenhower turned to his own intelligence apparatus and that of the British to devise a plan to fool the Germans in whatever action was devised. The first part of that plan was put into effect once Eisenhower arrived in London in January 1944 to meet with his British counterparts. Unknown to the general, a German spy, code-named Tate, sent a message to his controller back in Hamburg reporting the arrival of the allied commander. What Eisenhower would learn was that Tate was a "turned" German agent who had been captured by the British Secret Service upon his arrival in England. Tate was under the control of the British Double Cross System, a top-secret organization that was responsible for the capturing of German agents inside the country.

The "turned" German spies were given a choice: either work as double agents for the British or be hanged as spies. All decided on the former. What the Double Cross System did was to use these German agents to send back to their homeland, real and imagined intelligence information fed by the British. The quality of the information returned to Abwehr HQ appeared accurate and the agents received praise from their controllers in Germany.

It was the job of MI-5, the British internal security agency (like our own FBI) to pinpoint all German spies arriving inside the country, and they did so without a hitch. The section tasked with the challenge of running these doubles was BI-A, under the overall direction of John Masterman who ran Double Cross. (In the end, more than 120 German agents were captured.)

How the British discovered the identities of all the agents coming into Britain was due to the information gathered by their use of the Ultra Secret. What the Germans did not realize was that British codebreakers working out of Bletchley Park had broken the German military codes by way of Enigma and knew the daily order of battle that the German military was preparing.

The Americans provided another intelligence bonanza used by the allies to the British via their eavesdropping on Japanese diplomatic messages between Baron Oshima, the Japanese Ambassador to Berlin, and his foreign minister in Tokyo. U.S. codebreakers read the reports of Baron Oshima's conversations with Hitler in which the Nazi leader described the defenses of the German forces, particularly where the Germans believed an allied attack against Europe would take place (it wasn't Normandy).

One of the most proficient double agents was Juan Pujol, a Spaniard, given the code name Garbo. Garbo was the best spy the Germans had in England (although they did not know he was working for the British), sending them 315 letters via Lisbon, in one year. Garbo made up his own fictitious army of spies whom he "ran," and reported their "progress" to the Abwehr. In reply to one of his lengthy messages, the Germans sent him this answer, "Your activity and that of your informants gives us a perfect idea of what is taking place over there; these reports, as you can imagine, have an incalculable value and for this reason I beg of you to proceed with the greatest care so as not to endanger in these momentous times either yourself or your organization."

In early 1944, the Germans turned to Garbo for news on the upcoming allied invasion of Europe, especially the size of army units, sea, and air forces, the dates of operations, etc. Using information provided by the British, Garbo sent what the Germans believed to be vital information concerning allied intentions.

One of the deception operations devised by the allies in the entire Overlord plan was a guise called Fortitude. Fortitude was divided into two parts: Fortitude North was the supposed invasion of Norway, and Fortitude South was the fake invasion of the Pas de Calais (the area in which the allies wanted the Nazis to think the "real" invasion was to take place).

The base of the two Fortitude plans was the creation of a fictitious British Fourth Army in Scotland, labeled Fusag. Fusag, as far as the Germans were concerned, was located in southeastern England near Dover. (The real invasion force slated for Normandy was the 21st Army Group, then in wait west of Dover.)

Fusag, in reality, was comprised of about 400 men sending false radio messages to each other, with the call signs of a real army. Using a code that the Germans could intercept, the fake Fusag men alerted the Germans to a fictitious British 58th Division, mountain training (in order to lull the Germans into believing that an attack on Norway was imminent), another fake unit, the 55th Division, all of whose activities were reported on by Garbo.

Fortitude South received one of its early coups in the person of captured German General Hans Kramer. Kramer had been captured in North Africa and was being sent back to German lines via Sweden. During his travels, Kramer was taken right through the heart of the allied build-up. When asked where he was, he was purposely misled by his captors, being told that Dover, Kent was "just over the hill," strategically placed near the coast, within striking distance of the Pas de Calais.

Garbo also told of row after row of planes, tanks, ships, and trucks along the ports of the English Channel. In reality, these were nothing more than fakes, constructed of plywood, developed by allied engineers. This army in waiting was photographed (up to a point) by high-flying German airplanes.

The man in command of Fusag was George Patton, the controversial, no-nonsense general who would later be immortalized in film. In order to make Fusag more powerful, the counterfeit British Fourth Army was merged under Patton's control.

Through the work of Garbo and the other agents of the Double Cross System, the Germans believed that the allies had a total of 80 divisions in Britain (only eight actually existed). With all the false information pouring forth, the Germans sent 280,000 crack troops to Norway, awaiting an invasion that never took place. In another bit of subterfuge on the part of the allies, these troops were sent to France 10 days after the June 6 invasion. These soldiers were directed to the Pas de Calais, not Normandy.

Even before the massive allied deception process began, the German commanders, including Field Marshall Gerd von Rundstedt, believed that the attack would come "across the narrower part of the Channel." This was the area closest to the Pas de Calais, with strategic importance to the Germans.

Adolf Hitler himself believed he knew the source of the attack, "I have decided," said Hitler, "to reinforce the defenses in the West, particularly at places from which we shall launch our long-range war against England. For those are the very points at which the enemy must and will attack: there—unless all indications are misleading—will be fought the decisive invasion battle."

His mention "of places which we shall launch our long-range war against England" was the Pas de Calais, the site of the launch pads for the powerful V-1 rockets which were to reign death and destruction upon English cities.

Hitler and his generals' belief that Pas de Calais would be the ideal launching pad for an invasion lay in the fact that it was the narrowest part of the English Channel, near Belgium and almost approaching the Straits of Dover, a short, 20-mile distance for aircraft flying from Britain, and a direct line to the heart of Germany's economically vital Ruhr Valley.

The allies, too, had a tough decision to make as to where the invasion was to take place. Other sites under consideration were Holland, Belgium, and the French Mediterranean. Holland and Belgium were too heavily defended and too close to Germany to be of any value. The Pas de Calais was defended by the almost impregnable Atlantic Wall, a series of long, highly fortified military posts stretching for miles, directly facing the sea. That left only one alternative—Normandy.

Normandy was an attractive site as it was close to the vital port of Caen, an offloading point for ships and supplies coming from the large flotilla offshore. Inland there were a number of navigable rivers to divert any German forces they encountered. After weighing all the alternatives, General Eisenhower decided that Normandy would indeed be the site of the invasion. With the Normandy determination made, all the various plans called for in Operation Bodyguard were put into effect with startling results.

As Eisenhower mulled over when to make the attack, he only had a three-day window of opportunity in which to work with—June 5, 6, and 7, 1944. The one intangible that Eisenhower could not control was the weather, and the situation worsened when a powerful Atlantic storm began on June 4, causing a postponement. With thousands of men and ships lying off the coast of France, conditions could not have been worse. But the next day, June 5, the weather suddenly cleared enough to give Eisenhower the chance he needed to launch the attack.

The Germans inadvertently aided the allies when the few weather stations they once maintained along the coast of France were removed, thus denying them information concerning the patterns in the region.

Not believing that Eisenhower would give the go-ahead because of the inclement weather near the Channel, the Germans did not make further military preparations to fortify their troops in the region. The Germans swallowed the bait completely, and on June 6, 1944, the greatest invasion the world had ever seen stormed along the beaches on the Normandy coast.

Through the use of Ultra, the allies knew that the enemy had little fuel in reserve and thus were able to mount successful attacks against the French port of Cherbourg and the entire Contentin peninsula.

It was now that Garbo would plant the decisive seed that would ensure the success of the D-Day deception. He radioed his controllers in Germany saying that three of his fictitious agents, "Donny, Dick, and Dorick," had vital news for him. Garbo sent a message saying that the landings at Normandy were a "diversionary maneuver designed to draw off enemy reserves in order to make an attack at another place. In view of the continued air attacks on the concentration area mentioned, which is a strategically favorable position for this, it may very probably take place in the Pas de Calais, particularly since in such an attack the proximity of air bases will facilitate the operation by providing continued strong air support."

Hitler's military commanders agreed with Garbo's assessments, going even further by stating that the probable venue for the invasion was in Belgium. Garbo's news was backed up by a report arriving at Abwehr HQ from a German spy in Stockholm who said that "authoritative military sources" in London said that the invasion would start in the Pas de Calais. That strategically important deception plan delayed the arrival of the lst SS Panzer Division in Normandy until June 16, 10 days after the attack began. (If the lst Panzer Division had been at Normandy when the troops landed, they would have been mauled.)

Within two months of the June 6, D-Day landings the allies had liberated Paris, which fell on August 25. Twelve months after the D-Day landings, Berlin fell, Hitler committed suicide in his Bunker, the Japanese surrendered, and World War II was over.

(*See Also*: D-Day Deception; Garbo; Double Cross System; Masterman, John; Enigma; Ultra; Twenty Committee; Kennedy, Joseph, P.)

Operation Corn Flake

Operation Corn Flake was an audacious plan run by the OSS's Moral Operations Department, in conjunction with their office in Berne, Switzerland to undermine the morale of the German people by the use of fake postage stamps that were clandestinely put into the German mail system.

Bill Donovan put Operation Corn Flake into business using the Berne OSS office as its headquarters. The purpose of the mission was to produce fake postage stamps with an altered face of Adolf Hitler on the "Death Head" stamp, with the false inscription printed on it which read, "Futsches Reich," or Ruined Empire. The stamps used for this purpose were the 12pf and 6pf issues, which were forged by OSS master craftsmen using the material of a real German postal stamp.

The OSS used the 6pf and 12pf Hitler head stamps in sheets of 50 rather than the original covers. The stamps were altered due to their dull surface. Once the stamps were ready, the next question was how to get them into circulation? That answer came from the OSS and the Army Air Corps.

It was decided by the OSS and the Air Corps that the German mail trains were to be attacked as often as possible. In the confusion following these attacks, other American planes would fly over the area and drop large amounts of mail sacks containing letters with the "Futsches Reich" stamps on them. Once the bombed-out trains were back on track, the fake mail, along with the real messages, were sent on their way.

The OSS used real-time German phone directories to cull thousands of names of people in various cities, and affixed the fabricated stamps to the letters. OSS researchers were able to duplicate up to a T, the exact type of mailbags used in the German postal system, along with any official marks then in effect. Over the course of many months, unsuspecting citizens picked up thousands of these Death Head stamps as they opened their mail.

Operation Corn Flake came to light after the war with the sale of President Roosevelt's private stamp collection. FDR was an avid stamp collector, spending many hours in the solitude of the White House cataloging his private collection. The OSS, too, kept many of these Death Head stamps in its files for its historical records.

Today, the ardent stamp collector can purchase these bits of wartime history in prices ranging in sets from $50 to $175. Operation Corn Flake was just one example of MO operations.

Operation Griffin

Operation Griffin was the operational name given by MI-6 to one of its foremost agents to undertake a mission. The man in question was a brilliant Austrian scientist named Paul Rosbaud who, by the time the war was over, would reveal some of the most valuable intelligence information coming out of Germany.

Paul Rosbaud was born in Austria in 1897. His father deserted the family when Paul was young, and he grew up in a home minus a loving father figure.

When World War I broke out, Paul joined the army and was captured by the British in 1917. As a young man, his first love was science; and as an adult, he pursued his passion with a vengeance.

Once the conflict ended, he enrolled in the Darmstadt Technical University and through hard work won a fellowship at the Kaiser Wilhelm Institute in Berlin where he did groundbreaking work in the field of X-ray cinematography. He also received his doctorate degree from the Berlin Technical University.

With his reputation as one of the best scientific minds in Europe fixed, Paul Rosbaud gained entry into the inner world of Germany's most influential scientists and mathematicians. To that end, he began gathering articles from the best minds of the day which he began publishing and disseminating throughout the scientific community. In time, he was sought out for the breath and knowledge of his work.

But for all of Rosbaud's brilliant work, he was troubled by the rise of Hitler's National Socialist Programs and the virulent anti-Semitic dictates that began to filter down into everyday life in Germany.

Rosebaud, whose wife was Jewish, decided that she would be safer if she left Germany, and he went to the British Embassy in Berlin in the hope of getting a visa for her. At the embassy, Rosbaud met with Francis Foley, the passport control officer (that was his cover position in the embassy—he was actually an officer for MI-6). Foley gladly gave Mrs. Rosbaud a visa to travel to England, and when asked if he, too, would like to leave, Paul declined. In their conversations, the two men hit it off at once, and Rosbaud openly told Foley of his distaste for Hitler and what was happening in Germany.

Foley managed to get Rosbaud's agreement to deliver to him any significant information he could gather in his talks with his fellow scientists. In a meeting held by Rosbaud and Foley in December 1938, Rosbaud revealed that fellow scientist Otto Hahn explained the rudiments of fission—the first step in the development of an atomic bomb. In what proved to be a blunder on the part of the German government, the results of the fission plan were published in a scientific journal. After Great Britain entered the war, Rosbaud's access to Foley was severely curtailed, and a new way of contacting him was needed. This problem was solved by the use of friendly Norwegian students studying in Berlin, who took Rosbaud's messages to Foley.

Paul Rosbaud was now in a position to reveal some of the guarded scientific data coming out of Berlin, all of which he shared with Francis Foley and the British. Among the new developments that Rosbaud brought to life were a new rocket-propelled glider controlled by a plane using electronic signals and information on a proposed anti-aircraft missile.

By 1942, Rosbaud was given his most important assignment: he was to monitor the nascent German atomic bomb project. The next year proved vital for Operation Griffin. Rosbaud reported that the heavy water used in the process of building an atomic bomb was being worked on in a plant in Norway. With this information in hand, the British mounted a successful air operation against the facility, as well as a commando raid conducted by elements of the Norwegian resistance, which crippled the plant and its sensitive work.

Rosbaud also delivered plans of the ME-262, the first jet airplane which the Germans hoped to put into production, as well as new safety measures concerning the U-boat fleet. His intelligence was instrumental in the British destruction of the German facility at Peenemunde, the location of Germany's fleet of V-1 rockets that reigned destruction upon London.

After Germany surrendered, the British welcomed Rosbaud to England, where he joined his wife. For the rest of his life, he wrote, taught, and resumed a life of anonymity, keeping out of the public eye, until his death in 1963.

Operation Kondor

Operation Kondor was a German infiltration mission established out of Cairo, Egypt, in 1942. It involved the activities of two Abwehr agents, the actions of the British army, and a number of highly placed Egyptian military officers who were involved with the Germans.

By 1942, the Germans had a substantial number of troops, especially those under the command of the Desert Fox, General Erwin Rommel, and his Africa Korps, among the desolate dunes and terrible heat of the Egyptian desert. Rommel knew that if he could defeat the British in Egypt, then the vitally important Suez Canal could be used as a springboard to further Nazi military success across the entire Mediterranean.

In May 1942, the unsuspecting German agents, Peter Monkaster and Hussein Ghafer, found their way into a remote British army camp near the town of Assuit, Egypt. They received food and were directed to a station for the train to Cairo. After the departure of Monkaster and Ghafer, the radio-man at Assuit sent a coded message to British military HQ in Cairo, alerting them that the men had just left the camp and were headed their way.

In reality, both men were not whom they claimed to be. Peter Monkaster was really Hans Gerd, and Hussein Ghafer was Johann Eppler. Eppler was born in Alexandria, Egypt, and lived the good, privileged life of a well-to-do young man, with plenty of available money. Eppler was initiated into the Abwehr in 1938, a good catch for the Germans. He spoke Arabic and was instructed to become a "sleeper," an agent who would live a normal life, just waiting for the call activating him. That summons came in March 1942, when he was brought back to Germany for intelligence training.

Eppler was matched with another Abwehr agent, Hans Gerd, and they were given an assignment: to set up a radio link in Cairo and report back via Eppler. They were issued false papers, and more importantly, $80,000 in British pounds, and sent on their way.

At the same time that Eppler/Gerd were heading toward Cairo, the Germans had scored a major intelligence coup. They managed to break into the secure communications of the British forces in Egypt and sent back all their information to General Rommel. They managed another intelligence bonanza when they were able to tap into the communications of U.S. Colonel Bonner Fuller, the U.S. military attaché in Cairo. This, too, was relayed to Rommel.

Eppler was instructed to send his findings to his German counterparts in the Egyptian deserts, using a code book based on a best-selling book of the day, *Rebecca*, written by Daphne du Maurier.

What the unsuspecting Eppler and Gerd did not realize was the fact that the British, via Ultra, had zoomed in on their whereabouts and were tracking them at a feverish pace. Upon arriving in Cairo, the two German spies met with a beautiful Egyptian belly dancer named Fathmy, who found them suitable living quarters.

As soon as Eppler/Gerd began transmitting their messages, British listening stations intercepted their signals, and were able to arrest two other German agents. Among the accessories found on them was a copy of *Rebecca*. Using special inks, British intelligence found that the book was paid for in Portugese currency, and that six copies of the same title had been purchased in a Lisbon bookstore by the wife of the German military attaché at the German Embassy.

Eppler was by now spending lavishly in Cairo's nightspots. He lost thousands of the British pounds given to him as operating expenses. What the sloppy Eppler did not know was that some of the money given to him was bogus currency, part of the German counterfeiting scheme called Operation Bernhard. British agents went to the various casinos in Cairo and eventually were able to learn the identity of the high-spending playboy—Johann Eppler.

While all this transpired, Eppler had clandestine meetings with a number of anti-British Egyptian military officers, among them an up-and-coming soldier named Anwar Sadat. These Egyptian officers decided that Germany would provide a better partner than the hated British, especially if the Germans won the war.

In time, Eppler, Gerd, Sadat, and the belly dancer Fathmy were arrested. Eppler decided to cooperate with the British and became a double agent, relaying bogus information to the Desert Fox. Eppler's biggest contribution came when he purposely withheld from Rommel the fact that British forces were planning to attack an obscure town called El Alamein. During that decisive battle, Rommel's Panzers were destroyed, thus giving the British total control over Egypt and the Suez Canal.

Johann Eppler spent his final years operating a bookstore in Germany. Hans Gerd, too, returned to Germany but disappeared. Anwar Sadat would become president of Egypt, and prove indispensable in beginning the peace process with Israel. He would tragically meet his fate at the hands of an assassin in 1981.

(*See Also*: Operation Bernhard)

Operation Pastorius

Operation Pastorius was the code name of a detailed Nazi plan to wreak havoc and sabotage inside the United States during 1942. Admiral Wilhelm Canaris, who was responsible for the training and execution of the plot, also conceived it. Operation Pastorius was the first attempt by the Germans to infiltrate directly onto American soil, and by the time the mission was completed, Canaris's future would be in doubt, the plot to blow up American factories, a dismal failure.

On the dark night of June 13, 1942, 21-year-old coast guardsmen John C. Cullen was patrolling the silent beaches off Amagansett, Long Island, some 105 miles from New York City. The stretch of Atlantic beach that Cullen was working was far from the battles raging a continent away. Or so he thought. Out of the darkness, Cullen heard the rustle of noise and men's voices coming his way. Cullen spotted four men, the leader walking directly toward him. He confronted the stranger. The man said he was a fisherman from Southampton whose boat had run aground. The fisherman said that his name was George Davis.

John Cullen, growing suspicious of the four strangers, asked Davis if he would come with him to the coast guard station to file a report. Davis refused. He then offered Cullen a bribe of $300 if he would forget he ever saw them and threatened to kill him. Cullen was in no position to take any action, and he watched as the four men headed inland. They would later be seen at the Amagansett train station of the Long Island Rail Road boarding a train for New York City.

Cullen went back to his station and reported on what had just transpired. Cullen, along with a number of coast guardsmen, returned to the spot where the encounter had taken place. What they found corroborated his story. Strewn across the dunes were German marine uniforms, cigarettes, boxes of explosives, bombs made out of clay, and other German-related items.

Just as they were about to leave, their attention was turned to the sea and the sight of a conning tower of a German submarine diving beneath the waves. What the coast guardsmen saw was the German U-boat 202, which had just dropped off Davis and his men.

Immediately after the incident took place, the coast guard in Amagansett called the New York office of the FBI, who took over the investigation, and more importantly, the search for the German agents.

In reality, George Davis was George Dasch, a 39-year-old German who had previously lived in the United States from 1922 to 1941. Dasch was the leader of an undercover mission called Operation Pastorius, named after Franz Daniel Pastorius, the leader of one of the early groups of German settlers to immigrate to the United States during the 1600s.

Preparations for Operation Pastorius lay in the hands of Colonel Erwin von Lahousen, the director of the Abwehr's sabotage unit. Colonel Lahousen chose Lieutenant Walter Kappe to find suitable men who were fluent in English and who knew American customs for their planned sabotage operations inside the United States. Kappe had previously lived in the States from

OPERATION PASTORIUS

1925 to 1937. After an exhaustive search conducted by the DAI, "Deutsches Ausland-Instiut," eight men were selected. They were then sent to the Abwehr sabotage school located at Quenz Lake Farm, outside the city of Brandenburg. For several months, they were trained in demolitions, the use of explosives, and the study of American magazines and newspapers. They were given false identities, including genuine American social security and selective service cards.

Shortly before their training was completed, they were given their targets, in the United States: the Aluminum Company of America plants in Tennessee, Illinois, and New York. Other secondary targets were the Philadelphia Salt Company's cryolite plant in Philadelphia, as well as the disruption of Newark, New Jersey's railroad terminal, the locks around the Ohio River, and the vital reservoirs supplying New York City.

With the final preparations for Operation Pastorius completed, each team leader was given $50,000 in U.S. bills to cover expenses.

It was decided by the Abwehr that two targets of opportunity would be selected for operations inside the United States. To that end, the team left by submarine from the German naval base at Lorient, France. The first group, led by Edward Kerling, departed by sub on May 26, 1942, bound for Ponte Verda Beach, Florida, 25 miles from Jacksonville.

Kerling, then 33, had lived in the United States, working as a chauffeur and other odd jobs. He returned to Germany in 1940 and got a job as a translator for English language broadcasts.

The U-202, carrying Dasch and his men, set out to sea on May 28, 1942. Kerling's team arrived off the Florida coast on June 17, while Dasch's U-202 reached shore off Amagansett on June 13.

George Dasch was born in Speyer-am-Rhein, Germany in 1903 and came to Philadelphia in 1922. For many years, he shuttled between New York, Miami, Los Angeles, and San Francisco, working as a waiter. He married Rose Marie Guille in 1930. Once the war started, however, Dasch and his bride returned to Germany, where he took up the Nazi cause. Once home, Dasch met Lieutenant Walter Kappe, who worked for the Abwehr. Kappe got Dasch a job tracing American broadcasts in Germany (the same job as Kerling), and it was through Kappe that George Dasch was assigned to Operation Pastorius.

The other men who took part in Operation Pastorius besides Dasch and Kerling were: Ernst Burger, a native of Augsburg; Richard Quirin, who lived in Berlin before arriving in the U.S. in 1927 and worked in upstate New York as a mechanic; Heinrich Heinck, born in Hamburg in 1907, an illegal immigrant to the U.S. in 1926; Hermann Neubauer, also from Hamburg, who worked in the U.S. as a cook and in the hotel industry, going back in 1940;. Werner Thiel, born in Dortmund in 1907, who lived for a time in

Philadelphia, Detroit, and Los Angeles and joined the Bund in the U.S., and was given an all-expenses-paid trip to Germany in 1939; Herbert Hans Haupt, who lived as a youth in Chicago and worked making eyeglasses. All these men took training at the Abwehr run Quentz Lake facility.

After making their getaway from Amagansett, the raiders arrived in New York City and divided themselves into pairs. George Dasch found himself with Ernest Burger. They checked into a hotel under assumed names. Then, the most unlikely and still unresolved event took place. George Dasch called the FBI on June 14, saying that he was "Franz Daniel Pastorius" and that he had information he could give only to J. Edgar Hoover.

The FBI man thought the call was a prank. Dasch said that he would come to Washington to personally give his information to the director. Dasch arrived in Washington on June 18 and checked into the fashionable Mayflower Hotel. It was from there that he called FBI headquarters once again. This time, though, the bureau was aware of the incident on Long Island, and agents were at Dasch's hotel within minutes. He was taken into custody and told his story.

Dasch confessed the history of the Abwehr plan to infiltrate the United States, testified about the second landing in Florida, and gave the names of all his accomplices. Within days, all eight Germans were arrested and proceeded to stand trial.

The Germans were put on trial on orders from President Roosevelt on July 8, at the Justice Department Building in Washington, D.C. The proceedings were kept secret from the public, with only a few in the administration aware of it. Attorney General Francis Biddle and the army's Judge Advocate General (JAG), General Myron Cramer, headed the prosecution. Colonel Carl Ristine was Dasch's attorney, while Colonels Casius Dowell and Kenneth Royall represented the other defendants.

The defense attorneys tried to petition the court for a change of venue, i.e., that no overt act of sabotage was committed and that the trial should not be held in a military court. Defense Counsel Royall, in a highly unusual move, managed to get the members of the Supreme Court, who were all on summer break, to reconvene in an emergency session to deliberate on the issue of whether or not the military should have jurisdiction over the case. The Supreme Court judges agreed that the Germans were indeed an invasion force and let the military commission stand.

The trial took less than a month to make a decision. On August 3, 1942, they sent their decision to the president. Five days later, FDR's decision regarding what action to take was carried out.

On August 8, 1942, Edward Kerling, Richard Quirin, Herbert Haupt, Heinrich Heinck, Werner Thiel, and Hermann Neubauer were executed.

The military tribunal, however, asked that the death penalty be waved in the cases of George Dasch and Ernest Burger, because of their cooperation in exposing the case to the FBI. Burger was given a life sentence, while Dasch was sentenced to 30 years.

Both men served only six years of their prison term. In April 1948, President Harry Truman commuted their sentences, and both men were sent back to Germany, now an ally of the United States.

It was not until years later that the American public was told the entire story of the landings at Amagansett and Jacksonville. What was obvious that summer of 1942 was that the United States was now directly in the line of fire, its people and industries ripe for invasion.

Operation Sauerkraut

Operation Sauerkraut was a Moral Operations (MO) mission, run in conjunction with Company D, based out of Caserta, Italy. The purpose was to distribute false information to the German troops in Italy. Its secondary aim was the collection of intelligence for OSS use. It was this second phase of Operation Sauerkraut that caused a rift between the OSS and the army as far as which branch would have operational jurisdiction over its assignments.

The main duty of the Sauerkraut exercises was to "disseminate propaganda material among German troops, place posters and leaflets wherever it might be suitable in and around military installations, in bivouac areas, supply posts, etc. All of the material was presumed German subversive propaganda turned out by German-Austrian and Czech underground movements."

A majority of the men used in the Sauerkraut operations were members of the local resistance who were currently active and under OSS control. A number of them were then living undercover in the liberated areas of Italy and were in close contact with allied forces. When recruiting these men, the OSS had to use a certain amount of subterfuge in order to win them over.

Their work was requested by a representative of the different German resistance movements. When giving briefings, no official U.S. Army representative was in attendance. A civilian member of the OSS conducted the meetings, and the army was never mentioned. They were placed under the direction of German-speaking American civilians who were presented to the agents as the true spokespersons of the German underground.

The agents were not told the name of the organization they were working for, or were they under any strict military discipline or orders. The agents were told that the army was interested in any secondary intelligence that they might collect in the carrying out of their work, and upon completion of their assignments, they should report anything of value to their supervisors.

By February 1945, a feud over who would run Operation Sauerkraut erupted between the OSS and the army via Company D, responsible for covert missions using army personnel. Memos written to Lieutenant Colonel David Rosen, the S-2 of the 2677th Regiment OSS, from Eugene Warner, Chief MO (Moral Operations) Branch, tells the story.

Lieutenant Colonel Rosen, Warner, and Major Shuling agreed to give total responsibility for Sauerkraut Operations to Company D for a 60-day period. After that time, the situation regarding Sauerkraut would be reevaluated. The MO Division further said that they were in the process of procuring numerous items of equipment from the OSS's Research and Development (R&D) for Company D's use.

Colonel Rosen wrote, "the Sauerkrauts are not to be primarily for intelligence purposes that they are going for MO propaganda purposes." The OSS succinctly responded, "If MO doesn't want to play ball let's call off the whole MO deal. Neither Army nor we understand the MO attitude. It's embarrassing."

OSS documents in the National Archives reflect the bad blood regarding Sauerkraut. Eugene Warner's memo states that Major Suhling wanted to take over all MO agents for intelligence purposes. "The past record will show that MO originated, equipped and launched the first Sauerkrauts despite a negative and perhaps hostile attitude by Suhling and some army officers. For weeks and months, Suhling made clear that he did not desire this type of operation. For its part, army ordered the agents removed from the forward area, and they had to be taken back to Rome. As far as intelligence for the army is concerned, MO has always processed its agents thru tactical interrogations in order to give [the] Army the utmost cooperation and every chance to gain intelligence. The early Sauerkraut's run by MO produced intelligence of value."

In January 1945, MO stopped any further Sauerkraut operations, mostly due to bad weather, as well as the protection of "OSS security." "Another important reason, of which Major Suhling is apparently unaware, is that the source of our propaganda is seemingly still undiscovered by the enemy; and to risk capture of these agents might well blow the entire MO effort of the past year by revealing it as of Allied origin."

In time, these divergent positions were settled, and Sauerkraut missions proceeded on schedule.

The use of undercover operatives after hostilities stopped was discussed, and plans for their deployment devised. "If OSS is to continue undercover operations in the Reich after the armistice and in the postwar years, it seems obvious that a network of native Germans of a reliable type will have to be recruited and spotted at points where they can best serve our interest. One source of tried and tested men will be MO PWs who have finished their tour of duty on the front lines."

OPERATION SUSSEX

An out-of-the-way site to hold these men was proposed for southern Italy or "some island off the coast where these men can be held in safety and where they can at the same time, be schooled and trained for our purpose."

During the Cold War years, the CIA had a number of in-place agents in Europe to be used in case of war with the Soviet Union. The men who took part in the World War II Sauerkraut missions were the precursor of this super-secret body.

(*See Also*: Italian Patriot Bands)

Operation Sussex

Operation Sussex was an allied espionage mission linked to the D-Day invasion of Normandy on June 6, 1944, one of many planned to coincide with the main thrust into Europe.

The mission was under the direct supervision of General Eisenhower and run by the OSS/SI division. OSS agents would be attached to Army Group and army headquarters in the field, with cooperation coming from the army's intelligence unit, G-2. In the development of the plan, both British and French components were added but with severe restrictions placed on French participation.

The Sussex Plan was a combined British-American operation developed by the British SIS and OSS/SI in collaboration with the French SIS. The purpose of the operation was to obtain information by the use of undercover agents in enemy-occupied territory. The plan contemplated the introduction of specially trained agents into certain localities on the continent prior to D-Day. SHAEF Headquarters was responsible for the actual location of where the agent were to be infiltrated. A majority of the men used in Sussex were previously held in areas in the United Kingdom by the OSS, ready for instant deployment.

Another aspect of Sussex called for the recruitment of prospective new men in the field and training of such people at OSS/SI field bases in Great Britain.

Once in enemy territory, the Sussex agents relied on radio communication with OSS/SI stations in England. The information they gleaned was also forwarded to U.S. Army G-2. Upon completion of their missions, all briefings of agents were to be conducted by representatives of the U.S. Army's G-2 (intelligence unit).

The number of Sussex agents assigned to each operational unit comprised 10 officers and 12 enlisted men. However, once they were deployed under Army Group Headquarters, four officers and six enlisted men were withdrawn.

In formulating Sussex missions, political considerations weighed in as far as French operational participation was concerned. Animosities lay behind the scenes at allied headquarters as to how much and to what extent French forces would take part in the liberation of Europe. The Americans and the British were still wary of the participation by French generals and politicians aligned with the Vichy regime of Marshal Philippe Petain and his relationship with Hitler. Consequently, it was determined to place effective controls on French involvement in Sussex.

Upon the start of each Sussex mission, a French liaison officer would be allowed to provide any assistance in furtherance of the plan. It was then, however, that restrictions began to be applied.

The G-2 was responsible for recruiting any personnel in the field, despite any of the French liaison's objections.

Under the discretion of the OSS leader in the field, an agent could be sent to another location, not to the satisfaction of the French officer. Such orders stood, but the French liaison would be able to report his disagreement to OSS London.

If the French officer disapproved of the use of an individual considered to take part in any field operation, he would not sign the "order of mission, but OSS could use the individual at its own discretion. In such instances, it will be remembered that the French assumed no responsibility for the pay, pension, etc. of such agents, since they would not be enrolled as members of the French Army."

The French liaison officer did have control over the handling of the agents intended for tactical intelligence purposes. OSS documents say, "their activities have no bearing on any other intelligence operations of either BCRA or OSS."

Despite these rather severe restraints placed upon them, the French resistance groups played a critical role in slowing down front line German troops prior to and just after the Normandy landings.

(*See Also*: French Resistance Movements)

Oster, Hans

Hans Oster (1888-1945), was a top deputy to Admiral Wilhelm Canaris in the Abwehr and a prime participant in the back channel plots to kill or remove Hitler from power.

Hans Oster was born in Dresden, Germany, in 1888. His family was a member of the Protestant faith, one that he kept all his life. He served in World War I, attaining the rank of general. With Germany defeated, Oster entered the small espionage organization called the Reichswehr. This was his first taste of the life of a spy, and for the rest of his military career, Oster would ply that most ancient of trades.

In 1933, he entered the War Ministry with the rank of colonel and was soon promoted to head the Second Department of the Abwehr, a mostly administrative position. However, one of his tasks was to keep track of all agents then working for Germany.

When war broke out, Admiral Canaris picked Oster to be his deputy at Abwehr headquarters. In Oster, Canaris found a like-minded man when it came to seeing the horrors inflicted upon Germany at the hands of Hitler. In short order, Oster became a leading figure along with his boss Canaris and other high-ranking German military officers' far ranging plots to remove Hitler from office.

The spark igniting Oster's treason was the trumped-up charges brought by Hitler against General Werner von Fritsch, the chief of the army command. General Fritsch withdrew his support of Hitler during the Czech crisis of 1939, in which Germany annexed territory. In retaliation, false charges that Fritsch was homosexual were brought up and the much-decorated general was indicted. After a three-week trial in which the defense proved the charges against General Fritsch were a fabrication, Hitler summarily dismissed him as that country's military chief.

The Fritsch affair put officers who were opposed to Hitler's policies on notice that the same thing could happen to them. Among them were Wilhelm Canaris and Hans Oster.

The removal of General Fritsch was the catalyst that set both Oster and Canaris to begin planning for the Führer's end. Oster held meetings with Colonel General Ludwig Beck, who was general chief of staff of the army. Beck, a World War I veteran, was an early supporter of Hitler until the Czech Crisis. Beck told his fellow officers that if Germany found itself at war with both England and France, then Germany would lose.

With Beck and other staff officers on their side, Canaris gave Oster the go-ahead to plan the dismissal of Hitler. To that end, Oster began contacting many of the organized resistance groups who were anti-Hitler. He provided them with secret intelligence from Abwehr files on Hitler's plans and his whereabouts during his trips. Commander Franz Leidig, head of the Abwehr's naval intelligence branch, later wrote about how important Oster was in the war against Hitler. He was "the center of gravity for resistance within the German military."

The two most influential resistance leaders with whom Oster was in contact were Count Wolf Heinrich von Helldorf, the head of the Berlin Police, and Arthur Nebe, a Gestapo officer who worked in the Criminal Investigation Department.

Oster quickly engaged the support of two influential government officials, State Secretary Baron Ernst von Weizsacker, and Erich Kordt of the foreign ministry who headed the Bureau of Information. Oster asked von Weizsacker to ask the British to take a hard line in the upcoming talks scheduled to take place at Munich between Hitler and then British Prime Minister Neville Chamberlain.

When this diplomatic channel failed, Oster and his fellow conspirators put another plan into action. They planned to stage a coup in Berlin with the assistance of Lieutenant Colonel Friedrich Heinz whose assigned task it was to capture Hitler. Heinz went one step further, telling Oster that if he was lucky enough to get to Hitler, he was going to kill him. When the plotters failed to receive assurances from the British and the French that any German attack on Czech territory would lead to war, the scheme was stopped.

As early as 1938, and into the Czech crisis of 1939, both Oster and Canaris were sending secret messages via their conduits in other countries to the Western democracies, warning them of an imminent attack on both France and England. These missives were largely ignored, especially by Chamberlain who did not believe that Hitler would dare attack Czechoslovakia.

As Germany's plans to invade Poland came closer, Oster, along with four other members of the resistance group—General Beck, Dr. Carl Goerdeler, the German Ambassador to Rome, Ulrich von Hassell, the army chief of economic warfare, and General Georg Thomas—dispatched an urgent letter to Field Marshall Keitel, chief of the German High Command, urging that no military action be taken against Poland. They argued that if such an event occurred, then both France and England would declare war against Germany.

On September 1, 1939, German troops marched into Poland, setting off the war that so many of Hitler's generals were working to prevent.

In April of 1940, German plans to attack Norway were put into motion, with the code name "Operation Weser-Exceise." When Oster found out about them, he took immediate action to inform the Norwegian government. He contacted an old friend, Colonel Gijsbertus Jacobus Sas, the Dutch military attaché in Berlin, informing him that hostilities against his nation were going forward. To their ultimate discredit, Oster's information was not sent to Oslo, the Norwegian capital. In days' time, the Nazis attacked Norway, taking a large number of casualties, before ultimately overrunning the country.

By March, 1943 Oster had brought into his cabal another ranking German officer, 42-year-old General Henning von Tresckow, chief of staff to Field Marshall von Kluge. When it was learned that Hitler was planning an inspection trip to Kluge's headquarters at Smolensk, von Tresckow devised a plan to assassinate Hitler by blowing up his plane. Upon a successful completion of the plan, a coup would be staged at General Kluge's military headquarters, at which point the army would come under his control (by this time, Hitler had appointed himself commander-in-chief of the German armed forces, taking that responsibility away from his generals).

The bomb was clandestinely put on Hitler's aircraft by a Colonel Brandt, one of his aides. It was hidden in two brandy bottles. Unfortunately for the plotters, the bomb failed to go off. In a scramble to remove the evidence before anyone on the plane could find it, one of the plotters, Lieutenant Fabian von Schlabrendorff, a lawyer by trade, managed to get on board and take it away.

Oster and Canaris were also responsible for saving the lives of many Jews, whom they took under Abwehr control. Oster gave them jobs as his personal agents and sent them to Switzerland with the knowledge that they would then seek political asylum. In time, the Oster-Canaris connection helped more than 500 Dutch Jews escape to points in South America.

In April 1943, Oster and Canaris's treachery were finally unmasked by the Gestapo. Gestapo agents found documents linking Oster to the smuggling of the Jews out of Germany. In what turned out to be a lucky break for Oster, he was spared harsh punishment and was only given a slap on the wrist, convicted on charges of "inefficiency." Oster was removed from his Abwehr post, his loss a terrible blow to the resistance.

One final attempt on Hitler's life took place on July 20, 1944, in what came to be known as Operation Valkyrie. While Hitler was at his headquarters at Rastenburg, East Prussia, the plotters, led by Chief of Staff Colonel Claus von Stauffenberg, placed a bomb in the room where Hitler was conducting a meeting. The bomb went off, but Hitler survived. In the immediate purges that followed, many of the conspirators including Hans Oster and his boss Wilhelm Canaris were arrested. In the wake of the abortive assassination attempt, nearly 5,000 people connected in any way to the plot were killed, including Hans Oster.

P

Pack, Amy Thorpe aka "Cynthia"

If Mata Hari (Margaretha Zelle) was World War I's most seductive female spy, than her counterpart in World War II was a beautiful American named Amy Elizabeth Thorpe. During the war, she would work for both the OSS and the British BSC (British Security Coordination, run by William Stephenson), using her considerable charms to lure information from highly placed enemy diplomats in Washington, and other duty assignments.

Amy Elizabeth Thorpe was born on November 22, 1910, in Minneapolis, Minnesota. Her father was George Thorpe, a decorated U.S. marine. Her mother was a highly educated woman, attending school at the University of Michigan and the Sorbonne in France. From her father, Amy got hooked with the life of adventure and made the most of it when she traveled with her parents to far away places. At age 11, she penned a romantic novel titled *Fioretta*.

Amy had the privileged life of wealth, attending school in both France and the United States. When not at school, she spent her summers at a fashionable retreat at Newport, Rhode Island. It was during this period that Amy met her future husband, Arthur Pack, the secretary at the British Embassy in Washington. They were married in April 1930. The couple had two children, although neither one lived for long with them. The children were sent to boarding schools and later to foster homes.

In 1938, Arthur Pack was transferred to Warsaw, Poland, on the eve of World War II. Once in Warsaw, Amy had a number of sexual encounters with men from the Polish Foreign Office who unknowingly spilled secrets to her.

By now, Amy Thorpe had been vetted by the British Secret Service and was acting as an undercover agent for the Crown. When Arthur was transferred to Madrid at the beginning of the Spanish-Civil War, Amy went with him and helped move Red Cross supplies to Franco's forces. She also aided in the evacuation of the British Embassy personnel out of Spain. With

Arthur Pack troubled with a variety of illnesses, Amy had every reason to leave home, and she made most of her opportunities.

She was able to obtain a copy of a map of Czechoslovakia which included the new borders the Germans hoped to have, once they invaded that country.

Her most important contribution came when she formed a relationship with Josef Beck, the Polish Foreign Minister. Beck had a clandestine relationship with the German military and shared a number of its secrets with her. One of Beck's aides was privy to this information, and he dispensed the news to his lover, "Cynthia," who learned that the Poles were able to break the most secret code of the German military—Ultra. With their knowledge of Ultra, British code breakers working out of Bletchley Park broke the German Enigma cipher, and were now in a position to read communications sent to and from their ships at sea and their ground forces in the field. The breaking of Enigma was a key strategic development as far as the British were concerned and led ultimately to victory.

After her successful mission in Warsaw, British intelligence sent Amy out of harm's way and assigned her to Chile in 1940. She remained there only a short time and was reassigned to Washington.

Taking up residence in the Georgetown section of Washington, Amy began a relationship with Alberto Lais, an admiral, and the naval attaché at Italy's Washington embassy. They both knew each other at an earlier date, and the admiral was more than pleased to renew their friendship. Using her charm, "Cynthia" was able to pry loose from him the Italian navy's code and cipher books, as well as plans to incapacitate Italian ships that were then berthed in U.S. ports.

At this time, Amy was introduced to 48-year-old Ellery Huntington, Jr., one of Bill Donovan's top men in the OSS. Huntington was ordered to conduct an illegal break-in of the Vichy French Embassy in Washington in order to steal the French naval code books locked in the embassy's safe. The person Huntington turned to was his number-one agent, Amy Thorpe Pack. The importance of these code books was not lost on both the OSS and the BSC, as they contained the plans for the disposition of Vichy French forces in Africa.

"Cynthia" promptly contacted the French Embassy, talking with Charles Brousse, the press attaché. She told Brousse that she was an freelance journalist after a story and requested an interview. One was granted immediately. Over time, a relationship between them began, and "Cynthia" eventually revealed that she was working for the Americans. She soon learned that Charles Brousse was an ardent anti-Nazi and he agreed to cooperate with her.

Soon, elaborate plans were worked out between Huntington and

"Cynthia" for the burglary of the safe in the Vichy embassy. The OSS used the talents of an expert safe cracker dubbed the "Georgia Cracker," for the entry.

Brousse bribed the night watchman at the embassy to let him and "Cynthia" inside the building for their sexual trysts. They spent several nights making love, with the watchman never in sight.

On the night of the actual burglary, the guard was given knockout drops, and the safe cracker went to work, but couldn't complete the job. A second try worked to perfection, with "Cynthia" and the "Cracker" able to photocopy the all important French naval ciphers, all of which were handed over to William Stephenson's BSC and Bill Donovan's OSS.

The purloined ciphers were indispensable when the Americans invaded North Africa in 1942.

After the death of Arthur Pack, Amy married Charles Brousse and lived in France.

Amy Thorpe Pack died on December 1, 1963 of cancer.

Pan Am Clipper Plot

In 1942, the Wehrmacht, acting under orders from Hitler, devised a plan to blow up the Pan Am Clipper, which took passengers from Europe and the United States to Portugal. What Hitler and his commanders did not know was that their orders were to be thwarted at the very beginning.

During the war, Portugal was one of the significant neutral countries on the European continent. The city bustled with shops filled with goods not then available in war-torn Europe. The city was also a hotbed of espionage activities, with spies from many countries seeking information. With German U-boats controlling the Atlantic sea lanes, the Pan Am Clipper was the safest means of transportation for Americans and other nationalities entering Europe.

German spies kept a close watch at the landing site of the aircraft, noting all who disembarked. The Pan Am Clipper was a large amphibious plane with a wingspan of 130 feet. The Clipper fleet carried passengers across the Pacific, as well as the Atlantic, stopping in ports such as Midway and Wake Islands, Honolulu, Hong Kong, and Manila. The Clippers carried a total of 74 people, along with spacious suites for their well-heeled clientele.

The assignment to destroy the plane was given to the chief of the Abwehr, Admiral Canaris by Field Marshal Keitel. The ever-wary Canaris disapproved of the plan but was powerless to publicly protest the order. Canaris and a three-man team gained easy access to the parked Clipper and planted the bomb inside the plane. Once the Clipper was airborne, it would explode, killing all onboard.

Canaris arrived in Lisbon to oversee the operation. It was then that the Abwehr chief dramatically ordered the plan aborted. Without explaining why, he enjoined two of his men to reboard the plane and disarm the bomb.

Within hours of the removal of the bomb, the Clipper took off for New York, making a successful voyage.

Canaris was never punished for his part in the Clipper operation, but would suffer the ultimate penalty after the abortive plot to assassinate Hitler at his East Prussian headquarters.

(*See Also*: Oster, Hans)

Pearl Harbor Attack

On December 7, 1941, carrier-based aircraft from the approaching Japanese strike force heading for Hawaii, suddenly, without warning, attacked the American fleet based at Pearl Harbor. The attack caught the sleeping crews and their ships completely by surprise and when the raid was over, the American fleet in the Pacific had been almost destroyed. Eighteen ships, including eight battleships were struck, 2,400 sailors, soldiers and airmen were killed, and another 1,100 were wounded. The only saving grace was that the main aircraft carriers were out on patrol when the Japanese struck.

Could the attack on Pearl Harbor have been avoided? That has been the nagging question for more than 50 years without a positive answer. Surely there were warning signs, but they were either ignored or sloppily mishandled. In the historical prism of a half century, what were the omens that should have warned American commanders in the Pacific and the policy makers in Washington that events were about to drastically happen?

U.S.-Japanese diplomatic relations had turned for the worse over the course of the 1930s. The U.S. saw the Japanese military presence in Asia, particularly in China and Korea, as a potential battleground with the United States in later years. In July 1941, the U.S. cut off the export of raw material and scrap iron to Japan, thus creating a gaping hole in Japan's economic lifeline.

In 1941, William Friedman had broken the Japanese cryptosystem called Purple, which allowed this country to read all the diplomatic traffic coming from Tokyo to its outposts around the world. Besides the Purple intercepts, the navy's intelligence unit called OP-20-G was reading Japanese radio transmissions to and from its ships at sea and to its agents in their embassies around the globe. The navy was able to intercept communications from Japan to its primary agent in Hawaii, Takeo Yoshikawa, asking for the disposition of the ships anchored at Pearl Harbor, whether or not the ships were protected by anti-torpedo nets, and if the U.S. sent aloft balloons to check the sea beyond the base.

By the fall of 1941, U.S. intelligence listing posts in the Pacific and at the West Coast of the United States, spotted a huge movement of the Japanese fleet from their home bases and suspected that they were about to invade either the Philippines or Indo-China (the thought that Pearl Harbor might be the target was never even considered by U.S. commanders). American radio intercepts also noted instructions from Tokyo to the Japanese Ambassador in Washington to set a deadline of November 24, 1941, as the last day for any possible negotiations between the United States and Japan to try to curtail any outbreak of hostilities. After that, the decoded messages say in part, "that things are automatically going to happen." All these messages were made available to the aides in the Roosevelt administration, but not the commanders in Hawaii.

In the first week of December, 1941, the U.S. learned that the Japanese government gave instructions to its Washington embassy to start destroying its codes, a clear sign that diplomatic relations were about to be broken. On December 6-7, U.S. code breakers intercepted a 14-part message, the so-called "War Warning," which ended with orders to break off any further talks with the Americans at precisely 1:00 PM Washington time (7:30 AM Hawaii time) on December 7.

None of these intercepts culled from the Magic decrypts were either given to the military commanders in Hawaii, Admiral Husband Kimmel or General Walter Short. (Another person not in the Magic loop was Bill Donovan.) Over the years, conspiracy theories have been put forth laying the blame on the Pearl Harbor attack directly on the feet of President Roosevelt in order to get the United States into the war. What is clear is that the military commanders did not have adequate warnings pointing to an attack on Pearl Harbor and that a considerable amount of vital intelligence was not given to them.

On November 15, 1941, the Japanese sent a special envoy to Washington to aid in the bilateral peace talks. After the November 29th deadline ended without an agreement, the envoy received several messages from Tokyo stating even though the negotiations were "de facto ruptured, the Japanese delegation should continue the talks to prevent the United States from becoming unduly suspicious."

On December 2nd, the navy intercepted a letter to its spy in Hawaii asking for a "day by day" report on the whereabouts of all the ships docked at Pearl Harbor.

Another indication that an attack was imminent was the so-called "Winds Message." This Open Code message was sent by Tokyo to its embassies in Washington, London and Moscow saying that in the event of hostilities, secure communications might have to be cut off at a moment's notice. If that happened, they would receive the news via radio referring to a weather report which would be the signal to destroy all codes. A November 19 message from Tokyo was intercepted relaying the words "East Wind Rain," a signal that hostilities were at hand.

The initial planning for the attack was carried out one year earlier by Japanese Admiral Isoroku Yamamoto. In January 1941, reports of the plan were given to the American Ambassador in Tokyo by a source in the Peruvian Embassy, but was dismissed out of hand. By September 1941, Tokyo had cabled its espionage network in Honolulu asking for details of the types of vessels at anchor in Pearl Harbor. This message was decrypted on October 9, 1941, by U.S. analysts. Subsequent queries to Honolulu from Tokyo were picked up by army and navy code breakers in the latter part of November, as well as the first week of December.

During the time period of November-December 1941, U.S. military analysts were tracking a large Japanese assault force heading for China or Indo-China and believed that was the area in which Japanese forces would make an attack.

On November 1 and December 1, U.S. analysts picked up a major difference in the call signs coming from the Japanese navy, making it uncertain where or when the Japanese would strike. What the U.S. military did not know was that on November 25, the Japanese aircraft carriers that would take part in the Pearl Harbor raid left their bases at the Kurile Islands of northern Japan, observing strict radio silence.

Long after the attack, the possibility was raised that the Japanese carriers did *not* maintain radio silence, as they said they did. In his groundbreaking book on the attack called *Infamy: Pearl Harbor And Its Aftermath,* author John Toland quotes a report by a Japanese documentary called the "Search For the Solution of the Pearl Harbor Puzzle," definitely rebuking the radio silence story once and for all.

The director of the show, Tsutomu Konno, interviewed Robert Haslach, who once worked for the Netherlands Embassy in Washington and was writing a book on Netherlands East Indies cryptology. Haslach provided an affidavit from a Dutch naval captain named Henning which was addressed to the Netherlands Royal Naval General Staff during the war saying that by studying the naval radio traffic of the Japanese, Dutch interceptors were able to ascertain that the Japanese fleet had in fact left their bases in the Kuriles and were heading toward Hawaii. If the Japanese had indeed stood firm with their policy of radio silence, then how did Henning know that they left the Kuriles?

Toland also refers to a letter from a Colonel Carleton Ketchum who lived in Pittsburgh, saying that FBI Director J. Edgar Hoover had prior knowledge of the attack. Ketchum's job during the war was to enroll a large number of men over the draft age for duty in the Air Force, for non-combat positions. Ketchum says that in 1942 he had a meeting in Washington with Congressman George Bender of Ohio and a number of other government officials. Bender told Ketchum that the FBI Director told him that President Roosevelt had foreknowledge of the Japanese plans to attack Pearl Harbor. Ketchum said that Hoover told Bender and the others that the intelligence regarding the attack came from the Dutch Secret Service in the Far East, and also information coming from the British Secret Service in Hong Kong.

Others in the Washington loop who knew about the impending attack were Harry Hopkins, the president's chief aide, as well as Secretary of the Navy Frank Knox. Ketchum says that the Magic intercepts were not passed on to Admiral Kimmel, General Short, or General George Marshall.

Colonel Ketchum revealed this information in a book he wrote called *The Recollections of Colonel Retread 1942-45* (Hart Books, 1976).

Another warning of Japanese interest in Hawaii came in early 1941 from a double agent, Dusko Popov. Popov was a German spy who defected to Britain and was used by them as a double agent. The Germans sent Popov to the United States from Portugal to set up an intelligence net. Upon arriving in New York City, Popov contacted the FBI. The Japanese asked their German counterparts to ask Popov to find out as much information as he could on the dispositions of the American fleet at Pearl Harbor. Popov was asked to locate ammunition dumps, airfields, the depth of the water at Pearl Harbor, and the sailing schedules of the fleet. All this information was saved on a microdot, a photographic reduction of information that was used to hide its contents from the unsuspecting reader. Popov's information was given to FBI Director J. Edgar Hoover, but he refused to believe him, saying that he was really working for the Germans, and any information coming from him was suspect.

Almost two weeks after the attack, Washington began a long series of investigations of the sneak attack. The first panel was chaired by Supreme Court Justice Own Roberts and called the "Roberts Commission." When the panel ended its probe on January 23, 1942, it concluded that Admiral Kimmel and General Short were derelict in their military duties. They were subsequently relieved of their posts, and they retired from active duty.

The army and navy conducted their own fact-finding missions into the raid, but it was the large-scale Congressional investigation that began on November 14, 1945, that proved the most comprehensive. Once again, they pinned the blame on Short and Kimmel, saying that they disregarded the warnings given to them by Washington, failed to take adequate measures to protect the fleet and the airfields in Hawaii, said that they made "errors of judgement" and were guilty of "dereliction of duty."

One direct result of the Pearl Harbor attack was the introduction after the war of the first, professional United States intelligence agency: the CIA. The advent of modern-day computers and satellites in space now makes a repeat of the Pearl Harbor disaster almost impossible.

Conspiracy theorists have had a field day over the years concerning the possibility that President Roosevelt knew about the attack and let it happen in order to get the U.S. into the war. The most logical answer is that the U.S. intelligence services at the time were derelict in their duty, and ignored repeated warning signals until it was too late.

(*See Also*: Hoover, J. Edgar; Popov, Dusan; Hypo, Station; Kuhn, Bernard; Layton, Edwin; Yoshikawa, Takeo; Magic; Lanikai & the Isabel; Rochefort, Joseph)

Philby, Harold A.R. (Kim)

In the history of 20th century espionage, Harold "Kim" Philby (1912-1988) ranks as the preeminent spy who worked as a double agent for the Russians against his British homeland. Philby's name is associated with the infamous Cambridge Spy Ring comprised of his fellow British traitors, Anthony Blunt, Guy Burgess, and Donald MacLean. It is ironic that this man who was trusted with the most sensitive secrets of the British government during World War II, and during the height of the Cold War, was almost chosen as "C," the head of the British Secret Service. No one knows how history would have been changed if "Kim" Philby had been given the ultimate power in the British Secret Service.

"Kim" Philby was born in 1912 in Ambala, India. He was given the nickname of "Kim" after the character in one of Rudyard Kipling's novels. His father was the noted spy and adventurer, Harry St. John Philby, assistant commissioner in the Punjab district of India, when that country was part of the British empire. The elder Philby married in 1910 while stationed there. It was during his stint in India that his first son, Adrian, was born.

Harry St. John Philby was one of his day's fascinating personalitie and was primarily responsible for the choice of a profession his son would later take. He served in Mesopotamia during World War I for British military intelligence, in time, forming a strategic and personal relationship with King Ibn Saud.

Kim Philby attended the Westminster school and graduated in 1928. He then went on to Trinity College at Cambridge, where he was to meet his fellow traitors: Anthony Blunt, Guy Burgess, and Donald MacLean. During their time at Cambridge, they recruited into the NKVD, the Russian espionage service. In the early 1930s, Philby traveled to Germany, France, and Austria where he observed firsthand, the fast-changing political situations that would ultimately lead to war.

His first marriage was to Alice Friedman in Vienna, Austria, on February 24, 1934. His new wife was a communist who was on the run from the police. By marrying Philby, she was now a British subject and was given a passport which allowed her to legally leave that country. Philby did not tell his bride of his pro-communist connections, one of the first betrayals he was to become so used to.

During the Spanish Civil War, Philby worked for *The Times* of London, covering the war, allowing his pro-Franco sympathies to show. In 1939, he and Alice were divorced. He was transferred to Germany as *Times* correspondent and spent most of his free time spying for the Russians against the Germans.

When Britain entered the war, Philby joined the British Expeditionary Force as a reporter and was sent to France. After the fall of France, Philby returned to England, and it was then, according to him, he was approached by MI-6 to become one of their own. Other sources in the know said that St. John Philby pulled strings to get his son into the secret service. Whatever the case, young Kim was now inside the bowels of the British Secret Service, an unsuspected double agent who would remain in that role until the early 1960s.

Philby's first posting was with Section V, the counterespionage section of SIS. He would become the leader of the Iberian subdivision of Section V, responsible for running agents in such countries as Spain, Portugal, Italy, and North Africa.

Philby, however, had more important chips up his sleeve, and the plan he devised was sanctioned by his controllers in Moscow. As the war grew to a close, both the U.S. and England feared Russia as a potential enemy once the conflict was over. The intelligence services of both countries wanted to keep a close watch on Russia. Philby asked that he be allowed to set up a subsection within Section V, whose primary duties were to monitor Soviet intelligence. This was immediately agreed upon, and Philby was now in a position to funnel highly informative intelligence emanating from the British SIS to Anatoli Lebedev, his Soviet controlling officer. The name given to this desk by Philby was called "Section 5." In order to show his progress, Philby unmasked for British intelligence the name of a long-time Soviet spy operating in England, Boris Krotov. By the time of Philby's report, Krotov had departed for Moscow and was unreachable. What Philby did not say in his missives was that Boris Krotov was not only his handler but controlled Burgess and MacLean as well.

PHILBY

Philby's treachery was also seen regarding the anti-German plots then being hatched inside Germany. Philby was aware of the plots by Admiral Canaris and others to overthrow Hitler, as well as their negotiations with the West to secure a separate peace. This turn of events sent shock waves inside the Kremlin. The last thing the Soviets wanted was a non-Hitler country allied with the United States and Great Britain against the Soviet Union.

Philby began to plot against Admiral Canaris, even going so far as to devise a scheme that he proposed to "C," Stewart Menzies, to have the admiral killed while he was in Spain. Philby's pathological desire to see Canaris removed was his fear of an entente between Britain and Germany. This, Philby vowed, would not happen.

While working in Section V, an internal report was written concerning the rift between the German General Staff and officers surrounding Hitler. The study chronicled the role played by Canaris and his conspirators. The supposed author was Stewart Hampshire of Section V. Its main thrust was that if the British gave enough incentives to the anti-Hitler plotters to overthrow Hitler, the war could come to an early end. All leaders of Section V asked that the paper be circulated among all personnel of the department except one, Kim Philby. Philby, for obvious reasons, forcefully rejected the idea of passing on the report and even managed to persuade his superior, Section V Chief, Major Felix Cowgill, to back his censoring of the document.

The document was suppressed, despite the uproar it created. However, the story doesn't end there. One copy was made and was forwarded by Hugh Trevor-Roper, then a member of Section V, to a personal aide of Prime Minister Churchill. Churchill called in Stewart Menzies who admitted that he had no knowledge of the report. The aftershocks of the scandal were felt directly in Section V, with the removal of Trevor-Roper. Philby had succeeded completely.

Philby's handiwork in preventing contacts between the British and the German conspirators can be seen in the Otto John case. John was an Abwehr colleague of Hans Oster who participated in the plans to kill Hitler. John gave Colonel Henning von Tresckow the blueprints for the plane that Hitler was to be traveling on. Henning planned on blowing up the plane, killing Hitler and all aboard. John made covert contact with a British agent called "Tony" who worked in the British Embassy in Lisbon. In January 1944, John tried to contact "Tony," but when he was unavailable, John was put in touch with a member of his staff named Rita. Rita told John that under no condition would there be any meetings with the anti-Hitler plotters. In reality, the "Rita" instructions came from Philby.

Another of his assignments that aided the British Secret Service was his relationship with the so-called "Lucy Ring," a group of Soviet espionage agents operating from neutral Switzerland.

In October 1944, Philby was assigned another job in the SIS which required him to ferret out communist penetrations of the British intelligence service.

In August 1945, just at the end of the war, Philby's cover was almost blown. A Russian named Konstantin Volkov, working as vice counsel in Istanbul, Turkey, defected. He said that he had information about a number of Soviet moles inside the British espionage establishment, one of whom worked inside the London counterespionage section (Philby).

Philby got wind of the Volkov defection and personally took over the file on him. Philby told his controllers about Volkov, and soon the defector was never heard from again. (It is believed that he was killed by Russian assassins.)

In 1949, Philby was posted to Washington, where he took over the job as the liaison between the FBI and the newly created CIA. He made friends with the CIA's director, James Jesus Angleton, and sent back a hoard of both CIA and NATO information to Moscow.

In May 1951, Philby learned that MI-5 was about to arrest Guy Burgess and Donald MacLean. After Philby alerted them, both men made a quick escape to Moscow. Philby was called back to England and was confronted by accusations made by another defector named Ismail Akhmedov-Ege, a Turk, who had been a colonel in the KGB. Akhmedov-Ege was now working for the CIA, and he told them that Philby was a Russian mole. After a long investigation in which Philby denied he was a Russian agent, he decided to retire from government service. He denied any relationship with either Burgess or MacLean, and his story was believed by many top men in the British government.

In the 1950s, Philby got a job as a reporter covering the Middle East for the British newspapers, *The Observer* and the *Economist*. It was at this time that a defector named Vladimir Petrov said that Philby was the "Third Man," along with Burgess and MacLean.

Philby's final unmasking came in 1961-62 with the defection to the CIA of Anatoly Golitsyn, a ranking KGB officer. Golitsyn provided enough details of Philby's conspiracy that he was finally confronted by the British. Philby admitted to being a Soviet spy, and in one final act of defiance, managed to flee from Beirut, on a Russian-bound ship to Odessa. On July 3, 1963, the Soviet regime announced that Philby had been given political asylum in Russia and made a Soviet citizen.

His new wife Eleanor joined him in Russia but soon found out that he was having an affair with the wife of Donald MacLean and took off. Melinda MacLean left Philby in 1966. He later married a Russian woman, Rufina

Ivanova, in 1971.

He lived out his life in Russia, dying in May 1988, a revered figure in the Soviet Union, an unforgiving traitor to all those who once gave him their undying trust.

(*See Also*: Cambridge Spies; MacLean, Donald; Cairncross, John; Burgess, Guy)

Popov, Dusan

On August 12, 1941, a dashing, 29-year-old disembarked at New York's La Guardia Airport from the Pan Am Clipper that had just arrived from Estroil, Portugal. After checking through U.S. immigration, the man took a cab to the Waldorf Astoria Hotel overlooking Park Avenue and checked in. He arranged his clothes so that he would notice any disturbance when he returned. The man then walked out of the hotel and into New York City's bright lights. (When he came back, his suitcases had been moved.)

The man in question was Dusan Popov (1912-1982), a Yugoslav by birth, a man of many talents, his most recent that of being a double agent working for British Intelligence. Popov was then in the employ of the German Abwehr but so disliked the ruin brought upon Germany by Hitler that he offered his services to the British as a double agent. Popov was given $58,000 from the Abwehr to go to the United States in order to set up an espionage ring. He also had on him $12,000 that he had won in the gaming tables at Estoril.

Popov had been recruited into the Abwehr by a German friend, Johann Jebsen. His first assignment was to go to France and report on political leaders who might be helpful to the Nazis. Popov agreed, gave the required information to the Abwehr, and also gave a copy to British Intelligence. Popov was run by the so-called Double Cross System, a part of British intelligence who were responsible for the running of all the captured German spies who were trying to infiltrate that country. Popov decided to play the double game because of his hatred of the Nazis and agreed to spy for the British. He was given the code name Tricycle.

Preceding his trip to the United States, the Abwehr gave their prize spy a vital, new piece of spy paraphernalia. It was a list of questions written on a microdot that would allow pages of information to be reduced to the size of a pinhead. The microdotted information carried by Popov was written on a telegram which he kept with him.

Before leaving for the United States, Popov spent lavishly at the posh casinos at Estoril, making a killing at the tables. One of the men watching him at the tables was Ian Fleming, then working for British Intelligence. (Later, Fleming would use the Popov-casino scene in his James Bond novels

—and later movie—*Casino Royale*.) One day after his binge at the casinos, Popov boarded Pan Am Clipper No. 314 headed for New York.

Upon his arrival in New York, Popov contacted the FBI and asked that someone come to talk with him. To his chagrin, he had to wait five long days until the bureau responded. He was met by James Foxworth who was the FBI's bureau chief in New York. Popov handed over the microdot questionnaire provided to him by the Abwehr. As agent Foxworth began to read its contents, he knew he had something extraordinary. The paper contained a list of questions that the Germans wanted answered for their allies, the Japanese. Among the queries were information on American defenses at the giant naval base at Pearl Harbor, including the exact locations of the airbases at Hickam, Wheeler, and Kaneohe airfields, sketches of Pearl Harbor, the depths of its harbor, and the number and locations of any anti-torpedo nets.

Foxworth knew that he had important information on his hands. He immediately gave the information to his boss, FBI Director J. Edgar Hoover. Hoover did not trust Popov, believing that he was still working for the Abwehr. Another strike against Popov, according to Hoover, was the man's playboy lifestyle. Popov moved into a luxurious apartment overlooking Fifth Ave., had numerous affairs with attractive women, including the actress, Simone Simone (and her mother), and spent lavishly of the Abwehr's money.

Popov's every move was watched closely by the FBI, and what they noticed was that after three months of living the high life in New York, Popov had not contacted any German agents in New York. The Abwehr, too, now had second thoughts about their prize spy. They pleaded with Popov to show some results for his work and began to think that he might have been "turned."

Popov transferred the intelligence information to the FBI under orders from MI-6. His case was personally supervised by Stewart Menzies, head of MI-6. Menzies contacted J. Edgar Hoover and "loaned" Popov to the Americans.

In regard to Popov's Pearl Harbor questionnaire, the FBI Director did a curious thing. Instead of handing it over to Bill Donovan, the head of COI, or more importantly, to President Roosevelt, Hoover doctored the questions, gave nothing to Donovan, and omitted the Pearl Harbor queries when he finally sent them along to the White House.

In late November 1941, under the ever watchful eye of the FBI, Popov received orders from the Abwehr, sending him to Rio de Janeiro. He was contacted by the Abwehr man in Rio and was told to establish a radio link between Rio and Lisbon, Portugal. Popov was to concentrate on seeking information on war production, the destination of allied convoys, and news he could glean on anti-submarine warfare.

Popov was in Rio on December 7, 1941, when the Japanese attacked Pearl Harbor. He returned to the United States one week later and handed over a second set of microdots to the FBI. A sampling of the queries from the Germans concerned the types of powder used for ammunition and a seven-page list of questions concerning America's atomic bomb research.

One of the nagging queries in the Popov case is whether or not he actually met personally with J. Edgar Hoover. FBI documents shed no light on this matter, and persons on each side have differing opinions. In his memoirs, Popov said that he "encountered J. Edgar at the FBI office in New York." After Hoover's death, the FBI stated flatly that there had been no face-to-face meeting between the two men. William Stephenson, the head of the BSC in New York during the war, wrote of his conversations with "Intrepid" concerning Popov. The BSC chief did in fact say that Hoover met with Popov. "Our conversation was not for publication at the time. But he was very clear. He said Popov had indeed met Hoover—he knew all about it....Stephenson had no doubts about Popov's credibility, and he thought the FBI had totally failed to pick up on what Popov was trying to tell them about Pearl Harbor."

Popov's British case officer, Colonel Robertson, said that during his debriefing session, Popov had told him that he met with Hoover. Another person in British intelligence who told the same story was Chole MacMillan. MacMillan worked in Portugal during the war. He said that when he met Popov in later years, Tricycle said that he in truth met Hoover and that Hoover was negligent in not believing him regarding the Japanese plan for Pearl Harbor.

One year after his arrival in the United States, the FBI returned Popov to MI-6 control, calling him a "liar," saying that he was "too expensive to justify his retention." By 1943, he was back in England, working for the Double Cross System.

Historians are still debating why Hoover failed to give the leaders of the U.S. government the contents of Popov's entire microdot transmission, as well as knocking Popov's bona fides. Long after the war, Dusan Popov wrote about his wartime experiences in a book called *Spy/Counterspy.*

He died in 1982, age 70.

(*See Also*: Hoover, J. Edgar; Pearl Harbor Attack; Double Cross System; Stephenson, William; Fleming, Ian)

Prosper Network

The Prosper network was a multi-faceted operation run by British intelligence—SIS and SOE—whose main object was to create a national insurrection in France at the time of the allied invasion. In reality, the Prosper program became a high-level feud between the two British intelligence agencies, a blown operation, and more importantly, serious allegations that one part of the intelligence services purposely blew the operation to the Germans.

The two protagonists in the Prosper plan were Stewart Menzies, "C," the head of the SIS (Secret Intelligence Service), and Colin Gubbins, the chief of SOE (Special Operations Executive). Both men had a grudging respect for each other, yet were wary of cooperating too much with their rival organizations. At one time during the war, Gubbins took over operational control of Menzies "Section D," the sabotage and special operations unit, without consulting him.

Gubbins also had an ally in the powerful William Stephenson, head of the BSC operating out of New York. As the war advanced, both SIS and SOE were rivals in carrying out secret missions in Germany.

During the war, the French section of SOE was run by Maurice Buckmaster. His main job was to send British agents into France to wreak havoc on the German military infrastructure and to act as liaison with the resistance groups. One of Buckmaster's most sensitive projects was to oversee the entry and exit of RAF pilots who ferried agents into and out of France. These pilots also took with them secure mail containing information for the wireless operators for their correspondence with London. One of the most trusted of these aircraft handlers was Henri Dericourt, who controlled all secret air traffic into Paris and the surrounding countryside.

Dericourt served from 1939 to 1940, in the French air force as a test pilot, as well as a courier operator. He was introduced to the SIS and during his interrogation, he revealed that he had been a messenger for the SD, a section of the German espionage service. His German contact at SD HQ was Hans Boemelburg, then head of Section IV in Paris. Dericourt was brought into the British secret service by Claude Dansey, vice chief of the SIS, a man with so little regard for human life that he was reviled by most of the people who knew him. Despite Dericourt's assurances that he was not a German agent, Dansey picked him to mole his way into SD HQ in Paris. (He was also given the rank of flight lieutenant in the RAF).

Dansey offered Dericourt's services to Buckmaster as the "air movements officer" for the Paris area but failed to notify him about his alleged SD ties.

Dericourt was dropped into France on January 22-23, 1943, and made a beeline to Paris. Upon arrival, he contacted various members of the SD, and it is reported that he was assigned an SD case officer. Dericourt then proceeded to give the location of 14 clandestine airfields from which airdrops into occupied France originated.

It was now that another major player was added to the mix, as well as preparations for a large allied deception project called Starkey, a deception operation designed to fool the Germans into believing that the allies were going to invade northwest Europe in 1943, and that military maneuvers in Italy and Sicily were just diversions.

The main participant was Major Frances Suttill, then 32 years old. In 1943, Suttill was dropped into France and made his way to Paris. His task was to set up F Section's largest network in France, called Prosper. One of the first men to aid Suttill was the suspicious Henri Dericourt. The pilot ferried Prosper agents, as well as mail from England to France. His secondary undertaking was to gear up the resistance networks for the invasion of Europe.

In a surprise move, Dericourt was recalled to London on April 22-23, 1943, and spent over two weeks in meetings with his controllers. It has been conjectured that Dericourt was told of the planned invasion of Europe. Speculation has been rife all these years concerning Dericourt's next moves. Did he reveal the Starkey plan to his SD controllers? Furthermore, did Claude Dansey reveal the Starkey news to him?

Upon Dericourt's return to Paris, it was Suttill's-Prosper turn to go to London. In his memoirs, Buckmaster said that Suttill met with Winston Churchill, who told him that the allies planned an invasion of Europe in 1943 (the actual invasion did not take place until one year later in June 1944). Others in the Prosper network said that Suttill told them that the invasion was planned for a few months in the future (1943).

On June 24, 1943, less than two weeks after his departure from London, Suttill was arrested by German police outside of his Paris home. Who betrayed Suttill-Prosper? M.R.D. Foot, the official historian of the SOE in France, charges that Claude Dansey was responsible for the betrayal of Suttill. He said that, "it was widely believed in France that Suttill's circuit was deliberately betrayed by the British to the Germans even directly by wireless to the Avenue Foch (German military HQ in Paris)."

Intercepted British decrypts tell that Hitler himself took time out daily to be briefed about Prosper and ordered that Suttill's group be arrested.

Suttill was brutally interrogated and executed at the Sachsenhausen concentration camp. But who ultimately sold out Prosper and was responsible for his arrest?

William Stephenson of the BSC, said that he was told by Colin Gubbins that the culprit was Claude Dansey. "Gubbins advised me that Dansey had betrayed to the enemy a number of his key agents in France, and that the casualties were extremely heavy....I believed this, for I myself had formed the impression that Dansey was an evil man who would stop at nothing to get someone out of his way." Stephenson claimed that he met with Menzies regarding the Gubbins allegation and that "C" said that action would be taken.

Another person who points the finger at Dansey was Patrick Reilly, Menzies's assistant. "Dansey came into my room and asked me with delight all over his face: 'Have you heard the news, Reilly?' '…No…,' Dansey replied as if this was the most important moment of his career had come. SOE's in the shit. They've bought it in France. The Germans are mopping them up all over the place. I felt sick inside and I then realized that Dansey was the most evil and the most wicked man I had met in public service, and nothing since then has made me change my mind."

Among the many scenarios concerning the elimination of the Prosper network is the possible compromise of the mail onboard the British planes under the direction of Henri Dericourt. Did the Frenchman turn over this prized material to the SD? What is certain is that the SD, through its spy Dericourt, knew every move the SIS made. It is possible that Suttill was arrested via this information. An Abwehr counterespionage officer named Hugo Bleicher said that Prosper was arrested because of the SD's knowledge of the British mail.

Dericourt was ordered back to London in February 1944 and faced hostile interrogation concerning his knowledge of the Prosper affair. Despite his obvious Nazi ties, no punitive action was taken against him. The treachery in the death of Major Frances Suttill and the end of his web of agents, remains one of the unsolved stories of World War II.

(*See Also*: Dansey, Claude; French Resistance Movements)

Q

Quigley, Martin

Martin Quigley was an OSS agent sent to the Vatican City in 1944 on the personal orders of William Donovan. His mission was to sound out Japanese diplomats about the possibilities of negotiations for an end of the war in the Pacific.

Martin Quigley was a long-time friend of Bill Donovan, and when the war began, Donovan had asked him to take on certain confidential work for the United States. Quigley also called among his contacts, President Roosevelt and Francis Cardinal Spellman, Archbishop of New York, one of the most powerful Catholic leaders in the country.

Quigley worked in the Hollywood movie industry, and had contacts among the producers and actors. In January 1943, after a meeting with an OSS officer, Frederic Dolbeare, on Donovan's instructions, Quigley provided certain information to the OSS. Quigley said that he still maintained indirect communications with persons in European countries who might be of help to the OSS. "People who have connections with men of political interest in this country (the U.S.), individuals who might be willing to serve abroad, wholly untrustworthy characters, and people who might know, in definite terms, matters of scandal relating to official people in enemy countries."

Mr. Dolbeare wrote to Donovan regarding his meeting with Quigley. It reads in part: "I see no possible harm in attempting a survey of the possibilities of that area, provided the name of OSS is left out of it." Donovan, however, had another, more important mission for Quigley to perform.

In the fall of 1944, Donovan met with Quigley in Washington and, over lunch, gave him his new orders. He was to go to the Vatican and make contact with the Japanese, via his connection with the Holy See, to sound out the Japanese about ending the war. His Vatican assignment was not Quigley's first work for the OSS. He had previously served in Ireland in 1943 under the cover of a representative of the American Film Industry. In reality, he was an undercover agent in that neutral country, spying on any possible German penetration of the Emerald Isle.

Using the same commercial cover in Italy, he sailed for Europe in December, departing from Newport News, Virginia, on a 14-day voyage to Naples, arriving in Rome a few days later. He found an expensive apartment owned by Dr. Ing Giovianni Pasini, located at 162 Via Po. His formal instructions from the OSS were to "establish and maintain the commercial cover and acquire intelligence of direct or indirect military or strategic value." He had access to a local taxi driver who would take him on his rounds, and had two locations for his "drops" of dispatches and other correspondence. As soon as Quigley was settled in Rome, he began his American and Vatican contacts.

Three of the men whom he took under his wing were Father McCormick, Engineer Pietro Galeazzi, and most important, Monsignor Egidio Vagnozzi.

Father McCormick once served as the Rector of the Gregorian, a large international seminary in Rome. He was then in Rome as an important member of the Jesuit headquarters, specializing in American relations. He also served as Pope Pius XII's English language specialist.

Pietro Galeazzi was the architect of the Vatican, as well as the chief operating officer of Vatican City, and one of the Pontiff's best friends.

Quigley's other middlemen in Rome who did not know of his OSS ties were Dr. Thomas Kiernan, the Irish Ambassador, and a second diplomat, Michael MacWhite, the Irish envoy to the Italian government.

Egidio Vagnozzi, one of the top members of the Church hierarchy, spoke English, had lived in the United States for 10 years, and was on good terms with the ecclesiastical advisor to the Japanese Ambassador, Reverend Benedict Tomizawa, a fact duly noted by Quigley. It was Monsignor Vagnozzi whom Quigley would contact as his intermediary with the Japanese.

When Quigley called Monsignor Vagnozzi, the prelate knew who he was. They had met before, and the American asked if he could arrange a meeting as early as possible. Quigley came to Monsignor Vagnozzi's residence and over drinks, presented his case. He began by saying that with the European war now over, it was only a matter of time before Japan would be defeated. He told the priest of his Catholic background, and the fact that his family knew William Donovan, a name Vagnozzi knew all too well. He then told the monsignor of his OSS ties.

He described his instructions from Donovan: to see if he could open up a channel of communications with the Japanese for possible peace initiatives. He went on to say that the Vatican would be the most logical place to begin negotiations. Quigley then made his pitch. Would he, Monsignor Vagnozzi, be the intermediary with the Japanese? He then went on to ask if the monsignor would see his friend, Benedict Tomizawa, who lived in the same building. Vagnozzi was reluctant to get involved in international politics, saying that he would try, but promised nothing. Quigley said that if the prelate agreed, he would be the communications tie between the U.S. and Japan.

Monsignor Vagnozzi met with Father Tomizawa and in cautious language relayed what his unnamed American visitor told him. The Japanese priest seemed stunned but agreed to pass along Monsignor Vagnozzi's offers. What neither Quigley nor Vagnozzi was aware of was that the Emperor of Japan had given Ambassador Harada instructions to listen to any peace feelers that might come his way (Harada was the Japanese Ambassador to Rome).

Father Tomizawa had a hurried meeting with Ambassador Harada at which time they debated Quigley's offers. A third person was called into the discussion, the Secretary of the Mission, a man named Kamayama (also a Catholic). They drew up a list of the pros and cons regarding the peace feelers before making a decision on whether or not to recommend to Tokyo that any further action be taken.

In the end, Ambassador Harada rejected Quigley's offer, saying in part, "At the present time I believe that Japan does not seek to hasten the coming of peace. Furthermore, it goes without saying that we cannot discuss such questions with a person whose official position and identity are unknown to us."

Martin Quigley's long-shot peace proposal failed to end the war. It would take the dropping of two atomic bombs on Japan to finally end the bloodshed in the Pacific Theater.

(*See Also*: Japanese Peace Feelers)

Quisling, Vidkun

In the long history of World War II, one person's name is synonymous with treason: Vidkun Quisling of Norway. Quisling served as the puppet master of Norway, at Hitler's beck and call, and for his own lust for power turned over his country to the Nazis.

Vidkun Quisling was born in 1887 in Tyrdesdal, Norway, the child of a local preacher. He always wanted to become a soldier, and he attended the local military academy. Through hard work, he rose in the ranks, eventually becoming a captain on the Norwegian Army's General Staff. His first posting was as the military attaché in the Russian city of St. Petersburg.

In 1922, he left the army and went to work for Fridtjof Nansen, a socially compassionate person who aided refugees from the Russian Revolution. Quisling did not last long in the employ of Nansen, and he soon left for other pursuits.

Quisling joined a group of like-minded, disgruntled men who sought revolution to cure the world's ills. He detested the Russian form of Bolshevism and formed Norway's National Unity Party in 1931. This organization was modeled on Adolf Hitler's slowly rising National Socialists in Germany. He shared Hitler's hatred of the Jews, saying that they were responsible for all the troubles then plaguing European society.

In Germany, Quisling's name was known by ranking Nazis, and he was approached by Alfred Rosenberg, Hitler's ideologue. In 1939, Quisling traveled to Berlin and had his first meeting with Rosenberg. Quisling told the German that Norway was of strategic interest to the Germans, and that Hitler would be wise to turn his attention to that nation. He also said that he would be willing to aid Hitler. That same year, a number of Quisling's men arrived in Germany for schooling in the policies of National Socialism.

Norway was then a neutral country, and hoped to stay that way, even while the rest of Europe warred. The Norwegians believed that their country would be protected by the might of the British navy in case of attack. Their policy was that in case of war, Norway was not to be brought in on Germany's side.

Quisling went to work for Admiral Schniewind, chief of staff for Grand Admiral Erich Raeder. Raeder wanted Hitler to consider an invasion of Scandinavia, and he even brought Quisling to have a personal meeting with the Führer. Hitler eventually put the plans for an invasion of Norway into motion, and ordered Quisling back home to become the central agent in the conquest.

The Germans moved against Norway under the constant threat that the British might stage a "friendly" invasion to stop a Nazi takeover. Under the guise of a training mission called "Operation Weser Excerise," plans for the invasion of Norway got underway. Using agents planted into many of Norway's seaports like Oslo, Narvik and Christiansand, German spies reported on all ocean traffic and the sailing schedules of Norwegian ships.

On April 9, 1940, German troops and ships invaded Norway. The Norwegian's resisted the seaborne attack and inflicted heavy losses on the invaders.

As the Germans overran the country, the legitimate national government fled, and Quisling, now a puppet of the Germans, proclaimed himself head of the Norwegian government. He vainly ordered his new "subjects" to surrender, and help the encroachers at all levels.

For the remainder of the war, Quisling ran Norway under Hitler's strings. Under his regime, a number of Jews were deported, and he encouraged men of fighting age to take up arms for Germany.

In the end, the treason undertaken by Quisling led to his own downfall.

QUISLING

Instead of meekly complying with the German occupation, a national resistance movement sprung up, which eventually ousted the Germans.

For his treason, Vidkun Quisling was executed.

R

Raisin Mission

The OSS Raisin mission, running out of headquarters in Brindisi, Italy, was one of the successful and daring operations of the war. It accomplished the rescue of a number of high-ranking allied officers from enemy hands, as well as establishment of a radio network in Italy.

The Raisin Team was part of an elite unit dubbed Combined "Λ" Force Ops. One of its leaders was Captain Max Corvo, a leader of the Secret Intelligence Branch of OSS. He was instrumental in the recruitment of a number of Italian Americans of Sicilian heritage for OSS duty in North Africa and Italy. Another person in the "A" Force chain of command was Vincent Scamporino, also operating out of Brindisi.

The Raisin team's most productive military mission began in February 1944, when they entered Northern Italy. The method of transportation was by submarine, and they were transferred to shore by a rubber boat.

Their first communication with OSS HQ was made on July 27, 1944. From that date on, they were able to transmit more than 150 messages from the field and posted a large intelligence windfall. From that heady start, things began to go asunder. The Germans somehow located where the Raisin team were making their broadcasts and managed to capture the lead radio operator, as well as their cipher plans. Despite this setback, the remainder of the team made it to safety. In October 1944, a successful airdrop of supplies was made to Raisin at their new location.

"The Raisin Team has been an outstanding mission," reports OSS documents, "from the day of its first contact. It has not limited itself to the gathering of intelligence, which is its primary job, since there were too many elements which were friendly to the Allies, in the Raisin Zone, and which were in need of help. Since Raisin had the method of communications to Allied Occupied Italy, and since a great organizer led the team, this help was given, and proved to be of enormous significance."

In May 1944, OSS sent the Raisin Team its most significant set of instructions. They were to rescue five Allied General Officers (English), as well as one Allied consul trapped behind enemy territory. The only location in the documents put the generals somewhere in German-occupied Italy.

The Raisin Team made contact with the British "A" Force quarters and made the rescue in the second week in May. The Raisin Team brought the allied officers out on the night of May 23rd, "south of the mouth of the Poci Dell Adige." They rendezvoused at 11:00, and were instructed to remain in that position until 1:30. The generals were taken back to OSS HQ at Bari.

"The generals cannot stop thanking us. I have sent Captain Clemente to interview them and ask how our boys are getting along. As soon as he gets back, I am sure we will have the names of the officers and all other pertinent information." Speaking of the role of Raisin in the springing of the generals, the documents say that, "the Raisin leader, realizing this feat, did all in his power to facilitate the rescue and even sent as guides two of his own agents."

The Raisin mission was also responsible for establishing a courier service from German occupied Italy. In a daring adventure, plans were made for a meeting on the high seas between a submarine and a fishing boat to be sent by Raisin. The result was the first time that this type of operation in the Adriatic and in the entire Italian theater of operations was carried out. In the history of OSS operations in Italy, Raisin was, by far, the most successful. (*See Also*: Corvo, Max; Italian Patriot Bands)

Red Orchestra

The Red Orchestra was a successful anti-German spy networks run by the Soviet Union during the war. Also called the "Rote Kapelle," its members were some daring and public figures, although their reputation among historians is still being debated.

The Red Orchestra got its impetus even before the Germans broke their peace treaty with Stalin and invaded Russia. A deep animosity between Stalin and Hitler was just under the surface, and when Operation Barbarosa, the code name for the Nazi attack on Russia occurred, the Russians took immediate steps to spy on their new enemy.

The founding members of the group were Harro Schulze-Boysen and Arvid Harnack. Schulze-Boysen was an intelligence agent with the German Air Ministry. In the 1930s, he taught economics at Giessen University and secretly organized a communist underground ring. He was arrested in 1933 for his political views but was released through the intervention of important family members. It was then that he wound up working for German military intelligence. In January 1941, he was named as the liaison to the Luftwaffe Chiefs of Staff.

Harnack was recruited into the Russian NKVD in 1935. He met Schulze-Boysen in 1941 and took him into his organization. Over a number of months, both Boysen and Harnack were able to make intelligence inroads by taking on agents from the most vital areas of the German military. Among the offices where they received information through their secret sources were the Air Ministry, the Foreign Office, the Economic Ministry, Ministry of Labor, among others.

Soon, members of the Red Orchestra began operations in Belgium, France, and the Netherlands. All of their information was sent via radio. At certain times during their transmissions, German listening stations were able to hear their signals but at first were not capable of fixing their exact position.

As hundreds of radio messages from the group were being sent to Moscow, it was only a matter of time before German counterintelligence were able to locate them. Schulze-Boysen and Harnack were arrested during the last week of August and September 1942. By December 1942, many hundreds of their group were apprehended. Many of them were tortured to death.

The man who ran the Red Orchestra was Leopold Trepper, called the "Grand Chef" by his group. Trepper began working for the Russians in 1939, and it was in that year that he came to Brussels, Belgium, under the cover of a Canadian businessman, to begin preparations for espionage activities in France and Scandinavia. He started a business called the Foreign Excellent Raincoat Company, a front. When the Nazis conquered Belgium, Trepper moved his organization to France. Like the good executive he was, Trepper ran seven spy rings in France, sending back vital military and industrial information to Moscow. He was also able to relay facts on the locations of German troops in the field, as well as statistics on the Atlantic Wall, then being built in anticipation of an allied invasion. Trepper also utilized members of the French Communist Party for his intelligence.

In order to counter the Red Orchestra, Hitler ordered a number of his counterintelligence agencies including the Abwehr, and the Gestapo, to bring them down. Using sophisticated direction finders, they were able to round up dozens of "pianists," the name given by the Germans to the senders of radio transmissions by Trepper's group. On December 5, 1942, Leopold Trepper was arrested at the office of his dentist in Paris. Almost one year after his capture, he was able to escape his jailers and hide until the war was over.

Sandor Rado ran another component of the Red Orchestra, code-named Dora, which operated out of neutral Switzerland. Working from headquarters in Geneva, Rado employed a number of highly successful agents, among them, Rachel Dubendorfer, code-named Sissy, George Blum, and Otto

Puenter. Historians of World War II also called the Switzerland web the "Lucy Ring."

Rachel Dubendorfer's most productive agent was Rudolf Roessler, a German who went to Lucerne, Switzerland in 1933 to create a publishing house. The Swiss knew about Roessler's front activities and in 1939 recruited him into their own service. Roessler acquired information from the Swiss, as well as a number of his own agents, the best source being a German code-named Werther. Roessler was eventually arrested and found guilty but never served time.

While the Red Orchestra proved to be a vital link in the Soviet's intelligence connection, Stalin never really trusted their work, believing that a majority of the group were double agents working for the Germans. A prime example was when the Red Orchestra provided Stalin with concrete information warning them of a German invasion of Russia in June 1941. Stalin never took their admonition seriously, and paid dearly for his mistake.

Many years after the war ended, the CIA conducted a major study on the activities of the Red Orchestra, highlighting their functions, and taking a shot at identifying the source, or sources, of their mole inside the German government. (This study is now declassified and can be found at the National Archives.)

(*See Also*: Foote, Alexander; Roessler, Rudolf; Werther)

Rochefort, Joseph

Joseph Rochefort (1898-1976), one of the navy's most important cryptanalysts during World War II, headed the vital code-breaking station located at Pearl Harbor. The messages he and his team decrypted were responsible for the navy's intelligence success at the battle of Midway. They also compiled a voluminous amount of deciphered radio communications regarding the whereabouts of the Japanese fleet in the weeks before Pearl Harbor.

Joseph Rochefort graduated from the University of California and joined the navy during World War I at age 17. He was promoted to ensign and served on destroyers. After the war, Rochefort headed the Code and Signal Section of the Office of Naval Communications. He was an avid fan of crossword puzzles as well as cryptography, and his talent landed him in one of the growing fields of naval intelligence. He was promoted to lieutenant and assigned to duty with Lieutenant Commander Lawrence Safford who was in command of the fledgling Navy Communications Section. He was later sent to Japan where he remained for three years, learning the language and studying Japanese culture. During the 1930s, Rochefort was sent to the Pacific, where he worked under the direction of the Pacific Fleet commander. In 1941, Rochefort was given control of the Combat Intelligence Unit of the

Fourteenth Naval district in Pearl Harbor. It was from this spot that he would play a role in the events leading up to the Pearl Harbor attack.

He was responsible for Station Hypo, a U.S. Pacific monitoring section of the navy, which listened in on radio communications from various Japanese sources, including the Imperial Navy. Rochefort's Station Hypo had the obligation of keeping track of the Mid-Pacific Communications Intelligence Network, which was comprised of 140 communications workers. Station Hypo also worked closely with other navy intercept stations located on Midway Island, and Dutch Harbor, as well as one listening post in Hawaii. Station Hypo kept track of intercepts coming from Japanese naval communications.

By October 1941, Rochefort's analysts at Station Hypo were beginning to intercept a large number of signals coming from Japanese naval sources, leading them to believe that a change in Japanese operational orders was imminent. They picked up a plain language message from Tokyo saying that the Japanese First Fleet, comprised of submarines as well as surface ships, was leaving the port of Hitokappu Bay. Hypo also reported that, in their opinion, Japan was planning a naval maneuver from the Kurile Islands.

One of Rochefort's main competitors in the intelligence-gathering pecking order in Hawaii was the army's Station Five located at Fort Shafter on Oahu. General Walter Short ran Station Five. Short never cooperated with Rochefort's Hypo, and an intense rivalry between the two materialized. When General Short learned that Five had intercepted the "Japanese telegraphic code," he ordered Rochefort to break the code. Rochefort ignored the general's orders. On December 17, 10 days after the attack on Pearl Harbor, General Short was relieved of his command.

Rochefort was also in the middle of breaking the Japanese 5-Num Code. "Throughout 1941 and 1942, the United States naval cryptographers and intercept operators referred to Code Book D as the 5-Num Code, because a group of five numbers represented a Japanese word or phrase. Japan's navy assigned thousands of different five-number combinations to represent their language for radio transmission purposes."

As the Japanese plans for Pearl Harbor took root, Rochefort's code analysts were able to track their progress. Through radio intercepts, they were capable of ascertaining that Admiral Yamamoto, the architect of the attack, had reorganized his Combined Fleet into eight distinct sections. This information was sent to Admiral Husband Kimmel at Naval HQ at Pearl Harbor. The fleet consisted of aircraft carriers, submarines, troop transports, minelaying ships, cruisers, as well as destroyers. These ships were part of his overall plan to counter the U.S. in the Pacific, as well as position them for strikes against the Philippines and other allied targets once hostilities began. Part of this fleet was destined to attack Pearl Harbor.

U.S. Navy intercept stations were able to decipher messages coming from the fleet saying that the, "combined fleet will observe radio communication procedures as follows: 1) except in extreme emergency, the main force and its attached forces will cease communicating, 2) other forces are at discretion of their respective commanders."

Rochefort's greatest success in using the 5-Num code came when he was able to identify three Japanese military units called "Keibii 51, Keibii 52 and Keibii 53." These units were dispatched from the naval base at Maizuru, an amphibious landing training base used by the Japanese navy. These troops were part of the force that attacked Wake Island on December 11, 1941, and were repelled by the waiting U.S. marines.

Rochefort testified before the Pearl Harbor investigations of 1944 to 1946, with harsh words for the navy's lack of preparedness before December 7, 1941. He said that on numerous occasions he informed Admiral Kimmel regarding his station intercepts. For whatever reason, Rochefort stopped reporting to the admiral on November 16, 1941—the very day that the Japanese strike force began gathering at their collection points for the Pearl Harbor attack. He next brought up the code on December 19, 12 days after the Japanese attack. Rochefort knew all too well that the Japanese naval forces were on the move from their home bases to points unknown in the Pacific.

Rochefort spotted another puzzle to the attack in the two months prior to the strike when they intercepted Japanese communications placing their merchant fleet at the disposal of the navy. He then ordered his Mid-Pacific Communications Network on an "eight-day" work schedule. This added another watch to the radio transmission operation.

Rochefort's daily intelligence summary regarding Japanese moves in the Pacific led Washington to take an interesting set of actions. In late November, the U.S. Navy ordered a "Vacant Sea" alert, removing all U.S. ships out of the area from which the Japanese naval communications were coming from. The ships were sent to the Torres Strait in the South Pacific, near Australia and New Guinea. This was done, according to the navy, "when we believed that war was imminent."

The fact that Joseph Rochefort was a controversial figure in the events leading up to Pearl Harbor led to more contention after the war. Admiral Chester Nimitz recommended that he be awarded the Distinguished Service Medal for his work. Unfortunately, the navy turned down the request. In October 1942, he was released from his code-breaking duties and was given another assignment.

Joseph Rochefort died in 1976. In 1986, in an effort to clear the record, then Navy Secretary John Lehman, awarded him the DSM posthumously in recognition of his vital wartime service.

(*See Also*: Hypo, Station; Pearl Harbor Attack)

Rockefeller, Nelson

Throughout our history, Latin America has played a vital role in the affairs of the United States. From the Monroe Doctrine to FDR's hands-off policy regarding foreign intervention in the region, American presidents have kept a keen eye on the political and military developments to our south.

When World War II began, the FBI was the only American intelligence-gathering agency. It began to monitor Nazi intelligence activities throughout South America. President Roosevelt believed that if Germany won the war, the vital interests of this continent would be in great danger. In order to counteract German espionage activities in South America, the president turned to one of his oldest political friends, Nelson Rockefeller, to create a new agency that would counter German activity.

In August 1940, he appointed Rockefeller to "The Office of the Coordinator of Commercial and Cultural Relations among the American Republics." This agency would later be dubbed "The Coordinator of Inter-American Affairs."

Rockefeller's job was to use his considerable worldwide business interests to counter German political activities in the area. Specifically, the new group was to persuade, by all means necessary, American companies from doing business in South America if that firm had any connections with German-leaning commerce in that region. In addition, the Coordinator's office tried to persuade any American company which had employees sympathetic to the Germans, and operated in Latin America, to be removed from their jobs.

In Nelson Rockefeller, FDR had picked a most capable agent. Rockefeller, whose family controlled the giant Standard Oil Company, had influence unmatched in the American business community. Standard Oil's tentacles reached far and wide, and when Rockefeller made a pitch, the government listened. But the fledgling Rockefeller organization did not work alone. Operating along with the Coordinator's Office, was the British spy organization operating in the United States, the BSC, run by William Stephenson.

Stephenson's BSC had agents throughout South America reporting on all aspects of German activity. The British, through the BSC, provided Rockefeller with the information they needed to counteract German programs relative to American interests. The FBI was also involved in this venture.

J. Edgar Hoover had no love for either Rockefeller or Stephenson and wanted total control over all facets of U.S. intelligence functions. Hoover, however, had to go along with his two intelligence competitors on the direct orders from the White House.

Rockefeller's agents, working in tandem with both the FBI and the BSC, covered Brazil, Argentina, Chile, the main countries in South America that had the largest number of German immigrants, along with a large and well-established clandestine intelligence network.

After the war, Nelson Rockefeller entered Republican politics and was elected governor of New York. He made an unsuccessful try for the Republican presidential nomination in 1960 (won by Richard Nixon) and was later appointed with the consent of the congress to vice president of the United States.

As a national politician, Rockefeller's name was well known. But few knew of his covert role in pre-Pearl Harbor espionage activities (*See Also*: BSC; Stephenson, William; Latin American Espionage; Nascimento, Tulio)

Roessler, Rudolf, "Lucy"

Rudolf Roessler (1897-1958), code-named "Lucy," was head of the "Lucy Ring," a tightly knit group of anti-Nazis that worked for the Soviet Union in Switzerland. The information sent back to the Soviet Union was so valuable that they failed to take most of it seriously, believing that Lucy and his team were double agents for the Germans.

Rudolf Roessler was born on November 22, 1897, in Kaufbeuren, Bavaria, near Munich. His father was a minor official in the local government. Rudolf went to school in the city of Augsburg, attending the Realgymnasium.

During World War I, he served in the German army. After the war, he became a newspaper reporter in Augsburg and later in Berlin. When Hitler came to power in Germany, Roessler moved to Lucerne, Switzerland, where he wrote anti-German articles. In time, he also established a small publishing company called the Vita Nova Verlag, which he would run as a cover throughout the war.

Not much is known as to how Roessler began his espionage career, but what is certain is that he had an all encompassing hatred of Hitler and a powerful interest in Stalin's Soviet Union. In Switzerland, Roessler made contacts with other anti-Nazis who aided him in his work. Roessler's initial contact in his spy career came in the person of Dr. Xaver Schnieper. Schnieper aided Roessler when the latter began writing for an anti-Nazi publication called *Die Entscheidung* (The Decision). Schnieper put Roessler in contact with Captain Hans Hausamann who worked for the Swiss intelligence service, Buro Ha. Another person with whom Roessler met was Roger Masson, then head of

Swiss military intelligence.

An informal arrangement among Roessler, Masson and Hausamann began, and the Swiss looked the other way when Roessler and his underground group began sending their intelligence to Moscow. It has been postulated that Roessler was working in direct contact with the Swiss, providing them the same information that they gave to the Russians.

By 1939, Roessler had informants in the highest places of the German military command, including sources in the OKH, the army high command, where military plans were set in motion. He had agents working directly in the offices of such leaders as Generals Franz Halder, Walther von Brauchitsch, and George Thomas.

One of Roessler's agents was a British spy named Alexander Foote. Foote worked in Geneva with a woman named Ruth Kuczynski, also known as Sonia. He was Sonia's radio operator and later reported to Sandor Rado, who worked alongside Roessler. The Lucy material to the Soviets came straight from Foote's mouth during the war, "Lucy provided Moscow with an up-to-date…order of battle of the German forces in East Russia, fighting with her back to the wall and scraping her last resources…vitally interested in trustworthy information regarding the armed forces ranged against her…this 'Lucy' supplied."

The code names for Lucy's agents inside the German military were "Teddy," "Bill," "Olga," "Anna," and his principal spy, "Werther." Werther worked inside the OKW, and told the Russians that Hitler was about to renege on his non-aggression pact with Stalin and invade Russia. "Teddy" worked in the OKH, the Army High Command, "Bill" served in the army's weapons office, "Olga" reported on army maneuvers, while "Anna" furnished news coming from the Foreign Office. Together, they sent more than 5,500 messages to Moscow during the war.

In sending his top-grade intelligence to Moscow, Roessler worked with a number of "cut-outs," the most trusted agents, who sent the information along a chain ending in Russia. Roessler sent his information to a friend named Christian Schneider. Schneider gave it to Rachel Dubendorfer, "Sissy." Neither Dubendorfer nor others in the Lucy ring knew the real identity of "Lucy"—Roessler, or any others in their circle.

While the "Lucy" ring sent messages on German military plans relevant to the Soviet Union, the office that oversaw Roessler began to have grave doubts about their operations. Rachel Dubendorfer wanted to distance herself and refused to follow the Center's instructions. The Center instructed Dubendorfer and Lucy to go to ground, as they received information saying that the Germans were on their trail. One message from Moscow said, "If you are interrogated by the Swiss police, deny everything categorically." The Center also instructed Sandor Rado to break his ties to Dubendorfer and begged her to reveal her sources to Moscow (this, she refused to do).

Rachel Dubendorfer believed that the Center was trying to take operational control away from her. They sent her this message showing their impatience: "Dear Sissy, We, the Center, which has its people everywhere and can determine what is happening in other countries and around you, have told you clearly and explicitly that we have hard evidence that the Gestapo knows that you work for us and will try to uncover your connections into Germany. You, however, deny this possibility and interpret it as an attempt to take the Lucy group away from you. You must understand, inasmuch as you assume this position, that you know nothing of the danger which threatens you and Taylor's [Lucy's] people, especially those in Germany. Your behavior is frivolous and irresponsible. We demand that you recognize the seriousness of the situation and place full confidence in our statements." In the end, Dubendorfer would not give up her sources, no matter how hard she was pushed by Moscow.

During the life of the Lucy ring, German counterespionage agents in Switzerland were following its every move, and it came as no surprise that they would eventually locate the sites of their communications. The Germans protested to the Swiss government, who arrested Lucy Ring principals, including Foote, Rado, and Roessler.

The Swiss, who were one of the major beneficiaries of the information provided by Lucy, were lenient in their treatment of their prized prisoners and by the fall of 1944, they were set free. Foote, Roessler and Dubendorfer were let go in September. Sandor Rado was never arrested, and the Germans at no time knew his true identity.

In the ensuing months, Foote and Rachel Dubendorfer met for the first time. While the Lucy Ring was now defunct, Dubendorfer told him that she was still in contact with Roessler who continued to receive intelligence from his prime source inside the German military. Werther and Roessler joined Foote and Dubendorfer many months later for their first face-to-face meeting. It was arranged for Foote to travel openly to Paris and take the intelligence material provided by Werther to the Soviet consulate. From that point, the material would be forwarded to Moscow.

The end of the war found Roessler still living in Switzerland, this time selling information to the allies. In the 1950s, he was again arrested by the Swiss on espionage charges and spent one year in prison. Rudolf Roessler, aka "Lucy," died in Switzerland in 1958.

(*See Also*: Foote, Alexander; Red Orchestra; Werther)

Rosenberg, Julius & Ethel

Almost 50 years have passed since the June 19, 1953, execution of Julius and Ethel Rosenberg in Sing Sing on espionage charges for their involvement in stealing America's atomic secrets during World War II. The case against the Rosenbergs still creates passionate debate over the death sentence, and to what extent Julius and Ethel were involved with the Soviet Union's espionage operations.

In the ensuing years, their now-grown sons, Michael and Robert Meeropol (they took on their adoptive parent's last name after the execution), have spent their lives trying to clear their parents' name. With the end of the Cold War, America's most prominent code-breaking service, the National Security Agency, as well as a former Soviet intelligence official who knew the Rosenbergs well, have shed new light on the role they performed for the Soviets during the war.

Julius Rosenberg was born on May 12, 1918, in New York City. His parents had emigrated from Poland at the turn of the century and raised five children. Julius attended schools in New York and graduated from Seward Park High School at age 16.

He attended City College of New York and joined the Young Communist League, where he would meet a number of other young men who shared his political views and who would later become part of the Soviet espionage apparatus: Morton Sobell, William Perl, and Joel Barr. Julius studied electrical engineering, instead of rabbinical studies that his father asked him to pursue.

Ethel Greenglass Rosenberg was two years younger than Julius and fancied herself going into the performing arts or a career in music. She, too, had radical political ideas. They met at a rally and were married in 1939.

In 1940, Julius went to work as a civilian employee for the U.S. Army Signal Corps and in 1942 attained the position of inspector. While he was working for the army, both joined the Communist Party U.S.A. In time, he served as the chairman of Branch 16B of the Party's Industrial Division. However, in 1943, Julius left the Communist Party to pursue his active espionage for the Soviet Union.

There have been conflicting accounts over who originally recruited Julius Rosenberg into the Soviet espionage orbit. The two leading candidates were Semen Semenov, a KGB agent who worked out of the Soviet trade organization called Amtorg, or Gaik Ovakimian, the NKVD's top agent in New York City.

Whatever the case, Julius began active spying in 1942. In 1943, Semenov returned to the Soviet Union, after it was discovered that he was under tight FBI surveillance. With Semenov gone, Rosenberg was assigned a new controller, Alexander Feklisov, then a promising agent working in the Soviet consulate in New York.

Through his Russian contacts in New York, Julius was put in touch with a member of the intelligence apparatus working out of the Russian consulate, Anatoli Yakovlev. Yakovlev's aim was the theft of America's atomic secrets. One of the men Yakovlev employed was Julius Rosenberg.

Julius used his brother-in-law, David Greenglass, a soldier assigned to the top-secret Los Alamos Laboratory in New Mexico, as his conduit for the transfer of material to the Russians. Greenglass worked for the Manhattan Project, the most sensitive project undertaken by the United States during the war.

Julius arranged for Harry Gold, a courier used by the Russians, to go to New Mexico and bring back information supplied by Greenglass. Another Russian mole working inside the Manhattan Project was British scientist Klaus Fuchs, a brilliant man and a fellow traveler. In 1945, while on leave, Greenglass arrived at Julius's apartment in New York and gave him a picture of a lens mold used for the detonation of the atomic bomb.

While Julius was active in the transfer of the atomic bomb intelligence, he was also involved in other facets of spying. He helped recruit a number of people in the American electronic industry who provided the Russians with highly technical data coming from U.S. factories. One of his major coups was the revelation to the Soviets of a working model of a so-called proximity fuse, which was used to shoot down aircraft without a direct hit. Julius was able to secure this device from his new employer, the Emerson Radio Company in New York during 1944.

Throughout the time that Julius was working for the Russians, the FBI had been intercepting an enormous amount of enciphered messages to and from the Soviet consulate in New York and Moscow. It was not until after the war, in 1947, that the messages were turned over to the Army Security Agency. In years of painstaking work by a crack team of cryptanalysts, U.S. code breakers were able to piece together the story. What they found shocked them to the core. They discovered that the Soviets had penetrated the Manhattan Project and that the prime leader was Klaus Fuchs. The British took Fuchs into custody, and he admitted his Los Alamos espionage activities. Fuchs in turn gave the British and the Americans, the name of his cut-out in the operation, Harry Gold. Gold turned in David Greenglass, and he was arrested. The circumstances of what happened next are still unclear. When questioned by the FBI, Greenglass told them that his sister, Ethel, and her husband, Julius, had recruited him into their Russian-controlled spy ring. On June 17, 1950, Julius was arrested on suspicion of espionage. Ethel was arrested shortly thereafter.

At their trial, which lasted from March-April 1951, Julius and Ethel were convicted of espionage. The other two defendants, David Greenglass and Morton Sobell, received a 15- and 30-year prison sentence.

Julius and Ethel were taken to Sing Sing Prison in New York, while their appeal process went on. Despite an uproar from numerous prominent world figures, the two were executed on June 19, 1953. (Ethel was the second woman in America to be put to death for wartime espionage. The first was Mary Surratt who was hanged for her alleged participation in the plot to kill President Abraham Lincoln).

In the 1990s, 50 years after their deaths, and after the end of the Cold War, new information relating to the role the Rosenbergs played during that time has come to light.

The U.S. intelligence used the Venona Project to spy on the Soviets. It was run out of Arlington Hall and taken over after the war by the newly created National Security Agency. The Venona decryption revealed Julius Rosenberg's role in Soviet wartime espionage.

The Russians gave Rosenberg two code names: Antenna and Liberal. From 1944 to 1945, the Venona analysts picked up 21 cables referring to Julius. What they learned was that by May 22, 1944, Rosenberg's network in New York was flourishing. Julius recruited Alfred Sarant, a classmate at CCNY, who had previously worked at the Signal Corps laboratory at Fort Monmouth, New Jersey. After working for the Soviets, he fled the U.S. in July 1950. The early Venona materials report that the Russians provided Julius with his own camera in order to copy stolen documents at his home.

Another man taken on by Rosenberg was Morton Sobell, who joined the group in 1944. He worked at the General Electric laboratory in Schenectady, New York, and passed on information on military radar. In 1950, Sobell went to Mexico, was arrested by Mexican police, and deported to the U.S. He was given a 30-year prison term and served 18 of those years.

Julius also brought in to his cell, a dynamic aircraft engineer named William Pearl. Pearl went to CCNY with Morton Sobell and supplied information from his job at the National Advisory Committee for Aeronautics. He provided the Russians with vital news on aeronautics and for his reward was given a $500 bonus in 1944. He was convicted of perjury and was given a five-year jail term.

As far as Rosenberg was concerned, the Venona materials report that while working at the Emerson Radio Company, Julius stole a complete set of a new, highly secret proximity fuse used for the military. For this action, he received a $1,000 incentive.

A retired Russian spy who was close to the couple during the war, Alexander Feklisov, provided more information on Ethel and Julius

ROSENBERG

Rosenberg's wartime espionage activities. In 1997, Feklisov gave a number of interviews to American news organizations regarding his knowledge of the Rosenberg case.

Feklisov said he met with Julius in the summer of 1946 in a New York restaurant. At that meeting he gave him $1,000 expense money. Prior to that date, Feklisov said that between 1943 and 1946, he met with Julius Rosenberg in New York more than 50 times, helping him to establish his espionage network.

He emphatically told his interviewers that while Ethel Rosenberg was aware of her husband's work for the Russians, she had no direct contact with any member of Soviet intelligence. Of Ethel Rosenberg, the Venona documents say that she "knows about her husband's work, but is in delicate health and does not work." When questioned about Julius's role in stealing America's atomic secrets, he said that he played only a minor role in the affair. (He alluded to the fact that Klaus Fuchs was the main participant in the theft of the Manhattan Project's secrets.)

During his tenure for the Soviet Union, Julius would meet with Feklisov at such places as Madison Square Garden, a Child's Restaurant, and other public places. The ex-Russian spy said that Julius once told him that, "I calculated the risks very carefully. What I was risking was only one-hundredth of what a Red Army soldier risks when he attacks a tank."

The new information supplied via the Venona Project and Alexander Feklisov adds new details to the case. Their trial came at a time in American history when the Cold War hysteria and McCarthyism were at their height. The Korean War had just begun, and Americans were looking for scapegoats. Whether they were its first victims or pawns in a larger game of cold-war politics is still debatable. History, in the Rosenberg case, is still ongoing.

(*See Also*: Bentley, Elizabeth; Fuchs, Klaus; Gold, Harry; Golos, Jacob; Greenglass, David; Manhattan Project)

S

SOE (Special Operations Executive)

When France fell in June 1940, the event sent shock waves throughout London. Prime Minister Churchill knew that Great Britain's armies alone would not be able to defeat Germany directly on the battlefield. Other, non-traditional means would be needed. In response to that challenge, Churchill, on July 16, 1940, established a covert, paramilitary force to, in his words, "set Europe ablaze." The means to carry out his assignment was called SOE, Special Operations Executive.

SOE's primary purpose was to aid the resistance fighters in occupied Europe through assassination, sabotage, guerrilla operations, and hit-and-run raids against military facilities.

SOE's first director was Sir Hugh Dalton, who also served as Minister of Economic Warfare. The new agency was given responsibility for Military Research, Propaganda, and the action arm of the service, Section D of the Secret Intelligence Service. The man put in charge of Section D was Major L.D. Grand. Sir Colin Stuart, a former executive of the *London Times*, ran the propaganda section, and Major J.C. Holland, a man well versed in guerrilla operations, took over the covert section, M.I.R.

SOE's headquarters operated out of offices at 64 Baker Street in London. Candidates for possible entry into SOE were culled from recommendations from the SIS, as well as from advertisements in local papers. Interviewees were screened at the Northumberland Hotel, were quizzed in French, and told up front about the dangers the work entailed. After each applicant passed a rigorous security check, they were sent for four weeks of intensive training at Wandsborough Manor, where they were taught map reading, small arms training, and other paramilitary skills. From there, they were shipped to Ringway, Manchester, for two weeks of parachute training. Students took their final grooming courses at a mansion on the west coast of Scotland called Inverness-Shire where they were taught commando tactics, and radio operations.

SOE operated two overseas training bases, one called Camp X in the forested country near Lake Ontario, Canada (called STS 103), the other at Tanjong Balai (STS 101) in Singapore. Throughout the life of SOE, more than 13,000 men and women joined its ranks.

From August 1940 to September 1943, two men headed SOE: Sir Frank Nelson and Sir Charles Hambro. In September 1943, Brigadier Colin Gubbins was picked to be the new chief of SOE. Gubbins, born in Japan in 1896, had his roots in Scotland. He served in the Royal Artillery in World War I, saw service in Russia, Ireland, and India. Gubbins quickly became versed in resistance tactics, guerrilla operations and, in June 1940, organized a guerrilla force of British troops called Auxiliary Units, which was to be used in case of an invasion of England.

Gubbins actively took over all aspects of SOE, overseeing training and beginning a relationship with the fledgling U.S. spy agency, the OSS. If Gubbins had good relations with Donovan, the same could not be said concerning his counterpart at SIS HQ, Stewart Menzies. Menzies originally took to the idea of a new sabotage and undercover unit. The only problem was that Menzies wanted to direct it himself. According to Menzies's thinking, his SIS, was diametrically opposite the boom and bang techniques of SOE. Churchill however, decided against giving "C" overall control of SOE and made it a separate entity. As the war progressed, both SIS and SOE agents came to near physical blows, fighting among themselves.

SOE also had a special relationship in the United States under the umbrella of William Stephenson's BSC, British Security Coordination. BSC's mandate was to coordinate intelligence operations in the Western Hemisphere and eventually encompass other intelligence services such as SIS and MI-5. One of the tasks conducted by SOE in the United States was the covert war targeted against anti-British groups. Among those U.S. groups given covert support were the Non-Sectarian Anti-Nazi League, The Free World Association, The American Labor Committee to Aid British Labor, among others.

Stephenson's BSC also allowed SOE to send its agents into Latin American countries to set up wireless listening posts tracing enemy transmissions. By October 1942, SOE had launched eavesdropping stations in Venezuela, Chile, Uruguay and Argentina.

SOE agents worked in all parts of the world. A large SOE operation was run out of Spain. SOE agents in Spain helped downed allied airmen escape to England or France, and served as a liaison with dissident factions in the region. A number of operations run out of Spain included the smuggling of material from Gibraltar, the use of private companies to transport contraband to SOE agents, and a propaganda campaign in which rumors were spread that a German government in exile was being set up in Argentina and Ireland.

SOE's operations in Germany concerned some of the most highly guarded, as well as the most dangerous missions of the war. One mission in particular was called Operation Foxley, an SOE operation to kill Hitler. Another proposed caper—code named Little Foxley—was a plan to kill Joseph Goebbels in 1944.

In 1997, Peter Mason, a member of SOE, gave an interview to the *Sunday Times* of London, revealing facts on his role in the hunt for Nazis after the war's end. Mason said that in 1945, he had been assigned to hunt down and kill Nazis who had murdered SOE agents. Working out of a base in the Black Forest, Mason and his team were given the names of their targets from the files of the Nuremberg War Crimes Tribunal. Once a target was located, they used German made weapons including Walther P381s, and Luger P08s on their victims.

The SOE closed its doors in 1946.

(*See Also*: French Resistance Movements; Menzies, Stewart)

Skorzeny, Otto

Otto Skorzeny (1908-1976) was one of Hitler's most flamboyant underlings, a man of ruthless courage and self-discipline. He was nicknamed "the most dangerous man in Europe" by friends and foes alike.

Otto Skorzeny, born on June 12, 1908, in Vienna, Austria, studied at the University of Vienna to learn engineering. He was an ardent supporter of Hitler and his policies of bringing Germany back from its depths after World War I.

While in his twenties, he joined the Nazi Party. He took part in many personal duels and once was cut on the cheek. It was then that he got the nickname of "Scarface" that he would carry all his life.

At the start of World War II, Skorzeny entered the Waffen SS, joining their elite ranks on February 21, 1940. An enlisted man, he rose to the rank of officer. He saw duty in Holland, France and Russia, but was sent home with an inflamed gall bladder. He was awarded the Iron Cross for bravery. Others in the German military knew of Skorzeny's bravery and they planned his next assignment.

He was put in charge of a new unit and promoted to the grade of SS-Hauptsturmführer. Skorzeny had studied British commando operations and persuaded his superiors to allow him to form Germany's own special force. He recruited the best soldiers in the army and received his first assignment directly from Hitler: the freeing of Italian dictator, Benito Mussolini.

Mussolini had been overthrown in July 1943 and held captive by anti-fascist partisans at a heavily guarded hotel called Grand Sasso, high in the Italian mountains. In a daring operation, Skorzeny and his elite group composed of 12 gliders touched down in a large clearing near the hotel. Storming the building, they located Mussolini and whisked him by air to safety in Vienna. Skorzeny's reputation had been made.

In the aftermath of the failed attempt to kill Hitler in July 1944 by dissidents and with rumors of the Führer's death circulating, Skorzeny brought his force of commandos to Berlin. Throughout the confusion that reigned that day, he was able to stabilize the situation until Hitler could restore order.

Skorzeny's next assignment came in September 1944. The Hungarian leader, Miklos Horthy, was making direct contacts with the Russians to negotiate a separate peace with the Kremlin. Hitler ordered Skorzeny into Hungary, where they captured President Horthy's son. Horthy was given an ultimatum: resign or have his son killed. Horthy refused to give up, and Skorzeny's troops made an unsuccessful attempt to kidnap him. In the end, Hungary remained loyal to Germany.

In December 1944, Skorzeny showed his military audacity during the Battle of the Ardennes. Hitler ordered major units to attack the Americans in this region and then strike at the strategic port of Antwerp, which supplied tons of material to Allied troops. If Antwerp could be taken, the war might turn in Germany's favor.

Skorzeny organized numbers of English speaking German soldiers (3,000 in all), to infiltrate behind allied lines. Dressed in American uniforms, using captured U.S. military vehicles, their object was to disrupt through sabotage, assassination, and other covert means, the allied advance through the Ardennes.

In a stroke of luck, the U.S. First Army Intelligence detachment captured orders linking the fake English-speaking Germans directly to Skorzeny. American soldiers tracked down Skorzeny, and he was arrested in Austria in 1945. At trial, he was found not guilty, testifying that allied troops also carried out secret operations wearing the uniforms of the enemy. In a stroke of luck, he escaped from prison on the morning of July 27, 1948.

From Austria, he made his way to South America via a Nazi underground movement called "Odessa," or De Spinne. He settled for a time in Argentina, where he helped the oppressive regime of Juan and Eva Peron. He later moved to Spain, where he operated a Nazi-linked import-export business.

He died in Madrid on July 7, 1975.

Sorge, Richard

Richard Sorge (1895-1944) was one of the memorable spymasters to emerge from World War II. He worked for the Russian NKVD in both China and Japan and was instrumental in providing the Russians vital information on both Germany and Japan's wartime policies. Reports from Sorge enabled Stalin to shift front-line troops from the plains of Siberia to Moscow as a defense against German invasion.

Richard Sorge was born on October 4, 1895, in Baku, Russia. His mother was Russian, and his father a German mining engineer who immigrated to the Soviet Union. In 1898, the Sorge family moved to Berlin, where he attended the University of Hamburg, getting a degree in political science in 1920. He fought in World War I and was wounded a number of times, receiving the Iron Cross for his bravery. It was during his recovery process that Sorge became deeply involved in the ideas of Karl Marx and joined the Communist Party. Sorge's paternal grandfather was once the personal secretary to Karl Marx, the founder of modern-day communism. Sorge read everything he could get his hands on concerning the communist doctrine, and he realized that he would do anything to aid the system.

Sorge was taken on by the NKVD, the Soviet intelligence service, in 1920 and sent to Moscow for training. Over the next 10 years, Sorge would travel to the United States, Germany, England, and the Scandinavian countries under the cover of a teacher or journalist to gather intelligence.

Working as a journalist for a German newspaper called the *Frankfurter Zeitung,* Sorge was sent to Shanghai, China, with instructions to set up a large Russian spy network. Using an alias, "William Johnson," an American, Sorge established an espionage net across China. His main purposes was to secure information on the nationalist leader, Chaing-Kai-shek, and a young communist newcomer named Mao Tse-tung.

The most important intelligence gleaned by Sorge was the fact that Germany was about to sever its long-standing political ties with China, shifting them to a new and potentially powerfully ally in Asia, Japan.

One of Sorge's most trusted spies was a beautiful American woman named Agnes Smedley. Smedley worked as the American correspondent for the *Frankfurter Zeitung,* and the two soon became lovers. Another person recruited by Sorge was a Japanese newspaper writer named Hotsumi Ozaki, who worked for the *Asahi Shimbun.* Ozaki provided Sorge with entry to the communist underground movement in China, including access to radio-transmitting equipment, and those able to use it. Ozaki would later have an important position in the office of the Japanese premier. Ozaki would provide Sorge with an abundance of political intelligence concerning Japanese foreign policy.

The Chinese never questioned Sorge's accomplished reporting (although they had deep suspicions concerning Ozaki) and allowed him free reign in traveling across the country. Sorge met and befriended Chaing and wrote laudatory articles about his movement.

Sorge was recalled to Moscow in December 1932. He didn't stay there long and was given another high-profile assignment: he was to travel to Japan and establish a far-flung espionage agency. His instructions by the Fourth Department of Russian intelligence prior to his departure were to learn if the Japanese intended to attack the Soviet Union.

However, before he went to Japan, Sorge made a highly risky trip to Berlin, where he took all necessary steps to create a profile for himself. Using his background as a journalist and his father's German citizenship, he secured a German passport, despite his communist leanings. He finally arrived in Yokohama, Japan, on September 6, 1933.

Once in Japan, Sorge used the services of two GRU (Russian military) officers to aid him in his spying: Max Klausen, a German who would serve as his radio operator, and Branko de Voukelich, a Yugoslavian and intelligence expert. He also renewed his contact with Ozaki, who had returned to Japan from China.

From Yokohama, Sorge arrived in Tokyo and, using his new persona as an ardent Nazi, cultivated the military attaché at the German Embassy, Eugene Ott. Soon, Sorge began beguiling Ott with his expertise on Japanese culture and history and, more importantly, gave him bits and pieces of information of interest to his country.

Sorge learned that the Germans were going to attack Russia and sent this information to Moscow, which decided not to take it seriously. Ozaki gave Sorge the vital information that Japan was about to attack the Dutch East Indies and French Indochina in latter 1941. Stalin took this information in earnest, and he ordered a Siberian army base transferred to the capital to defend the city during the German siege of Moscow.

Sorge was also able to learn from Ozaki that the Japanese were planning to send its fleet out into the Pacific in the fall of 1941, coming close to the U.S. naval base in Hawaii.

The Japanese espionage service, *Kempi Tai*, were tracking the radio transmissions coming from Tokyo but did not know who the senders were. The Kempi Tai sent its agents to trail Ozaki because of his communist reputation and was able, through him, to track down Sorge as the man responsible for the transmissions to Moscow. Sorge, hiding his clandestine activities, used a sailboat to relay his messages, going from one port to another.

The beginning of the end of the Sorge spy ring came when the Kempi Tai interrogated a Japanese communist named Yotoku Miyagi, associated with Sorge. Under intense questioning, Miyagi broke and gave away Sorge's name and location. Ozaki was arrested on October 14, 1941.

On the night of October 16, 1941, after dining with German friends, Sorge was arrested as he entered his home. Sorge was tried in a secret court, found guilty and spent three years undergoing intense questioning. He ultimately confessed to being a spy for the Russians, and when his usefulness to the Japanese was ended, he was hanged on November 7, 1944. For his gallant actions, Richard Sorge was posthumously awarded the Hero of the Soviet Union medal in 1964.

Spanish "TO" Ring

Shortly after the Japanese attacked the United States, the State Department ordered the Japanese Embassy closed and their diplomats sent home. Leaving their Washington base, the Japanese lost a valued staging post in which to spy on the United States. But that did not deter them from carrying out espionage tactics. A formal, secret understanding was made between the Japanese and the Spanish government in which the latter, after taking over the now-abandoned embassy, would carry on espionage activities.

The organization, which was run from Madrid, was called "TO," the Japanese word for "door." The Japanese informed the Spanish that $500,000 had been left in the safe in their old residence. This money would be used to bankroll their spy apparatus.

The records available through the declassification process via the National Security Agency do not reveal the names of the individuals who took part in the "TO" Ring, only which jobs they performed.

Among those involved in the operation were the attaché in the Spanish Embassy in Washington, the consuls in New Orleans, New York and San Francisco. Among the Americans who worked for the "TO" Ring were an officer attached to the Army Air Corps, a teacher at the Merchant Marine School in New London, CT, and unnamed civilians working in defense plants in Pennsylvania, among others.

Among the intelligence given to them were sailing schedules of American ships and "special training" courses being given to foreign allied troops in the United States. This information was also passed on to Japan's envoy to Spain.

The United States learned about the "TO" Ring's operations via its Magic intercepts, which enabled American cryptographers to read all Japanese diplomatic and military plans.

Money was smuggled into the U.S. by the Spanish via diplomatic pouch for "TO" Ring purposes. In a bit of chicanery by parties unknown, two large sacks of high-grade pearls were sent by the Japanese via Buenos Aires, Argentina to fund the group. The route of the pearls took them to New Orleans, winding up at the door of the Spanish Ambassador in Washington. Under mysterious circumstances, the pearls never arrived.

The surrogate "TO" Ring continued to operate in the U.S. during the war under the eyes of U.S. intelligence.
(*See Also*: Magic)

Station Hypo

In the wake of the 1941 Japanese attack, it was imperative to the United States to gather intelligence on Japanese military and diplomatic moves in the Pacific. This was the pre-war era before computer and satellite espionage. In mid-1942, the navy established an extensive communications center called JICPOA: Joint Intelligence Center Pacific Ocean Area. Among the material collected at JICPOA were maps, charts, booklets, and all sorts of original documents on the Japanese military.

There was a separate intelligence center, Pacific Ocean Area (ICPOA), also known as Station Hypo. Hypo was the Combat Intelligence Center. In its prime, it was known as the Fleet Radio Unit Pacific (FRUPAC), but as the war progressed its activity changed from intelligence gathering to communication intercepts. As new research on the pre-Pearl Harbor attack intelligence shows, Station Hypo sat in the middle of the most important Japanese intercepts.

Station Hypo dates back to 1936, when Lieutenant Thomas Dyer of the United States Navy, began his operation in Hawaii. In time, Dyer would be promoted to Lieutenant Commander, and was second in command and Station Hypo's chief cryptographer. This secure facility was located on the second floor of Building Number One at the 14th Naval District at Pearl Harbor. It soon moved to the basement of the building.

In the weeks and months following America's entry into World War II, Station Hypo's duties took on a more urgent task. Joseph Rochefort was put in command of the Code and Signal Section of the Office of Naval Communications from 1925 to 1927. He was well versed in the Japanese language and went to Japan for further study from 1929 to 1932. In June 1941, six months before the Pearl Harbor attack, he was given the command of the Combat Intelligence Unit. His mandate was to collect communications intelligence concerning the location and operations of the Japanese navy.

Station Hypo was in charge of the Mid-Pacific Network, which comprised the largest naval communications section in that part of the world. It employed 140 radio intelligence operators, as well as 32 technical officers who monitored Radio Direction Finding (RDF) stations in such places as Dutch Harbor, Alaska, Midway Island, Samoa, and two bases on Oahu. At the height of the war, Station Hypo was processing over 1,000 Japanese military intercepts per day. Their mandate was only to intercept Japanese naval communications, not diplomatic missives.

Physically, Station Hypo was located 15 feet underground, in a sweltering room with little ventilation. In the middle of the room was a powerful IBM sorting machine with its own air-conditioning system.

Rochefort's most important task at Hypo was radio detection finding (RDF). "By means of radio detection findings," wrote the Hypo commander years later, "you ascertain the geographical position of the enemy force. That's called direction finding—DF. That's a part of radio intelligence."

Despite Hypo's importance, it did not share its intelligence findings with another important intelligence unit, the Army's Station Five, an intercept station located at Fort Shafter on Oahu. Station Five was commanded by General Walter Short and worked only on Japanese diplomatic messages. In 1942, after General Short learned of Japanese radio messages obtained by Station Hypo, he asked if Rochefort would train his analysts in their decoding. Rochefort refused the general's request.

Station Hypo was also caught in the middle of important secret messages decoded by U.S. intercept facilities in the Hawaiian Islands. They discussed Japanese moves against Pearl Harbor prior to the attack on December 7, 1941.

The event in question was the "Bomb Plot" affair that set off a detailed investigation by the Roosevelt administration. The man who touched off this series of events was Tadashi Morimura, a Japanese spy attached to the Hawaiian consulate. Morimura's real name was Takeo Yoshikawa, an ensign in the Japanese navy. He was under diplomatic cover, but his real purpose was to spy on the Pearl Harbor naval base. On his trips around the islands, Morimura was indiscreet, drinking in bars and boasting of his secret work.

He was able to pinpoint the Pacific fleet at anchor at the naval base. He sent information back to Japan concerning 53 of the navy's docks, for planning torpedo attacks against the docked U.S. fleet. He also filed detailed sketches of the locations of each large battleship, repair facilities, and other important military facilities. Morimura sent an encoded bomb plot message, which was picked up by a messenger and sent to Tokyo.

Unknown to Morimura, his message was intercepted by a number of U.S. listening stations in Washington State, Virginia and Corregidor. After his successful spy operation, he was arrested for drunkenness. He was released but not before the incident was reported to the FBI.

President Roosevelt received word of the Morimura affair and personally sent David Sarnoff, President of RCA, to Hawaii. From Roosevelt's perspective, if Sarnoff's RCA had been the facility where Morimura sent his bomb plot messages, then the letters must be in their system. He met with military commanders: Admiral Husband Kimmel, Lieutenant General Walter Short, and Hypo's Joseph Rochefort. Sarnoff provided the Hawaii commanders copies of all of RCA's notes sent by Morimura. After the war, Rochefort testified that Hypo had the facilities to decode these messages but failed to do so.

It is clear from the historical record that the Rochefort/Hypo nexus had warnings from Morimura that Pearl Harbor was the target of a possible Japanese attack.

A second area in which Hypo was involved in the pre-Pearl Harbor episode concerned the Japanese fleet. For years, the historical record stated that the U.S. had no knowledge of the Japanese fleet bound for Hawaii, because it maintained radio silence and that intelligence failed to pick up its signals. In his new book on the intelligence failure at Pearl Harbor, *Day of Deceit: The Truth About FDR And Pearl Harbor*, author Robert Stinnett tells a different story.

U.S. Station Cast in the Philippines listened in on Japanese naval broadcasts from December 1st through the 5th, 1941, and determined the new call signs of the approaching vessels in mid-Pacific. Cast analysts sent this information to Hawaii, where Hypo was given a copy. Rochefort, for whatever reason, failed to give these messages to Admiral Kimmel. Rochefort later wrote, concerning the Cast reports, "that there was no information on the carriers of the First Air Fleet. Not one carrier has been identified."

Hypo was also involved in a message sent to Washington on November 26th, 1941, one week prior to the attack. This incident involved Rochefort, Admiral Kimmel and Rear Admiral Claude Bloch. The two admirals were informed by Rochefort's Hypo that intercepted radio communications detected a large Japanese fleet containing submarines and patrol craft heading eastward toward Hawaii from Japan.

Kimmel and Bloch arrived at Rochefort's Hypo office to discuss further actions. A summary of the intercepts was sent to Washington. Parts of the report read as follows: "…There is believed to be strong concentration of submarines and air groups in the Marshalls which compromise Airron twenty-four. At least one carrier division unit plus probably one third of the submarine fleet. Evaluate above to indicate strong force component may be preparing to operate in South Eastern Asia while parts may operate from Palao and Marshalls."

This message was sent to Washington to the Chief of Naval Operations, then to the White House via Lieutenant Commander Arthur McCollum, FDR's routing officer. Internal White House records indicate that FDR received this material from his naval aide, Captain Beardall.

Two days after receiving the alert from Hypo, FDR prepared the armed forces for war. This is the only document directly linking the president to information gathered by Hypo, one that has immense historical significance.

Hypo was instrumental in gathering signals intelligence on Japanese naval movements in the Coral Sea. Hypo analysts deciphered the American-designated Japanese naval code JN-25. One of their major breakthroughs was identifying the Japanese signal "AF" for Midway. With their knowledge of "AF," the U.S. Navy delivered a punishing blow to the Japanese navy at the battle of Midway, thus changing the conduct of the war in the Pacific.

(*See Also*: Pearl Harbor Attack; Magic; Rochefort, Joseph; Kuhn Spy Family)

Stephenson, William, Sir

William Stephenson occupied one of the most sensitive positions in the British intelligence establishment. He headed the BSC (British Security Coordination), operating out of New York City's Rockefeller Center. From there, BSC men and women tracked down agents in South America and other parts of the Western Hemisphere, as well as establishing a working relationship with the OSS and the FBI. It was from his efforts that the "myth of Intrepid" (his cover name) was established.

William Stephenson was born on January 11, 1896, in Point Douglas, Manitoba, Canada. Growing up, he took to anything electric, built model airplanes, learned Morse Code, and was an expert in the operation of a wireless set. He graduated high school in 1914. During World War I, he joined the Royal Canadian Engineers, seeing service in France. He quickly rose in rank from lieutenant to captain. He was wounded in a gas attack.

While convalescing in England, Stephenson volunteered to the Royal Flying Corps and shot down 26 German planes in combat. After one sortie, he was shot down, captured, and made a daring escape to allied lines. For his bold exploits, he was awarded the Distinguished Flying Cross, as well as the French Legion of Honor.

During the 1920s and 1930s, Stephenson became an acclaimed boxer, winning the amateur lightweight championship. He also was a professional flyer, competing in various air races. It was during this period in his life that he developed a patent for a new type of can opener, established it worldwide, and became a millionaire.

He married Mary Simmons, and the newlyweds traveled through Europe in the years prior to World War II. Returning to London, Stephenson reported to British intelligence all he had seen and heard in Germany. When Britain declared war, Stephenson was appointed by Prime Minister Churchill in May 1940, as his personal representative to President Roosevelt and was sent to the United States to open up a covert espionage agency, the British Security Coordination, BSC.

Stephenson's cover was that of Passport Control Officer. His predecessor in that position was Commander James Paget. Stephenson arrived in New

York on April 2, 1940, supposedly working for the Ministry of Supply. He met with FBI Director J. Edgar Hoover who grudgingly agreed to work with him on direct orders from FDR

Stephenson moved his HQ to a small office in room 3603 in Rockefeller Center (the Rockefeller family charged BSC one cent in rent). His mandate was to subvert German activities in South America, overthrow pro-Nazi governments, watch the ports of the United States for enemy sabotage and make direct links to the OSS and FBI to ensure their continued support.

By the time Stephenson arrived in New York, his proposed activities had caused a great deal of dissension among the president's advisors. FDR had given Stephenson carte blanche to use America in his counterespionage activities. The president failed to notify Congress about Intrepid's dealings on American soil. But if the Congress didn't know about Stephenson, two other men who would play an important part in the Stephenson-BSC story surely did.

They were J. Edgar Hoover and the newly appointed head of the Office of the Coordinator of Information, William J. Donovan. Donovan and Stephenson (called "Little Bill" and "Big Bill") worked closely together to their mutual advantage. Hoover, on the other hand, saw Stephenson's role in America as conflicting directly with his own domination over all U.S. intelligence functions.

Stephenson directed his cadre of spies throughout North America, setting up a secret training facility dubbed "Camp X" in the Canadian wilderness, where agents were schooled before setting off for missions in Europe. Personally supervising the rigorous training schedule, Stephenson prowled the grounds of Camp X, overseeing radio communications techniques and operating stations in Bermuda, where code breakers intercepted transmissions. Stephenson, according to legend, brought his friend and fellow agent Ian Fleming with him on his tours of Camp X.

But other objective historians take a somewhat different view of Stephenson's importance in the running of the BSC. They point out that the BSC was really operated by Britain's sabotage organization, SOE, Special Operations Executive. SOE was responsible for "setting Europe ablaze," sending sabotage teams throughout Nazi-occupied Europe to disrupt the German military activities. Stephenson's BSC, these skeptics say, was used to recruit agents for SOE's use for its own clandestine activities.

The doubters concerning Stephenson's role in wartime espionage point to his supposed actions at Camp X. They say that SOE actually had operational control over the training at the facility and that Stephenson never had any command on a daily basis.

To Stephenson's credit, he did have a close, working relationship with

Donovan, with information jointly shared. Stephenson's major backer was FDR, who was kept abreast of BSC's work.

After the war, Stephenson retired to Bermuda where he spent the rest of his life. Whether or not Stephenson's role in espionage activities was as definitive as he had hoped is still a subject of debate among scholars of the war. What is not debatable, however, is the continuing "Intrepid legend."

William Stephenson died in Bermuda on January 31, 1989, age 93.

(*See Also*: BSC; Camp X; Donovan, William; Hoover, J. Edgar; SOE)

T

"Target FDR"

In 1943, a daring plan to assassinate FDR was hatched in Berlin during the conference at Teheran, Iran. The man chosen to carry out the assault was Otto Skorzeny: Hitler's trusted confidant and the man who rescued Mussolini from a castle in the Alps. The code name for the operation was "Long Pounce."

On November 13, 1943, the U.S.S. *Iowa*, carrying FDR and his party, left its berth and made its way toward the open Atlantic Ocean. The president, accompanied by such aides as Harry Hopkins, Army Chief of Staff, George Marshall, Admiral Ernest King, and General "Hap" Arnold, were en route to Oran in North Africa, their first stop before heading for Cairo, Egypt, and then on to Teheran.

The Teheran summit of Roosevelt, Stalin and Churchill would prove to be crucial in defining where and when the allies would attack Fortress Europe. Disputes had arisen between FDR and Churchill's advisors as to where the invasion would take place and how it was to be accomplished. To that end, the British, led by the Prime Minister, left England onboard the HMS *Renown*, sailing for Cairo where the two Western leaders would hold a mini-summit.

The American delegation arrived in Cairo on November 22, 1943, and under heavy guard was whisked to their secure quarters. The next day, FDR and Churchill met at the Mena Palace Hotel, one of the finest in the city. While their respective advisors had heated discussions over strategy, FDR and Churchill agreed on positions which they would present to Stalin.

The president's party arrived in Teheran on November 27. After retiring to his quarters, Stalin visited Roosevelt and gave him surprising information. Stalin told the president that Soviet intelligence had learned that a plot was afoot to kill him during the Teheran Conference. The plan, continued Stalin, was to be carried out by Otto Skorzeny, called "the most dangerous man in

Europe." Roosevelt reported the information to Mike Riley, chief of the U.S. Secret Service who had accompanied FDR on the trip.

Riley took the report very seriously and arranged for the presidential party to stay in the secure grounds of the Soviet Mission, avoiding a long and potentially dangerous motorcade through the heart of Teheran.

At the same time that the Big Three were meeting in Teheran, events in another part of the country added fuel to the assassination rumor. An unidentified agent of the OSS, the Office of Strategic Services, code-named C-12, dropped from the sky, in the middle of the Iranian desert. The agent, fluent in Kurdish, was to pass himself off as an Arab, live amongst the tribesmen, and gather information on the political and military situation in Iran. C-12 soon gained local confidence. One day he heard reports of Germans arriving in the desert. C-12, through his informants, was introduced to these commandos, learned about their mission, and through guile and luck convinced the hit-squad to hire him as their driver to Teheran.

After a long and arduous journey to Teheran, C-12 obtained a hotel near the route where the presidential caravan would travel. The Nazi team began digging a tunnel to the street, carried explosives within reach, and waited for their target to emerge.

Unknown to Skorzeny's men, C-12 made off with the detonators, essential for the explosives.

At just the right moment, C-12, still dressed in Arab garb, made his way to the U.S. Embassy compound and managed to persuade the armed sentries to allow him entrance. Within hours, U.S. soldiers took up positions around the hotel where the Germans were lodged and arrested them.

The plot to kill FDR was foiled by the brave exploits of C-12, his identity a mystery even today.

Twenty Committee

The Twenty Committee was the policy-making body of the British operation known as the Double Cross System. The Double Cross System was the organization primarily responsible for the running of all captured German agents sent into Britain during the war. These "turned" agents, under the penalty of death, sent misinformation back to Germany in order to mislead their controllers.

The Twenty Committee took its name from the Roman numeral XX signifying the sign of the double cross. The Twenty Committee had its first formal meeting on January 8, 1941. The Twenty Committee did not run the captured agents. It did, however, collate and gather intelligence which was then passed on to MI-5, and MI-6, and sent on to the double agents for transmission to Germany.

TWENTY COMMITTEE

The initial meeting of the Twenty Committee took place at Wormwood Scrubs Hospital. Its written mandate was to "1) obtain information from the enemy, 2) to mislead the enemy, and perhaps to deflect his plans, by handing out false information." Five conferences were held during the first month of its existence. After a short while, the members changed their meeting place to 58 St. James Street.

An integral part of the Twenty Committee was a subdivision called the "W" Board. This commission was comprised of Directors of Intelligence, a spokesperson from the Security Service (Captain Guy Lidell), and a representative from the Civilian Ministries Board. Originally the W Board had responsibility of controlling deception operations from England into enemy hands. In time, however, the W Board took on all counterespionage operations against German targets in the UK, and soon assumed responsibility for the entire Double Cross System. "The W Board represented the controlling body of the Twenty Committee and developed policy regarding the Double-Cross System."

The man put in overall charge of the Double Cross/Twenty Committee was John Masterman. Masterman, formerly an Oxford professor, had spent four years in a German prison camp during the First World War.

Masterman and the Twenty Committee fed false information to the Germans concerning the effect of their relentless bombing campaign against British cities and civilian targets. To this outcome, double agents sent misleading information reporting RAF airfields serving a number of planes and much military equipment (which they did not). Unfortunately, the Germans did not carry out extensive attacks against these targets.

A majority of the Twenty Committee's work concentrated on deception operations leading to the invasion. The deception phase of the plan was called Operation Fortitude, whose main purpose was to lull the Germans into thinking that the main attack would be at the Pas de Calais area, not Normandy. To that effort, the Twenty Committee concentrated all its double agents. Two of its primary agents in this massive misinformation project were "Tricycle" and "Garbo."

"Tricycle" was the Yugoslav businessman and playboy, Dusan Popov. Popov was originally recruited by the Abwehr but soon became a double agent working for the British. "Tricycle" and other agents were run under the direction of MI-5 and its subdivision called B1. B1's chief of operations was Lieutenant Colonel T.A. Robertson. The Twenty Committee was called into a hurried meeting to discuss the "Tricycle" case, due to the enormous amount of material provided to him by the Abwehr. They instructed Popov to send back false information regarding the disposition of mine fields on England's East coast in case the country was invaded. (The proposed invasion of the

British Isles was called Operation Sea Lion, but the invasion plan was canceled.) In time, Popov traveled to the United States to set up an espionage net with the full knowledge of the FBI.

Another double agent who was followed closely by the Twenty Committee was Juan Pujol Garcia, aka "Garbo." Garcia was used by the Double Cross System and turned out to be one of the outstanding agents employed during the war. Garbo came to the UK in April 1941 and made up a large, fictitious network of spies, all of whose bogus material he fed to Germany.

The Garbo incident showed just how compartmentalized the British Security Services had become. MI-6 had access to all the Garbo traffic, culled via Enigma. But they failed to provide B1 and the Twenty Committee with this information. After many days of acrimonious haggling between the services, a deal was arranged relating to double agents. The Twenty Committee had now won its turf battle.

The Twenty Committee worked throughout the war, successfully operating and deceiving the Abwehr. The first public information concerning the Twenty Committee and the Double Cross System came to light when John Masterman published his memoirs in 1972, entitled *The Double Cross System in the War of 1939-45*.

(*See Also*: Double Cross System; Garbo; Masterman, John; Popov, Dusan; Operation Bodyguard)

U

Ultra

Ultra was the name given by British cryptanalysts to the mass of inter-cepted German communications intelligence culled via Enigma, translated into plain English at Bletchley Park. The use of Ultra was the most valuable intelligence tool obtained and was vitally important in defeating the enemy.

In order to handle secure communications, the Germans developed a complicated machine containing two rotors. When the operator typed a let-ter on the keyboard the signal was sent via battery to a system of moving rotors. A light then came on behind the rows of letters, which was then received by a different Enigma machine. The operator on the other end had a key list informing him of which letter on his typewriter corresponded to the one sending. The receiver was then able to decipher messages and rewrite them in plain language.

Throughout the war, the Germans were convinced that their Enigma communications were invulnerable and believed the allies would never be able to break their codes. This changed when in 1939, a German clerk by the name of Hans Thilo-Schmidt, who worked in the OKW (German High Command), sold a sample Enigma machine to the French Secret Service, the *Deuxieme Bureau.*

The French paid Thilo-Schmidt $10,000, which he spent rashly. Despite their windfall, the French were unable to understand how the machine func-tioned. They passed the Enigma machine to the British, but they, too, were unable to solve it. The French then contacted the Polish Secret Service called *Biuro Szyfrow 4*, an arm more than willing to try at cracking the puzzle. The Poles had successfully been reading both the Russian and German radio com-munications for a number of months in order to kept abreast of what their enemies were doing. The job of analyzing Enigma was given to Gwido Langer, the chief of *Biuro Szyfrow 4.*

With a brain trust of the best mathematicians available, Langer and his team broke Enigma by December, 1932. By 1938, with war imminent, the Poles decided to share their breakthroughs of Enigma with both the British and the French. (During the war, the British gave the U.S. access to Ultra material, but not all top-level American intelligence leaders were allowed to see it.)

The location where British cryptographers worked to break Enigma was the Government Code and Cypher School at Bletchley Park. Using a huge staff, as well as access to their own captured Enigma machine, hundreds of skilled workers operated around the clock, listening to all radio communications emanating from German military units in the field, as well as from their ships and U-boats, above and below the seas. In time, American code breakers were brought to Bletchley Park to partake in the deciphering process.

The first major setback to Ultra took place in 1942, when the German navy constructed a new Enigma machine for communicating with its U-boats. The analysts and Bletchley Park were unable to break this new code. For months, the silent U-boats inflicted heavy damage on allied shipping in the Atlantic, especially those ships bringing needed supplies from the United States. Then, in a stroke of luck, the British navy was able to capture a new, intact Enigma machine from a damaged U-boat during an attack in the mid-Atlantic.

In an assault by a number of British warships, including the *Bulldog* and the *Aubretia*, the German U-boat, U-110, was depth charged and suffered serious damage. A boarding party managed to find the Enigma machine and took it back for study. With the new Enigma machine now in the hands of the analysts at Bletchley Park, the current German naval code was broken, and the Battle of the Atlantic shifted to the allies.

By 1944, it was obvious that the war was turning and preparations were being made in London and Washington for the upcoming European invasion. It was decided by the British government that the time had come to share its Ultra secret with the United States.

The man in charge of the allied army ready to strike was General Eisenhower. Ike was called to a personal meeting with Prime Minister Churchill upon his arrival in London and was told about Ultra and the success that the British had gleaned from its use. Another person who had input in bringing Eisenhower to Ultra was "C," Stewart Menzies, head of British Intelligence.

In order to coordinate both countries' intelligence take, the U.S. and Great Britain made a pact called "MSS," or "Most Secret Source," which was "the designated term for highly secret information obtained by intercepting enemy messages which have been enciphered in cryptographic systems of a high security classification"—Ultra.

Only those messages relating to Ultra material would have the word "Ultra" stamped in the body of the text, which was then handled by a separate team of interpreters. Sixteen pages of regulations were written and given to those in the need for ultimate Ultra dissemination.

Other severe restrictions were placed on Eisenhower's handling of Ultra material, including the stipulation that Ike could not put Ultra into effect in order to save American lives or to plan attacks against the enemy. After reading Ultra material, all documents were to be destroyed. Also, the team Ultra was not to be discussed by any of Ike's officers, or were men privy to Ultra put in a position where they were likely to be captured. Ike also had to allow a British intelligence officer on his staff. This officer would deliver Ultra documents to the Americans.

Another high-ranking American officer privy to Ultra was Ike's deputy, General Mark Clark. Both men were allowed to read top-grade Ultra, including minutes of meetings between Hitler and Field Marshall Wilhelm Keitel, and communications from Field Marshall Albert Kesselring, the supreme commander of German forces in the Mediterranean. They were also given access to data from the "Desert Fox," General Erwin Rommel. For his part, General Clark did not have faith in the Ultra material being provided to him. Despite General Clark's misgivings, Eisenhower followed the limitations placed upon him by the British regarding Ultra, and no leaks occurred from his headquarters.

One man not privy to Ultra was America's chief spymaster, William Donovan. A decision was made not to give Donovan, then head of COI, entree to Ultra, one which rankled him. Instead, all Ultra material went to the U.S. Joint Chiefs of Staff. Donovan, however, planned a separate course which would allow him access to communications intelligence.

The COI formed a secret communications intelligence unit called the FBQ Corporation. Its purpose was as a "means of or instrumentality by which certain properties and facilities might be acquired and operated in the United States of America without public disclosure." FBQ worked out of a New York address at 52 Wall St., under the pseudonym of Lanson & Tamblyn.

FBQ's job was to secretly purchase two commercial wireless listening posts, one located at Reseda, California, the other in Bellmore, Long Island. Donovan hired a talented cryptographer, Alfred Sheinwold, to run the operation. Over the course of several months, Donovan hired a large staff whose job it was to monitor and intercept maritime communications of all European nations. They succeeded in intercepting radio communications from many countries.

The FBQ operated under Donovan's control during the war. Despite this fact, Donovan was never allowed entry into the world of Ultra, largely out of decisions made by his superiors, most of all, by George Strong, head of military intelligence.

The allied success in taking advantage of Ultra relied in no small part on the lack of security by the Germans. They never believed that their vaulted Ultra intelligence was vulnerable to attack and took very few countermeasures to even change codes or put in new Enigma machines. They were shocked when it was revealed, many years after the war ended, that the allies were reading all their prized secrets during most of the conflict.

The successful use of Ultra during World War II was the genesis that lay behind the modern-day computer. The man most responsible for this feat was a brilliant, dysfunctional, British cryptologist, Alan Turing. Turing, working at Bletchley Park, built a duplicate Enigma machine and cracked many of the codes. Turing and his partner, Gordon Welchman, designed the world's first programmed computer which they called "Colossus." Alan Turing never lived to see his infant called Colossus grow into today's modern, super-chip computer industry. He died of self-poisoning in 1954. (*See Also*: Bletchley Park; COI; Donovan, William; Enigma; Menzies, Stewart)

The United States Navy v. the Chicago Tribune

On June 7, 1942, a correspondent for the *Chicago Tribune* dispatched a story to his editor concerning the just completed American victory on Midway Island. The writer, Stanley Johnston, wrote that our naval forces had prior knowledge of the whereabouts of the Japanese fleet and were thus able to wait for it in ambush. What Stanley Johnston was writing about, and which was one of the most guarded secrets in the American military, was that the United States had broken the Japanese secret codes and was aware of every move they made. How Stanley Johnston got his information and what happened next concerned freedom of the press, the security of America's wartime secrets and the lengths powerful individuals would go to embarrass the administration of President Franklin D. Roosevelt.

The banner headline in the June 7, 1942, edition of the *Chicago Tribune* read as follows. "Navy Had Word of Jap Plan to Strike at Sea. Knew Dutch Harbor Was Feint." The article went on to say that the just completed naval engagement was a decisive victory for the United States and that our naval commanders knew the exact location of the Japanese battle group beforehand.

The battle of Midway was a turning point in the war in the Pacific. The Japanese hoped that a victory at Midway would be a springboard for further advances across the Pacific, ranging from Australia to the Dutch East Indies.

UNITED STATES NAVY

Unknown to the Japanese, American cryptographers, working from covert radio direction-finding stations in Hawaii and Dutch Harbor, had broken their secure communications and were reading their order of battle during "real time." Knowing where the Japanese navy was going, U.S. ships waited in ambush positions, and on June 4, 1942, sunk four Japanese carriers and one cruiser. Japanese losses included 250 planes. After Midway, the tide of battle in the Pacific turned in favor of the U.S., and Japanese control of the Pacific was lost for the duration of the war.

The term used by U.S. code breakers in cracking the Japanese ciphers was called Magic. The Japanese used a coding machine called Purple to send their secure information. Purple was broken in 1940, thanks to the hard work by William Friedman, the army's chief cryptanalyst. Magic was known to only a limited number of people, and no civilian had access to this information. How then, did Stanley Johnston get hold of it?

Stanley Johnston, born in Australia, served in World War I in Egypt and lived the life of a modern-day adventurer. He crisscrossed the South China seas, looking for riches that he never found. He left the Orient in 1936, made his way to New York City and married. He found a job as a journalist with the *Chicago Tribune*, detailing his adventures. When the U.S. entered the war, he was assigned to the paper's Honolulu office and officially became a U.S. citizen. He was assigned to cover the navy, sailed on the *Lexington,* and was rescued when the ship was sunk by Japanese warships.

Johnston and the other lucky sailors were rescued by the U.S. Navy ship *Barnett* and made passage home. On board the *Barnett,* Johnston became friendly with one of the ship's officers, who allowed him to see secret communications intelligence regarding the Midway attack. Upon his return to the States, Stanley Johnston filed his blockbuster news story.

Besides the *Chicago Tribune,* three other U.S. newspapers reprinted Johnston's story: the *New York Daily News, San Francisco Chronicle,* and the *Washington Times-Herald.*

The *Chicago Tribune* was owned by one of President Franklin D. Roosevelt's severest critics, Colonel Robert R. McCormick. McCormick's editorials in the *Tribune* raged against the domestic policies of FDR, especially the controversial Lend Lease agreement whereby the U.S. gave England old destroyers from our fleet in exchange for bases in the Caribbean. McCormick said that FDR was a tool of the European powers and charged that the president was blunting freedom of the press after the U.S. entered the war. Three days before the Pearl Harbor attack, December 4, 1941, McCormick's paper published a story saying that the U.S. Army and Navy were getting ready for "active participation" in the European war. The story also said that the U.S. wanted the total destruction of Germany. This report was based on classified material and after it was written, Attorney General Francis Biddle wanted to prosecute the paper as being in violation of the Espionage Act. The Pearl Harbor attack made the matter mute.

Despite the war, many government leaders wanted to make the *Chicago Tribune* and Robert McCormick, its anti-FDR publisher, pay—and pay dearly. Lawyers in both the War and Justice Departments believed that by printing the Midway story, McCormick had broken the Espionage Act by the "willful intent to aid, or reason to believe, and providing the enemy with useful information relating to the nation's defense."

The Navy's Public Affairs Office, in the person of Lieutenant Commander Paul Smith, said that "the navy's advantage in knowledge of the enemy's code and the security of our own code were both lost through the publication."

The first concrete action taken by the government against the *Chicago Tribune* was a citation for violating the Censorship Code that was put into effect during the war. The Censorship Code was a temporary act which called upon the press not to aid the enemy through the dissemination of news stories that would affect the fighting men abroad. Part of the Censorship Code called for the "press and radio to abstain voluntarily from the dissemination of detailed information of certain kinds, such as reports of the movements of vessels and troops," a clear reference to what the *Chicago Tribune* had written.

The navy now began its own, official investigation of the *Chicago Tribune's* actions. The first *Chicago Tribune* executive to appear before the board was J. Loy Maloney, the managing editor. Maloney said that Johnston received his information from other unnamed Naval sources whom he had cultivated over the years.

The next man to testify was the author himself, Stanley Johnston. Johnston told the assembled naval officers that he had originally obtained his information from news accounts provided by the Associated Press, saying that the American fleet inflicted a decisive defeat for the Japanese navy.

On August 7, 1942, the inquiry took on added emphasis. Attorney General Francis Biddle asked the Justice Department to urge that a federal grand jury be empaneled to look into the possibility that the paper had broken a criminal statute when it published the article.

Colonel McCormick countered by saying that the Roosevelt administration was out to get him and was violating his constitutional right to a free press. Soon, Republican members of the Senate took up McCormick's cause, even threatening a congressional investigation.(Nothing came of the threat.)

The grand jury began taking witnesses on August 14, 1942, by calling to the stand Captain Thomas Shock of the U.S.S. *Barnett,* the vessel that Johnston was traveling on. The jurors wanted to know how Johnston gained access to classified material. The captain told them that the documents in question were just "left around" in a place accessible for Johnston's viewing. The navy had planned to bring an intelligence officer into court to tell them about how the ciphers were used during the Midway planning, but that design was dropped due to national security considerations. In view of these new conditions, the grand jury had no choice but to drop the investigation.

In 1964, 22 years after the incident, both the Justice and the Navy Departments came out with a rather strange statement neither acknowledging nor denying any official connection to the *Chicago Tribune* affair.
(*See Also*: Hypo, Station; Magic; Midway)

V

Vatican Intrigue

Historians have called the period of time between the German invasion of Poland and the opening of hostilities with France and England as the "Phoney War." This was a time in which the Germans solidified their rule in Poland and waited for a response from the West. This was also a time when the internal German resistance movements, especially generals who were opposed to Hitler's invasion of Poland, had time to contemplate what actions to take. What the anti-Hitler officers hoped for was the aversion of full-scale European war. To that effect, they began covert contacts with different Western factions to block further bloodshed.

The prime mover in these intrigues was Abwehr chief, Canaris. Canaris, aware of the atrocities that had been inflicted by German troops during the invasion of Poland, made sure that members of the High Command were made well aware of what had transpired. He and his deputy, Hans Oster, brought the evidence of mass murders on both civilian and armed troops to officers in the SD and SS. These Hitler loyalists brushed off Canaris's news, leaving him in the lurch.

Unknown to many of these Nazis, Canaris was part of a group of conspirators called the Schwarze Kapelle (Black Orchestra), who had many followers in the German armed forces. Schwarze Kapelle members planned to take over the government, oust Hitler, and seek an end to the war. One of Canaris's underground links was to sympathetic ears in the Vatican.

One of the first moves made by Canaris was to inform his sources in the pope's palace of a plan to attack Norway and Denmark. The man who received the notice was the Belgian Ambassador to the Vatican. The high official who provided this information was Hans Oster, Canaris's deputy. Oster, in turn, passed this intelligence to Joseph Muller, a Catholic lawyer in Munich, and a personal friend of Pope Pius XII. Muller was also on good terms with other men in the Vatican, such as Father Robert Leiber, and

VATICAN INTRIGUE

Monsignor Ludwig Kass, a Vatican official. Father Leiber was in contact with members of the OSS, as well as a courier of documents to and from Rome.

Oster approached Muller and asked him if he would serve as an intermediary between the Schwarze Kapelle and the British government, via the Vatican. Muller quickly accepted.

The German resistance, in order to be believable in the eyes of the Western powers, required someone who would pass along their intentions to the West. The man they chose was Pope Pius. The pope was a firm believer in the German people, but detested Hitler, and his gross slaughter of the innocent. The code name given to this Vatican connection by Canaris and Oster was called "Operation X."

The resistance received encouraging news when Father Leiber brought word that the pope would help "when conditions justify it." This meant, when Hitler was removed. The pope, with all his influence, was on their side.

Father Leiber then notified the British Ambassador to the Vatican, Sir Francis d'Arcy Osborne, of the approaches made by the Schwarze Kapelle, and of the pope's response. d'Arcy Osborne was also told that the pope would serve as the intermediary only if the British and French promised not to interfere in domestic German politics if a new regime came into being.

Lord Halifax, the British Foreign Secretary, contacted the pope and told him that Ambassador d'Arcy Osborne had His Majesty's permission to consult with the resistance. The euphoria, nonetheless, did not last long.

Ambassador Osborne listened to what the resistance leadership had to say, but was unconvinced. Osborne told His Majesty's government that he'd recommend continued contacts only if the Hitler regime was gone and the Germans promised to return lands conquered in recent cross-border incursions, and only if Germany agreed to return the Sudetenland to Czechoslovakia.

In another communication to Osborne from the pope, His Holiness said that he learned that elements of the German army were poised to stage a coup, but only on the condition that the merger of Austria and Germany would be guaranteed. Foreign Secretary Halifax responded by saying that France and Britain would not be party to any blackmail, and more importantly, that the Austrian populace should have self-determination in their future.

The X Report, originally drafted by Canaris and Hans Oster, now made its way among the resistance leaders. Others who now were adding clauses to The X Report were Joseph Muller, Hans von Duhnanyi, a Ministry of Justice official, and Generals Georg Thomas and Franz Halder.

These men told the British that the foundation of any plan was based on prompt removal of Hitler. General Halder, in a move that he later regretted, gave a copy of the X Report to Walther von Brauchitsch, the commander in chief of the German army. Halder was shocked when General von Brauchitsch all but labeled him a traitor and warned him to ignore the report.

For the Schwarze Kapelle, the cold shoulder given to them by General von Brauchitsch was the last straw in any possible deal involving the Vatican in trying to end the war. Hitler was now prepared to invade France, Norway, Denmark, and eventually, Great Britain.

While the Schwarze Kapelle was working with the Vatican, Reinhard Heydrich's SD was following intently. The mole was a Benedictine monk named Hermann Keller who lived and worked in an abbey called Beuron, high in the Swabbian Mountains. Keller was Heydrich's informant, and through intrigue on Keller's part, was able to oust the Arch Abbot of the monastery, Rafael Walser, and virtually rule on his own terms.

The same Joseph Muller who was part of the resistance was ordered to investigate Keller, and he proved that the monk had initiated trumped-up charges against the Arch Abbot. Keller was sent to Jerusalem, where he was once again put under the command of the SD.

Keller traveled to Basel, Switzerland, in October 1939, and it was there that he met a Berlin lawyer, Dr. Hans Etscheit. Etscheit was then working for Admiral Canaris's Abwehr, and had no idea that the monk was working for the rival, SD. After hours of conversations, Etscheit told Keller about the Vatican connection, believing that his secret was safe with the monk. Keller had learned from Etscheit that Muller was the middleman with the Vatican, and Keller traveled to Rome where he confronted Muller about his Vatican contacts.

Canaris and Oster wrote their own version of the Muller-Etscheit allegations, playing down any conspiracy and leaving out the most critical names of those involved. Canaris personally brought the report to Hitler, who after reading it, called it "nonsense."

By a stroke of ill luck, the Vatican conspiracy ended in a whimper, not a bang. It did, however, show the lengths to which many German officials would go to prevent an all-out European war, as well as to remove Hitler.
(*See Also*: Black Orchestra; Canaris, Wilhelm; Dulles, Allen; Leiber, Robert, Father; Oster, Hans; Quigley, Martin; Venlo Affair)

Venlo Affair

The Venlo Affair was a successful sting operation on the part of the SD, run by Major Walter Schellenberg, against two MI-6 officers in the town of Venlo, near the Dutch-German border. The aftermath of the Venlo Affair led to the destruction of most MI-6's operations in many parts of Europe, as well as the impetus leading up to the German invasions of Denmark, Norway, and then France.

Soon after the German invasion of Poland in September 1939, a number of general officers in the German army made plans to topple Hitler before the European continent could be plunged into war. MI-6, the covert British spy organization, contacted disgruntled German officers to aid them in their furtive plots.

Walter Schellenberg, of the counterintelligence unit also known as Department IV, or foreign intelligence, had infiltrated the plot on Hitler's life and knew who was involved in the conspiracy. MI-6, however, was not aware of Schellenberg's intrigues, and it was during this time period that a number of anti-Hitler generals contacted MI-6 seeking help in dealing with Hitler.

Schellenberg knew that the plotters were meeting with the British, and he took steps to infiltrate their organization and wreck the conspiracy. To that effect, Schellenberg asked one of his best agents, who also happened to be a double agent working for the British, a Dr. Fischer, to contact London and commence the negotiations.

The British recruited two of their most capable agents to be their representatives to the resistance: Captain S. Payne Best and Major H. R. Stevens. Major Stevens, in charge at the SIS Hague station, was previously stationed in India, where he was an intelligence officer, while Captain Best also served in the Hague as the representative of a spy group called the Z Organization.

He also went by the code number 55. Best operated a dummy corporation called the Continental Trading Company, which hid his spying activities. The Z Organization began operations in 1935 as a separate intelligence entity to the Secret Intelligence Service (SIS). Most heads of station who worked as SIS employees served in their host countries under the cover of Passport Control Officers.

These Passport Control Officers were well known to the intelligence services of the countries in which they operated, and the Z Organization was organized to hide these officers' identities. While the two men worked closely together, Major Stevens was unaware that Captain Best was representing the Z Organization.

Major Stevens took it upon himself to act as the representative between Dr. Fischer and MI-6. Dr. Fisher told Major Stevens that he had contacted the resistance and that a meeting was to be set up at a Dutch village. Dr. Fischer also informed Walter Schellenberg of what had transpired, and Schellenberg told him to proceed with caution.

Major Stevens was in steady contact with Stewart Menzies, the head of SIS regarding the resistance, and Menzies told Stevens to organize a covert meeting with the other side for October 17, 1939. On that day, one man came to meet with the British. General von Wietersheim was the commander of the Fourteenth Panzer Corps, then stationed in Poland. The general said that he would work with the British but wanted their terms for an armistice agreement. He said that he would meet with them three days hence on October 20. Menzies concurred and gave the orders for the rendezvous.

On the appointed day, Major Stevens, Captain Best, and an officer from the Dutch intelligence service, Dirk Klop, arrived in the town of Dinxperloo, where they met two members of the resistance. The two Germans identified themselves as "Colonel Seydlitz and Colonel Grosch." The men then proceeded to the city of Arnhem, where further discussions took place. Best and Stevens told their German visitors that then Prime Minister Neville Chamberlain was willing to end the war only if the territory seized by Germany at the outbreak of the war (Poland) was returned. The Germans promised that with a successful coup, Hitler would be imprisoned, and new leadership, friendly to the allies, would be installed in Berlin.

All this information was funneled back to Menzies by Best, who told the MI-6 chief that he believed that Colonels Seydlitz and Grosch were working for the SS. Menzies, for his part, shared Best's instincts and told him to keep a close watch on their activity when they next met.

While Best and Stevens were making preparations for their clandestine meeting with the generals, an event took place in Germany that had a direct bearing on the outcome of their plan.

On the night of November 8, 1939, an assassination attempt was undertaken on Hitler's life. Hitler was dining in a Berlin beer hall with a number of aides when a bomb exploded. There were casualties, but Hitler escaped unhurt. In the aftermath of the assassination plot, the Germans arrested George Elser, a 36-year-old mechanic from the city of Wurttemberg.

In order to milk the most propaganda out of the attempt, the German government put the blame squarely on the shoulders of British Intelligence. In reality, the plot was hatched by dissident elements of the German army.

In the wake of the attack, it was decided by military leaders in Berlin that when the generals next met with Stevens and Best, they would be kidnapped in retaliation.

Through their secret middlemen, Best, Stevens, and Lieutenant Klop from the Dutch military, headed for their rendezvous at the Dutch-German border town of Venlo on November 9, 1939. Instead of the dissident German generals that Best and Stevens believed they were going to meet, Walter Schellenberg, along with a group of soldiers, came instead.

Schellenberg, introducing himself as "Major Schaemmel," along with two other officers, met with Best and Stevens at a café in Venlo, saying that they were representing the dissenters. Schellenberg then excused himself.

This was his signal for the raiding party that was stationed on the German side of the border to proceed. On Schellenberg's signal, the team, led by his right-hand man, Alfred Naujocks, raced past the startled Dutch border guards, their guns blazing.

In a furious fire fight lasting only a few minutes, Naujocks and his men captured Best and Stevens and spirited them across the border. In the ensuing fight, Lieutenant Klop was shot and killed. During the battle, a German guard almost killed Schellenberg, unaware of his identity.

The aftereffects of the Venlo Affair were no less than an intelligence disaster on the part of MI-6. Best and Stevens were taken to a concentration camp, where they would remain until freed by American GIs at the war's end. Under intense interrogation, Best and Stevens broke, giving vital information about MI-6 operations across Europe. Soon, the MI-6 station was closed. But the disaster did not end there.

MI-6 removed all its agents from its stations in Prague, Berlin, Warsaw, and Bucharest. The only surviving British agents were those working in Germany, men not under the control of Best and Stevens. Another casualty was the ending of the Z Organization

Six months after the Venlo Affair, German troops invaded Holland on May 10, 1940. France was the next target of the German blitzkrieg, and German troops entered Paris the following month.

George Elser, the fall guy in the attempt on Hitler, was executed.

S. Payne Best returned to England and wrote a book on the incident called appropriately, *The Venlo Affair*. He died in 1978 at the age of 93.

Richard Stevens passed away in 1965.

Walter Schellenberg was captured by the allies in 1945, tried at the Nuremberg War Crimes Tribunal, served five years in prison, and was released in 1950. He died two years later.

(*See Also*: Menzies, Stewart; Vatican Intrigue; Oster, Hans)

Venona

On February 1, 1943, a group called the U.S. Army Signal Intelligence Service, forerunner of the modern-day National Security Agency, began a project to intercept and analyze Soviet diplomatic traffic. The undertaking went by the code name Venona. It is only now that the NSA has been releasing portions of its files on the Venona Project, and what we are learning changes the way historians have been viewing Soviet penetration of U.S. espionage agencies. The files also shed a bright light on the mentality of the Cold War that dominated U.S. foreign policy for almost 50 years.

Venona was the brainchild of Colonel Carter Clarke, the chief of the United States Army's Special Branch, a division of the War Department's

Military Intelligence Division. During 1943, Colonel Clarke picked up signals that a possible Soviet-German peace deal was in the works, and Clarke wanted to find out if the rumor had merit. Colonel Clarke ordered his small code-breaking unit to read all Soviet diplomatic messages being sent from the U.S. to Moscow. The colonel's code breakers were able to pick up copies of Soviet messages via international cable traffic being sent over the wires. Through hairsplitting months of trial and error, the analysts were able to crack the Soviet code. What they found was not information leading up to a separate peace, but a large-scale, well-organized Soviet espionage penetration of the highest levels of the American government.

The headquarters of the Venona Project was a remote cite in Virginia called Arlington Hall. It was from here that code breakers worked on the thousands of pages of cables being intercepted from Soviet diplomatic missions around the world.

The Soviet official entrusted in 1943 with handling these messages was Pavel Fitin, chief of the foreign intelligence directorate of the KGB in Moscow. (He would keep that position until 1946.) Fitin ran five different espionage branches in the United States: 1) commercial ties like the Soviet Amtorg company handling all information coming from the U.S. Lend Lease program to the Soviet Union, 2) the use of Soviet diplomats as intelligence agents, 3) direct relations with KGB HQ in Moscow, 4) the running of GRU-Soviet Army General Staff Intelligence Directorate, and 5) the GRU-Soviet Naval Intelligence Staff.

By the time the Venona analysts made headway breaking Soviet traffic, the war had ended. But what they did learn in the early 1950s was that the Soviet Union had penetrated the Manhattan Project in which U.S. scientists developed the atomic bomb.

Nineteen-hundred and forty-five was a pivotal year as far as information from Venona was concerned. In that year, a Soviet code clerk working in the Russian Embassy in Ottawa, Canada, Igor Gouzenko, defected to Canadian authorities with hundreds of top-secret documents. Gouzenko told the Canadians that the Soviets had a mole inside their intelligence system. He also named numerous officials who were working for the Soviet Union, passing national secrets. Among them were Alger Hiss, Harry Dexter White, the second-highest-level person in the Treasury Department, Lauchlin Currie, one of FDR's confidants, and the atomic espionage ring led by Julius Rosenberg.

The arrest of Julius Rosenberg would eventually lead to the jailing of his wife, Ethel, her brother, David Greenglass, Harry Gold, and British scientist Klaus Fuchs, among others. Another person who came forward to document Gouzenko's claims was Elizabeth Bentley, a former KGB courier in Washington.

VENONA

Another major breakthrough was the unmasking of another Soviet penetration of Western spy agencies known as the Cambridge Five, consisting of Kim Philby, Donald MacLean, Guy Burgess, John Cairncross, and Anthony Blunt.

Venona analysts were able to match the cover-names originating from the Soviet cables to real people and places. For example, "Kapitan" was FDR, "Antenna and Liberal" were Julius and Ethel Rosenberg, "Enormoz" was the Manhattan Project, "Babylon" was San Francisco, and "Good Girl" was Elizabeth Bentley.

One of the analysts at Arlington Hall in 1946 was Meredith Gardner, who was able to decipher messages going between KGB headquarters in Moscow and their consulate in New York. Among the clues Gardner found was the fact that the KGB had its spies operating in Latin America, and that they had many discussions about the 1944 U.S. presidential election. From 1947 through 1952, Arlington Hall analysts broke all KGB traffic between the Soviet Union and the United States. In 1953, U.S. analysts were aided considerably in their work when they managed to get a copy of a semi-burned Russian codebook relating to this message traffic.

For the Soviet's part, they did have a general inkling of what the people at Arlington Hall were doing. When Elizabeth Bentley went over to the FBI, she reported that Kim Philby had given them some details concerning Venona in 1944. When Philby was working in Washington in the early 1950s, he often went to Arlington Hall and was privy to the intelligence.

Besides the Manhattan Project, Venona was one of the most highly secret programs operating during the war. The senior members of the army and FBI curbed knowledge of Venona to only a few with a need to know. In fact, the CIA was not brought into the fold until 1952, and even then did not receive all deciphered messages until 1953.

Even President Truman was not told the extent of the material retrieved from Venona. He was given this information only from his regular briefings from the FBI and the Justice Department.

By the time the Venona Project ended, more than 3,000 letters from the Soviet Union to their personnel in the United States had been read. The Freedom of Information Act led to the opening up of the Venona files, and it was only in 1995 that the world learned fully of its contents.

The historical significance of the Venona files is incalculable. They show without a shadow of a doubt that Alger Hiss was a Soviet agent, and that Julius Rosenberg ran a highly successful espionage ring in the U.S.

On the other side of the coin, by hiding the facts culled from Venona, the Rosenbergs were executed, never giving their lawyers the information needed in their defense.

As time goes on, more of the Venona traffic is being released, giving 21st-century historians a better look at one of the most turbulent times in our history.

(*See Also*: Bentley, Elizabeth; Burgess, Guy; Cambridge Spies; Fuchs, Klaus; Gold, Harry; Greenglass, David; Hiss, Alger; MacLean, Donald; Manhattan Project; Philby, Kim; The Rosenbergs)

Vessel Case

He OSS had numerous undercover operations with the Vatican during the war, trying to use the Holy See as an intermediary in negotiating peace terms. In 1944, the OSS was immersed in Vatican intrigue in a case known as Vessel, whose information reached upper levels of the American government, right into the oval office of President Roosevelt. By the time the Vessel case was over, it would prove to be one of the most embarrassing and unproductive affairs conducted by the OSS during the war.

The earliest cooperation between the OSS and the Vatican began in 1941, when Bill Donovan established an informal working relationship with a Father Morlion, the leader of an anti-Nazi group called the European Catholic anti-Comintern. This organization was also an intelligence service named Pro Deo. Donovan gave funds to the Pro Deo, who supplied him with insight into the political thinking of Vatican officials.

The Vessel case began when Vincent Scamporino, the OSS SI (Secret Intelligence) chief stationed in Rome, obtained intelligence coming from inside Pope Pius XII's palace. After receiving this information which he called "Z," he sent it on to Washington for evaluation. Scamporino had been a veteran of the State Department, served in the New Hampshire legislature, and was an expert on Italy.

Upon reading the news imparted by Scamporino, most of which concerned Japanese foreign policy, it was deemed of great value, and the OSS X-2, counterintelligence unit was called in to protect the source, now called Dusty. Dusty was paid up to $500 per month. The Dusty-Vessel case was overseen by Brigadier General John Magruder, the director of all OSS intelligence services.

As Donovan and his men studied the information coming from Vessel, they could only wonder at their good fortune. They read the minutes of meetings from the branches of the Vatican, including the Secretariat, the Department of Extraordinary Affairs (the foreign affairs branch), the Propaganda division, and the writings of the pope himself.

If Donovan was enamored by Vessel, James Angleton, the head of OSS X-2 in Rome, saw it differently. Angleton was generally wary of sudden influxes of intelligence, especially from people whose bona fides he did not know. Angleton did, however, check out the middleman who brought the Vessel material to OSS, a Russian named Dubinin. Angleton's investigation showed that Dubinin was working for the British and the French, and he told Donovan that he did not approve the Vessel affair.

The first impressive Vessel intelligence reached the OSS in January 1945, regarding a conversation between the pope and Pietro Cardinal Fumasoni-Biondi, the director of the Propaganda Department. Their exchanges covered the possibility of a mediation of the Vatican with the Japanese for the ending of hostilities and also a cancellation by the Soviet Union of its non-aggression pact with Japan and what type of deals the Japanese might make in any peace talks.

Later that month, Vessel sent another intelligence bonanza to the OSS of conversations between the pope and Cardinal Fumasoni-Biondi. In it, the Japanese agreed that in return for peace, they would give up claims to all the territory they conquered except Hong Kong and Hainan, that Japan would regain lands controlled before the Sino-Japanese war of 1894; Japan believed that they were the "victor" in the war, and the allies should consider them as such, and finally, that the Philippines should become an "independent regime."

Later news reports from Vessel began to shift from political to military matters. In one memo, it was learned that the Japanese had put a new, heavily fortified battleship into service, and that it was heading to Nagasaki in December. Later communiques referred to the fact that U.S. air raids caused many injuries to factory workers and that there were rumblings that the government was responsible for making defeat inevitable.

While Vessel was providing the administration with what seemed serious material, a rift between the X-2 and SI developed regarding the handling of Vessel. At the same time that Vincent Scamporino was receiving his reports, James Angleton was getting similar stories from his own source in the Vatican, Fillippo Setaccioli. For his part, Angleton wanted to control all Vessel information, not wanting to share it with his colleagues in SI. The rift between the two espionage branches of OSS finally received the attention of the Roosevelt administration. They now decided to double check the Vessel material, and what they found was nothing less than a hoax being perpetrated.

In February 1945, Vessel sent a report to Washington regarding a meeting attended by Myron Taylor, the president's personal envoy to the Vatican, and Harada Ken, the Japanese Ambassador to the Vatican. When asked to confirm his meeting with Ambassador Ken, Myron Taylor denied having met him. The minutes of this meeting supplied by Vessel had the Japanese saying that they would not negotiate on any allied terms and that they saw no likelihood of an early end to the war. Another part of the news report had the

Russians telling the Japanese that they would put pressure on the allies to negotiate a peace treaty.

These Vessel documents finally sent up red flags in both the OSS and the Roosevelt White House. Donovan was informed by his two associates handling Vessel material, General Magruder and Whitney Shepardson, that they had "grave doubts as to the validity" of Vessel's reports. A full-scale investigation was undertaken.

Vessel, it turned out, was the Italian writer and confidence man Virgilio Scattolini. Scattolini, the author of a number of pornographic books, was a former reporter for the Vatican newspaper *Osservatore Romano*. After being fired by the paper when they found out about his pornographic writings, he took to creating and selling bogus information on Vatican affairs to anyone who would pay his high fee. Scattolini was tried in an Italian court for crimes against the Vatican, found guilty and served seven months in jail. After leaving prison, Scattolini disappeared.

The Vessel case was an embarrassment to the OSS. Virgillio Scattolini not only had fooled America's spymasters but taught them a powerful lesson in how a source should be handled and how the vetting process of prospective agents should be dealt with when creating secret, counterintelligence operations.

(*See Also*: OSS Italy; Vatican Intrigue)

Vlassov Movement, The

Of all the battles fought in Europe, some of the bloodiest campaigns took place in the East, as German and Russian troops and tanks cut each other to pieces. In 1942, the Wehrmacht decided that the military campaign had to be supported by political activity among the population of the conquered territories. It was suggested by the commanders that they should scour the population of their Russian POW camps to locate a well-known, anti-Soviet figure who would be able to rally the anti-Russian elements then in custody.

The man given the job of finding such a person was Hauptmann Strickfeld, who, after a long and arduous search, found the one he was looking for: General Andre Vlassov. After intensive talks with Vlassov, it was decided that he filled all the requirements for the task.

The documents on the Vlassov case report little or no activity between the general and the Germans from 1942 to 1944. In 1944, however, conditions became ripe for Vlassov's help.

During 1944, anti-Soviet deserters from the Russian army, mainly Ukrainians, Georgians, and other ethnic minorities, were fighting in German units. These men were growing restless and were worried that in the event of a Russian victory, they would stand no chance of returning to their homes. The Wehrmacht renewed its contacts with General Vlassov and sent a staff officer named Gunter D'Alguin, the former editor of the paper *Schwarze Korps,* and during the war, the director of the Propaganda Staff of the Waffen SS, to meet with Vlassov.

D'Alguin realized that the war could not be won strictly in military terms alone, and he soon came to recognize that Vlassov could provide the leadership for all anti-Soviet elements then aiding Germany.

In September 1944, Vlassov met with Heinrich Himmler, the dreaded head of the SS, to form an alliance. Himmler told Vlassov that the Germans wanted three things from him: "1) the formation of strictly Russian units to fight with the army in the East, 2) the infiltration of Russian nationals behind Soviet lines to spread anti-Russian propaganda, and 3) an increase in anti-Soviet propaganda amongst the Russian workers in Germany."

If Vlassov was to become a traitor to his country, he had certain conditions that he demanded from the Germans. He insisted that the status of all minorities should be put off until the Bolsheviks were out of power and that these groups should have the majority of power in a new Russia.

He also set military conditions for his cooperation. He wanted to command all Russian forces fighting in German units and wanted to be allowed to recruit volunteers from Eastern workers in Germany. He promised to raise an army of one million men to fight for Germany, including elements of the refugee community. A decision was made to let Vlassov create two divisions, with a third in preparation.

Vlassov made other demands on Himmler. He wanted better treatment of Russian workers in the East, better food, and the prohibition of the wearing of special patches on their clothing.

He now went further, wanting to create a manifesto which outlined his basic plans for the overthrow of Stalin. His goal was immediately met with skepticism from the leaders of the Ukrainians and the Georgians who were unwilling to serve under him. These men accused Vlassov of trying to create a "Greater Russia," in which minority groups would be underrepresented.

Despite the opposition from these men, a meeting of the "Committee of Liberation of the People of Russia," under Vlassov's tutelage, was held in Prague in November 1944. The handpicked delegates passed the "Vlassov Manifesto," giving him total control over the group.

With Germany providing the necessary arms and equipment, two newly created divisions of Vlassov's troops began training at the city of Muensing in February 1945 and were sent into combat on the Oder front.

German security forces placed a careful watch on all members of the Vlassov movement, as well as providing protection to the general.

During the first days of 1945, Vlassov had personal meetings with the Nazi brass, including Goering, Goebbels, and Ribbentrop. These were purely social gatherings, and little official business was conducted.

OSS records indicate that in March-April 1945, with the Third Reich on the brink of defeat, Vlassov contacted the allies.

Documents indicate that Vlassov hadn't planned how a new Russia free of Stalin would be governed or how the problem of the minorities would be settled. What he did want is "the suspicion that Vlassov's aim was the creation of a Greater Russia with General Vlassov at its head."

W

Wallenberg, Raoul

One of the bright lights in a very dark and sorrowful history of World War II is the role played by a courageous Swedish diplomat named Raoul Wallenberg. Wallenberg is credited with saving the lives of more than a million Hungarian Jews from certain death in the concentration camps of Europe. Wallenberg's actions on behalf of the Jews of Europe were not for personal gain but for humanity.

Raoul Wallenberg came from a wealthy Swedish banking family founded by his uncle, Marcus Wallenberg. Marcus owned the prosperous Enshilda Bank, the largest in that country. Another uncle, Jacob Wallenberg, was also a director of the bank, which had trading rights with most of the other well-connected depositories in Europe, especially with those in Germany.

Raoul received his college education in the U.S., studying architecture at the University of Michigan, returning to Sweden after graduation. In 1938, he joined his family's banking firm but soon was to have a change of heart which would forever alter his life. In that year, he was sent to Palestine to open a branch and was met with a flood of Jewish refugees who were fleeing the beginning of Hitler's bloodbath in Europe. Caught by the enormity of the suffering he saw, Wallenberg returned to Sweden.

Once home, he met a new partner in the firm, a Hungarian Jew, who told him horror stories concerning the fate of his fellow Jews. This man could not return to Hungary, and Wallenberg went in his place. After seeing the conditions in Budapest, Raoul decreed that his work would be to help the Jews of Europe escape death.

Meanwhile, the family's Enshilda bank began a covert relationship with the Soviet KGB in order to broker a peace deal between Russia and Finland. Wallenberg also had a clandestine relationship with the British Secret Service and helped the struggling British in gaining access to Swedish raw materials without the knowledge of KGB or the Nazis. But his most notable success was the saving of more than 20,000 Hungarian Jews in 1944, using Swedish papers, the hiding of thousands of them in safe houses in Budapest, and succeeding in rescuing 70,000 Jews from extermination.

Unknown to Raoul, however, was the fact that the KGB had been tracking his movements, including meetings with German army officers.

On January 17, 1945, as Wallenberg was about to go to a conference with a ranking Soviet military officer in Budapest to discuss the distribution of food to the Jews of the city, he disappeared. Not since that fateful discussion has the fate of Raoul Wallenberg been known. Some reports have it that he was seen alive in Russia well into the 1970s and 1980s. Another account stated that he died shortly after a meeting in 1945. But in an article in the May 13, 1996, edition of *U.S. News and World Report,* new information on Wallenberg's links to the OSS have been confirmed.

The files show that Wallenberg was appointed with the approval of President Roosevelt to be an intelligence asset of the U.S. His wartime job was to provide the OSS with information on the anti-Hitler resistance, and to help in the release of Jews in Europe. According to the *U.S. News and World Report* article, "…it is a reasonable conclusion that Raoul Wallenberg was of benefit to American intelligence." Donald Jameson, a former CIA official, calls this statement, "a virtual admission that Wallenberg was used by us. It is a minimum statement the CIA can make and still be plausible."

According to the newly released files, Wallenberg was used by the OSS as a penetration agent assigned to make reconnaissance missions into Hungary, where Bill Donovan's secret soldiers had no direct "in." In today's spy parlance, Wallenberg was a "contract agent," not formally on the OSS payroll but subject to its laws. The newly available files also report reliable sources seeing Wallenberg alive in Russia decades after his "official" death.

A recent article in the July 25, 2000, edition of *The New York Times* sheds new light on his mysterious disappearance. According to the article, an investigation by Swedish diplomat Ambassador Jan Lundvik reveals that the Russian government has changed its mind in saying that Wallenberg died a natural death while in Soviet hands. The new Russian government now says that Wallenberg was probably killed while in Soviet custody. The article went on to say that in all probability, Stalin would have had to have given the order for execution.

With the ending of the Cold War and the breakup of the Soviet Union, the "true" events concerning the mystery of Raoul Wallenberg may finally come to light.

Wenner-Gren, Alex

Alex Wenner-Gren's wartime activities involved a wide cast of characters, including a German spy operating in the United States, a beautiful Nordic woman suspected by the FBI, and a future president of the United States. In 1941, Alex Wenner-Gren, the owner of Electrolux, was 59, and one of the richest men in the world.

He also held interests in Sweden's largest paper companies, was a stockholder in newspapers and mines, and was also part owner of the Bofors armaments company. He was opposed to the war and active in various German peace initiatives. When Neville Chamberlain was British Prime Minister, Wenner-Gren served as a courier between the Crown and Herman Goering. In 1940, he had a personal meeting at the White House with FDR, at which time he passed along the minutes of conversations from Berlin.

All these activities made Wenner-Gren's name well known to the FBI—who kept a detailed file on him—the Office of Naval Intelligence, and William Stephenson's BSC. It was suspected by all three agencies that the wealthy Swede was a Nazi agent or at the least a man who conspired with them.

In early 1940, Wenner-Gren bought a huge estate on Hog Island in Nassau, Bahamas. He established the Bank of the Bahamas, which had a working relationship with the Stein Bank in Cologne, Germany. Later in the war, it would be learned that Wenner-Gren's bank funneled funds from Germany. After the war, one of his partners, Harry Oakes, would be murdered under circumstances still unexplained today.

Another of Wenner-Gren's friends was the Duke of Windsor, the governor of the Bahamas, and his personal banker. The Duke's relationship with the Germans was an open secret. Both men opposed the war and sought to create alliances with the Germans against the Soviets.

As Wenner-Gren's links to Germany's intelligence agencies became more apparent, the U.S. State Department placed him on a "Black List" of firms with whom U.S. companies were forbidden to work.

Immediately after the Japanese attack on Pearl Harbor, Wenner-Gren was placed on a blacklist by the U.S. government. He was denied an entry visa to America. He then moved his operation to Mexico, where he was seen on many occasions meeting with representatives of Admiral Canaris's Abwehr.

The FBI also placed under observation Wenner-Gren's spacious yacht, the *Southern Cross,* bought from Howard Hughes. Wenner-Gren had made suspicious changes. He put in high-powered radio and communication equipment, installed long-range fuel tanks, and armed it with machine guns and rifles.

Captain Samuel Hunter of Office of Naval Intelligence wrote, "the American Navy was…convinced that the yacht was being used for refueling U-Boats."

If the FBI had some doubts about Wenner-Gren's association with

Hitler, the Swede's next move left no doubt in their minds. With the blitzkrieg controlling most of Europe, the Nazis took over its vast wealth. They had to transfer huge amounts of cash and gold to banks outside the continent. To that end, they established relationships with dummy corporations and banks in such countries as Brazil and Argentina. From Europe, the funds were also sent to banks in Mexico.

To facilitate the process, the Germans turned to two men who would aid them in their scheme: Alex Wenner-Gren and the Duke of Windsor. Huge sums of money from Wenner-Gren's Bank of the Bahamas went to a bank in Mexico called Banco Continental. The owner of Banco Continental, Maximinio Camacho, had agreed to the scheme. Although British law forbade the transfer of currency to Mexico, the Duke invested a million pounds in the Mexican bank.

In Mexico, Wenner-Gren had meetings with the known German agent, William Rhodes Davis. Hoover's FBI and Bill Stephenson's BSC were monitoring the shady activities of both William Rhodes Davis and Alex Wenner-Gren. As if all this espionage wasn't enough, another twist was about to be revealed.

One of Wenner-Gren's business confidants was Paul Fejos. Fejos, who had come from Hungary, was a naturalized American citizen and accomplished explorer. In 1936, he married a beautiful woman named Inga Arvad. Arvad was born in Denmark, schooled in England, and returned to Copenhagen where she studied dance at the Royal Theater.

Inga was a stunning beauty who won many pageants in Denmark. She was much sought after in both high society and politics. Inga worked for a time as a journalist and traveled to Germany on numerous occasions. She interviewed leaders including Hitler, Goering, and Goebbels. Inga made such an impression on Hitler that he invited her to his private box during the 1936 Winter Olympics.

These meetings gave the FBI reason to consider Inga Arvad a possible German espionage agent. According to a January 21, 1942, FBI memo to the Attorney General, "The combination of these facts indicate a definite possibility that she may be engaged in a most subtle type of espionage activities against the United States."

In February 1940, Inga came to the United States. She settled in New York and enrolled at the Columbia School of Journalism. After graduation she moved to Washington, D.C., to work at the *Times Herald* newspaper writing a popular column in which she interviewed prominent people in business and government.

In December 1941, the FBI had begun a full-scale surveillance operation on Arvad. The agents watching her building saw a skinny, young U.S. Navy ensign enter her apartment, stay the night, and leave in the morning. Over the following months, while still married to Paul Fejos, Inga Arvad and "Jack" carried on a torrid love affair.

Hoover's agents passed along their surveillance reports to the Office of Naval Intelligence. Their own internal investigation revealed that "Jack" was the son of the former Ambassador to England, John F. Kennedy.

Ensign John F. Kennedy was working for ONI. The FBI and the navy soon began a double investigation concerning Lieutenant Kennedy and Inga Arvad. An FBI memo on their relationship reads as follows, "He called on the above date and stated that it had come to ONI's attention that Ensign Kennedy had been "playing around" with Inga Arvad and that steps had been taken to put an end to this relationship."

Ambassador Joseph P. Kennedy learned of his son's affair with his "Nordic Beauty," and pulled his considerable strings to have his son transferred out of Washington. Ensign Kennedy was sent to the naval base at Charleston, South Carolina. "Inga Binga," as Kennedy called her, went to visit him at Charleston, where they continued their affair.

The transfer of Kennedy to Charleston, however, did not end the romance. The investigation of Inga Arvad reached the Oval Office of the White House in a July 16, 1942, FBI memo written to the president's secretary, Marvin McIntrye. "Some weeks ago the president sent to me a personal note indicating that we should keep [an eye] on Inga Arvad. I thought I should let you know, as I thought the president might be interested in the matter." In another memo originating from the bureau, the agent who took over the Arvad case said, "it has got more possibilities than anything I have seen in a long time."

Inga Arvad hotly denied that she was a German spy, and no "smoking gun" was ever found to link her with German intelligence. Nevertheless, the Wenner-Gren-Arvad-Kennedy affair was among the tantalizing stories of the war.

Werther

One of the best-kept secrets in the intelligence world during the war was the "Lucy Ring," run by a group of anti-Nazis who were working for the Soviet Union in Switzerland. The man who ran the Lucy Ring was Rudolf Roessler. One of Roessler's best agents was a man who went by the code name "Werther." Werther was Roessler's key agent who operated from his position inside the OKW, the supreme headquarters from which Hitler, and his two generals, Wilhelm Keitel and Alfred Jodl, planned strategy. It was Werther who supplied Lucy with crucial battlefield intelligence of the war, keeping Stalin's troops one step ahead of the rapidly advancing German armies.

Throughout the conflict, the identity of Werther was kept secret; Roessler did not reveal the names of his agents to Moscow. Now, 50 years after the war, the individual called Werther may finally be known.

Werther worked in the OKW's high-command headquarters located at Zossen in southeastern Berlin. Werther was privy to German military tactics and the locations of its Panzer Corps, as well the dispositions of ground troops. The information supplied to Moscow allowed Stalin to counter the German thrusts, effectively gaining valuable time for Russian forces to regroup.

Werther sent his information to his contact, Rachel Dubendorfer, then on to Lucy, who directed his news via another man known as "Taylor." While most of the material sent to Moscow was high-grade intelligence, Stalin did not trust Lucy and failed to comprehend the information being sent to him. If Stalin had any reason not to trust Lucy, it came in one disastrous cable from Werther which ended in the German advance on Stalingrad, costing almost 100,000 Russian casualties.

If Werther was deadly wrong about the Stalingrad incident, he had made up for it concerning the German invasion of Russia, called Operation Barbarossa. From his position at OKW HQ, Werther sent a cable to Lucy stating that 100 German infantry divisions were poised along the German-Russian border. He offered information that the Germans were going to break their non-aggression treaty with Russia and launch an invasion on June 22, 1941. Moscow Center did not believe Werther's warning, calling it an "Abwehr trap." When Hitler's blitzkrieg stormed into Russia, Stalin could only wish he had listened beforehand.

Another intelligence bonanza from Werther came in December 1944, when he sent a radio message to Lucy, telling Moscow the exact number of replacement divisions the Germans were building up after their defeat at Stalingrad.

The fact that Werther was indeed a key member of Hitler's brain trust can be seen during the Third Reich's preparations for the battle of Kursk, a strategic victory for the Russians. Werther not only gave the numbers and locations of German forces preparing for Kursk, but intelligence on the personalities of the men heading the units. He was also able to relay the minutes of high-level meetings among Hitler, Goering, Halder, and other generals. One section of a message sent to Lucy by Werther reads as follows: "The conference opened under Goering's chairmanship without Hitler, then Hitler arrived and took part. The conference revealed the existence of fundamental differences of opinion between Goering on one hand and Halder on the other."

So then, who was Werther? The author of a book titled *Hitler's Traitor: Martin Bormann and the Third Reich*, written by Pulitzer Prize winner Louis

Kilzer, offers an answer. According to Kilzer's research, Werther was in fact Hitler's right-hand man, Martin Bormann!

Why Bormann? Kilzer writes that Bormann worked in the German High Command from 1941 through 1944. He was cognizant of the debate going on behind the scenes in the OKW, especially as it related to troop movements and the policy behind such actions. A code clerk would not have such access, writes Kilzer. He eliminates the other potential candidates for Werther, such as Hans Bernd Gisevius, Carl Goerdeler, and General Boelitz, all of whom were part of the Lucy Ring. These men did not have Bormann's entree to the OKW center.

Another man eliminated for consideration by Kilzer was Hans Oster, Admiral Canaris's deputy. Oster's use to the underground ended in the spring of 1943, and thus he couldn't have been providing information into 1944.

Others who worked in OKW HQ and were sacked by Hitler in the waning days of the war were General Halder, Walther Brauchitsch, the OKH commandant, General Erich von Manstein.

Unknown to Hitler, Bormann had been receiving the minutes of all staff meetings from the stenographers who transcribed notes. Bormann fit the bill as Werther for obvious reasons. No one would ever suspect him. He was Hitler's confidant, after only Speer, Goebbels, and Himmler. After the war, Albert Speer told the Americans that he had met with Herman Goering to plan ways of keeping Bormann from becoming Hitler's number-one gatekeeper, excluding anyone else.

As far as Bormann's motive, Kilzer writes that he was a socialist at heart, had great respect for Stalin, and fumed inwardly when Hitler made a speech decrying state socialism. He knew about the Lucy Ring, made covert contact with them, and became Werther.

(*See Also*: Lucy Ring; Oster, Hans; Roessler, Rudolph)

Winterbotham, Frederick

Frederick Winterbotham was an RAF (Royal Air Force) officer and the head of the air section of British intelligence during the war. He was also responsible for the distribution of all Ultra intelligence to allied commanders. After his retirement from the military, he wrote a best-selling book called *The Ultra Secret*, which revealed the story of Ultra.

Frederick Winterbotham served in the British army during World War I in the Royal Gloucester Hussars, a cavalry unit. In 1916, he transferred to the air section and was shot down by a German plane on July 13, 1917. He was imprisoned for more than 18 months.

Once back in civilian life, he studied law at Christ Church College, Oxford, and later worked on a farm. In December 1929, he was back in military service, this time as the RAF voice to MI-6, the Secret Intelligence Service. From 1934 to 1939, he traveled widely in Europe, especially Germany, where he met a number of the leaders of Hitler's new government. Using his cover as an expert on the use of military aircraft, Winterbotham was able to learn about the Luftwaffe, meeting with a number of their pilots (it was only in 1938 that the Germans would become aware of his MI-6 connections and refuse him further access to that country).

By 1939, Winterbotham began organizing a Scientific Intelligence group within the Air Section of MI-6. His team began studying new types of aircraft being developed by the Germans. As luck would have it, his air section was housed in the same building as the Government Code and Cypher School (GC&CS). This was his introduction to code breaking, the area that he'd specialize in throughout the war years.

Winterbotham's Air Section began planning for the expected invasion of Great Britain called Operation Sea Lion. With his knowledge of air tactics, he told his superiors that he believed London would be the first place hit in an invasion. He was also able to give the RAF the strength of the Luftwaffe (in 1939), which consisted of 927 long-distance aircraft and also that the Nazis would be able to fly 720 sorties per day, with a capacity of dropping 945 tons of bombs.

Winterbotham's legacy was his role in the handling of the Enigma traffic decoded by British analysts at Bletchley Park. He was given the job of distributing these intercepts to members of the government and military. He also developed secure levels of communications he called Special Liaison Units to deal with the Ultra material. During his tenure in handling the Ultra material, not one message fell into the wrong hands.

Winterbotham had a behind-the-scenes view of how the Ultra material was used in the destructive German air raid against the city of Coventry. Using the Ultra decrypts, the British knew of the impending German attack against that city. The government did not take any precautions to counter the raid in which Luftwaffe bombers devastated the city, killing more than 500 people, destroying 51,000 dwellings, and wounding hundreds.

He was also privy to the reactions of allied officials in the aftermath of the assassination of Vichy French leader Jean Darlan. Winterbotham was in Algiers meeting with Georges Ronin, the head of the air section of the French Secret Service, and Stewart Menzies, "C." During dinner, they were informed of Darlan's murder. Winterbotham would later relate that neither man seemed shocked at the news.

When he was in the process of writing his book called *The Ultra Secret,* his proposed memoir caused an uproar among the British Intelligence establishment. He had a lone ally in the person of Alastair Denniston, who headed the GC&CS at Bletchley Park. Despite threats that he was breaking the Official Secrets Act, *The Ultra Secret* became a worldwide bestseller. He later wrote another book on espionage called *The Nazi Connection*.

(*See Also*: Bletchley Park; Darlan, Jean; Lockheed Plane Affair; Ultra)

Wolff, Karl

Lieutenant General Karl Wolff was one of the most powerful men in the Waffen SS, and a deputy of Reichsführer Himmler. He was put in command of German forces located in rear combat areas in early 1945. He was the strong man in Hitler's general staff, as well as one of a number of high-ranking officers involved in making a separate peace with the allies.

During his exceptional military service in World War I, Wolff was awarded the Iron Cross. He rose in the ranks and by the time World War II began, he had risen to the post of Lieutenant General, with access to Hitler. OSS documents sent by Allen Dulles to Washington refer to Lieutenant General Wolff as, "a distinctive personality, and evidence indicates that he represents the more moderate element in Waffen SS combined with a measure of romanticism. He is probably the most dynamic personality in North Italy and, next to Kesselring, the most powerful."

Hitler must have agreed with Dulles's opinion of Wolff and he ordered him to headquarters for an unusual and daring mission. He ordered Lieutenant General Wolff to take a number of highly trained troops, head to the Vatican, and spirit Pope Pius XII out of the country. Hitler was aware of the pope's actions in trying to save a number of Jews from certain death by hiding them in safe houses around Rome. He also knew that a number of his high-level commanders had made covert contacts with the pope in order to end the war. General Wolff had no choice but to draw up detailed plans to kidnap the pope, including designs to take him to Liechtenstein. Unknown to Hitler, Wolff had no intention of carrying out the mission.

Wolff contacted two trusted emissaries in his search for a peaceful end to the war: Dr. Rudolf Rahn, the German Ambassador to Italy, and Ernst von Weizacker, the envoy to the Vatican. He told them of Hitler's brash plan and reassured them that he would never give the order for the mission to proceed. For Wolff's part, he sent a letter to the pope describing the kidnapping plot, and his reactions to it.

In December 1943, Lieutenant General Wolff met with Hitler regarding the current status of the mission. For hours, Wolff pressed his point, saying that if the pope was kidnapped, than all of Italy would be aflame, and that worldwide Catholic repulsion against Germany's actions would result in a huge propaganda defeat. A reluctant Hitler finally canceled the project.

With the Vatican plot now out of the way, Wolff turned his attention to making contact with the OSS representative in Switzerland, Allen Dulles.

On March 6, 1945, Wolff and a small number of men in whom he had the most confidence left from Milan, bound for Zurich. They were traveling under cover of an Italian-German trade group, all wearing civilian clothes. Others going along with them was a member of the Swiss Intelligence Service, Major Max Waibel, and Baron Luigi Parilli, who served as the intermediary with Dulles.

Upon their arrival in Bern, the OSS representative agreed to meet with Wolff but on one condition: Dulles wanted Wolff, then commander of German forces in Italy, to release two top Italian partisan leaders, allied with the U.S., Antonio Usmiani and Ferruccio Parri. Within a week, both men were freed.

Under strict secrecy, Wolff was taken to Dulles's home by Professor Max Hausmann, who hid the general and his men while in the city. Wolff got right to the point. He said that it was time for the war to come to an end, and told Dulles that he was going to try to persuade Albert Kesselring to cooperate with him. Wolff told Dulles that he had operational control over all German forces in the strategic areas of Western Austria, the Tyrol, and the Brenner Pass. Dulles wrote that, "Wolff feels that joint action by Kesselring and himself would have a vital repercussion on the German Army, particularly on the Western front, since many Generals are only waiting for someone to take the lead. Wolff made no request concerning his personal safety or privileged treatment from the war criminal viewpoint."

Wolff continued by saying that he would try to convince as many commanders in the field as possible to dissociate themselves from Hitler and Himmler, and try to arrange for the ending of hostilities in Northern Italy. He told Dulles that if Kesselring agreed, he would attempt to get him to join him in Switzerland to coordinate surrender terms. In order to show further good faith, Wolff told Dulles that he would stop hit-and-run attacks on Italian partisans by German troops, would release a number of imprisoned Jews, and would further assure the safety of 350 American POWs, including a number of sick and wounded held in Italy. Dulles listened intently to General Wolff and assured him that he would study the offer and get back to him in the near future.

General Wolff's discussions with Dulles caught the attention of Ernst Kaltenbrunner, the head of the Nazi security police, the SD. Kaltenbrunner warned Wolff not to interfere with the course of the war. What Wolff did not know was that Himmler too was in covert contacts with the Western allies via Carl Burckhardt, the president of the International Red Cross.

In March 1945, Wolff was again in contact again with Dulles saying that Kesselring had agreed to the surrender of German forces in Italy. He also told Dulles that his family was being "guarded," and that he feared for their lives if he continued his meetings with the OSS.

Amid this turmoil, Wolff was summoned to Hitler's bunker to explain his meetings with the Americans. Hitler told Wolff that his actions were tantamount to treason. Wolff countered by telling Hitler that he was acting on his own, and that he was trying to persuade the Americans to make an alliance with the Germans against the Russians. In the end, Hitler took no punitive action against Wolff, and he was free to proceed with his plans for the surrender of German troops in Italy.

General Wolff was contacted by Marshal Rodolfo Graziani, the Italian Minister of War, who assigned him the task of conducting the surrender of his armies. The ceremony took place on April 29, 1945, at allied HQ in the Royal Summer Palace in Caserta, Italy. The men who penned the capitulation orders were Lieutenant Colonel Viktor von Schweintz, and SS Major Max Wenner, General Wolff's spokesperson. More than a million German troops gave themselves up, in a ceremony that allowed the troops a sense of dignity.

Karl Wolff escaped certain death with Hitler's suicide in his bunker. His heroic actions in the Italian surrender saved hundreds of thousands of lives and contributed to the end of the war.

X

X-2 (Counterespionage)

X-2 was the counterespionage department of the OSS, the agency that protected the OSS from penetration of its secrets by other nations. A large part of X-2's work was a complex records system that kept track of all enemy agents, in all theaters of operation.

Before the United States entered the war, it did not have an organized intelligence system, let alone any counterintelligence organization. That effort was shared by a number of government agencies, including the FBI, G-2 (Army Intelligence) and ONI (Office of Naval Intelligence). The British aided the United States in any cases dealing with a potential foreign threat. When the United States entered the war, all that changed. The creation of Bill Donovan's infant intelligence organization, COI (Coordinator of Information), was the initial step in bringing about a centralized espionage network to the United States. In time, the OSS created its own counterespionage unit, called X-2.

The United States turned to the British Security Coordination based in New York to plan its initial steps in counterespionage. The basis of the British counterespionage success was its comprehensive security registry of enemy personnel or suspected agents. They agreed to turn over this mother lode of information to the Americans, only on the condition that they train their own personnel in how to handle the security of this material.

In an unprecedented security agreement between the United States and Great Britain, the Americans established a civilian counterespionage organization within the OSS, similar to the British MI-6 and MI-5. The first American representative arrived in London in November 1942 as the special liaison to British intelligence.

By March 1943, the OSS had sent four officers and four secretaries to London, whose sole purpose was to learn the British way of conducting CE (counterespionage) techniques and compile its own data base.

X-2

For its part, the OSS set up its own CE headquarters in New York, in the same building housing Bill Stephenson's BSC. At first, all CE material coming from OSS London and elsewhere were handled by the BSC, then given to the OSS for its own use.

On June 15, 1943, the CE department was given autonomous status as part of the OSS's SI, Secret Intelligence, system. This was the infant of the latter day counterintelligence division of the Central Intelligence Agency.

Throughout the war, London served as the headquarters for all X-2 operations in Europe. With the growth of the London operation, the need for their New York office diminished and most of its work was sent overseas. In September 1943, the research work at New York was ended. The OSS also set up an X-2 Registry in Washington, and most of its records from New York were transferred to that facility.

The OSS X-2 was divided into various departments, each with its own task to perform. They were: the Administrative Office who took care of budgets and financing, the Liaison Office who worked with the other American intelligence agencies, i.e., FBI, ONI, the Deputy Chief's office who hired military and civilian personnel for overseas work, an Operations Officer whose duties were to oversee all foreign operations, and the Director of Research whose main functions was the creation of "geographical desks"— divided into the various theaters of war—"whose reports were processed and marked for carding and for distribution." This section also had extensive files on enemy agents, and the organization for which they worked. This was further subdivided into other sections: 1) the Enemy Intelligence Organization, 2) the Watch List Unit, 3) the Insurance Intelligence Section, and 4) a CE Smuggling Section.

By far, the most important part of CE was its Central Registry in Washington. A spy agency, no matter how big or small, is only as good as the knowledge it accumulates from various sources, and OSS X-2 was no exception. By having an extensive filing system on all aspects of enemy operations, X-2 was able to prepare their agents for their own CE duties.

X-2 had its first big role following the Normandy landings in June 1944. A small, covert detachment arrived in Paris on August 15, 1944, before all German troops had left the city. This group set up its first X-2 headquarters for all of France. Their biggest victory was the capturing of a number of Germans who had infiltrated American territory, wearing GI uniforms, creating sabotage behind the lines. In time, X-2 was able to "turn" six of these men into their own CE assets.

X-2 Paris had much success in turning four former agents who were given the code names "Juggler, Hoch, Chariot, and Spook."

"Juggler" was a captured Abwehr agent who gave X-2 the locations of a vast amount of military equipment left by the Germans as they fled Paris.

"Hoch" was a sleeper agent who surrendered to the OSS. Before he could be used as a turned agent, he was murdered by locals in revenge for the horrors inflicted by their German occupiers.

"Chariot" was a man of Spanish descent taken into custody in Cherbourg after the allied invasion of France, and had the distinction of being the first case run by X-2 in Europe. As a turned agent, "Chariot" told his German controllers that he had obtained a job on the docks and was working as an interpreter for the Americans. He was allowed by the allies to travel to U.S. submarine bases along the French coast and radioed back false information given to him by X-2.

"Spook" arrived in the Verdun area by parachute from a Luftwaffe plane which dropped himself and another agent. Their purpose was to spy on allied troop strength in the area. Upon landing, they were captured and taken to an X-2 holding area. "Spook" was a radio operator, and he agreed to work with the Americans. Upon contacting his home base, he asked to be given the routes for his possible return to Germany. The U.S. Third Army was informed about these routes, and more patrols were added. Spook told his German base that he was going to attempt to try out one of these roads in an attempt to come home. He was "captured" by the U.S. Army, then released. Through the intelligence grapevine, the Abwehr learned about the arrest of "Spooks" and his subsequent escape. He later moved his base of operations to the area surrounding the Battle of the Bulge, and once again sent back bogus information. For his services, "Spook" was awarded the Iron Cross.

X-2 also worked closely with other departments within the OSS in combating German intelligence activities in Switzerland. The Safehaven Project, as it was called, worked under the direction of the Secret Intelligence Branch (SI) which was responsible for intelligence gathering in neutral countries, as well as German occupied Europe. According to a report on allied activities in Switzerland, "Safehaven thus emerged as a joint SI/X-2 operation shortly after its inception, especially in the key OSS outposts in Switzerland, Spain, and Portugal, with X-2 frequently playing the dominant role." By January 1945, a number of X-2 agents were working in Switzerland, monitoring the passage of looted gold and cash.

X-2's operations were shut down in October 1945. At its height, the agency had more than 650 employees and had agents operating in every major European and Asian country. In their two years and four months in business, X-2 protected the OSS from enemy penetration, and established a first-rate counterintelligence organization.

(*See Also*: BSC; COI; OSS)

Y

Yamamoto Assassination

One of the intelligence successes was the ability of the United States to intercept and decrypt Japanese broadcasts coming from its headquarters in Tokyo. U.S. code breakers were able to read the secret Japanese naval code called JN-25, which was used to communicate with all units of its navy. The target of the American intercepts was the architect of the Japanese attack on Pearl Harbor, Admiral Isoroku Yamamoto.

Yamamoto was the chief of the Japanese Combined Fleet and was ranked by U.S. military authorities as being the most capable of all Japanese commanders. Using JN-25, American intelligence officers were able to learn that Admiral Yamamoto was making a one-day inspection tour of Japanese bases in the Solomon Islands, most notably the tiny island of Bougainville on April 18, 1943. They were also able to learn the exact time of his arrival and the precise route his plane would be taking.

The White House was notified about Yamamoto's plans, and a meeting was held between Secretary of the Navy Frank Knox and President Roosevelt. In a highly debatable decision taken during hostilities, Roosevelt ordered that the plane carrying Admiral Yamamoto be shot down. The president issued the orders for the Yamamoto assassination attempt and passed them down the chain of command to Admiral Chester Nimitz, the Commander in Chief of the Pacific Fleet.

When making the decision, U.S. officials would have to weight the consequences that if successful, the Japanese would realize that the U.S. had broken their naval codes. But it was decided to go on with the plan.

The orders to carry out the mission was assigned to Major John Mitchell's 339th Fighter Squadron, as well as Captain Thomas Lanphier's 70th Fighter Squadron. The attack group left their base at Henderson Field on Guadalcanal early on the morning of April 18, 1943, headed for Bougainville. The planes flew low to the sea so as not to be spotted by high-flying Japanese aircraft.

Once over the rendezvous point, Captain Lanphier spotted the Betty bomber carrying Admiral Yamamoto. Before attacking the bomber, he confronted a Zeke (the newer version of the Japanese Zero) and shot the plane down. Captain Lanphier then raced to intercept the bomber and brought the plane down with a burst of shells hitting its wings. The plane caught fire and crashed into a nearby island, killing Yamamoto.

The raid was a complete success. The man who planned the Pearl Harbor attack was eliminated, and the security of JN-25 was never compromised. (*See Also*: Hypo, Statio; Pearl Harbor Attack)

Yatskov, Anatoly

The name of Anatoly Yatskov is not known to the casual student of espionage, but he loomed large in the Soviet penetration of America's atomic laboratory at Los Alamos, New Mexico.

Anatoly Yatskov, a KGB officer under diplomatic cover, worked in the Russian consulate in New York. His undercover mission in the United States was to oversee the gathering of scientific information via the Soviet moles then working inside the Los Alamos facility, the Manhattan Project. Yatskov personally handled a number of U.S. spies, including Harry Gold, the courier for Julius Rosenberg.

With the release of newly opened Russian archives covering their penetration of the Los Alamos facility during the war, new information concerning an as yet unnamed Soviet spy handled by Yatskov has come to light. In 1991, Colonel Vladimir Chikov, a press officer with the Russian intelligence service, wrote about two people who made it inside the New Mexico complex: Morris and Lona Cohen. The Cohens were communists who fled the United States in 1950 for Russia. They then moved to London and ran a used book store which was a front for espionage activities. In 1961, they were arrested by the British in connection with the Naval Secrets Case.

Vladimir Chikov wrote that Morris Cohen recruited a spy inside the Manhattan Project. The cover name given to this physicist was "Perseus."

In 1944, Harry Gold, one of the plotters of the atomic spy ring working out of Los Alamos, was transferred to the care of Yatskov. Yatskov became his mentor, nursing the shy Gold in his efforts for the Soviets. The Russian received information regarding the Manhattan Project via his other agents inside the facility, David Greenglass, and to a lesser extent, Julius and Ethel Rosenberg.

All that changed, however, when in 1945, the security of their agents broke down. With the exposure of the Rosenbergs, as well as Harry Gold now out in the open, the Russians instructed Yatskov to be diligently careful.

Yatskov received another crippling blow when Elizabeth Bentley defected to the FBI and brought with her tales of Soviet penetration of American intelligence during the war years.

The defection of Elizabeth Bentley caused the Soviets to instruct Yatskov to stop all further espionage activities in the United States and Canada. Despite this warning, Yatskov met again with Harry Gold on December 19, 1945. They discussed a man named Abraham Brothman, aka "Korn." Gold told Yatskov that Brothman knew him as "Frank Kessler," and knew that he lived in Philadelphia. When Yatskov told Gold that Brothman's espionage was known to the FBI, he seemed not at all concerned.

In 1946, Brothman hired Gold as a chemist in his new factory. Gold told Brothman all about himself, including the fact that he was not married (as Brothman thought he was). In one bit of nerve, Gold and Brothman went to the Soviet Purchasing Commissions office to see if they would be interested in buying Vitamin B, which Brothman's factory was working on.

When Yatskov found out about their business relationship, he scolded both of them for their indiscretions. Yakskov later wrote of the incident that Gold, "realizes he committed a grave mistake."

With the arrest of the Rosenbergs, Harry Gold and the others involved in the Manhattan Project, the New York KGB closed up shop. Anatoly Yatskov, the prime overseer of the most important Soviet spy ring of the 20th century, unobtrusively went home.

(*See Also*: Bentley, Elizabeth; Cohen, Lona & Morris; Gold, Harry; Greenglass, David; Manhattan Project)

Yoshikawa, Takeo

Takeo Yoshikawa (1914-1993) was Japan's master spy operating out of Hawaii in the year before the Pearl Harbor attack. Yoshikawa provided Admiral Yamamoto with the exact locations of the U.S. fleet at anchor, as well as other vital information concerning the dispositions of aircraft, as well as the safeguards put in place to protect the fleet. His messages back to Tokyo gave the Japanese strike force intelligence culminating in the successful surprise attack.

Takeo Yoshikawa had no formal intelligence training. He had dreamed of becoming an actor. He was well versed in the Japanese art of *Kendo*, a sport that consisted of stick fighting. He graduated from the Japanese Naval Academy, studied the English language at Nippon University, where he learned American history, as well as studying American naval strategy. He later served four years with the Third Bureau, the Naval General Staff's intelligence unit, and was assigned to the American desk. In time, he became an expert on American naval tactics, and had an encyclopedic knowledge of

American aircraft. As Admiral Yamamoto's plans for the attack intensified (code named Operation Z), he required a spy on the ground in Hawaii. The man he chose for this dangerous assignment was Takeo Yoshikawa.

Yoshikawa left Japan on board the Japanese vessel *Nita Maru*, which docked at Honolulu on March 14, 1941. His cover assignment was that of consul general, a job in name only. He also changed his name to Tadashi Morimura, one he would use during his activities around the islands.

Upon his arrival at the consulate, he gave his orders from Captain Bunjiro Yamaguchi, from the intelligence section of the Naval General Staff, to the highest ranking diplomat, consul general Nagao Kita. Kita was well aware of Yoshikawa's real purpose in Hawaii and gave him great leeway in his espionage activities.

Yoshikawa knew that an attack was being planned, but he did not know the exact date that it would take place. His job was to reconnoiter the vast American naval base, study the aircraft at Hickam Field, the home of the Eighteenth Bomber Wing, as well as the army airfield located at Ford Island, which had previously been taken over by the navy when the naval base was expanded.

Yoshikawa hired his own driver from the Royal Taxi Company, who chauffered him on his clandestine tours around the islands. Dressed in a loud Aloha shirt popularized by the thousands of tourists who flocked to the Hawaiian Islands, he fit in like any other traveler. For weeks on end, Yoshikawa would take scenic drives overlooking the naval base where he studied the layout of the ships at berth, recording their names and what armaments they carried. From atop the high hills on the islands, he would monitor the takeoffs and landings of hundreds of planes, noting their routes and schedules. He even took swims with a number of local girls whom he met on the beautiful beaches in Hawaii. But these outings were not all pleasure. He would learn the grade of the beaches in case the Japanese decided on an amphibious landing.

He did not work alone but was aided by others in the consulate. Among them were Richard Kotoshshirodo and Kohichi Seki, who had been doing secret work before his arrival. Another man who did leg work for Yoshikawa was a German named Bernard Otto Kuhn (along with his family).

Yoshikawa became a ladies' man, often being seen at many posh nightclubs with a beautiful woman on his arm. These women were selected from the consulate to be part of his cover story. He often was seen at the Spring Tide Restaurant, a Japanese eatery located on Alewa Heights. It was here that he would meet U.S. naval officers just arrived from sea duty, listen to their stories, and pick up abundant intelligence. He also recruited a local man who ran a soda fountain right outside the naval base. The owner reported any interesting conversations he heard and passed them on to Yoshikawa. He also took plane rides over the islands, where he had a panoramic view of all the air and naval bases around Oahu.

The FBI had a large office in Honolulu headed by SA Robert Shivers. Shivers had a number of his men trailing Yoshikawa and other possible spies around the islands. But since Yoshikawa had diplomatic immunity and was not caught entering any U.S. military facility, their efforts were limited.

By mid-November 1941, Yoshikawa's reports to Tokyo were increasing. From the safety of their consulate code room, his messages went via the cable companies operating in Hawaii. These intercepts were addressed to Japan's Foreign Minister. He, in turn, sent them on to the Third Bureau.

Yoshikawa sent a report in which he made a "grid" of Pearl Harbor. The grid was separated into various areas. Area "A" concerned the areas between Ford Island and the naval base, "Area B" was the waters south and west of Ford Island, "Area C" was the East Loch, "Area D" was the Middle Loch, "Area E" designated the West Loch. In his message to Tokyo, he further separated the identifications of the regions by making up his own codes. FGA stood for the east of Ford Island, FGB was the west side of the island, while FV stood for Ford Island. When broken down, Tokyo was told the exact number and names of the ships at dock, including "one Texas-Class battleship, One Indianapolis-Class Cruiser, two heavy cruisers, seven light cruisers, twenty-six destroyers, six submarines, one troopship, and two destroyers off Waikiki."

For the historians studying the attack, this was the so-called "bomb plot" message. American listening posts in Hawaii decoded this message and sent it along to Washington where it was read, but not acted upon by military brass. Admiral Husband Kimmel was not even given a copy of this message.

The backlog of Japanese intercepts, and the small staff to handle them, resulted in a total breakdown in the decoding of Yoshikawa's messages. On December, 6, 1941, one day before the attack, U.S. analysts had in their possession more than 200 messages sent by him to Tokyo.

On November 1, 1943, the Japanese liner *Taiyo Maru* arrived in Honolulu. What made this sailing different was the fact that the ship took the exact route that the attacking Japanese fleet would make in a month's time. What struck the ship's captain was that they encountered no other commercial ships during their voyage.

Onboard the *Taiyo Maru* was Lieutenant Commander Surguru Suzuki, an officer knowledgeable concerning aviation tactics. At the consulate, Suzuki met with consular general Kita and handed him a list of 97 questions that he wanted Yoshikawa to answer, all of them revolving around the defensives. Some of the queries and answers are as follows:

Q—On what day of the week would the most ships be in Pearl Harbor on normal occasions?

A—Sunday.

Q—How many large seaplanes patrol from Pearl Harbor at dawn and sunset?

A—About 10, both times.

Q—Each week, the fleet goes to sea. Where do they go? What do they do? Particularly aircraft carriers?

A—Mostly unknown.

Yoshikawa's answers were put in the diplomatic pouch and returned to the *Taiyo Maru* for its return voyage to Japan. This material was sent to the incoming Japanese invasion fleet then approaching Hawaii. This was the final intelligence straw for the Pearl Harbor attack.

Takeo Yoshikawa was sleeping in his bed on the morning of December 7, 1941, when he was awakened by the sound of planes overhead. He went to the window and saw the attack force fly overhead. In a matter of minutes, most of America's Pacific fleet lay in ruins, and the United States was at war with Japan. Following the attack, the Japanese consulate staff was sent home. Included among them was Japan's most famous spy.

(*See Also*: Hypo, Station; Kuhn Spy Family; Lanikai & the Isabel; Layton, Edwin; Pearl Harbor Attack; Rochefort, Joseph)

Yugoslavia Activities

For the late 1990s, the United States and her NATO partners turned their attention to the brutal civil war raging in the former Yugoslavia. In 1999, a U.S.-led coalition waged a limited war against the regime of President Slobodan Milosevic over his ethnic cleansing policies in Kosovo. In 2000, after President Milosevic lost a democratically waged election, he refused to give up power and was brought down by a popular revolt. The root causes of the troubles in the former Yugoslavia date back to World War II, and the policies of both the British and the United States in choosing one side over the other in the war. They also include the failure of both the OSS and the British intelligence services over who should represent the Yugoslav people after the war ended.

As Hitler's troops were storming across Europe, one Yugoslav patriot, General Draja Mikhailovich, the leader of the Chetnicks, declared his open resistance to Germany. His rival was Marshall Joseph Tito, the commander of the Partisan army. The British and the United States had contacts with both men, and a debate began in both Washington and London as to which side to back. In time, the United States sided with Tito, and a steady stream of military supplies began to be delivered. Over time, 100,000 rifles, 50,000 machine guns, 1,400 mortars, and clothing for Tito's troops were brought in.

YUGOSLAVIA ACTIVITIES

The decision to support Tito left General Mikhailovich out in the cold.

A propaganda campaign was then waged against Mikhailovich, linking him to the Germans. It was run by a number of pro-communists in both the British and American intelligence services. The few allied military officers who knew that Mikhailovich was not a collaborator were unsuccessful in trying to persuade their governments from abandoning him.

Before the West left Mikhailovich, the OSS sent a military mission to his headquarters under the command of Lieutenant Colonel Robert McDowell in 1944. This mission, code named Ranger, would leave scars not only between Mikhailovich and the U.S., but with the British, as well.

The order to send Lieutenant Colonel McDowell to Mikhailovich's headquarters was taken by Bill Donovan with the cooperation of the U.S. Joint Chiefs of Staff. The original mission was to send in a team of men to conduct *intelligence operations only* (italics by author), having nothing to do with the political situation then on the ground. The secondary purpose was to maintain contact with Mikhailovich's troops, as well as to send intelligence teams into Austria, Germany, and other central European countries.

The British saw the McDowell mission as an interference in their own, large intelligence-gathering operations in Yugoslavia and so stated publicly to President Roosevelt. If this was not enough, Mikhailovich's troops were waging their own, fierce battle with Marshall Tito's forces.

If this military/political situation were not fluid enough, a new element was added into the mix. In the summer of 1944, the American air corps was sending bombers across Yugoslavia to attack the vital Romanian oil fields. Dozens of these pilots were shot down and many were rescued by Mikhailovich's troops. From August 9, 1944, to December 27, 1944, 432 American flyers were evacuated from Yugoslavia, mainly due to the work of Mikhailovich's Chetnicks. As the Chetnicks began rescuing American flyers, they sent hurried wireless messages to the allies telling them that their pilots were safe. In many instances, this news was never delivered. In time, these signals were acknowledged, and the airmen were lifted out. (Some of these planes used for the rescue of allied airmen, also carried military supplies to Tito's troops.)

As preparations for the McDowell mission continued, the OSS met with Tito and told him of their decision to meet with Mikhailovich. Tito protested loudly. In order to placate Tito, Ellery Huntington of the OSS met with Tito on August 29, 1944, on the island of Vis. They discussed the ways in which OSS teams could be used in Yugoslavia and sought Tito's advice.

While Huntington was meeting with Tito, a behind-the-scenes clash between the United States and England was taking place. On September 1, 1944, FDR received a letter from Prime Minister Churchill objecting to the American plan to send a team to rendezvous with the Chetnick leader.

Churchill wrote to the president that, "If we each back different sides, we lay the scene for a fine civil war."

With McDowell now ready to bring his team into Yugoslavia, the nature of the mission began to change. Besides making contact with Mikhailovich's forces, McDowell was prepared to travel to Austria to meet up with various resistance groups. Robert McDowell was fluent in French and German, was a history professor at the University of Wisconsin, and was an OSS expert on the Balkans. With McDowell came Lieutenant Colonel Lanning Macfarland as the executive officer. Another man on the team was Captain John Milodragovich from the Secret Intelligence branch of the OSS, Captain Ellsworth Kramer, also from OSS SI, Sergeant Michael Rajachich, and Michael Devyak.

The Ranger's orders were to work with Mikhailovich "and collect data about the battle disposition of enemy and nationalist units, potential Chetnick collaboration with the occupying forces, armed encounters between Chetnicks and Partisans, and successful Partisan attempts to win over Chetnicks by force or by propaganda. The mission was also supposed to establish contacts with anti-Axis forces in Bulgaria and Hungary and to convey proposals for surrender to Allied forces."

With the McDowell mission on the ground, Mikhailovich began to see things differently than the Americans. He believed that the American aid was the precursor of "a broad political authorization" from the United States, which was not going to happen. McDowell also told the stunned Mikhailovich that no American military supplies were forthcoming and that the delegation was only an intelligence operation designed to bring back strategic information.

In a side move, Robert McDowell and the Chetnick leader, met secretly with a German named Rudi Starker in September 1944. Starker tried to persuade McDowell to use his influence for a united front between the Germans and the U.S. to fight Russia. In an unusual move, Starker and another German official, Hermann Neubacher, promised military aid to Mikhailovich which would be used to fight Tito's forces. After the war ended, Neubacher told American authorities that McDowell told him that he wanted to stop a Soviet invasion of the Balkans, to work against Tito, and give military assistance to the Chetnicks.

During this time, the German SD had secure radio communications with Mikhailovich's headquarters. This communication setup was used to request military supplies. These covert links with the Germans sent many at OSS headquarters into a panic, eventually doming the McDowell mission, and setting Mikhailovich adrift.

Washington was now receiving news from the British that Mikhailovich had been receiving military supplies from the Germans and requested that McDowell answer these charges. In response, McDowell said that this was not true.

In an attempt to quell the ever-growing political problems caused by the McDowell mission, FDR decided to bring him home. Bill Donovan wrote to the president saying that it was necessary to have an intelligence team on the ground in the Balkans in order to investigate allegations of coaction between the Chetnicks and the Germans. Despite Donovan's pleas, the order recalling McDowell was sent out on September 13, 1944. McDowell did not actually leave the region until November 1, 1944.

McDowell was sent to Naples, where he wrote a report on his time with Mikhailovich.

As far as the OSS was concerned, it made no attempts to evacuate Mikhailovich from Yugoslavia. On March 24, 1946, the new communist government of Yugoslavia arrested Mikhailovich. In June, he was put on trial, found guilty, and put to death by firing squad on July 17, 1946.

The McDowell mission had become an embarrassment to the OSS in all its varied military/political implications. For the United States and Great Britain, their treatment of the nationalist Mikhailovich eventually led to Tito's assumption of power in Yugoslavia. The decision to jettison Mikhailovich in 1944 would come back to haunt the West in the decades to come.

(*See Also*: OSS Italy)

Z

Zacharias, Ellis

Ellis Zacharias (1890-1961) was one of the notable names in the Office of Naval Intelligence, before and during the conflict. He took part in many of the early reconnaissance missions of the Japanese-held islands of the Pacific, developing the navy's first radio communications network in that part of the world.

Ellis Zacharias grew up in Jacksonville, Florida. Realizing his life-long dream of joining the navy, he attended the U.S. Naval Academy and graduated in 1912. He was a fast comer in the navy and in 1920 and was sent to Japan to learn the Japanese language, where he remained until 1924.

Zacharias received his first taste of intelligence training when, in 1921, the Japanese and the United States held a naval conference in Washington, D.C., which established how many capital ships each country could have, how much tonnage was allowed, the number of guns allowed on each ship, etc. Even in the early 1920s, the United States was keeping a wary eye on Japan, especially the growth of her navy, seeing that country as a possible military adversary in the future. From his outpost in Tokyo, Zacharias, and another U.S. Naval officer, Commander John Waller McClaran, were assigned by Captain Edward Watson, the American Naval Attaché in Tokyo, to represent the navy at the conference.

Prior to the Washington Naval Conference, the United States had broken the Japanese diplomatic code thanks to the diligence of Herbert Yardley and his "American Black Chamber." From this knowledge, American diplomats were able to counter any Japanese stonewalling regarding the allotment of capital ships. The work of Yardley's American Black Chamber gave the U.S. an unqualified success during the meeting.

Both Zacharias and McClaran, being advised of the Japanese negotiating position, talked terms with their counterparts, Captains Nomura and Nagano, into the compromise that was eventually worked out, mostly on American terms.

After his success at the Naval Conference, Ellis Zacharias was sent back to

Washington by the ONI on another undercover mission. His job was to keep track of the new Japanese Naval Attaché assigned to their Washington embassy, Commander Yoshitake Uyeda. Zacharias discovered that Uyeda was enjoying an affair with an American woman who worked as a secretary in the Navy Department. It was decided by ONI to let Uyeda alone, and concentrate on the other attaché, Lieutenant Commander Kiyoshi Hasegawa. Using women known to the navy, it was ascertained that a copy of the code book of the Japanese fleet could be obtained by covert means. Through the work of Zacharias and other ONI men, a successful raid on the Japanese building holding the code was made, and its contents were given to the navy. ONI analysts gave the code the designation of *JN-1*, but later referred to it as the "Red Book." This was an opportunity for the U.S. They now had inside knowledge of Japanese dispatch traffic.

In October 1926, Zacharias was given command of the ship *McCormick*, bound for the Yellow Sea. The *McCormick* was a new type of destroyer that had within its bowels, a system of aerials which were used to pick up signals from Japanese ships that were were cruising these sea lanes. The ship also had a compliment of six radiomen trained to man this new type of equipment. After the ship docked at Hong Kong, Zacharias left and proceeded to his next duty assignment.

He headed for Manila in the Philippines, where he was to revamp the way the navy used its radio stations in the Pacific for intelligence gathering. From Manila, he ventured to Shanghai, where he was responsible for turning the American radio center located in the American consulate for intercept functions. From 1927 onward, Commander Zacharias had operating a number of full-fledged radio intercept stations from the Philippines, Guam, and Shanghai.

When, in 1927, the United States Navy learned that their Japanese opposite numbers were planning large-scale maneuvers of its Combined Fleet in the fall, they decided to mount a reconnaissance operation to watch their travels. The U.S. learned that the Japanese were going to stage their maneuvers near the islands of Amami and Mihonoeski, and Zacharias made plans to track them.

His design was to send in a specially equipped U.S. warship that could listen in on all the Japanese radio traffic, right in the midst of their maneuvers. The vessel that the navy chose to use on this assignment was the U.S.S. *Marblehead*. Commander Zacharias was put aboard the *Marblehead*, in charge of the specialized espionage mission. On the night of October 16, the ship left Shanghai, China, with her sophisticated intelligence-monitoring equipment and headed to sea. The *Marblehead* was soon followed by a number of American ships which would watch the Japanese war games.

A large flotilla of 170 Japanese ships, divided up into two teams, one called the "Red Fleet" and the other the "Blue Fleet," fought a mock battle in the middle of the Pacific Ocean. The Japanese used aircraft in this mock show of force, something they would later use to their great advantage in their Pearl Harbor attack.

Commodore Zacharias, onboard the *Marblehead,* never actually saw the Japanese fleet, but her radio operators gleaned every ounce of intelligence from their powerful radios. Other ships from the American flotilla were able to see aerial maneuvers from the aircraft carrier *Akagi.* In his after-action report, Zacharias wrote that we were able to put "together the complete and accurate plan of the entire operation."

The *Marblehead,* with Zacharias onboard, arrived in Kobe, Japan, on a goodwill visit, where he turned over his report on the operation to U.S. Navy officials.

He was also peripherally involved in the case of a missing navy intelligence officer named Lieutenant Colonel Earl Ellis of the Marine Corps. In late 1922, Earl Ellis was living in Yokohama, Japan, posing as a businessman. Zacharias, in his position as the assistant naval attaché in Tokyo, knew of Ellis and kept a watch on him. When Ellis collapsed, he was taken to the U.S. Naval hospital in Yokohama and was treated for drunkenness. Ellis's condition worsened, and he was given the opportunity to go back to the United States. Instead, Ellis, checked himself out of the hospital.

Ellis, in fact, was an agent for the U.S., on a mission to develop plans for gaining control of the many Japanese-held islands in the Pacific in the event of war between the two nations.

Ellis was not a prime candidate to be an intelligence agent. He suffered from a malady of psychological ailments and a nervous disorder. After a frantic search, it was learned that Ellis had gone to the island of Koror in the Carolines, where he died under mysterious circumstances.

With Zacharias's approval, Lawrence Zembsch, who knew Ellis well, was sent to Koror to retrieve his body. When Zembsch returned to Japan, Zacharais found him huddled in a drunken stupor inside his ship's cabin, along with the cremated remains of Earl Ellis. It is believed that Ellis was killed by the Japanese and that the same treatment was meant for Zembsch.

During World War II, Ellis Zacharias took command of a number of ships, including the *Salt Lake City,* from November 1940 to May 1942. He was also involved in battles in the Gilbert and Marshall Islands.

In 1942, he went stateside and was appointed as the deputy director of ONI (Office of Naval Intelligence), in which he served until 1943. He was later the skipper of the battleship U.S.S. *New Mexico.* He ended his naval career as the chief of staff for the Eleventh Naval District. He retired from the navy in 1946 and wrote a book called *Secret Missions.* He died on June 27, 1961.

BIBLIOGRAPHY

Books

Albright, Joseph & Kunstel, Marcia. *Bombshell: The Secret Story of America's Unknown Atomic Spy Conspiracy.* N.Y. Times Books, 1997.

Allen, Thomas & Polmar, Norman. *Spy Book: The Encyclopedia of Espionage.* Random House, NY, 1997.

Ambrose, Stephen. *Ike's Spies: Eisenhower and the Espionage Establishment.* University Press of Mississippi, Jackson, 1999.

Bearse, Ray & Read, Anthony. *Conspirator: The Untold Story of Tyler Kent.* Doubleday, NY, 1991.

Breuer, William. *Hitler's Undercover War: The Nazi Invasion of the U.S.A.* St. Martin's Press, NY, 1989.

_____.*Unexplained Mysteries of World War II.* John Wiley & Sons, NY, 1997.

_____.*Top Secret Tales of World War II.* John Wiley & Sons, NY, 2000.

_____.*Undercover Tales of World War II.* John Wiley & Sons, NY, 1999.

_____.*Hoodwinking Hitler: The Normandy Deception.* Praeger, Westport, Ct., 1993.

_____. *MacArthur's Undercover War.* John Wiley & Sons., NY, 1995.

Brown, Anthony Cave. *Wild Bill Donovan: The Last Hero.* Times Books, NY, 1982.

_____."C": The Secret Life of Sir Stewart Menzies. Spymaster to Winston Churchill.* Macmillian Publishing Co., NY, 1987.

_____. *Bodyguard of Lies.* Harper & Row, NY, 1975.

Chalou, George, Editor. *The Secrets War: The Office of Strategic Services in World War II.* National Archives & Records Administration, Washington, D.C., 1992.

Clausen, Henry & Lee, Bruce. *Pearl Harbor. Final Judgement.* Crown Publishers, NY, 1992,

Farago, Ladislas. *The Broken Seal.* Bantam Books, NY, 1967.

BIBLIOGRAPHY

_____. *Burn After Reading.* Pinnacle Books, Los Angeles, CA, 1961.

_____. *The Game of Foxes. The Untold Story of German Espionage in the U.S. and Great Britain During World War II.* David McKay Co., NY, 1971.

Fisher, David. *The War Magician: The Incredible True Story of Jasper Maskelyne And His Magic Gang.* Berkley Books, NY, 1983.

Ford, Corey. *Donovan of the OSS.* Little Brown, Boston, MA, 1970.

Gentry, Curt. *J. Edgar Hoover: The Man And The Secrets.* W.W. Norton, NY, 1991.

Goodwin, Doris Kearns. *The Fitzgeralds and the Kennedys: An American Saga.* Simon & Schuster., NY, 1987.

Harrington, Dale. *Mystery Man: William Rhodes Davis. Nazi Agent.* Brassey's, Dulles, VA, 1999.

Haynes, John Earl & Klehr, Harvey. *Venona: Decoding Soviet Espionage in America.* Yale University Press, New Haven, CT, 1999.

Heidking, Jurgen & Mauch, Christof. *American Intelligence And The German Resistance to Hitler: A Documentary History.* Westview Press, 1996.

Hinsley, F.H. *British Intelligence In The Second World War. Vol. 4. Security & Intelligence.* Cambridge University Press, NY, 1990.

Jakub, Jay. *Spies And Saboteurs: Anglo-American Collaboration and Rivalry In Human Intelligence Collection and Special Operations 1940-45.* St. Martin's Press, NY, 1999.

Kahn, David. *Seizing The Enigma. The Race to Break the German U-Boat Codes, 1939-1943.* Houghton Mifflin Co., Boston, MA, 1991.

Kilzer, Louis. *Hitler's Traitor: Martin Bormann and the Defeat of the Third Reich.* Presidio Press, Novato, CA, 2000.

Kross, Peter. *Spies, Traitors and Moles: An Espionage and Intelligence Quiz Book.* Illuminet Press, Lilburn, GA, 1998.

Layton, Edwin, Rear Admiral, Pineau, Roger, Captain, & Costello, John. *"And I Was There." Pearl Harbor And Midway-Breaking The Secrets.* William Morrow, Inc., NY, 1985.

Lee, Bruce. *Marching Orders. The Untold Story of World War II.* Crown Publishers, NY, 1995.

Lycett, Andrew. *Ian Fleming: The Man Behind James Bond.* Turner Publishing Co., Atlanta, GA, 1995.

McIntosh, Elizabeth. *Sisterhood of Spies: The Women of the OSS.* Naval Institute Press, Annapolis, MD, 1998.

Melton, H. Keith. *The Ultimate Spy Book.* DK Publishing Co., NY, 1996.

Miller, Nathan. *Spying For America: The Hidden History of U.S. Intelligence.* Paragon House, NY, 1989.

Nash, J. Robert. *Spies: A Narrative Encyclopedia of Dirty Deeds and Double Dealing From Biblical Times To Today.* M. Evans & Co., New York, 1997.

O'Toole, G.J.A. *The Encyclopedia of American Intelligence and Espionage: From The Revolutionary War To The Present.* Facts on File., NY, 1988.

Persico, Joseph. *Piercing The Reich: The Penetration of Nazi Germany by American Agents During World War II.* Ballantine Books, NY, 1979.

_____. *Casey: The Lives And Secrets of William Casey. From OSS to the CIA.* Penguin Books, NY, 1990.

Powers, Richard Gid. *Secrecy And Power: The Life of J. Edgar Hoover.* The Free Press, NY, 1987.

Prange, Gordon. With Goldstein, Donald & Dillon, Katherine. *Pearl Harbor: The Verdict of History.* McGraw Hill Co., NY, 1986.

Quigley, Martin. *Peace Without Hiroshima: Secret Action at the Vatican in the Spring of 1945.* Madison Books, NY, 1991.

Readers Digest Association. *Secrets And Spies: Behind the Scenes Stories of World War II.* Pleasantville, NY, 1964.

Rhodes, Richard. *Dark Sun: The Making of the Hydrogen Bomb.* Simon & Schuster, NY, 1995.

Richelson, Jeffrey. *A Century of Spies: Intelligence in the Twentieth Century.* Oxford University Press, NY, 1995.

Riebling, Mark. *Wedge: The Secret War Between The FBI And CIA.* Alfred Knopf, NY, 1994.

Roosevelt, Kermit, Introduction By. *War Report of the O.S.S.* Walker & Co., NY, 1976.

Rusbridger, James & Nave, Eric. *Betrayal At Pearl Harbor: How Churchill Lured Roosevelt Into World War II.* Summit Books, NY, 1991.

Russell, Francis. *The Secret War.* Time-Life Books, NY, 1981.

Sayer, Ian & Botting, Douglas. *Nazi Gold.* Congdon & Weed, NY, 1984.

Seth, Richard. *Some of My Favorite Spies.* Chilton Book Co., NY, 1968.

Shoemaker, Lloyd. *The Escape Factory: The Story of MIS-X, America's Ultra-Secret Masterminds of World War II's Greatest Escapes.* St. Martin's Press, NY, 1990.

Simmons, Dan. *The Crook Factory.* Avon Books, NY, 1999.

Srodes, James. *Allen Dulles: Master of Spies.* Regnery Publishing Co., Washington, D.C., 1999.

Stafford, David. *Camp X. OSS "Intrepid" and the Allies North American Training Camp for Secret Agents, 1941-45.* Dodd, Mead & Co., NY, 1987.

Stinnett, Robert. *Day of Deceit: The Truth About FDR And Pearl Harbor.* The Free Press, NY, 2000.

Summers, Anthony. *Official and Confidential. The Secret Life of J. Edgar Hoover.* G.P. Putnam, NY, 1993.

Troy, Thomas. *Wild Bill And Intrepid: Donovan, Stephenson and the Origin of the CIA.* Yale University Press, New Haven, CT, 1996.

BIBLIOGRAPHY

Waller, John. *The Unseen War in Europe: Espionage and Conspiracy in the Second World War.* Random House, NY, 1996.

Weinstein, Allen & Vassiliev, Alexander. *The Haunted Wood: Soviet Espionage in America-The Stalin Era.* Random House, NY, 1999.

West, Nigel, Introduction By. *British Security Coordination: The Secret History of British Intelligence in the Americas, 1940-45.* Fromm International, NY, 1999.

Williams, Robert W. *Klaus Fuchs: Atom Spy.* Harvard University Press. ,Boston, MA, 1987.

Wires, Richard. *The Cicero Spy Affair: German Access to British Secrets In World War II.* Praeger Publishing Co., Westport, CT, 1999.

Government Documents

U.S. Government Record Group 226: Papers Relating to OSS Activities During World War II. Located at the National Archives, College Park, MD.

Periodicals

Ardman, Harvey. *The Ship That Died Of Carelessness.* American Heritage, December 1983, Vol. 351. No.1. Pp. 61-69.

Bittner, John R. *Undercover: A Racing Car's Sudden Appearance, Shots, and a "snatch" would mark the "Venlo" Incident.* World War II, Vol. 5, No.1. Pp. 8, 64-66.

Bratzel, John F. & Rout, Leslie, Jr. *"FDR and the Secret Map.* The Wilson Quarterly, New Years, 1985. Pp. 167-173.

C.I.A. *Masterman Revisited.* Studies in Intelligence. Vol.18. No.1. Spring 1974.

Cohen, Joel. *FDR's Spies.* Back Channels. Vol.1 No.1. October, 1991. Pp. 7-8.

Deac, Wilfred. *Amy Elizabeth Thorpe, Code-named "Cynthia" was a World War II version of the legendary Mata Hari.* World War II, February 1996.

Frank, Larry. *The United States Navy V. The Chicago Tribune.* The Historian. Vol. XLII, February 1980, Pp. 284-303.

Hellen, Nicholas. *British Hit Squad 'executed' Nazis.* The Sunday London Times, December, 28, 1997.

Kross, Peter. *The Arvad-Kennedy Affair.* Back Channels. Vol. 1 No.4, Summer 1992.

_____. *Moe Berg. The Spy Behind the Plate.* Back Channels. Vol 3 Nos. 1&2, Fall/Winter 1993-94. Pp. 12-14.

_____. *Ian Fleming: The Real 007.* Back Channels. Vol.1 No. 2. Winter 1992. Pp. 12-13.

_____. *The Old Man and the Secret.* The Trenton Times. October 3, 1999. Section CC.

_____.*Hitler's Gold.* Back Channels. Vol.1 No. 3. Spring 1992.

Lownie, Andrew. *Tyler Kent: The Spy In The Code Room.* Back Channels. Vol 1. No. 3, Spring 1992, Pp. 16-17.

Martin, David. *The Mikhailovich Story: A Retelling.* World-Wide Web.www.suc.org/culture/history/Draza Mikhailovich.

Miller, Joan. *Nazi Invasion.* American History Illustrated. No Date. Pp. 42-49.

O'Toole, Thomas. *Spanish Diplomats Spied on U.S. for Japan in WW2; Spaniard's Spied on U.S. for Japan in WW2, NSA Code Data Show; Documents show codebreaking Bared "To" Ring!* Washington Post, September 10, 1978.

Oursler, Fulton, Jr. *Secret Treason.* American Heritage. December, 1991.

Oxford, Edward. *Prelude in the Pacific.* American History Illustrated. Date unknown. Pp. 52-63.

_____. *Intrigue in the Islands.* American History Illustrated. Date unknown. Pp. 50-66.

Stafford, David. *Intrepid: Myth and Reality.* Journal of Contemporary History, Beverly Hills, Vol. 22, 1987, Pp. 303-317.

Swanberg, W.A. *The Spies Who Came In From The Sea.* American Heritage, April, 1970, Pp. 66-69 & 87-90.

Trefousse, Hans. *Failure of German Intelligence in the United States, 1935-1945.* The Mississippi Valley Historical Review. Vol. VLII. Pp. 84-100.

U.S. News & World Report. *The Angel Was a Spy. Sweden's Raoul Wallenberg was a U.S. Espionage Asset.* May 13, 1996.

Weeks, Albert. *Undercover: In Operation Aphrodite, explosive-laden aircraft were to be flown against German Targets.* World War II. May, 2000. Pp. 66-68.

Wilson, William. *Code Talkers.* American History. February, 1997. Pp. 16-20 & 66-67.

Wrixon, Fred. *Undercover: The industrius Kuehn family Spied for Japan in Hawaii between 1935 and 1941.* World War II. March 2000. Pp. 16-24.

Zabecki, David. *Undercover: The Man Who Never Was.* World War II. November, 1995.

No Author. *Russia Concedes a Point on Wallenberg's Fate.* New York Times, July 25, 2000.

INDEX

INDEX

INDEX

INDEX

INDEX

OSS officers worked secretly in both Burma and China. Gen. Douglas MacArthur refused OSS entry into the Pacific Theatre of Operations, using instead his own intelligence officers to monitor Japanese troop and ship movements.

Italy was the cornerstone of a myriad of OSS operations in southern Europe. OSS men made contact with various Italian resistance movements via clandestine radio networks. The American mafia was used in the successful allied invasion of Sicily.